Computational Risk Management

Series Editors

For further volumes:
http://www.springer.com/series/8827

Desheng Dash Wu
Editor

Modeling Risk Management in Sustainable Construction

Springer

Editor
Prof. Desheng Dash Wu
University of Toronto
RiskLab
Toronto, ON M5S 3G3
Canada
DWu@Rotman.Utoronto.Ca

ISSN 2191-1436 e-ISSN 2191-1444
ISBN 978-3-642-15242-9 e-ISBN 978-3-642-15243-6
DOI 10.1007/978-3-642-15243-6
Springer Heidelberg Dordrecht London New York

Library of Congress Control Number: 2010938731

Cover design: eStudio Calamar S.L

Printed on acid-free paper

Springer is part of Springer Science+Business Media (www.springer.com)

Preface

We are living in a risky world, and it is getting riskier and riskier. As one of my fundamental claims that have been delivered to various audience including scholars, practitioners and government officers, first, risk avoidance system in today's world is becoming so interconnected; second, it is fully supported by a great of risk issues that have been addressed in this edited volume. Such risk issues, to name a few, include typical financial risk such as credit risk and market risk, construction risk management, supply chain risks, energy risk assessment, environmental risk analysis, risk management and sustainable development. These risk issues altogether form a risk checklist that could support my second claim: risk is unavoidable and business exists to cope with risks in their area of specialization. In William Sharpe's CAPM (capital asset pricing model) theory, investments are evaluated in terms of both risk and return relative to the market as a whole; the riskier a business stock, the greater profit potential. Thus risk implies opportunity and business exists to seek such risk-based opportunities.

Prediction of extreme risk events is almost unlikely. In Taleb's 2007 book titled "Black swan", extreme risks are said to be unpredictable like a black swan that lies beyond the realm of normal expectations. Many firms experienced difficulties from black swan bubbles. The most spectacular failure in the late twentieth century was probably that of Long-Term Capital Management [1], but that was only a precursor to the more comprehensive failure of technology firms during the dot.com bubble around 2001. The problems of interacting cultures demonstrated risk from terrorism as well, with numerous terrorist attacks, to include 9/11 in the U.S.

The third claim is that effective risk management needs integration of various risks facing the organization. National Research Council has two red books on risk analysis and management: one is from that 1983 titled "Risk Assessment in the Federal Government: Managing the Process" and the other from 2009 titled "Science and Decisions Advancing Risk Assessment". One of our observations is that the updated version "Recommends that risk management would become more integrated with the risk assessment process and focuses attention on improving the utility of risk assessments to better inform risk management decision-making"

[2, 3]. Enterprise risk management has been defined as a process that uses integrated, systematic approaches to manage risks that faces the organization. Therefore, enterprise risk management has been deemed as an effective risk management philosophy.

In the past, we have tried to discuss different aspects of risk, to include finance, information systems, disaster management, and supply chain perspectives [4, 5, 6]. In this edited volume, we present the state-of-the-art views of the perspective of enterprise risk management, to include frameworks and controls in the ERM process with respect to supply chains, constructions, and project, energy, environmental and sustainable development risk management.

The bulk of this volume is devoted to presenting a number of modeling approaches that have been (or could be) applied to enterprise risk management in construction from the 1st International Conference on Sustainable Construction and Risk Management in Chongqing Municipality, P. R China. We include decision analysis models, auction models to better enable risk managers to trade off conflicting criteria of importance in their decisions. Monte Carlo simulation models are the obvious operations research tool appropriate for risk management. Rough Set and fuzzy set theories are employed. Dynamic models such as dynamic AHP and Bayesian Networks are used to handle risky project management when achieving sustainable development purpose. We hope that this book provides some view of how quantitative models can be applied by more readers faced with enterprise risk.

Toronto, ON
July 2010

Desheng Dash Wu

References

1. Lowenstein, R. (2000). *When Genius Failed: The Rise and Fall of Long-Term Capital Management*. New York: Random House.
2. Wu D. and Olson DL. 2009. Introduction to the special section on "optimizing risk management: Methods and tools, Human and Ecological Risk Assessment 15(2): 220–226.
3. Wu D. and Johnson B. L. 2010. HERA emphasizing risk management: An editorial, Human and Ecological Risk Assessment.
4. Olson, D.L. and Wu, D. (2008a). *Enterprise Risk Management*. Singapore: World Scientific Publishing Co.
5. Olson, D.L. and Wu, D. (2008b). *New Frontiers in Risk Management*. Heidelberg: Springer.
6. Olson, D.L. and Wu, D. (2010). *Enterprise Risk Management Models*. Heidelberg: Springer.

Contents

Contributors

Hongwei Bai Shaanxi Fast Gear Co., Ltd, Xi'an, People's Republic of China, hevin_bai@163.com

Bo Cao Economics and Management School of Beijing, University of Technology, Beijing 100124, People's Republic of China, caobobjut@163.com

Yi Cao College of Civil Engineering, Hebei University of Technology, Beichen District, Tianjin, People's Republic of China, 313328565@qq.com

Albert P.C. Chan Department of Building and Real Estate, The Hong Kong Polytechnic University, Kowloon, Hong Kong, SAR, China, bsachan@polyu.edu.hk

Weng Tat Chan Department of Civil Engineering, National University of Singapore, 1 Engineering Drive 2, E1A 07-03 Singapore, 117576, Singapore, cvecwt@nus.edu.sg

Liwen Chen School of Management, Hebei University of Technology, Tianjin, People's Republic of China, lwchen@hebut.edu.cn

Pei Chen College of Civil Engineering, Hebei University of Technology, Beichen District, Tianjin, People's Republic of China, l03y@163.com

Qiaoyu Chen School of Management, Chongqing Jiaotong University, Chongqing 400074, People's Republic of China, qiaoyu.chen@yahoo.com.cn

Weijie Chen School of Economics and Business Administration, Chongqing University, Chongqing 400044, People's Republic of China, chwj721@163.com

Yueyue Chen School of Civil Engineering, Lanzhou Jiaotong University, Lanzhou 730070, People's Republic of China, chenyue-chenyue@163.com

Benkun Chi School of Management, Jilin University, Changchun 130025, People's Republic of China,

Jie Chi School of Management, Chongqing Jiaotong University, Chongqing Municipality 400074, People's Republic of China, cjwcjcmcj@126.com

Miao Chi School of Management, Chongqing Jiaotong University, Chongqing Municipality 400074, People's Republic of China, miachi871012@gmail.com

Yuanying Chi North China Electric Power University, Beijing 102206, People's Republic of China; Changchum University of Technology, Changchun 130012, People's Republic of China

Ligang Cui School of Management, Chongqing Jiaotong University, Chongqing 400074, People's Republic of China, cligang@126.com

Jie Ding School of Economics and Management, Tongji University, Shanghai 200092, People's Republic of China, dingjie_2010@126.com

Xiuli Du The College of Architecture and Civil Engineering, Beijing University of Technology, Beijing, People's Republic of China, duxiuli@bjut.edu.cn

Xiaobiao Fan Maritime College, Chongqing Jiaotong University, Chongqing 400074, People's Republic of China, fanxiaobiao@sina.com

Yong Fang School of Management, Chongqing Jiaotong University, No. 66 Xuefu Road, Nanan District, Chongqing Municipality, People's Republic of China, fangyongcqu@sohu.com

Yongheng Fang School of Management, Xi'an University of Architecture and Technology, Xi'an 710055, People's Republic of China, yhfang@xauat.edu.cn

Luo Fu-zhou School of Management, Xi'an University of Architecture & Technology, Xi'an, People's Republic of China, luofz@163.com

Linjie Gao School of Naval Architecture, Ocean and Civil Engineering, Shanghai Jiao Tong University, 800 Dongchuan Rd., Shanghai, People's Republic of China, ljgao@sdju.edu.cn

Yunhao Gao The College of Architecture and Civil Engineering, Beijing University of Technology, Beijing, People's Republic of China, gaoyunhao200704025@emails.bjut.edu.cn

Yun-li Gao Department of Civil Engineering and Architecture, Dalian Nationalities University, Liaoning Dalian, People's Republic of China, yunligao@163.com

Li Guo School of Management, Xi'an University of Architecture & Technology, Xi'an, Shanxi 710055, People's Republic of China, fair@126.com

Shufen Guo School of Management Science and Engineering, Shanxi University of Finance and Economics, Taiyuan 030006, People's Republic of China

Shurong Guo Shandong University of Technology, Zibo, Shandong 255049, People's Republic of China, zbshur@sina.com

Xiaohong Guo School of Management, Chongqing Jiaotong University, Nan'an, Chongqing 400074, People's Republic of China, chq-gxh@126.com

Hong He School of Economics and Management, Tongji University, 1239 Siping Rd, Shanghai, People's Republic of China, sophiestream@hotmail.com

Jimmie Hinze M.E. Rinker, Sr. School of Building Construction, University of Florida, Gainesville, FL, USA, hinze@ufl.edu

Li Huang International Office, Chongqing Jiaotong University, Chongqing 400074, People's Republic of China, orioleli@hotmail.com

Liwen Huang College of Navigation, Wuhan University of Technology, Wuhan 430063, People's Republic of China, lwhuang@whut.edu.cn

Eddie C.M. Hui Department of Building and Real Estate, The Hong Kong Polytechnic University, Hong Kong, China, bscmhui@inet.polyu.edu.hk

Zhouping Jia School of Management, Xi'an University of Architecture and Technology, Xi'an 710055, People's Republic of China, jiazhoupingping@163.com

Chuanjing Ju Faculty of Construction Management and Real Estate, Chongqing University, Chongqing, People's Republic of China, jcjandjcf@yahoo.com.cn

Zhicai Juan Antai College of Economics & Management, Shanghai Jiao Tong University, 535 Fahua Zhen Rd., Shanghai, People's Republic of China, zcjuan@sjtu.edu.cn

Yongjian Ke Department of Construction Management, Tsinghua University, Beijing 100084, People's Republic of China, kyj05@mails.tsinghua.edu.cn

Craig Langston Mirvac School of Sustainable Development, Bond University, Gold Coast, Australia, clangsto@bond.edu.au

Wang La-Yin School of Management, Xi'an University of Architecture & Technology, Xi'an, People's Republic of China, xjdwanglayin@sina.com

Feng Li School of Water conservancy and Environment, Zhenzhou University, Zhenzhou, Henan Province 450002, People's Republic of China, lifeng9406@126.com

Jiabo Li 91439 Army Unit, PLA, Dalian, 116041, People's Republic of China, lijb@163.com

Qiming Li Department of Construction Management and Real Estate, Southeast University, Nanjing, People's Republic of China; Department of Construction Management and Real Estate, Southeast University, Nanjing, People's Republic of China, njlqming@163.com

Shun-yong Li School of Management, Chongqing Jiaotong University, Chongqing 400074, People's Republic of China, lsypub@gmail.com

Sulei Li Shandong University of Technology, Zibo, Shandong 255049, People's Republic of China, lsulei@163.com

Xiangyang Li China's Power Investment Group Company, Beijing 100053, People's Republic of China,

Zong-Kun Li School of Water Conservancy and Environment, Zhengzhou University, Zhengzhou, Henan Province 450002, People's Republic of China, ramones123@126.com

Bangyin Liu Chengban Science and Technology Development Ltd, Nan'an, Chongqing 400060, People's Republic of China, bpl99@hotmail.com

Zaiming Liu School of Mathematics, Central South University, Changsha 410075, People's Republic of China, math_lzm@csu.edu.cn

Caiwu Lu School of Management, Xi'an University of Architecture & Technology, Xi'an, Shanxi 710055, People's Republic of China; Research Center for Industrial Organization, Southeast University, Najing 211189, People's Republic of China, lucaiwu@126.com

Ying Lu Department of Construction Management and Real Estate, Southeast University, Nanjing, People's Republic of China, luying_happy@126.com

Biyu Lv School of Economics and Management, Tongji University, 1239 Siping Rd, Shanghai, People's Republic of China, eabesy2529@163.com

Xuyao Ma Northwestern Polytechnical University, Xi'an, People's Republic of China, maxuyao@sina.com

Marek Mihola Faculty of Civil Engineering, VSB – Technical University of Ostrava, Ludvika Podeste 1875, 70833 Ostrava, Czech Republic, marek.mihola@vsb.cz

Dongxiao Niu North China Electric Power University, Beijing 102206, People's Republic of China

Hua Pan Vocational College Of Architecture Engineering, Chongqing 400039, People's Republic of China, Panhua2009@163.com

Yuhong Pan School of Management, Chongqing Jiaotong University, Chongqing, People's Republic of China, panyuhong3@hotmail.com

Dan Peng School of Mathematics, Hunan University of Science and Technology, Xiangtan 411201, People's Republic of China, danpengdanpeng@126.com

Hosein Piranfar Business School (RDBS), University of East London, University Way, London E16 2RD, UK, H.Piranfar@uel.ac.uk

Xiansheng Qin Northwestern Polytechnical University, Xi'an, People's Republic of China, qinxiansheng@163.com

Hua Shang School of Management, Dalian University of Technology, Dalian 116024, People's Republic of China, dlutshanghua@163.com

Yan-ting Sheng China Airport Construction Group Corporation of CAAC Northwest Branch, Xi'an, People's Republic of China, syt19831013@163.com

Jing Shentu School of Management Science and Engineering, Shanxi University of Finance and Economics, Taiyuan 030006, People's Republic of China

Xiaoxia Shi Beijing Key Laboratory of Logistics Systems and Technology, Beijing 101149, People's Republic of China; Beijing Wuzi University School of Logistics Beijing Wuzi University, Beijing 101149, People's Republic of China, shixx897@gmail.com

De-shan Tang College of Water Conservancy and Hydropower, Hohai University, Nanjing 210098, People's Republic of China, tds808@163.com

Fengming Tao College of Mechanical Engineering, Chongqing University, No. 174 Shazheng Street, Shapingba District, Chongqing Municipality, People's Republic of China; Henan Province Water conservancy Scientific Research Institute, Zhenzhou, Henan Province 450002, People's Republic of China, taofengming@cqu.edu.cn

Xiaoyu Wan School of Economic & Management, Chongqing University of Posts and Telecommunications, Chongqing 400065, People's Republic of China, wanxy@cqupt.edu.cn

Hongxia Wang Faculty of Construction Management and Real Estate, Chongqing University, Chongqing, People's Republic of China; Department of Economic and Trade, Chongqing Education College, Chongqing, People's Republic of China, whx1255@tom.com

ShouQing Wang Department of Construction Management, Tsinghua University, Beijing 100084, People's Republic of China, sqwang@tsinghua.edu.cn

Yan-Rong Wang North China University of Water Conservancy and Electric Power, Zhengzhou 450011, People's Republic of China, wyr223@126.com

Yongguang Wang School of Management Science and Engineering, Shanxi University of Finance and Economics, Taiyuan 030006, People's Republic of China,

Jinying Wei School of Economic and Management, Chongqing University of Posts and Telecommunications, Chongqing 400065, People's Republic of China, wjynjupt@163.com

Lian-yu Wei College of Civil Engineering, Hebei University of Technology, Beichen District, Tianjin, People's Republic of China, xiaoyi82031203@126.com

Qingqi Wei Chongqing University, Chongqing, People's Republic of China; NorthWestern Polytechnical University, Xi'an, People's Republic of China, weiqingqi@163.com

Guofeng Wen School of Management, Hebei University of Technology, Tianjin, People's Republic of China; Shandong Institute of Business and Technology, Yantai, People's Republic of China, wengf_sdibt@yahoo.com.cn

Francis K.W. Wong Department of Building and Real Estate, The Hong Kong Polytechnic University, Hong Kong, China, bskwwong@inet.polyu.edu.hk

Min Wu Department of Real Estate and Construction Management School, The University of Hong Kong, Pok Fu Lam, Hong KongChina, wu@hku.hk

Yue Wu Beijing Key Laboratory of Logistics Systems and Technology, Beijing 101149, People's Republic of China, wuyue@m165.com

Jianchuan Xianyu College of Economics and Management, Shanghai Dianji University, 88 Wenjing Rd., Shanghai, People's Republic of China, jianchuanxy@gmail.com

Wei Xiao Chongqing Jiaotong University, Chongqing, People's Republic of China, xiao98612343@163.com

Zhi Xiao School of Economics and Business Administration, Chongqing University, Chongqing 400044, People's Republic of China, xiaozhi@cqu.edu.cn

Danfeng Xie Shandong University of Technology, Zibo, Shandong 255049, People's Republic of China, xiedanfeng2001@126.com

Linlin Xie School of Civil Engineering and Transportation, South China University of Technology, Guangzhou, People's Republic of China, llxie@scut.edu.cn

Xiao-dong Xie College of Economy & Business Administraction Chongqing University, Chongqing 400044, People's Republic of China; School of Management Chongqing Jiaotong University, Chongqing 400074, People's Republic of China, xiexd@cquc.edu.cn

Yi-long Xiong School of Economics and Management, Beijing University of Technology, Beijing, People's Republic of China, yilong7826@emails.bjut.edu.cn

Maozeng Xu School of Management, Chongqing Jiaotong University, Chongqing 400074, People's Republic of China, xmzzrxhy@cquc.edu.cn

Qiao-Ling Xu North China University of Water Conservancy and Electric Power, Zhengzhou 450011, People's Republic of China, qiaoling1026xu@126.com

Min-Ren Yan Department of Business Administration, Chinese Culture University, No. 231, Sec. 2, Jianguo S. Rd., Da-an Dist., Taipei City, Taiwan, ROC, mjyen@sce.pccu.edu.tw

Ying Yan Traffic safety Laboratory, Automobile Institute, Chang'an University, Xi'an, People's Republic of China, yanying2199@sohu.com

Chuan-Bin Yang The Second Water Bureau of Henan Province, Zhengzhou, Henan Province 450016, People's Republic of China, yangchuanbin@126.com

Lin Yang School of Civil Engineering, Lanzhou Jiaotong University, Lanzhou 730070, People's Republic of China, yanglin5@yeah.net

Xingming Yang School of Economic & Management, Chongqing University of Posts and Telecommunications, Chongqing 400065, People's Republic of China, Xinming.Yang@alcatel-sbell.com.cn

Yu Yang Faculty of Construction Management and Real Estate, Chongqing University, Chongqing, People's Republic of China, cquyangyu@163.com

Zhen Yang School of Management, Xi'an University of Architecture & Technology, Xi'an, Shanxi 710055, People's Republic of China, yangzhen-2005@hotmail.com

Fei Ye School of Economics and Management, Beijing University of Technology, Beijing, People's Republic of China, yefei@bjut.edu.cn

Gui Ye Faculty of Construction Management and Real Estate, Chongqing University, Chongqing, People's Republic of China, yegui760404@126.com

Yang Yu Economics and Management School of Beijing, University of Technology, Beijing 100124, People's Republic of China; Research Center for Industrial Organization, Southease University, Nanjing 211189, People's Republic of China, yangyu.seu@gmail.com

Dan Zhang College of Navigation, Wuhan University of Technology, Wuhan 430063, China; Maritime College, Chongqing Jiaotong University, Chongqing 400074, People's Republic of China, ekindan@tom.com

Guo-jun Zhang Faculty of Infrastructure Engineering, Dalian University of Technology, Liaoning Dalian, People's Republic of China, zhanggj8686@163.com

Han Zhang Beijing Key Laboratory of Logistics Systems and Technology, Beijing 101149, People's Republic of China, zhanghan56@263.net

Jian Zhang Department of Civil Engineering, National University of Singapore, 1 Engineering Drive 2, E1 08-20 Singapore, Singapore, g0800227@nus.edu.sg117576,

Jiantong Zhang School of Economics and Management, Tongji University, 1239 Siping Rd, Shanghai, People's Republic of China, zhangjiant@163.com

Mingju Zhang The College of Architecture and Civil Engineering, Beijing University of Technology, Beijing, People's Republic of China, zhangmj@bjut.edu.cn

Wen-jin Zhang Business School, Hohai University, Nanjing 210098, People's Republic of China, zhangwenjin@yahoo.cn

Yu-hui Zhang Liaoning Communication Survey and Design Institute, Shenyang, People's Republic of China, lu20009693@126.com

Zi-jian Zhang College of management, Chongqing Jiao tong University, Chongqing 400074, People's Republic of China, kenzijian2000@yahoo.com.cn

Guohao Zhao School of Management Science and Engineering, Shanxi University of Finance and Economics, Taiyuan 030006, People's Republic of China, gzhao1958@yahoo.com.cn

Li-xiang Zhao School of Economics and Management, Beijing University of Technology, Beijing, People's Republic of China, zhaolixiang@bjut.edu.cn

Yanlong Zhao School of Economics and Management, Lanzhou Jiaotong University, Lanzhou 730070, China, zhaoyl@mail.lzjtu.cn

Part I
Enterprise Risk Management in Supply Chains

An Improved Approach for Supplier Selection in Project Material Bidding Procurement

Maozeng Xu, Qiaoyu Chen, and Ligang Cui

Abstract A multi-attribute group decision making method composed of intuitionistic fuzzy set and TOPSIS will be introduced into project material bidding procurement. First, the opinions of experts about bidders and indicators' attributes are expressed by linguistic terms, and then turned into intuitionistic fuzzy numbers, which can be used to obtain the weights of the indicators' attributes and experts. Based on the opinions of decision makers and IFWA operators, an aggregated intuitionistic fuzzy decision matrix is formulated. In the end, the bidders are ranked by TOPSIS method.

Keywords Bidding procurement · IFS · IFWA operator · Project material · TOPSIS

1 Introduction

The cost of material procurement impacts the economic benefits of construction enterprises directly. So bidding procurement is of great important to of construction enterprises' benefits. But whether we can find the best bidder which eventually meet the requirements for the supplier has a great relationship with evaluation methods.

At present the bidding methods have been improved by many scholars can overcome the shortcomings and insufficiencies (Hu 1992; Sheng et al. 2008). Atanassov (1986, 2000) put forward the concept of intuitionistic fuzzy sets, and studied its character and its computing. Gau and Buehrer (1993) proposed the concept of Vague sets; Bustince (1996) and others pointed out that the Vague set is intuitionistic fuzzy sets. Chen and Tan (1994) had applied fuzzy Vague sets to the multi-objective decision-making problems. Based on Chen's research, Hong and

M. Xu (✉), Q. Chen, and L. Cui
School of Management, Chongqing Jiaotong University, Chongqing 400074, People's Republic of China
e-mail: xmzzrxhy@cquc.edu.cn, qiaoyu.chen@yahoo.com.cn, cligang@126.com

D.D. Wu (ed.), *Modeling Risk Management in Sustainable Construction*, Computational Risk Management, DOI 10.1007/978-3-642-15243-6_1,

Choi (2000) used exact function to solve multi-objective decision-making problems. Li (2003) and Xu (2007a, b, c) and some others have also done a great deal in this area. In this paper, traditional TOPSIS method combined with the IFS will be used to evaluate and select the supplier in project material bidding procurement.

2 The Basic Theory of Intuitionistic Fuzzy Sets

The intuitionistic fuzzy sets substantially is the extension of fuzzy set theory currently widely used in medical diagnosis, decision-making, pattern recognition applications and many other fields (Boran et al. 2009).

Fuzzy sets A in a universe of discourse X is defined as: $A = \{\langle x, \mu_A(x), \nu_A(x)\rangle | x \in X\}$, where $\mu_A: X \to [0,1]$ and $\nu_A: X \to [0,1]$ are membership and non-membership of x to A, and $0 \le \mu_A(x) + \nu_A(x) \le 1, \forall x \in X$ Besides, $\pi_A = 1 - \mu_A(x) - \nu_A(x)$ is the indicator or hesitation degree of intuition of x to A, it is the degree of uncertainty of x. It is clear that for each $x \in X$, $0 \le \pi_A(x) \le 1$. The greater π_A is, the wider the range of uncertainty of x on the set A becomes.

Let the A and B be the intuitionistic fuzzy sets in a universe of discourse X, the multiplication operator is defined as follows (Atanassov 2000):

$$A \otimes B = \{\mu_A \bullet \nu_B, \nu_A + \nu_B - \nu_A \bullet \nu_B \,| x \in X\} \tag{1}$$

3 Supplier Selection Model on Project Materials Bidding and Purchasing

Let experts $D = \{D_1, D_2, \ldots D_l\}$ be the decision-making group, A = (A_1, A_2, ..., A_m) be a set of bidders, and X = (X_1, X_2, ..., X_n) be a set of criteria. The experts evaluate the bidders respectively on the X = (X_1, X_2, ..., X_n) attribute indicators by language assessment, and then converted them into a number of intuitionistic fuzzy number. Combining with IFWA operator, the bidders IFPIS and IFVIS distance can be got, and the relative closeness degree to get rank of the suppliers can be calculated. The steps of the intuitionistic fuzzy multi-attribute group decision making TOPSIS method for project material supplier selection are given as follows:

(i) Determine the weights of decision-makers. Assume that the Committee evaluation have l experts, the importance of each expert is considered as linguistic terms expressed in intuitionistic fuzzy numbers. The relationship between linguistic terms and IFNs are show in the following Table 1:

Table 1 The relationship between linguistic and IFNs

Linguistic terms	Intuitionistic fuzzy numbers
Very important	(0.90, 0.10)
Important	(0.75, 0.20)
General	(0.50, 0.45)
Unimportant	(0.35, 0.60)
Very unimportant	(0.10, 0.90)

Table 2 The relationship of linguistic terms and Intuitionistic Fuzzy number

Linguistic terms	Intuitionistic fuzzy number	Linguistic terms	Intuitionistic fuzzy number
Best/high/far	(1.00, 0.00)	General	(0.50, 0.40)
Much better/high/far	(0.90, 0.10)	Bad/low/near	(0.40, 0.50)
Better/high/far	(0.80, 0.10)	Very bad/low/near	(0.25, 0.60)
Very good/high/far	(0.70, 0.20)	Worse/low/near	(0.10, 0.75)
Good/high/far	(0.60, 0.30)	Worst/low/near	(0.10, 0.90)

Let $D_k = [\mu_k, v_k, \pi_k]$ be the intuitionistic fuzzy number of kth bidding evaluation experts, the weight of the experts is (Boran et al. 2009):

$$\lambda_k = \frac{\mu_k + \pi_k\left(\frac{\mu_k}{\mu_k + v_k}\right)}{\sum_{k=1}^{l}\left(\mu_k + \pi_k\left(\frac{\mu_k}{\mu_k + v_k}\right)\right)} \tag{2}$$

And $\sum_{k=1}^{l} \lambda_k = 1,\ \lambda_k \in [0, 1]$

(ii) Set up the intuitionistic fuzzy decision matrix based on the opinion of experts. Expert evaluation bidders under each indicator by the linguistic terms, the relationship between linguistic terms and intuitionistic fuzzy number are as Table 2. Then change the linguistic terms into IFNs, set up the intuitionistic fuzzy decision matrix $R = (r_{ij})_{m\times n}$, combined with the weight of each expert through the IFWA (intuitionistic fuzzy weighted average) operator.

$$R = \begin{bmatrix} r_{11} & r_{12} & \cdots & r_{1n} \\ r_{21} & r_{22} & \cdots & r_{2n} \\ \vdots & \vdots & \vdots & \vdots \\ r_{m1} & r_{m2} & \cdots & r_{mn} \end{bmatrix}$$

$$= \begin{bmatrix} (\mu_{A_1}(x_1), v_{A_1}(x_1), \pi_{A_1}(x_1)) & \cdots & (\mu_{A_1}(x_n), v_{A_1}(x_n), \pi_{A_1}(x_n)) \\ (\mu_{A_2}(x_1), v_{A_2}(x_1), \pi_{A_2}(x_1)) & \cdots & (\mu_{A_2}(x_n), v_{A_2}(x_n), \pi_{A_2}(x_n)) \\ \vdots & \vdots & \vdots \\ (\mu_{A_m}(x_1), v_{A_m}(x_1), \pi_{A_m}(x_1)) & \cdots & (\mu_{A_m}(x_n), v_{A_m}(x_n), \pi_{A_m}(x_n)) \end{bmatrix} \tag{3}$$

where

$$\begin{aligned} r_{ij} &= IFWA_{\lambda}(r_{ij}^{1}, r_{ij}^{2}, \cdots r_{ij}^{l}) \\ &= \lambda_1 r_{ij}^{1} \oplus \lambda_2 r_{ij}^{2} \oplus \lambda_3 r_{ij}^{3} \oplus \cdots \lambda_l r_{ij}^{l} \\ &= \left[1 - \prod_{k=1}^{l} (1 - \mu_{ij}^{k})^{\lambda_k}, \prod_{k=1}^{l} (v_{ij}^{k})^{\lambda_k}, \prod_{k=1}^{l} (1 - \mu_{ij}^{k})^{\lambda_k} - \prod_{k=1}^{l} (v_{ij}^{k})^{\lambda_k}\right], \end{aligned}$$

$$r_{ij} = (\mu_{A_i}(x_j), v_{A_i}(x_j), \pi_{A_i}(x_j))(i = 1, 2, \cdots m; j = 1, 2, \cdots n)$$

(iii) Determine the weights of evaluation indicators. Let $w_j^{(k)} = \left[\mu_j^{(k)}, v_j^{(k)}, \pi_j^{(k)}\right]$ be an intuitionistic fuzzy number assigned to indictor X_j by the kth expert. By using IFWA operator we draw the weights of the attributes is Xu (2007a, b, c):

$$\begin{aligned} w_j &= IFWA_{\lambda}(w_j^{1}, w_j^{2}, \cdots w_j^{l}) \\ &= \lambda_1 w_j^{1} \oplus \lambda_2 w_j^{2} \oplus \lambda_3 w_j^{3} \oplus \cdots \oplus \lambda_l w_j^{1} \\ &= \left[1 - \prod_{k=1}^{l} (1 - \mu_j^{k})^{\lambda_k}, \prod_{k=1}^{l} (v_j^{k})^{\lambda_k}, \prod_{k=1}^{l} (1 - \mu_j^{k})^{\lambda_k} - \prod_{k=1}^{l} (v_j^{k})^{\lambda_k}\right] \end{aligned} \quad (4)$$

where

$$W = [w_1, w_2, w_3, \cdots, w_j], w_j = (\mu_j, v_j, \pi_j)(j = 1, 2, \cdots n)$$

(iv) Set up the aggregated intuitionistic fuzzy decision matrix. The aggregated intuitionistic fuzzy decision matrix is calculated from intuitionistic fuzzy matrix multiply fuzzy weight matrix (Boran et al. 2009):

$$R \otimes W = \{\langle x, \mu_{A_i}(x) \bullet \mu_w(x), v_{A_i}(x) + v_w(x) - v_{A_i}(x) \bullet v_w(x) \rangle | x \in X\} \quad (5)$$

$$\pi_{A_i} \bullet w(x) = 1 - v_{A_i}(x) - v_w(x) - \mu_{A_i}(x) \bullet \mu_w(x) + v_{A_i}(x) \bullet v_w(x) \quad (6)$$

The aggregated intuitionistic fuzzy decision matrix is:

$$R' = \begin{bmatrix} r'_{11} & r'_{12} & \cdots & r'_{1n} \\ r'_{21} & r'_{22} & \cdots & r'_{2n} \\ \vdots & \vdots & \vdots & \vdots \\ r'_{m1} & r'_{m2} & \cdots & r'_{mn} \end{bmatrix} \quad (7)$$

where $r'_{ij} = (\mu'_{ij}, v'_{ij}, \pi'_{ij}) = (\mu_{A_i} w(x_j), v_{A_i} w(x_j), \pi_{A_i} w(x_j))$.

(v) Obtain intuitionistic fuzzy positive ideal solution and intuitionistic fuzzy negative ideal solution.

$$IFPIS = (\mu_{A^+} w(x_j), v_{A^+} w(x_j)) \quad (8)$$

$$IFNIS = (\mu_{A^-} w(x_j), v_{A^-} w(x_j)) \quad (9)$$

The IFPIS and IFNIS of benefit indicators and cost indicators are expressed by (10) and (11):

$$\begin{aligned} \mu_{A^+}w(x_j) &= \max_i \mu_{A_i}w(x_j) \\ v_{A^+}w(x_j) &= \min_i v_{A_i}w(x_j) \\ \mu_{A^-}w(x_j) &= \min_i \mu_{A_i}w(x_j) \\ v_{A^-}w(x_j) &= \max_i v_{A_i}w(x_j) \end{aligned} \tag{10}$$

$$\begin{aligned} \mu_{A^+}w(x_j) &= \min_i \mu_{A_i}w(x_j) \\ v_{A^+}w(x_j) &= \max_i v_{A_i}w(x_j) \\ \mu_{A^-}w(x_j) &= \max_i \mu_{A_i}w(x_j) \\ v_{A^-}w(x_j) &= \min_i v_{A_i}w(x_j) \end{aligned} \tag{11}$$

(vi) Calculate the separation between the positive and negative ideal solutions (Szmidt and Kacprzyk 2000):

$$s^+ = \sqrt{\frac{1}{2n}w^2(x_j)\sum_{j=1}^{n}\left[(\mu_{A_i} - \mu_{A^+})^2 + (v_{A_i} - v_{A^+})^2 + (\pi_{A_i} - \pi_{A^+})^2\right]} \tag{12}$$

$$s^- = \sqrt{\frac{1}{2n}w(x_j)\sum_{j=1}^{n}\left[(\mu_{A_i} - \mu_{A^-})^2 + (v_{A_i} - v_{A^-})^2 + (\pi_{A_i} - \pi_{A^-})^2\right]} \tag{13}$$

(vii) Calculate the relative closeness coefficient to the intuitionitic ideal solution:

$$C_i^* = \frac{s_i^-}{s_i^+ + s_i^-} \tag{14}$$

where $0 \le C_i^* \le 1$.

4 Empirical Study

A highway project needs to purchase large quantities of steel. Firstly, several qualified suppliers are selected from the company's database to hold a bidding procurement, and then expert committees are arised to rank the suppliers. To simplify the calculation, we assume that the evaluation of three experts D = (D_1, D_2, D_3) involves four evaluation indicators of $X = (X_1, X_2, X_3, X_4)$ on four bidders $A = (A_1, A_2, A_3, A_4)$ to select the best suppliers. Combined with the project characteristics, evaluation indicators are selected as follows: X_1 = product quality; X_2 = price; X_3 = delivery performance; X_4 = the industry's reputation. Specific selection process is as follows:

(i) Determine the weight of the experts. It is assumed that all experts on the fuzzy language evaluation are shown in Table 3. According to (2), the weights of the experts are as follows: $\lambda_{DM1} = 0.356$, $\lambda_{DM2} = 0.238$, $\lambda_{DM3} = 0.406$.

(ii) Set up the intuitionistic fuzzy matrix. Expert opinions about each bidder are shown in Table 4.
According to Table 3, the linguistic terms are changed into intuitionistic fuzzy numbers. We can get the aggregated intuitionistic fuzzy matrix as follows:

$$R = \begin{bmatrix} (0.780, 0.118, 0.102) & (0.687, 0.203, 0.100) & (0.615, 0.282, 0.103) & (0.764, 0.132, 0.104) \\ (0.728, 0.170, 0.102) & (0.526, 0.374, 0.100) & (0.543, 0.356, 0.101) & (0.746, 0.151, 0.103) \\ (0.644, 0.254, 0.102) & (0.578, 0.321, 0.101) & (0.626, 0.272, 0.101) & (0.596, 0.302, 0.102) \\ (0.668, 0.231, 0.101) & (0.663, 0.236, 0.101) & (0.740, 0.156, 0.104) & (0.708, 0.184, 0.108) \end{bmatrix}$$

(iii) Calculate the weights of evaluation indicators. The experts evaluation linguistic terms is shown in Table 5.
Linguistic terms are converted into intuitionistic fuzzy numbers. According to (4), the weights of is as follow:

Table 3 Linguistic terms of experts

	D_1	D_2	D_3
Linguistic terms	Important	General	Very important
Intuitionistic fuzzy number	(0.75, 0.20)	(0.50, 0.45)	(0.90, 0.10)

Table 4 Experts' opinions

	DM_1	DM_2	DM_3
	$X_1/X_2/X_3/X_4$	$X_1/X_2/X_3/X_4$	$X_1/X_2/X_3/X_4$
A_1	Best/high/general/better	Good/higher/better/better	Better/higher/far/good
A_2	Good/general/general/good	Better/higher/general/good	Good/general/farther/better
A_3	Better/higher/farther/general	Better/general/farther/good	Good/higher/farther/better
A_4	Better/high/farther/better	Good/high/farther/good	Good/better/far/better

Table 5 Linguistic terms of evaluation indicators

Indicators	DM1	DM2	DM3
X1	Very important	Important	Very important
X2	Important	Very important	Important
X3	Important	General	Important
X4	General	Important	General

Table 6 Separation measure and the relative closeness. Coefficient of each bidder

	X_1	X_2	X_3	X_4
S^+	0.073	0.023	0.087	0.106
S^-	0.091	0.117	0.063	0.038
C*	0.555	0.836	0.724	0.264

$$W_{\{X_1,X_2,X_3,X_4\}} = \begin{bmatrix} (0.876, 0.118, 0.006) \\ (0.799, 0.170, 0.031) \\ (0.705, 0.242, 0.053) \\ (0.576, 0.371, 0.053) \end{bmatrix}^T$$

(iv) According to (5) and (6), we get the aggregated intuitionistic fuzzy matrix:R'. According to (8) and (9), we can obtain FPIS and FNIS.

(v) According to (10)–(13), we calculate the distance of the bidders between positive and negative ideal point and the relative closeness coefficient of each bidder. See Table 6:
Then the bidders are ranked as: $X_2 > X_3 > X_1 > X_4$. Thus the best supplier for the highway project's steel bidding procurement is X2.

5 Conclusion

We introduced a scientific and reasonable evaluation process including IFS, IFWA and the TOPSIS method. IFS was used to express expert opinions without affecting the experts' preferences. It was combined with IFWA to get a intuitionistic fuzzy matrix. TOPSIS method was used to rank the project material procurement bidders. The process is useful for the construction enterprises to choose ideal suppliers.

References

Atanassov K.T.: Intuitionistic fuzzy sets. Fuzzy Sets and System. Vol. 20 (1986), p. 87–96

Atanassov K.T.: Two theorems for intuitionistic fuzzy sets. Fuzzy Sets and System. Vol. 110.3 (2000), p. 267–269

Bustince H., Burillo P.: Vague sets are intuitionistic fuzzy sets. Fuzzy Sets and System. Vol. 79 (1996), p. 403–405

Chen S.M., Tan J.M.: Handling muhieriteria fuzzy decision-making problem based on vague set. Fuzzy Sets and System. Vol. 67 (1994), p. 163–172

Boran F.E., Genē S., Kurt M. and Akay D.: A multi-criteria intuitionistic fuzzy group decision making for supplier selection with TOPSIS method. Expert Systems with Applications. Vol. 36 (2009), p. 11363–11368

Gau W.L., Buehrer D.J.: Vague sets. IEEE Transactions on Systems, Man, and Cybernetics. Vol. 23 (1993), p. 610–614

Hong D.H., Choi C-H.: Multicriteria fuzzy decision-making problem based on vague set theory. Fuzzy Sets and System. Vol. 114.1 (2000), p. 103–113

Hu J: Government procurement tender evaluation methods in the DEA. Statistics and Decision. Vol. 9 (1992), p. 125–127

Li D.F: Fuzzy multiobjective Many-person Decision Making and Games. Beijing: National Defence Industry Press (2003)

Sheng Song-tao, Mao Jian-ping and Su cun-an: Application of fuzzy comprehensive evaluation method in bidding assessment of water conservancy works. Yangtze River. Vol. 39.3 (2008), p. 104–106

Szmidt E., Kacprzy K.J: Distances between intuitionistic fuzzy sets. Fuzzy Sets and Systems. Vol. 114 (2000), p. 505–518

Xu Z.S: Intuitionistic fuzzy aggregation operators. IEE Transaction of Fuzzy Systems. Vol. 15 (2007a), p. 1179–1187

Xu Z.S: Intuitionistic preference relations and their application in group decision making. Information Sciences. Vol. 177 (2007b), p. 2363–2379

Xu.Z.S: Models for multiple attribute decision making with intuitionistic fuzzy information. International Journal of Uncertainty. Fuzziness and Knowledge-Based Systems. Vol. 15 (2007c), p. 285–297

Modeling the Out-of-Stock Risk and the EOQ–JIT Cost Indifference Point

Min Wu

Abstract The most important advantage of an economic order quantity (EOQ) system is its ability to handle the unexpected demand. A model for comparing the inventory costs of purchasing under the EOQ system and the just-in-time (JIT) order purchasing system in existing literature concluded that JIT purchasing was virtually always the preferable inventory ordering system. By expanding the classical EOQ model, taking into account out-of-stock risk, which was not considered by previous researchers, this paper shows that it is possible for an EOQ system to be more cost effective than a JIT system when the out-of-stock risk associated with the JIT purchasing system is high or the annual demand is either too low or too high.

Keywords Cost indifference point · EOQ · JIT · Out-of-stock · Risk

1 Introduction

The successful implementation of just-in-time (JIT) purchasing policy in various industries has prompted many companies that still use the economic order quantity (EOQ) purchasing system to ponder whether they should switch to the JIT purchasing policy. This decision is, however, difficult to be made.

Fazel (1997) and Schniederjans and Cao (2001) made significant contributions in developing EOQ–JIT cost indifferent point functions. Fazel (1997) suggested that JIT was only preferable when demand was low. The "fixed costs" such as rental, utilities and personnel salaries were omitted from the EOQ–JIT cost difference function by Fazel (1997).

M. Wu
Department of Real Estate and Construction Management School, The University of Hong Kong, Pok Fu Lam, Hong Kong, China
e-mail: wu@hku.hk

D.D. Wu (ed.), *Modeling Risk Management in Sustainable Construction*, Computational Risk Management, DOI 10.1007/978-3-642-15243-6_2,

Schniederjans and Cao (2001) argued that those "fixed costs" items were not fixed and thus should not be left out from the EOQ–JIT cost difference function. Schniederjans and Cao (2001) further argued that in situations where plants adopting the JIT operations experienced or could take advantage of physical plant space square meter reduction, to include a single cost item, namely, the physical plant space factor into the EOQ–JIT cost difference function would substantially increase the EOQ–JIT indifference point. Hence, the existing physical plant space could not hold the revised indifference point's amount of inventory. Consequently, additional physical plant space has to be purchased. This would again force "... a new round of additional facility space costs favoring a JIT system ..." (Schniederjans and Cao 2001, p.117). Schniederjans and Cao (2001) further suggested that saving space and using it to house additional increasing amounts of inventory to meet larger annual demand were juxtaposed issues. Schniederjans and Cao (2001) then concluded that the inclusion of a single cost item that was omitted by Fazel (1997) would prove that the JIT system was always preferable to an EOQ system (Schniederjans and Cao 2001). However, Schniederjans and Cao (2001) had difficulty to either scientifically or empirically ascertain the capability of an inventory facility to hold the EOQ–JIT cost indifference point's amount of inventory.

The most important advantage of an EOQ system is its ability to handle the unexpected demand. This paper expands the classical EOQ model, takes into account out-of-stock risk, which was not considered by previous researchers, and shows that it is possible for an EOQ system to be more cost effective than a JIT system when the out-of-stock risk associated with the JIT purchasing system is high or the annual demand is either too low or too high.

2 Harris' (1915) EOQ Model

Both Schniederjans and Cao's (2001) and Fazel's (1997) EOQ–JIT cost difference functions were based on Harris's (1915) EOQ model, namely, the classical EOQ model. The classical EOQ model aims to minimize the total of ordering and holding costs, while assuming some inventory operating costs such as rental, utilities, and personnel salary, etc are "fixed" costs. The total annual cost of the classical EOQ system, TC_E, is the sum of the inventory ordering cost, inventory holding cost, and the cost of the actual purchased units, or:

$$TC_E = \frac{kD}{Q} + \frac{Qh}{2} + P_E D \tag{1}$$

where Q is the fixed order quantity, h is the annual cost of holding one unit of inventory in stock, k is the cost of placing an order, D is the annual demand for the item, P_E is the purchase price per unit, $\frac{D}{Q}$ is the annual ordering frequency, $\frac{Q}{2}$ is the annual average inventory level in the inventory facility. The first ratio is the inventory ordering cost item. The second ratio is the inventory holding cost item.

The last item is the annual purchasing cost component. Suggested that k and h are the most subjective components in (1). Nevertheless, k usually includes the inventory delivery charges and transaction costs of clerical paperwork. h often includes opportunity cost of the working capital tied up in purchased goods, taxes and insurance paid on inventory items, inventory spoilage cost and inventory obsolescence cost. The classical EOQ model provides appropriate inventory ordering decisions only when its assumptions can be met. These assumptions are: (1) the inventory operating costs, rental, utilities and personnel salary, etc are constant; and (2) h the annual cost of holding one unit of inventory in stock and k the cost of placing an order are constant. It should be noted that although the term "the total annual cost of an inventory item under an EOQ system" is widely used to refer to "TC_E" in (1), "TC_E" is not the actual total annual cost of an inventory item under an EOQ system. The actual total annual cost of an inventory item under an EOQ system should be the sum of "TC_E" and the "fixed costs".

As mentioned earlier, that the so called "fixed costs", including "rental, utilities, and personnel salary" were excluded from the inventory holding cost item in (1) was also an important assumption made by Fazel (1997) and Schniederjans and Cao (2001) when they derived their EOQ–JIT cost indifference points. However, since (a) It is agreed that the so called "fixed costs" were left out from the so called "total annual cost of the EOQ system", and (b) Gaither (1996) suggested that the annual inventory holding cost should include the opportunity cost of the working capital tied up in purchased goods, taxes and insurance paid on inventory items, inventory spoilage cost and inventory obsolescence cost, together with the cost of physical storage, and (c) Schonberger (1982) and Wantuck (1989) etc proved that the so called "fixed costs" would no longer be constant during JIT operations, and (d) Schniederjans and Olsen (1999) and Schniederjans and Cao (2001) observed that the saved inventory facilities can be rented out when the annual average inventory level dropped, then there is a reason to include all components of inventory holding costs into the holding cost item, when comparing an EOQ system with a JIT system. To sum up, one of the assumptions of the classical EOQ model, namely, the so called "fixed" costs are excluded from the holding cost item need to be revised, and the traditional EOQ model need to be expanded when comparing an EOQ purchasing system with a JIT purchasing system.

3 Revised EOQ Model

The revised EOQ model was identified from the ready mixed concrete (RMC) industry in land-scarce Singapore. The expensive land rental promoted the RMC suppliers to reduce the size of their inventory facilities to save on inventory holding costs of the raw materials for mixing RMC. "An inventory facility", in this study, is defined as a physical plant place where raw materials, goods or merchandise are stored. An inventory facility can be a storehouse, a warehouse, an aggregates depot, a cement terminal, or a sand yard. The total cost under the revised EOQ model is thus:

$$TC_{Er} = \frac{kD}{Q} + \frac{HQ}{2} + P_E D \tag{2}$$

TC_{Er} is the sum of the inventory ordering cost, the expanded inventory holding cost, and the cost of the actual purchased units. TC_{Er}, with the inclusion of the so called "fixed costs", is the actual total cost of the EOQ ordering system and is thus greater than TC_E, in (1). $H$is the expanded annual cost of holding one unit of inventory in stock. "H", with the inclusion of the additional inventory holding costs, is thus significantly greater than "h" in (1). The revised EOQ model assumes that the so called "fixed costs", including rental, utilities and personnel salary are proportion to the annual average inventory level. This assumption is possible, particularly when the square meter area of an inventory facility is designed in proportion to its annual average inventory level and the rental, utilities and personnel salary are in proportional to the size of the inventory facility. The revised EOQ model is particularly suitable for the scenarios in which the so called "fixed costs" are not fixed, for example during the feasibility study stage and design stage of an inventory facility, or the excess inventory facility space can be rented out when the annual average inventory level drops, as observed by Schniederjans and Olsen (1999) and Schniederjans and Cao (2001).

By taking the first order derivative with respect to Q of (1) and setting it to equal to zero, the optimum order quantity of the classical EOQ model, Q^*, can be derived as:

$$Q^* = \sqrt{\frac{2kD}{h}} \tag{3}$$

By taking the first order derivative with respect to Q of (2) and setting it to equal to zero, the optimum order quantity of the revised EOQ model, Q_r^*, can be derived as:

$$Q_r^* = \sqrt{\frac{2kD}{H}} \tag{4}$$

The optimum order quantity of the revised EOQ model, Q_r^* is significantly less than the optimum order quantity of the classical EOQ model, Q^*, as H the annual cost of holding one unit of inventory in the revised EOQ model is substantially greater than h the annual cost of holding one unit of inventory in the classical EOQ model, supposing the values of the other parameters, namely, D and k are the same.

To sum up, the revised EOQ model is different from the classical EOQ model on four counts. Firstly, the so called "fixed costs", such as rental, utilities, personnel salaries, etc, are considered in the inventory holding cost item in the revised EOQ model, thus $H \succ h$. Secondly, the so called "fixed costs" are also included into the total annual inventory costs in the revised EOQ model, thus $TC_{Er} \succ TC_E$. Thirdly, the revised EOQ model prefers small lot sizes and frequent deliveries. Last, but not least, the revised EOQ model aims to reduce the actual total inventory ordering and holding cost, while the classical EOQ model aims to reduce the sum of the inventory ordering cost and a part of the inventory holding cost. The last point makes it very clear that the revised EOQ model is more suitable than the classical EOQ model to represent the total cost under the EOQ system when comparing the EOQ system with the JIT system.

4 Revised EOQ–JIT Cost Indifference Point

Equation (4) results in a total annual optimal cost under the EOQ purchasing approach of:

$$TC_{Er} = \sqrt{2kDH} + P_E D \tag{5}$$

It is essential to note that (5) is valid only when two conditions are concurrently satisfied. Firstly, k the cost of placing one order and H the annual cost of holding one unit of inventory are constant. Secondly, the inventory is ordered at its economic order quantity.

Under the JIT system, the ordering cost and holding cost, including the so called "fix costs" are mainly transferred to the supplier. The total annual cost under the JIT system, TC_J, suggested by Fazel (1997) is therefore given by:

$$TC_J = P_J D \tag{6}$$

where P_J is the unit price under the JIT system. P_J is greater than P_E. This is to partially reflect the holding costs and ordering costs that have been transferred to the materials suppliers (Fazel 1997; Schniederjans and Cao 2001). However, JIT purchasing systems are time sensitive. JIT purchasing requires precise level schedules and rely on frequent transportation, as they are generally unable to cope with significant fluctuation in demand. This can be seen in situations arising from the Kobe earthquake in Japan (Low and Choong 2001), the strike on the West Coast of American and the 2003 Iraqi War (Singh 2003). Thus, the risk parameter, namely the out-of-stock costs, should be considered. Let $\gamma\beta$ represents the additional out-of-stock costs under a JIT purchasing system comparing to that under an EOQ purchasing system, where γ represents the number of additional working hours that may be affected in a JIT system than that in an EOQ system, β represents the value created in one working hour. $\gamma\beta$ is a penalty for using JIT purchasing instead of EOQ purchasing. The revised total annual cost under the JIT system, TC_{Jr}, is therefore given by:

$$TC_{Jr} = P_J D + \gamma\beta \tag{7}$$

To make a comparison between the total costs under the EOQ system and the JIT system, a $Z_r$model that combines the total annual optimal cost under the EOQ system in (5) and the revised total annual cost under the JIT system in (7) can be presented as:

$$Z_r = \sqrt{2kDH} + P_E D - P_J D - \gamma\beta \tag{8}$$

Z_r represents the cost difference between an EOQ purchasing system and a JIT purchasing system.

When setting Z_r equal to zero, the roots of (8) are the revised EOQ–JIT cost indifference points, D_{indr1} and D_{indr2}. The values of D_{indr1} and D_{indr2} are given by:

$$D_{indr1} = \frac{kH - (P_J - P_E)\gamma\beta - \sqrt{k^2H^2 - 2kH\gamma\beta(P_J - P_E)}}{(P_J - P_E)^2} \tag{9}$$

$$D_{indr2} = \frac{kH - (P_J - P_E)\gamma\beta + \sqrt{k^2H^2 - 2kH\gamma\beta(P_J - P_E)}}{(P_J - P_E)^2} \tag{10}$$

5 Conclusion

JIT purchasing of raw materials is one important technique of the JIT philosophy. However, JIT purchasing is not always more cost effective than the EOQ purchasing system. By expanding the classical EOQ model, this study suggests that it is possible for an EOQ purchasing system to be more cost effective than a JIT purchasing system in the scenarios where demand is too low, or where demand is extremely large and the order costs cannot be economically split, or the out-of-stock costs associated with the JIT purchasing system is high.

References

Fazel, F. (1997), "A comparative analysis of inventory cost of JIT and EOQ", International Journal of Physical Distribution and Logistics Management, Vol. 27 No. 8, 496–505.

Gaither, N. (1996), Production and Operations Management, Duxbury Press, Belmont, CA.

Harris, F.W. (1915), Operations and Cost – Factory Management Series, A.W. Shaw Co, Chicago.

Low, S.P. and Choong, J.C. (2001), "Just-In-Time management of precast concrete components", Journal of Construction Engineering and Management, Vol. 127 No. 6, pp. 494–501.

Schniederjans, M.J. and Cao, Q. (2001), "An alternative analysis of inventory costs of JIT and EOQ purchasing", International Journal of Physical Distribution & Logistics Management, Vol. 31 No. 2, pp. 109–123.

Schniederjans, M.J. and Olsen, R.J. (1999), Advanced Topics in Just-in-Time Management, Westport, Conn: Quorum Books.

Schonberger, R.J. (1982), "A revolutionary way to streamline the factory", The Wall Street Journal, 15 November, pp. 24.

Singh, K. (2003), "Just-In-Time systems thrown into chaos suppliers rush to meet orders", The Streats Time, 20 March, Singapore.

Wantuck, K.A. (1989), Just-In-Time for America: A Common Sense Production Strategy, The Forum Ltd., Milwaukee, WI.

A Partner Selection Method Based on Risk Evaluation Using Fuzzy Soft Set Theory in Supply Chain

Zhi Xiao and Weijie Chen

Abstract Risk management in supply chains has received increasing attention in both academia and industry, so taking the risk evaluation into consideration to the partner selection problem is greatly meaningful. However, partner evaluation and selection considering risk factors are difficult under uncertain supply chain environment. In this paper, we present a new algorithm based on the fuzzy soft set theory and relative difference function to partner selection problems which has considered risk factors. A numerical example is employed to substantiate the algorithm.

Keywords AHP · TOPSIS

1 Introduction

Nowadays, the competition among enterprises has evolved into the competition among the supply chains, but the supply chains are exposed to different kinds of risks that increase along with globalization. Supply chain risk management (SCRM) is therefore a field of escalating importance. A number of mathematical models have been developed for modeling the partner selection problems, but there are few articles that deal with the partner selection process under risks. Wang et al. [1] described a risk-based subcontractor selection problem and designed a rule-based genetic algorithm for solving it. Huang et al. [2] discussed a possible Risk Breakdown Structure (RBS) for virtual enterprises and suggested a risk evaluation method. Wu et al. [3] proposed a fuzzy multi-objective programming model to decide on supplier selection taking risk factors into consideration.

Z. Xiao (✉) and W. Chen
School of Economics and Business Administration, Chongqing University, Chongqing 400044, People's Republic of China
e-mail: xiaozhi@cqu.edu.cn, chwj721@163.com

D.D. Wu (ed.), *Modeling Risk Management in Sustainable Construction*, Computational Risk Management, DOI 10.1007/978-3-642-15243-6_3,

A useful methodology for potential partner evaluation and selection must be able to deal with both vagueness and impreciseness. Soft set theory is a newly-emerging tool to deal with uncertain problems. The concept of soft-set theory was proposed by Molodotsov [4] to deal with the uncertainties. In recent years, research on soft set theory has become active, and its application has boomed. Maji et al. [5] described the application of soft set theory to a decision-making problem. Mushrif et al. [6] proposed a new classification algorithm of the natural textures which was based on the notions of soft set theory. Roy and Maji [7] proposed a decision-making application of fuzzy soft sets. Although the algorithm was proved incorrect by Kong et al. [8], the fuzzy soft sets and multi-observer concept are valuable to successive researchers. Zou and Xiao [9] presented location a data analysis approach of soft sets under incomplete information. Xiao and Gong [10] proposed a combined forecasting approach based on fuzzy soft sets.

The remainder of the paper is organized as follows: Sect. 2 introduces the basic principles of fuzzy soft sets and relative difference function. Section 3 gives a description of the fuzzy soft set decision-making method and algorithm to cope with the partner selection problem based on risk evaluation. Section 4 exams the proposed method with an example. Finally some conclusions from the research are presented in Sect. 5.

2 Preliminary

2.1 *Relative Difference Function Model*

Assume $X_0 = [a, b]$ is the attraction domain of variable fuzzy set $\underline{V}$ on the axis, and $X = [c, d]$ is one of range section that includes $X_0 (X_0 \subset X)$, which can be shown in Fig. 1 as follows [11].

In Fig. 1, both $[c, a]$ and $[b, d]$ are the rejection domain, M is one dot belonging to attraction domain $[a, b]$, whose degree of membership $u_A(x)$ equals 1. Assume x is an arbitrary point. When x is on the left of M, then the relative function formula is shown in (1) as follows:

$$D_A(u) = \begin{cases} \left(\dfrac{x-a}{M-a}\right)^{\beta} x \in [a, M] \\ -\left(\dfrac{x-a}{c-a}\right)^{\beta} x \in [c, a] \end{cases} \tag{1}$$

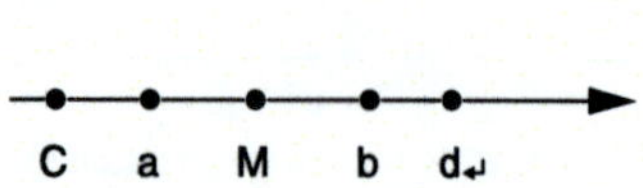

Fig. 1 The Location of X, M, $[a, b]$ and $[c, d]$

When x is on the right of M, then the formula is shown in (2) as follows:

$$D_A(u) = \begin{cases} \left(\frac{x-b}{M-b}\right)^{\beta} x \in [M,b] \\ -\left(\frac{x-b}{d-b}\right)^{\beta} x \in [b,d] \end{cases} \tag{2}$$

When $x \notin [c,d]$,

$$D_A(u) = -1 \tag{3}$$

β is nonnegative index, where $\beta = 1, M = \frac{a+b}{2}$.

Using (1), (2) and (3) we can calculate the relative membership degree, with (4) as follows:

$$u_A(x) = \frac{1 + D_A(u)}{2} \tag{4}$$

2.2 Soft Set and Fuzzy Soft Set

Let U be an initial universe set and let E be a set of parameters.

Definition 2.1. *(see [4]). A pair (F,E) is called a soft set over U, where F is a mapping given by $F: A \to P(U)$.*

Definition 2.2. *(See [12]). If (F,A) and (G,B) be two soft sets then "(F,A) OR (G,B)" denoted by $(F,A) \vee (G,B)$ is defined by $(F,A) \vee (G,B) = (O, A \times B)$, where $O(\alpha,\beta) = F(\alpha) \cup G(\beta)$, $\forall(\alpha,\beta) \in A \times B$.*

Definition 2.3. *(See [13]). Let $A_i \subset E$. A pair (F_i, A_i) is called a fuzzy soft set over U, where F_i is a mapping given by $F_i : A_i \to \mathscr{P}(U)$.*

3 Combined Risk Evaluation and Decision-Making Model Based on Fuzzy Soft Set

3.1 Establishment of Risk Factors Set

According to supply chain partnership system constitution, there are 11 individual risk factors affecting the supply chain partner selection, and they can be divided into three tiers [14], which can be commonly expressed as follows : $E = \{A,B,C\}$, and the single-factor sets are $A = \{a_1,a_2,a_3,a_4\}$, $B = \{b_1,b_2,b_3,b_4,b_5\}$, $C = \{c_1,c_2\}$ as show in Fig. 2.

Fig. 2 Supply chain partnership risk

Table 1 The level of risk

1	2	3	4	5
0–0.1	0.1–0.3	0.3–0.5	0.5–0.7	0.7–0.9

3.2 *The Evaluation Model of Risk Level Coefficient*

In the model, it is presented that the level of supply chains partnership risk can be divided into five grades. Construct the value of interval matrix $I_{a,b}$

$I_{a,b} = ((a,b]_1, (a,b]_2, (a,b]_3, (a,b]_4, (a,b]_5) = ([0,20], (20,40], (40,60], (60,80], (80,100])$. According to $I_{a,b}$ structure changes, the scope of the value of interval matrix $I_{c,d}$ is $I_{c,d} = ([c,d]_1, [c,d]_2, [c,d]_3, [c,d]_4, [c,d]_5) = ([0,40], [0,60], [20,80], [40,100], [60,100])$.

Based on the historical data, each expert can give the assessment value x_{ij}. x_{ij} denotes that the *ith* expert evaluates value for the *jth* risk factor, x_j is the *jth* risk factor value of comprehensive evaluation ,where $x_j = \frac{1}{n}\sum_{i=1}^{n} x_{ij}$. Using (4), we can calculate the final risk level:

$$H = \sum_{h=1}^{5} \frac{u_{ij}}{\sum_{j=1}^{n} u_{ij}} h \tag{5}$$

where H denotes the final risk grade assessment and $h(h = 1,2,3,4,5)$ represents the risk grade. Comparing the calculation result of H with the level of risk in Table 1, we can calculate the risk level coefficient $V_A(u_{ij})$ of risk factor:

$$V_A(\mu_{ij}) = g_i^l + (H - h_i) \times 0.2 \tag{6}$$

where g_i^l denotes the lower value of *ith* risk grade.

3.3 Weight Determination Based on Fuzzy Soft Sets

Definition 3.1: *Let* (F,A) *denote the fuzzy soft set over a common universe.* $U = \{o_1, o_2, o_3, ..., o_n\}$, *where* U *represents the universal set of partners, and* $A = \{a_1, a_2, a_3, ..., a_m\}$ *denotes the set of risk factor parameters, and then* F *is a mapping given by* $F : A \rightarrow \mathcal{P}(U)$.

Definition 3.2: *Let* $\xi_{ij}(i = 1,2,...,n; j = 1,2,...,m)$ *be a fuzzy variable defined on the fuzzy soft sets* (F,A), *and then its membership function is defined as follows*

$$f(\xi_{ij}) = V_A(u)_{ij}. \tag{7}$$

Obviously, $f(\xi_{ij}) \in [0,1]$ *and* $f(\xi_{ij})$*is a measure of the extent to the partner belongs to the level of risk factor. We can represent it in Table 2.*

Definition 3.3: *Suppose a vector* $W = [w_1, w_2, w_3, ..., w_m]$, *in which* $w_j(j = 1,2,3,...,m)$ *denotes the weight of the jth risk factor,*

$$w_j = \frac{\sum_{i=1}^{n} f(\xi_{ij})}{\sum_{j=1}^{m}\sum_{i=1}^{n} f(\xi_{ij})} \tag{8}$$

3.4 Decision Algorithm

Step 1: According to historical data, each expert gives out the assessed value x_{ij} and we can construct the relative difference function model. Then we can calculate the final risk grade H of each risk factor using (5), and determine the risk coefficient $V_A(u)_{ij}$ by (6).

Step 2: Use (7) to construct fuzzy soft sets (F,A), (G,B), (H,C) respectively.

Step 3: Compute the corresponding resultant-fuzzy-soft-set (S,P) from the fuzzy soft sets (F,A), (G,B), (H,C) and place it in tabular form.

Step 4: Calculate each w_j with (8) and construct the comprehensive weights table $((S\omega),P)$ according to fuzzy soft set (S,P).

Step 5: Compute $c_{ij} = \sum_{k=1}^{m} (f_{ik} - f_{jk})$, where the membership value of object o_i for the *kth* parameter is f_{ik}, and calculate the relative score of o_i, $\forall i$, $r_i = \sum_{j=1}^{m} c_{ij}$. The decision is k if $r_k = \min r_i$.

Table 2 A tabular form of fuzzy soft set

U	a_1	a_2	a_3	...	a_m
o_1	$f(\xi_{11})$	$f(\xi_{12})$	$f(\xi_{13})$	...	$f(\xi_{1m})$
o_2	$f(\xi_{21})$	$f(\xi_{22})$	$f(\xi_{23})$	...	$f(\xi_{2m})$
...	...	...	...	...	...
o_n	$f(\xi_{n1})$	$f(\xi_{n2})$	$f(\xi_{n3})$	...	$f(\xi_{nm})$

4 A Numerical Example

For demonstration purpose, the proposed model will be applied to a numerical example. Here we can use supposed data to test the proposed method effective for risk decision.

4.1 Stage of Evaluation and Selection

According to the historical data, every expert estimates each risk factor's value with the scope of the interval of [0,100]. Now there are five experts involved in the risk

Table 3 The value of the experts' evaluation

–	o_1	o_2	o_3	o_4	o_5
U	$e_1, e_2, ..., e_{11}$	$e_1, e_2, ..., e_{11}$	$e_1, e_2, ..., e_{11}$	$e_1, e_2, ..., e_{11}$	$e_1, e_2, ..., e_{11}$
E_1	20, 32, ...,43	23, 43, ...,61	19, 43, ...,51	21, 39, ...,43	27, 51, ...,61
E_2	19, 30, ...,52	19, 41, ...,57	21, 41, ...,47	19, 45, ...,41	29, 49, ...,69
E_3	20, 30, ...,42	17, 41 ,...,57	23, 41, ...,55	17, 47, ...,39	31, 47, ...,57
E_4	20, 42, ...,67	22, 39, ...,60	17, 39, ...,49	20, 39, ...,40	25, 50, ...,59
E_5	17, 36, ...,32	21, 42, ...,59	20, 45, ...,50	15, 43, ...,41	27, 48, ...,63

Table 4 The tabular representation of the fuzzy soft set (F,A), (H,C) and (G,B)

(F,A)						(H,C)	
U	a_1	a_2	a_3	a_4	–	c_1	c_2
o_1	0.19412	0.33076	0.52556	0.15210	–	0.39412	0.47942
o_2	0.20588	0.41698	0.52728	0.18572	–	0.43914	0.58302
o_3	0.20000	0.42478	0.60298	0.19126	–	0.38846	0.5027
o_4	0.18846	0.43452	0.49592	0.20874	–	0.61962	0.41154
o_5	0.28418	0.49310	0.50548	0.22222	–	0.50000	0.62478
(G,B)							
U	b_1	b_2	b_3	b_4	b_5	–	–
o_1	0.40298	0.31126	0.50980	0.34590	0.58302	–	–
o_2	0.49310	0.38302	0.38846	0.30548	0.49866	–	–
o_3	0.60874	0.39126	0.49730	0.38572	0.39412	–	–
o_4	0.39072	0.40298	0.49166	0.37272	0.61962	–	–
o_5	0.50408	0.46378	0.49592	0.36316	0.42972	–	–

Table 5 The resultant fuzzy soft set (S,P) and weight of risk factor

U	$'e_{11} \vee c_1'$	$'e_{11} \vee c_2'$	$'e_{12} \vee c_1'$	$'e_{12} \vee c_2'$	...	$'e_{45} \vee c_1'$	$'e_{45} \vee c_2'$
o_1	0.40298	0.47942	0.39412	0.47942	...	0.58302	0.58302
o_2	0.49310	0.58302	0.43914	0.58302	...	0.49866	0.58302
o_3	0.60874	0.60874	0.39126	0.50270	...	0.39412	0.50270
o_4	0.61962	0.41154	0.61962	0.41154	...	0.61962	0.61962
o_5	0.50408	0.62478	0.50000	0.62478	...	0.50000	0.62478
ω	0.02480	0.02550	0.02210	0.02450	...	0.02450	0.02750

Table 6 A tabular form of comprehensive weight fuzzy soft set

U	$(e_{11} \vee c_1, \omega_1)$	$(e_{11} \vee c_2, \omega_2)$	$(e_{12} \vee c_1, \omega_3)$	$(e_{12} \vee c_2, \omega_4)$	...	$(e_{45} \vee c_1, \omega_{39})$	$(e_{45} \vee c_2, \omega_{40})$
o_1	0.0100	0.0122	0.0087	0.0118	...	0.0143	0.0160
o_2	0.0122	0.0149	0.0097	0.0143	...	0.0122	0.0160
o_3	0.0151	0.0156	0.0087	0.0123	...	0.0097	0.0138
o_4	0.0154	0.0105	0.0137	0.0101	...	0.0152	0.0170
o_5	0.0125	0.0160	0.0111	0.0153	...	0.0122	0.0172

Table 7 The comparison with TOPSIS and FSS

TOPSIS(similarity to ideal solution)			FSS(relative risk coefficient)
U	Weight of index confirmed by entropy and AHP	Weight of index confirmed by entropy and weighted average	
o_1	0.7488	0.7459	−0.1697
o_2	0.5556	0.5641	0.0048
o_3	0.6411	0.5664	−0.1082
o_4	0.4491	0.4520	0.1078
o_5	0.3739	0.3565	0.1653

evaluation for five candidates. It is supposed that the results of the experts' evaluation are listed in Table 3.

Using (4) and (5), we can get the grade of the risk factors, then calculate the risk level coefficient of each risk factor, which are showed in Table 4.

Now considering the fuzzy soft set (F,A), (G,B) and (H,C), we perform "OR" operation. Suppose $P = \{e_{11} \vee c_1, e_{11} \vee c_2, ..., e_{45} \vee c_2\}$ is the set of choice parameters of an observer. The tabular representation of resultant fuzzy soft set (S,P) will be as below (Table 5).

From the Table 6, we can obtain $r_1 = -0.1697$, $r_2 = 0.0048$, $r_3 = -0.1082$, $r_4 = 0.1078$, $r_5 = 0.1653$. The decision is k if $r_k = \min_i r_i$. So the decision is object o_1.

4.2 *Comparison with AHP and TOPSIS*

In order to examine the performance of this model, we employ the above data to compare the fuzzy soft set model with TOPSIS model.

Table 7 offers a comparison between TOPSIS with different weight and fuzzy soft sets decision method. The results reveal that FSS and TOPSIS are more or less equal performance, but due to subjective factors affects, different weights may result in different results. Applying FSS to the selection of supply chain partners is likely to yield more reliable partners and thus reduce disruption to the supply chain operations and improve the supply chain competitiveness.

5 Conclusions

This study develops a partner selection approach by applying fuzzy soft set theory. This paper uses the risk coefficient as the criterion of fuzzy membership. The proposed approach provides a general and flexible framework to form a fuzzy soft set decision model. The numerical example demonstrates that the proposed method can be useful for solving partner selection based on risk problems.

References

1. Wang D, Yung KL, Ip WH (2001). A heuristic genetic algorithm for subcontractor selection in a global manufacturing environment. *IEEE Transactions on Systems, Man and Cybernetics-Part C: Applications and Reviews*, 31(2), 189–198.
2. Huang H, Chen J (2005). A partner selection method based on risk evaluation in virtual enterprises. *2005 International Conference on Services Systems and Services Management*, 1–2, 608–612.
3. Wu DD, Zhang Y, Wu D, et al. (2010). Fuzzy multi-objective programming for supplier selection and risk modeling: a possibility approach. *European Journal of Operational Research*, 200, 774–787.
4. Molodtsov D (1999). Soft set theory-first results. *Computers & Mathematics with Applications*, 37, 19–31.
5. Maji PK, Roy AR (2002). An application of soft sets in a decision making problem. *Computers & Mathematics with Applications*, 44(8–9), 1077–1083.
6. Mushrif MM, Sengupta S, Ray AK (2006). Texture classification using a novel, soft-set theory based classification algorithm. *Lecture Notes in Computer Science*, 3851, 246–254.
7. Roy AR, Maji PK (2007). A fuzzy soft set theoretic approach to decision making problems. *Journal of Computational and Applied Mathematics*, 203, 412–418.
8. Kong Z, Gao L, Wang L (2009). Comment on "A fuzzy soft set theoretic approach to decision making problems". *Journal of Computational and Applied Mathematics*, 223, 540–542.
9. Zou Y, Xiao Z (2008). Data analysis approaches of soft sets under incomplete information. *Knowledge-Based Systems*, 21, 941–945.
10. Xiao Z, Gong K, Zou Y (2009). A combined forecasting approach based on fuzzy soft sets. *Journal of Computational and Applied Mathematics*, 228, 326–333.
11. Zhang C, Guo Y, Li W, Song W (2007). Use of variable fuzzy sets method for evaluating groundwater quality. *Water Resources and Power*, 25, 15–18.
12. Maji PK, Biswas R, Roy AR (2003). Soft set theory. *Computers and Mathematics with Applications*, 45, 555–562.
13. Maji PK, Biswas R, Roy AR (2001) Fuzzy soft sets. *Journal of Fuzzy Mathematics*, 9, 589–602.
14. Liu X (2008). On the analysis of risk factors of supply chain partnership. *Journal of Jilin Province Economic Management Cadre College*, 22, 62–63.

A Quantitative Analysis for Degree of Supplier Involvement Under Market Uncertainty

Zi-jian Zhang and Hua Pan

Abstract In this paper, we provide a quantitative analysis for the degree of supplier's involvement under market uncertainty. Taking the proportion of tasks assumed by supplier as an index of the involvement extent, we seek this optimized extent from supplier's point of view. Our analysis shows that, for the supplier's involvement, its participation is restricted by two sides' relative marginal profit, development ability and market uncertainty of the new product. When supplier involved and shared some manufacturer' design task, it has a optimized proportion to choose, this proportion is positive relation to its marginal profit and technology development ability, negative relation to manufacturer's marginal profit and technology development ability, and negative relation to market success probability.

Keywords Degree · Market uncertainty · Supplier involvement

1 Introduction

The growing sophistication of component technologies and the rising costs of product development require suppliers to involve in the design process in earlier stage of new product development. When the manufacturers and suppliers design products together, it obtains the advantages of integration of two complementary resources, reducing product development risk and development costs, increasing production flexibility and quality, etc. [1, 2].

Supplier involves in product development through establishing cooperative relations with the manufacturer. It is more flexible than the vertical integration,

Z.-j. Zhang (✉)
College of management, Chongqing Jiao tong University, Chongqing 400074, People's Republic of China
e-mail: kenzijian2000@yahoo.com.cn

H. Pan
Vocational College of Architecture Engineering, Chongqing 400039, People's Republic of China
e-mail: Panhua2009@163.com

D.D. Wu (ed.), *Modeling Risk Management in Sustainable Construction*, Computational Risk Management, DOI 10.1007/978-3-642-15243-6_4,

and more efficient than traditional trading relationships [3], in addition, suppliers are integrated into the production and design process systematically, so that the suppliers can be directly involved in the initial stages of the design and communication, and, through the establishment of a set of rules in order to facilitate inter-organizational knowledge sharing, so that providers can offer their technical knowledge and creativity, and to provide customers with development-related equipment and information of the new products, and make recommendations for new products. In contrast, the manufacturer can also provide relevant market information providers and knowledge, and the suppliers should also take the appropriate responsibility, including the development, design and engineering responsibility for a complete system or sub-system [4–6].

Although there is a substantial body of research emerging in this field using a range of different research methodologies, empirical findings regarding performance benefits differ quite significantly. There are also uncertainties as to the situations in which supplier involvement will reap the expected benefits. While supplier involvement in product development projects can contribute with valuable knowledge and expertise, such involvement also poses organizational and managerial challenges [7]. Under the supplier involvement, besides the business risk inherent in innovation from the technical and market uncertainty, firms may also face the partners' uncertainty arising from the relationship between the agency problems of risk.

Despite the apparent benefits of supplier involvement in NPD, research remains fragmented [8]. Literatures about supplier involvement are almost from manufacturer's point of view, deals mostly with how manufacture manage the supplier's involvement , and ignores the inclination of the supplier influence by its benefits and the effect of market uncertainty on its decision-making. In fact, supplier involve in product development and taking part of the innovation task should pay a certain cost, Meanwhile, R&D in most situation has features of uncertainty, complexity, high-risk and so on. Our paper, focused on the inclination of the supplier's involvement. We take the proportion of new product design afford by supplier as index of supplier's involvement degree, and from this degree, we can express desire of supplier's involvement.

Bidualt thinks that supplier's involvement is that one kind of degree concept [9]. The high degree of suppliers' participation means that suppliers must take full responsibility for a complete system or sub-systems, components and sub-assembly. When suppliers participate in low degree, they just provide customers with the necessary equipment and information, and only provide cost and quality of the recommendations. Swink defines supplier involvement as the suppliers can involve in the design and communication of the new products directly, and they may participate in it at design stage of new products [10]. Wynstra and Pierick give a definition of supplier involvement as the participation of customers of new product development projects, and the extent of participation can be decided by the design of the customer to enhance the customer's manufacturing capacity-building or to a specific part of a complete development, design and engineering responsibility [11]. Petersen et al. define involvement may range from simple consultation with suppliers on design ideas to making suppliers fully responsible for the design of components or systems they will supply [12].

This paper focuses on the decision of supplier's involvement degree, borrows some modeling elements from collaborative development literatures, but differs significantly in that it emphasizes quality improvement and market uncertainty. We evaluate supplier involvement decision making that focuses on product quality improvements through effort sharing arrangements between firms. We quantitatively characterize the supplier involvement inclination influence by manufacture and supplier's relative profits and technology capability, and look for the optimal degree of supplier's involvement.

2 The Model

Suppose the future market demand for new products is determined by new product design stage scale of the task, the more of product design work carried out by, the bigger that will be, the better of the new product performance, behave as the greater demand of market. However, they need greater investment of resources.

$$q(a) = q_0 + b \cdot a^{\gamma} \tag{1}$$

where b is the proportion constant and assume that $b>0$, implying that the market demand of new product $q(a)$ increasing with the scale of the task a. γ is a factor to measure the impact of system development cost on the new product and assume that $\gamma<1$, implying that the diminishing returns from R&D expenditures or to diseconomies of scale that, in practice, are associated with bureaucracies in a larger firm which stifle creativity and impede innovation.

Assume that the product architecture the manufacturer adopted is a standard interface, so suppliers do not need to carry out development of customized components. We assume that the Ia/λ is the cost in the design phase of new products. We could interpret I as the investment cost coefficient and λ as a measure of the firm's innate development capability, directly impacting the speed and consistency of the development process, and is assumed to be a constant parameter for analytical tractability.

Into the production phase, each new product unit produced and sold, the marginal profit of manufacturer to obtain is ρ_m. The profit should be the marginal benefits multiply the market demand for the product and minus the R&D expenses as follow:

$$\pi_m = \rho_m \cdot q(a) - Ia/\lambda_m - F \tag{2}$$

Assume that the manufacturer during product design is unsure of the product's future market conditions. The probability of the favorable market condition is v, probability of unfavorable conditions is $(1 - v)$. Considering the uncertainty of development, and we can derive the expected profit of new products for the manufacturer:

$$\pi_m{}^v = v \cdot \rho_m \cdot b \cdot a^\gamma - Ia/\lambda_m - F \tag{3}$$

Without loss of generality, assume that product development is divided into two phases: the design stage and production stages. As the product development projects carried out over time, uncertainty will gradually disappear. Assume that manufacturer must make R&D investment before the uncertainty of new product has been revealed, but can delay their production decision until the new product further information appears. If the market condition is unfavorable, manufacturer will not make the fixed investment F of commercial stage for the new product. Consider this option value, the manufacturer's expected profit as follow:

$$\pi_m{}^v = v \cdot (\rho_m \cdot b \cdot a^\gamma - F) - Ia/\lambda_m \tag{4}$$

Assume that the supplier agrees to share a fraction k of the total product design tasks which the manufacturer incurs. Therefore, we can obtain profits of manufacturer and supplier respectively as follow:

$$\pi_m = \rho_m \cdot q(a) - I[(1-k)a]/\lambda_m - F \tag{5}$$

$$\pi_s = \rho_s \cdot q(a) - I[ka]/\lambda_s \tag{6}$$

where λ_m and λ_s are the innate technical capacity of manufacturer and supplier respectively and assume that $\lambda_m > \lambda$ and $\lambda_s > \lambda$, implying that with the supplier involvement, each firm could offer more attention to the specialization area, so could have a better technical capacity.

Consider the uncertainty of R&D and the option value; we can obtain the expected profits of manufacturer and supplier respectively as follow:

$$\pi_m^v = v \cdot [\rho_m \cdot q(a) - F] - I[(1-k)a]/\lambda_m \tag{7}$$

$$\pi_s^v = v\rho_s \cdot q(a) - I[ka]/\lambda_s \tag{8}$$

The profit in whole supply chain is:

$$\pi^v = v \cdot \rho \cdot q(a) - vF - I_m[(1-k)a] - I_s(ka) \tag{9}$$

3 Involvement Degree Decision Process

When supplier involve in with relational risk, manufacturer and supplier could make two decisions: the extent of supplier's involvement k, determining the proportion of tasks the supplier agrees to afford, the scale of product design tasks a, determining the degree of product innovation manufacturer want to undertake. The sequence of decision making is as follows: The supplier determines, at first, the proportion of design task k it would like to afford when the manufacturer invites it to involve in. Subsequently, the manufacturer determines design task scale a to make its profit maximizing.

From (7), Differentiating π_m^v w.r.t to a, we can find the scale of design tasks a that maximizes the manufacturer profits. This optimal scale would be:

$$a^C = \left(\frac{v \cdot \rho_m \cdot b \cdot \gamma \cdot \lambda_m}{(1-k)I}\right)^{\frac{1}{1-\gamma}} \tag{10}$$

As can be seen here, $(\partial a/\partial k>0)$, the scale of product design a is increasing in the degree of supplier involvement k, applying the greater the proportion of design tasks supplier agree to afford, the bigger the level of innovation manufacturer would undertake.

Substituting (10) in (7), we have

$$\begin{aligned}\pi_m^v &= v \cdot \rho_m \cdot b \cdot \left(\frac{v \cdot \rho_m \cdot b \cdot \gamma \cdot \lambda_m}{(1-k)I}\right)^{\frac{\gamma}{1-\gamma}} \\ &\quad - (1-k)\left(\frac{v \cdot \rho_m \cdot b \cdot \gamma \cdot \lambda_m}{(1-k)I}\right)^{\frac{1}{1-\gamma}} - v \cdot F_1\end{aligned} \tag{11}$$

The new product project require the future expected profit ${\pi_m}^v$ at least not lower then the profit of not execute this project π_m^N, so, it must ensure that:

$${\pi_m}^v \geq \pi_m^N \tag{12}$$

From (12), we can have

$$v^C \geq \left[\frac{(1-k) \cdot F_1 \cdot I}{(\rho_m \cdot \delta)^{\frac{1}{1-\gamma}}\left(\gamma^{\frac{\gamma}{1-\gamma}} - \gamma^{\frac{1}{1-\gamma}}\right)\lambda_m}\right]^{\frac{1-\gamma}{\gamma}} = v_{th}^C \tag{13}$$

Consider investing in an enterprise product development in a particular time, there is a market success probability threshold v_{th}^C. When this threshold is smaller, it means developing more extensive range of options, so the project will be more likely to occur. Therefore, the probability of market success of companies represented range in new product development projects can be considered, the scope of that business success can only be selected in this probability range of products into projects for development.

From (13), we can see that $v_{th}^C/k<0$, it means the supplier involvement degree will influence the manufacture's product development threshold. When supplier have a deep involvement, it may pull down this threshold, and the manufacture's product development would more likely to carry on.

For the supplier, although its participation can promote the manufacturer's product development, but participation needs to pay their own costs, for supplier, it has an optimal level of participation.

Substituting (10) in (8), we have

$$\pi_s^v = v\rho_s \cdot b \cdot \left(\frac{v \cdot \rho_m \cdot b \cdot \gamma \cdot \lambda}{(1-k)I}\right)^{\frac{\gamma}{1-\gamma}} - k \cdot I \cdot \left(\frac{v \cdot \rho_m \cdot b \cdot \gamma \cdot \lambda}{(1-k)I}\right)^{\frac{1}{1-\gamma}} \Big/ \lambda_s \tag{14}$$

From first order condition of π_s^v w.r.t to k, we can find the degree the supplier involve in that maximizes the profit:

$$\begin{aligned} & v \cdot \rho_s \cdot b \cdot \left(\frac{v \cdot \rho_m \cdot b \cdot \gamma \cdot \lambda_m}{I}\right)^{\frac{\gamma}{1-\gamma}} \cdot \left(\frac{\gamma}{1-\gamma}\right) \cdot (1-k)^{-\frac{1}{1-\gamma}} \\ & - I \cdot \left(\frac{v \cdot \rho_m \cdot b \cdot \gamma \cdot \lambda_m}{I}\right)^{\frac{1}{1-\gamma}} \cdot (1-k)^{-\frac{1}{1-\gamma}} \Big/ \lambda_s \\ & - k \cdot I \cdot \left(\frac{v \cdot \rho_m \cdot b \cdot \gamma \cdot \lambda_m}{I}\right)^{\frac{1}{1-\gamma}} \cdot \left(\frac{1}{1-\gamma}\right)(1-k)^{-\frac{2-\gamma}{1-\gamma}} \Big/ \lambda_s = 0 \end{aligned} \tag{15}$$

The resulting extent of supplier involvement would be the following:

$$k = \begin{cases} \dfrac{\lambda_s\rho_s - v(1-\gamma)\rho_m\lambda_m}{(\lambda_s\rho_s + v\gamma\rho_m\lambda_m)}, & \lambda_s\rho_s > v(1-\gamma)\rho_m\lambda_m \\ 0, & \text{otherwise} \end{cases} \tag{16}$$

4 Result Analysis

4.1 Proposition 1

The supplier would involve in the product development only if the multiplication of technology development capability λ_s and relative profit margins ρ_s is above a certain threshold i.e., $\lambda_s\rho_s\eta > (\eta - \gamma)(\lambda_m\rho_m)$.

By (16) we can find that when Suppliers bear part of the design task even if they can promote the development of new products, increasing market demand for new products, thereby increasing their demand for the supply of components, but this increase in profits by paying less than the cost of compensation involved, the supplier will be unwilling to participate in.

Proposition 1 captures the impact of that even though suppliers bear part of the design task can increase the profits of manufacturer, for suppliers, which may not be attractive enough, unless the increase in end-market demand to achieve a certain level. As the relative profit margins ρ_s and technology development capability λ_s increase, motivation of supplier involvement increases, and when $\lambda_s \rho_s \eta > (\eta - \gamma)(\lambda_m \rho_m)$, supplier then would agree to involve in the product development.

4.2 *Proposition 2*

The degree of suppliers willing to involve positive correlate to its technology development capability and relative profit margins, negative correlate to the manufacturer's technology development capability and relative profit margins, meanwhile, it negative correlate to the uncertainty of the product development project.

Proposition 2 captures the impact of that the degree of supplier's involvement depends on both sides' technology development capability and relative profit margins, meanwhile, it depends on the market success probability. The degree of supplier's involvement positive relating to its marginal benefits, technology development capability is mainly due to that as the supplier's technological development capacity λ_s increasing, the cost required to pay will be reduced, at the same time, as supplier's marginal benefits ρ_s increasing, the benefit form involve in the manufacturer's product innovation will be greater, so its involvement motivation will be stronger. The degree k negative relating to v is due to that when v is smaller, the uncertainty is greater, the manufacturer's product development is more risky, therefore, the less the investment. Meanwhile, in order to ensure that manufacturers of product development so both sides can benefit, the supplier will need a greater degree of commitment to the manufacturer's development tasks, sharing the development risks.

5 Conclusions

In summary, suppliers can participate in manufacturer's R&D in certain conditions, which is conditioned by the relative profit margins by both parties and the development of capacity constraints. Sometimes they may not participate in the development of cooperation. Moreover, when suppliers involve in the product development, and sharing part of the design task of the proportion, the most appropriate degree, in this degree of participation, suppliers can get the most expected profit. The degree of participation best suited to their own profit margins with suppliers and technology development capabilities are related to, but not with the manufacturer's profit margin as well as technical development capacity negatively correlated with market uncertainty determined by the probability of market success of products negatively Correlated with the positive correlation coefficient of R&D investment.

Acknowledgement This research is supported by the funds project under Humanities and Social Sciences Foundation of Ministry of Education of China (No. 09YJC630248).

References

1. Clark K.B. (1998) Project Scope and Project Performance: The Effect of Parts Strategy and Supplier Involvement on Product Development, *Management Science*, 35[10], 1247–1263.
2. Dyer J.H. (1997) Effective Inter firm Collaboration: How Firms Minimize Transaction Costs and Maximize Transaction Value, *Strategic Management Journal*, 18[7], 535–556.
3. Pelton L.E., Strutton D. and Lumpkin J.R. (1997) *Marketing Channels – A Relationship Management Approach*, Chicago: Irwin.
4. Bonaccorsi A., Lippaini A. (1994) Strategic Partnerships in New Product Development: An Italian Case Study, *Journal of Product Innovation Management*, 11, 134–145.
5. Dyer J.H., Nobeoka K. (2000) Creating and Managing: A High-Performance Knowledge-Sharing Network: The TOYOTA Case, *Strategic Management Journal*, 21[3], 345–367.
6. Liker J.K., Kamath R.R., Watsi S.N. and Nagamachi M. (1996) Supplier Involvement in Automotive Component Design: Are There Really Large US Japan Differences, *Research Policy*, 25[1], 59–89.
7. Andersen P.H., Drejer I. (2009) Together We Share? Competitive and Collaborative Supplier Interests in Product Development, *Technovation*, 29[10], 690–703.
8. Johnsen T. E. (2009) Supplier Involvement in New Product Development and Innovation: Taking Stock and Looking to the Future, *Journal of Purchasing and Supply Management*, 15[3], 187–197.
9. Bidualt F., Despres C. and Butler C. (1998) New Product Development and Early Supplier Involvement (ESI): The Drivers of ESI Adoption, *International Journal of Technology Management*, 15[1 & 2], 49–69.
10. Swink M. (1999) Threats to New Product manufacturability and the Effects of Development Team Integration Processes, *Journal of Operations Management*, 17[6], 691–709.
11. Wynstra F., Pierick E.T. (2000) Managing Supplier Involvement in New Product Development: A Portfolio Approach, *European Journal of Purchasing and Supply Management*, 6[1], 49–57.
12. Petersen K.J., Handfield R.B. (2005) Supplier Integration into New Product Development: Coordinating Product, Process and Supply Chain Design, *Journal of Operations Management*, 23[3], 371–388.

Part II
Enterprise Risk Management in Construction

Dynamic Network Planning Simulation for Scheduling Risk Analysis Base on Hybrid System

Lin Yang, Yanlong Zhao, and Yueyue Chen

Abstract Scheduling risk analysis and measure is a critical problem in modern project management. The network planning techniques are the most popular tools for it. This paper discussing the limitations of current network planning and consider that neglecting the correlations in project system will result in deviation of Scheduling risk measure. Addressing this problem, a Dynamic network planning simulation model is proposed, it integrate PERTS (PERT SIMULATION) and SD (System Dynamics) base on discrete–continuous hybrid System. When mimic the process by using PERTS, SD capture the feedback to measure the correlations in project system and reflect to scheduling. Such model try to comprehensive analysis the scheduling risk. Finally, a foundation work process is modeled using the hybrid approach to illustrate the model how to work.

Keywords Hybrid system · Network planning technique · Scheduling risk analysis · Simulation

1 Introduction

The network planning technique developed in late 1960s. It has become very important tool for the quantitative schedule risk assessment. In summary, this technique has undergone three phase:

The first phase: during this phase, the deterministic model was applied to study a project scheduling. It divides a project process into a number of sub processes

L. Yang (✉) and Y. Chen
School of Civil Engineering, Lanzhou Jiaotong University, Lanzhou 730070, People's Republic of China
e-mail: yanglin5@yeah.net; chenyue-chenyue@163.com

Y. Zhao,
School of Economics and Management, Lanzhou Jiaotong University, Lanzhou 730070, China
e-mail: zhaoyl@mail.lzjtu.cn

D.D. Wu (ed.), *Modeling Risk Management in Sustainable Construction*, Computational Risk Management, DOI 10.1007/978-3-642-15243-6_5,

(or call activities), and then assume the duration of each activities in the project as a constant. Therefore, we can analyze these processes utilizing the approaches of deterministic mathematics. The typical method during this phase is CPM (Critical Path Method). However, these methods are not significant in the risk assessment because they are deterministic model.

The second phase: during this phase, CPM was regard too simple to measuring risk, so the activities in a project are not represented by constants, but variables. Thus, whole scheduling of project was modeled a stochastic process. However, the approaches of dealing with this stochastic process are still the deterministic mathematic methods. The typical method during this phase is PERT (program evaluation and review technique). A project manager can measure risk from the scheduling of project by PERT, although it is a approximate method for risk measuring.

The third phase: during this phase, the stochastic mathematic methods were applied to model a project processes. The typical method is PERTS (PERT SIMULATION), it is an improved method to PERT but is different from PERT essentially: a series of random numbers were generated and represented the durations of each activities. Such experiment was carried out for many times, and then we can get large numbers of sample dates. According to the Monte Carlo (MC) principle, some indexs representing information of scheduling risk were calculated out through these dates, it can help us understanding and measuring the risk of a project scheduling.

2 PERT Simulation

We take a construction project example to explain PERTS. There is a construction project illustrated in Fig. 1. It is a six-activates network about a foundation work including digging foundation pit, casting foundation-bed, bricklaying, earth moving, earth abandoning and backfilling. First, determine what probability distribution the duration of activities obeys. Usually, it assumes that the duration of an activity obey β distribution. Second, every activity gets a number obeyed β distribution which generated by the program of random numbers generating. The values of these numbers represent the duration, and it is said the construction project was mimicked once, and the result is showed in Fig. 1a. If we do it once again, we get another result showed in Fig. 1b. Following, we repeat it many times and will get great deal of dates which can be analyzed to measure the scheduling risk about this construction project.

3 The Limitations of PERTS

With the growing of understanding to the project system, the discussions on PERTS applying in scheduling risk analysis begin to focus on the "relations" in a project. The tradition network planning technique (including CPM, PERT and PERTS)

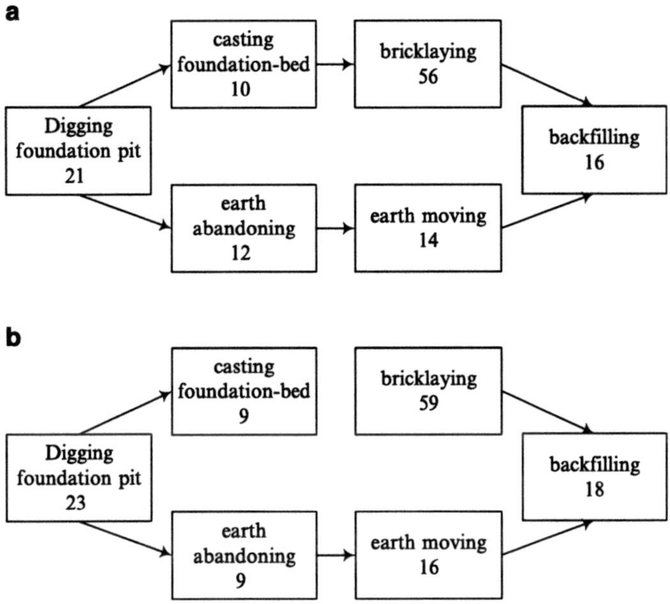

Fig. 1 A foundation work network diagram

neglect such relations, nevertheless, the relations (or say relate behaviors) are really exist in real project processes. For example, assume that some kind of delay occurred during the aforementioned casting foundation-bed, and it would lead to schedule slippage. In such a case, the project manager should not overlook this schedule discrepancy, but should take actions such as assigning more workers or issuing overtime work hours in next activity. So, the duration of bricklaying was reduced. In this case, there are some related behaviors between the casting foundation-bed and the bricklaying. Meantime, it causes the scheduling change. thus it can conclude that the non-correlated supposition in the tradition network methods is too simplify to help measure scheduling risk, that is say that sometimes the results these methods conclude probably are far away from the reality. Hence, a project manager will make decision-making mistake. The paper tries to address these issues in an effort. Following, a discussion will begin about what kinds of relations exist in project [1].

4 The Relations in a Project

Under the perspective of The System Theory, a system of project was composed of many entities (e.g. workers, machinery, project manager, materials, etc.) and a context surrounding these entities. Here, context represents the overall project-related behavior (e.g., staff skill level, collaboration level, motivation, inspection level, etc.), which interacts with scheduling and changes dynamically as a result of the feedback between the two. For example, any change in staff skill level (context) would affect how the project is carried out, and vice versa (e.g., where learning as a result of repetitive work operations can increase staff skill level, which will eventually cycle back to impact operation). The scheduling of a project is performed by the context and entities which interacting each other. Furthermore, each of entity has own attributes (for example, a worker has some attributes such as skill level, fatigue, etc.) [2]. In summary, there are three types of relations in a project scheduling (we explain the following terms through the aforementioned case of foundation work):

1. The correlations between processes and events: for instance, any deviation of the digging foundation pit process may cause the event which is hiring temporary workers to expedite this process
2. The correlations among processes: for example, a delay in the process of digging foundation pit would impact remaining processes such as bricklaying. The project manager would reduce the duration of bricklaying by hiring temporary workers and issuing overtime work. The goal is to realize the planned project duration.
3. The correlations among processes and the attributes of entities: for instance, the addition of temporary workers may be increase the production rate of bricklaying. However, there is a another probability is this policy may not increase the production rate as much as expected, as the additional workers may be low-skilled and will therefore require more time to complete the process. As well, the low-skilled workers may commit more errors and further slow the production rate.
4. And how to measure the scheduling risk caused by these relation behaviors in project? It is obviously that the tradition network approaches can't address these problems because they hypothesized that the activities in project are independent each other. In recent years, system dynamics (SD), a method applied widely in the social sciences, begins to be applied in realm of risk analysis because of its ability to effectively capture feedback.

5 System Dynamics

System dynamics (SD), a concept based on the notion of continuous simulation, it is capable of capturing feedback. Feedback here can be defined as the phenomenon whereby the output of a system is passed back through the system as input in a cyclical manner. The majority of complex dynamics arise from the feedbacks among the various components of the system, and not from the complexities of the components themselves. SD attempts to build the feedback, identifying cause and effect relationships between variables in the system. Focusing on this capability, SD has also been incorporated into diverse the risk analyses. One of the major

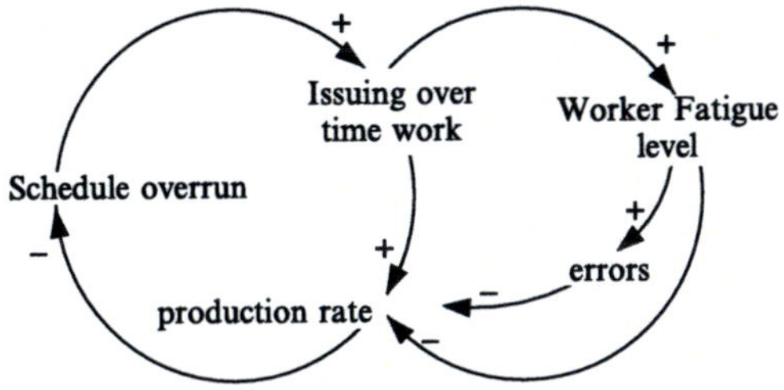

Fig. 2 SDs feedback processes caused by issuing over time work

areas that SD has targeted in the scheduling risk analysis of a project is the feedback between the entities' behavior and their surrounding contexts. For example, Fig. 2 shows SD's causal loop diagram, which aims at capturing this feedback process. In this previous digging foundation pit case, the overtime work can increase the production rate. However, feedback analysis suggests that some risk exist in this policy, because of the overtime work may be increase workers' fatigue lever and then the production rate will slow, then the schedule overrun [3].

6 Need for Integrating SD and PERTS

The significance of both processes and correlations of a project tells us that they should be taken into account simultaneously for a comprehensive understanding. Particularly with the modeling point of view, PERTS is able to mimic the process of a project but has a no capability to capture correlations in a project due to its hypothesis. On the other hand, SD can capture the feedbacks in a project, and capturing the many influencing factors with consistent time steps, by virtue of its continuous simulation; thus a hybrid approach that integrates SD and PERTS is needed in order to maximize their contributions, addressing both activities and correlations simultaneously. In light of this fact, this paper proposes a hybrid PERT–SD approach that can seamlessly addresses both activities and correlations [2].

7 Hybrid SD–PERTS Model

Essentially, to develop a hybrid PERT–SD model, project process are modeled by applying PERTS, their feedbacks with project context are modeled through the application of SD. However, one of the major challenges here is how to formulate interactions between PERTS and SD in a single model. PERTS is a kind of DES (Discrete Event Simulation), so it is based upon discrete time system. Meantime, SD is a kind of CVS (Continuous Variable Simulation) and it is based upon continuous variable system. For the purpose of interacting SD and PERTS, it needs that putting PERTS into an approximate continuous variable system. Therefore, to change simulation strategy is necessary. Three most common simulation strategies include event scheduling (ES), activity scanning (AS) and process interaction (PI) [4]. The strategy PERTS using is ES, which need that the simulation clocks' steps advance at irregular length according to the events schedule. However, in order to approximate continuous variable system, simulation clocks' step should advance at same length and which should be as short as possible. Hence, we must abandon ES but select AS. Under AS strategy, the simulation clocks' step length is a working day. For simulation advancement, AS scans activities for each work day and other start conditions, and then executes the activity that is due to happen.

8 Example of Modeling Hybrid PERTS–SD

To illustrate how hybrid PERTS–SD work, the aforementioned foundation work has been selected as an example of a possible application. We try to describe the program step by step:

1. Assume the daily output per worker is represented as a continuous variables, and it obey certain distribution. Moreover, we define some variables to represent process-related attribute of entities such as productivity, fatigue, schedule pressure, production rate, probability of error occurrence, probability of change occurrence, etc.
2. After the project start, scanning and checking all activities for start conditions. The activity digging foundation pit meet start conditions, then generate a random number (obey certain distribution) representing the output of first day. It means that the workers have carried out the work for a day. Naturally, some attributes of workers will change, for example, the lever of fatigue increase, the probability of error occurrence reduce, etc. we should define the feedback in these variables, and model the causal loop about these variables. With the PERT simulation process, there is a SD simulation process associating attributes of entities is working synchronously. Moreover, the hybrid model should consider that attributes changing also impact the processes of project. For example, lever of fatigue increase reduce production rate.
3. Compare the number with the workload of digging foundation pit and if it overrun the workload, digging foundation pit end.
4. Advancing simulation progress to next day.
5. Search for the unfinished and full condition activities. If digging foundation pit is unfinished, then generate a random number representing the output of second day.
6. Compare the accumulation of number first day and second day with the workload of digging foundation pit and if it overrun the workload, digging foundation pit end.

7. Advancing simulation progress to the next day.
8. Repeat the similar operation from step 5 to step 8 until there are no activities to execute.

9 Conclusion

This paper has discussed the need for a hybrid approach in order to comprehensive measure project scheduling risk. In past research, PERTS and SD have been addressed separately by means of discrete event simulation (DES) and system dynamics (SD), respectively, and as a result their dynamic interaction has not been thoroughly explored. In an effort to address this issue, the writers have proposed a hybrid PERTS–SD approach; in particular, the paper has introduce a case for demonstrating PERTS and SD how to work in a single model.

References

1. Lee S, Han S, and Peña-Mora F (2007) Hybrid system system dynamics and discrete event simulation for construction management. 2007 International Workshop on Computing in Civil Engineering, Pittsburgh, PA, 232–239.
2. Lee S, Han S, and Peña-Mora F (2009) Integrating Construction Operation and Context in Large-Scale Construction Using Hybrid Computer Simulation. Journal of Computing In Civil Engineering, ASCE, Vol. 23:2, 75–83.
3. Sterman J (2000) Business dynamics: System Thinking and Modeling for a Complex World. McGraw-Hill Publishing, New York.
4. Zhang H, Tam C M, Li H (2009) Activity Object-Oriented Simulation Strategy for Modelling Construction Operations. Journal of Computing In Civil Engineering, ASCE, Vol. 19:3, 314–322.
5. Bent JA, Thumann A (1994) Project Management for Engineering and Construction. Fairmont Press Publishing, Oklahoma.
6. Cassandras C, Lafortune S (2008) Introduction to Discrete Event Systems, Springer.

Research on the Integrated Risk Management Information System of Construction Project

Yun-li Gao

Abstract The integrated risk management of construction project must be based on the information system. The paper presented the frame of integrated risk management information system, which was composed of three subsystems: risk management subsystem, risk management database and external support subsystem. The content and the function of all the subsystems were elaborated and the relationship between information system and the external system was explained. Based on the hierarchical risk breakdown structure, the field and coding of risk database are designed. The information system could provide risk management platform for the project participants, accelerate the information flow and implement the integrated risk management.

Keywords Information system · Integration · Risk management

1 Introduction

The research concentrates on specific phase or some target of project management at present. It is emphasized to manage risk by a lot of mathematic model and other optimal model in these researches [1–3]. Furthermore, the participants of project respectively carry out their process of risk management, and these processes are separated. Obviously the isolated and separated risk management method has not been adapted to the demand of the new project. So it is necessary that the integrated risk management method be presented as a new research field from the overall point of view.

The integrated risk management process is accompanied with the information production, collection, treatment and delivery. The integrated risk management

Y.-l Gao (✉)
Department of Civil Engineering and Architecture, Dalian Nationalities University, Liaoning Dalian, People's Republic of China
e-mail: yunligao@163.com

D.D. Wu (ed.), *Modeling Risk Management in Sustainable Construction*, Computational Risk Management, DOI 10.1007/978-3-642-15243-6_6,

information system is mainly used to optimize the information flow, to improve degree of symmetry and real time. It can deliver appropriate information to the right person. The information system should be able to intercommunicate with other project information [4].

Based on the integrated risk management theory, the integrated risk management information system (IRMIS) is studied in the paper. The information system frame is built in this research and it includes three subsystems: risk management subsystem, risk management database and external support subsystem. The risk management subsystem is made up of risk identification, risk evaluation, risk handling and risk control. The risk management database is composed of risk database and risk handling measure database. The external support subsystem includes the risk management knowledge base, model base and case base. Their relationship and function is expatiated in the paper. In order to characterize the risk better, the field and coding of risk database are designed based on the hierarchical risk breakdown structure.

2 Integrated Risk Management Theory Model

The model of integrated risk management theory is shown in Fig. 1 [5].

The risk set is composed of the project risks. It is considered in the integrated risk management model that the risk, risk management organization, process and targets are varied dynamically along the project total lifecycle. On the other hand,

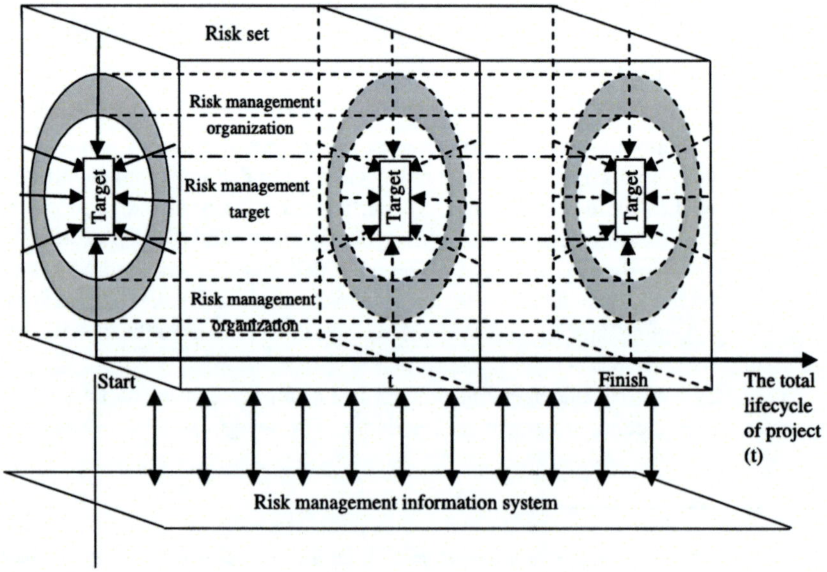

Fig. 1 Integrated risk management theory model of construction project

these elements are integrated at any time t. The project target can be set and optimized at some phase or some time, and the organization pattern can be found to achieve the target. The organization can utilize synthetically and choose the risk management method to manage the project risk at this time. The integrated risk management of construction project must base on the information system, which can provide the risk management platform for the project participants, and implement the integrated risk management.

3 Structure of the Integrated Risk Management Information System

It is implemented in the integrated risk management information system that risks identify, risks evaluate and control. The relevant risk handling measure can be given, and the project risks can be monitored. The integrated risk management information system is shown in Fig. 2.

The information system includes three subsystems: risk management subsystem, risk management database and external support subsystem. The risk management subsystem is made up of risk identification, risk evaluation, risk handling and risk control. The risk management database is composed of risk database and risk handling measure database. The external support subsystem includes the risk management knowledge base, model base and case base. Their relationship is shown in Fig. 3.

3.1 Function of the Integrated Risk Management Information System

3.1.1 Risk Management Subsystem

- Risk identification

The information that generated in the process of project management is identified and chosen. The potential risk will be found based on the deviation between actual data and plan.

- Risk evaluation

On the basis of the risk identification, the probability and consequence of risk is measured by the qualitative or quantitative methods and the risk evaluation model is given. The risk impact can be synthetically analyzed and the whole risk level can be determined.

- Risk handling

The risk trigger threshold is given according to the risk acceptability level. As the risk status is higher than the threshold, the risk handling will startup. The

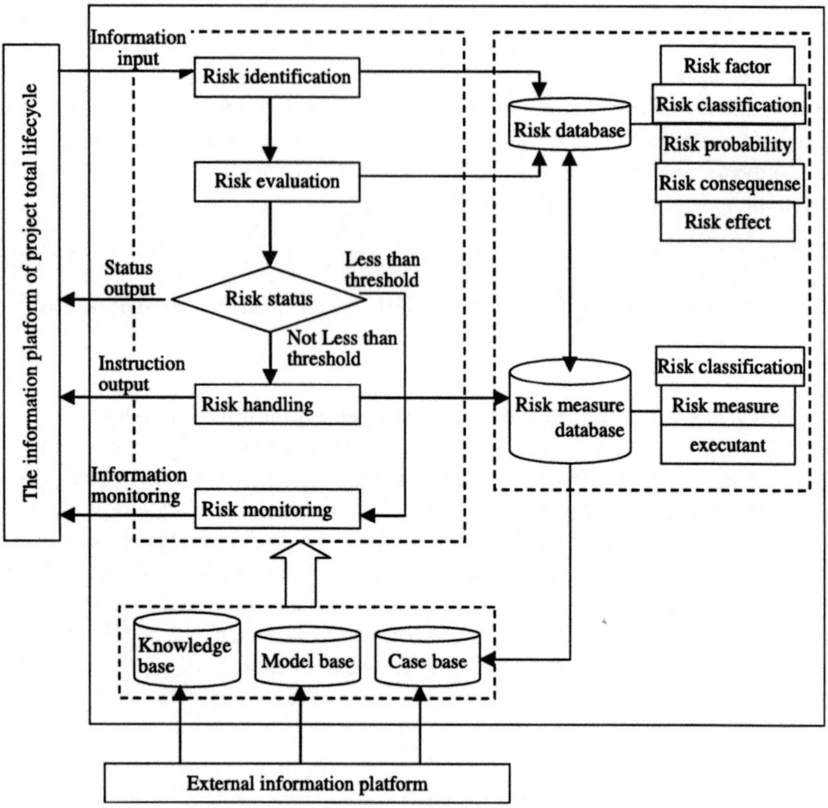

Fig. 2 Project integration risk management information system

relevant risk handling measure will be chosen and risk management action will be implemented.

- Risk monitoring

Risk monitoring system tracks the whole process of project risk management and controls it. Through the dynamic monitoring, the changes of information will be found. Once the changes vary beyond a certain range, the risk identification and evaluation will be startup. In addition, the risk monitoring system can check the effect of taking risk management measure at any time, adjust and revise the risk handling plan.

3.1.2 Risk Management Database

The risk management database is used to describe the overall project risk and it includes all risks data. The risk database is taken as memorizer that store up the risk

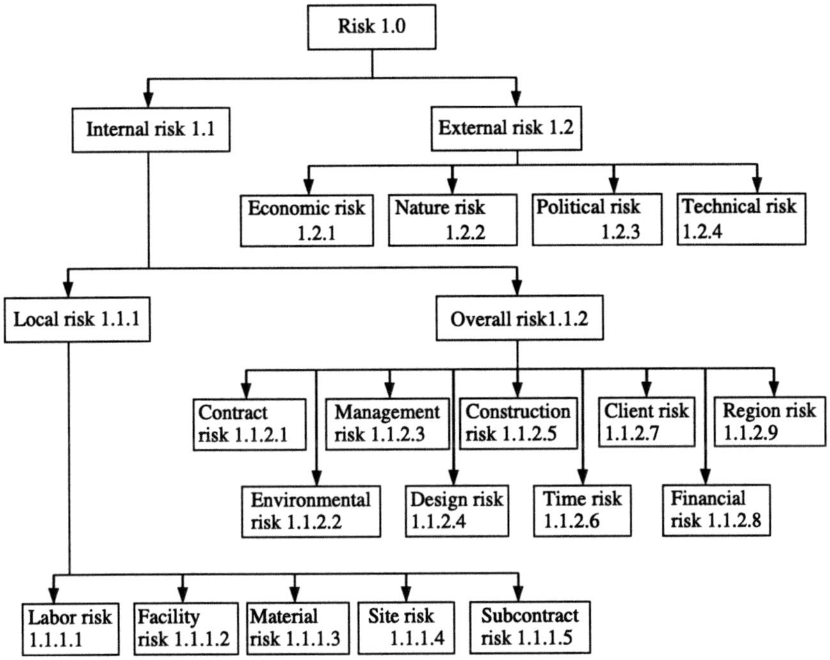

Fig. 3 Hierarchical risk breakdown structure

factor and its category, the probability and consequence of risk, and the impact to project target. The risk handling measure database mainly store up the risk handling measure and plan. The risk database is corresponding to the risk handling measure database. Namely, each probable risk status is accompanied with each risk handling measure.

3.1.3 External Support Subsystem of Risk Management

The integrated risk management information system is complex and dynamic. It needs to be supported by the expert's knowledge. The knowledge base accesses to expert's knowledge and makes knowledge reasoning. The model base includes all the technique, method and model of risk management. The history risk management data can be found in the case base.

3.1.4 Relationship of Three Subsystems

The risk management subsystem is a center in the integrated risk management information system. Using the subsystem, it is implemented that identification, evaluation, handling and monitoring of risk. All risk information is stored in the risk database and the relevant handling measure is stored in risk handling database. In the process of risk management, the method of risk identification, the technique and model of evaluation and other knowledge are needed. They are provided by the external support subsystem. When the project finished, the relevant data will be stored in the case base as the history data.

3.1.5 Relationship of IRMIS and the External System

The project total lifecycle information platform is the foundation of IRMIS. The information that used to identify risk is acquired from the platform and the output information of risk status also inflects on the platform. The user knows the risk status and gives the risk plan through the platform. The new risk that is triggered due to the information change is monitored real time by the risk monitoring system. It is necessary to update that the knowledge base, model base and case base in the external support subsystem.

All project information is reflected on the information platform and they are dynamic in the process of project. So the IRMIS is also dynamic and it will adopt different methods, models and plans that adapting to the changing information. On the other hand, the new method, model and plan will renew the external support subsystem.

3.2 Structure Design and Coding of Risk Management Database

3.2.1 Risk Breakdown Structure

The risk structure can be break down based on the method of hierarchical risk breakdown structure (HRBS) which Tah et al. presented [6, 7]. It is shown in Fig. 3

3.2.2 Designing Field and Coding of Risk Database

The communication about project risk among the participants is incomplete at present. Each participant adopts different languages to describe the same risk and use different techniques and method to analyze the risk. To the same risk, each participant has respective understanding and it is difficult for them to be consensus. So it is necessary that the same language of describing risk is used among the participants, such as fuzzy language or score.

In this paper we can code for the risk information based on HRBS. The field and coding of risk database and risk handling measure database is designed. They are shown in Tables 1 and 2.

Table 1 Field and coding of risk database

Risk field code	Risk factor	Risk classification	Probability	Consequence	Impact	Time	Description
R.1.1.1.1	...	...	...	...	...	...	...
R.1.1.1.2	...	...	...	...	...	...	...
...	...	...	...	...	...	...	...

Table 2 Field and coding of risk measure database

Risk measure code	Risk factor	Risk classification	Risk status	Measure	Cost	Executant	Effect	Description
RM.1.1.1.1	...	...	...	...	...	...	...	...
RM.1.1.1.2	...	...	...	...	...	...	...	...
...	...	...	...	...	...	...	...	...

The design of database standardizes the document and the process of risk management. As the database having more and more information, it can provide better function for future project.

4 Conclusion

Based on the project total lifecycle information platform of the project, it is found that all participants can enter into the risk management information system. All the project information that has been input system will be checked out. Risk information will be found. All participants can understand the process of risk management and discuss how to handle the risk. The effect of risk management can be observed through the system. Even if there is not so many experts and history documents, the risk will be intelligently handled based on the IRMIS. Certainly, the information frame is presented in the paper only, and how to structure and realize this system will be studied in our future research.

References

1. Yuan H., Apostolakis G. (1993) Conditional Influence diagrams in risk management. Risk Analysis 13:625–636
2. Poh Y.P., Tah J.H.M. (2006) Integrated duration-cost influence network for modeling risk impacts on construction tasks. Construction Management and Economics 24:861–868
3. Dikmen I., Birgonul M.T., Han S. (2007) Using fuzzy risk assessment to rate cost overrun risk in international construction projects. International Journal of Project Management 25:494–505
4. Xiang P.C., Xie L.L., Wang L. (2008) Research on the integrated risk management. Construction Economic 5:37–39

5. Gao Y.L., Li H.N., Li P. (2007) Research on the integrated risk management pattern. Construction Economic 3:24–26
6. Tah J.H.M., Carr V. (2001) Knowledge-based approach to construction project risk management. Journal of Computer in Civil Engineering 26:170–177
7. Tah J.H.M., Carr V. (2000) A proposal for construction project risk assessment using fuzzy logic. Construction Management and Economics 18:491–500

Sensitivity Analysis for the Relationship Between Toll Rate and Traffic Volume for Freeway

Lian-yu Wei, Yi Cao, and Pei Chen

Abstract In this paper, the relationship between the toll rate of roads and traffic volume assignment are analyzed based on traffic equilibrium assignment of different roads between an OD pair. And the application of sensitivity analysis is illustrated with a practical example, which shows the relationship between toll and traffic volume under the condition of competition among different sorting roads.

Keywords Equilibrium assignment · Sensitivity analysis · Toll rate · Traffic assignment

1 Introduction

With the construction of freeway and the development of highway-network system of our country, the situation that one or no less than one toll roads work meanwhile with other ordinary roads has been formed in present road network, so travelers have to make choices from a toll freeway and a free ordinary road. A survey shows that the operation of freeway is not very optimistic. It is to say that there is no absolute superiority in traffic volume for a toll freeway compared with its parallel free ordinary roads.

According to the theory of traffic planning, traffic demands is much more affected by generalized trip cost (including road toll and other types of trip costs) for different parallel roads between the same OD pair. For each single user, he is bound to choose the roads with minimum disutility. Therefore, the proper decrease

L.-y. Wei (✉), Y. Cao, and P. Chen
College of Civil Engineering, Hebei University of Technology, Beichen District, Tianjin, People's Republic of China
e-mail: xiaoyi82031203@126.com; 313328565@qq.com; l03y@163.com

D.D. Wu (ed.), *Modeling Risk Management in Sustainable Construction*, Computational Risk Management, DOI 10.1007/978-3-642-15243-6_7,

of road toll would absorb more traffic volume, and for different parallel roads, the change of traffic volume and the adjustment of road toll interact and affect with each other. Although traffic demands are not only decided by road toll, because factors – such as convenience, comfort, and security during trip – affect it too, road toll is the most important factor. Therefore, in transport market of road network, competition exists among different parallel roads, especially among freeways and ordinary roads.

It is obvious that road toll impact directly in traffic assignment among different parallel roads. Existing traffic facilities would be effectively made use of and the maximum economic benefits would be made if the administration of freeways sets a reasonable toll rate according to the relationship between road toll and traffic assignment.

After 20 years development, there are many effective measures of the theory of dynamic route choice. The research of variational inequality model of dynamic optimized route choice develops fast because of its advantages in dealing with asymmetry and its clear analysis characteristics [1]. Ran etc. raised a set of variational inequality models (2) of ideal dynamic user-optimized route choice problems based on road section from single-user perspective in 1996 [2]. Reference [3] analysis users' choice behavior to different roads, and establishes equilibrium model of users' choice among different roads.

In the text, sensitivity analysis measure is used in a traffic network with many different parallel roads (with different toll rate) between the same OD pair, to analysis the relation between traffic volume and road toll under competition condition. Logit model is used to get traffic volume of different parallel roads at equilibrium condition, and the relation of traffic demand and road toll (especially the charging price of a toll road) is figured out through sensitivity analysis. And the application of sensitivity analysis is illustrated with a practical example, which presents the relation between toll and traffic volume under the condition of competition of different sorting roads.

2 Traffic Assignment Among Different Parallel Roads

2.1 Trip Route Choice Mechanism Based on Utility Theory

Drivers' choices from different parallel roads are actually a trip-decision problem. Travelers don't easily make decisions when facing more than one road. In order to simulate travelers' mentality, a utility value or an absorb level – which reflects how much utility travelers would get if they choose a certain route – can be defined for each road.

Travelers always want to choose the road with maximum utility, but in practical problems, utility index is hard to get directly through observation or estimation. Factors that affect the utility are numerous and complex, and contain some random elements. So road utility is a random variable, and it is generally called random utility.

Assume that there are N different parallel roads available for travelers, the utility that travelers would get if choosing the road NO. $i(i \in N)$ can be indicated as:

$$U_i = V_i + \varepsilon_i \tag{1}$$

In this formula, U_i is the random utility of road NO. i, V_i is the utility which can be observed or defined of road NO. i, and ε_i is random error.

V_i is generally defined as:

$$V_i = \sum_{k \subset K} \alpha_i^k x_i^k \tag{2}$$

in this formula, x_i^k is the characteristic index "k" of the route NO. i (assume there are k different characteristics, such as ticket price, trip time, comfort, security and so on). α_i^k is an undefined parameter which can be calculated through statistical theory from observed data. Because utility of different roads is a random variable, it is actually a probability problem for travelers to choose from different routes. It means how much probability for a traveler to choose a certain route. It is obvious that this probability depends on the characteristics of utility function and the distribution of random error. The Logit model is the most wide-used model in route-choice problems. According to reference [1], assume that random errors ε_i of each toll function are independent from each other and follow Gumbel distribution. Route choice model (as follow) can be got under the travelers' utility maximization principle:

$$p_i = \frac{e^{\beta V_i}}{\sum_{i \in N} e^{\beta V_i}} \tag{3}$$

In this formula, p_i is the probability travelers choose the route NO. i, β is an adjustment parameter.

If we know the total traffic volume Q between the OD pair, the traffic volume of route NO. i is:

$$q_i = Q \bullet p_i = \left| \frac{e^{\beta V_i}}{\sum_{i \in N} e^{\beta V_i}} \right| Q \tag{4}$$

q_i is thc traffic volume of route NO. i between the OD pair. $N(i \in N)$ is the assembly of all roads between the OD.

2.2 Equilibrium Assignment of Traffic Flow Model of Different Parallel Roads Between the Same OD Pairs

Assume there are *N* parallel roads between one OD pair, including toll freeways and ordinary free roads. It is a traffic assignment problem of different sorting roads that travelers would consider which road to choose. In this paper, travelers are assumed to always choose the road with minimum generalized trip cost (including freeway toll, trip time, and comfort), and the traffic assignment would be ultimately stable and equilibrium among the different roads, as other equilibrium problems. It can be described as: among all the available routes between the same OD pair, all routes that travelers choose have the same generalized trip cost, and this cost is not more than that of unselected routes. This condition can be described as the following mathematics relation:

$$C_i \begin{cases} = C_\alpha, & \text{when } q_i > 0 \\ \geq C_\alpha, & \text{when } q_i = 0 \end{cases} \tag{5}$$

C_i is the generalized trip cost of road NO. $i(i \in N)$ between the OD pair, C_∂ is the average trip cost of all roads under equilibrium condition between the OD; q_i is the traffic volume of road NO. $i(i \in N), N$ is the assembly of all the roads between the OD pair. It can be described as the following mathematics planning model (*N*):

$$\min Z(q) = \sum_{i \in N} \int_0^{q_i} f(x)dx \tag{6}$$

$$s.t. \ \sum_{i \in N} q_i = Q \tag{7}$$

$$q_i \geq 0, i \in N \tag{8}$$

f is generalized cost function, and traffic flow of different roads are its independent variables, it means that $C_i = f(q_i)$. Different form of Generalized Cost function leads to different assignment modes of different roads between the OD pair. In traffic researches, the most common cost function forms are power function form and log function form. Q means the total traffic volume of all roads between OD pair under equilibrium condition. In this paper, this value can be got through Logit model (by relation (4)), and the condition of relation (7) is non-negative restriction of traffic volume.

Generalized cost function f increases as traffic volume increases, so it is a increasing function. Its derivative to Q is more than 0, so the Hessian matrix of the objective function of model (*N*) is a definite matrix, that is, the objective function is convex, as well as the constraint set, and model (*N*) is a convex-planning problem. It has the unique solution. Reference [2] proves the equivalence between the solution of model (*N*) and the conditions (5) of user-equilibrium. Model (*N*) can be solved through Frank-Wolf measures.

3 Sensitivity Analysis Measures in Multi-modes Traffic Network

Sensitivity analysis measure is mainly used in variational inequality, and derivatives of disturbed parameter in solutions of variational inequality is available by using this measure. In this paper, we defined this disturbed parameter as generalized trip cost of different roads between the same OD, including freeway toll, and other factors – such as trip time, comfort and security, which may affect traffic volume – are all measured in the form of cost. Therefore, this paper emphasizes in analyzing when time, comfort, and security are relatively stable, how the traffic volume changes if the toll changes. First of all, the equilibrium assignment model (*N*) can be expressed with following variational inequality:

$$f(q^*)^T(q-q^*) \geq 0, q \geq 0 \tag{9}$$

q^* is the equilibrium solution of model (N). Notice that all the variable of the above is described with radical vector, that is:

$$q = (q_1, q_2, \cdots\cdots q_N)^T,$$

$$q^* = (q_1^*, q_2^*, \cdots\cdots q_N^*)^T,$$

$$f(q_i^*) = (f(q_1^*), f(q_2^*), \cdots\cdots, f(q_N^*))$$

Then consider the common case that there are disturbed factors $u = [u_1, u_2, \cdots\cdots, u_N]^T$ in $f(q)$, that is, $f(q, u)$, the above variational inequality transforms as:

$$f(q^*(u), u)^T(q - q^*(u)) \geq 0 \tag{10}$$

assume the solution $q^*(u^*)$ of formula (10) is unique and already known when $u = u^*$, according to the reference [3], the necessary condition of the solution (when $u = u^*$) is:

$$f(q^*(u), u) - \mu = 0 \tag{11}$$

$$Q \bullet p_1 = \delta^T \bullet q_1{}^*(u_1) \tag{12}$$

μ is a Lagrange multiplier vector with *N* same elements. Assume that,

$$y(u) = [q(u), \mu(u)]^T \tag{13}$$

$J_y(u)$ refers to the Jacobian matrix of (11) and (12) to $[q, \mu]$, and $J_u(u)$ is Jacobian matrix of (11) and (12) to u. According to reference [3], we get the results:

$$\nabla y(u) = J_y^{-1}(u)[-J_u(u)]^T \tag{14}$$

Then we can get the relation between traffic volume of different roads and toll based on tailor expanded formula:

$$y(u) = [q(u^*), \mu(u^*)]^T + [J_y^*]^{-1}[-J_u^*] \bullet [u - u^*] \tag{15}$$

J_y^* and J_u^* are respectively the figure of $J_y(u)$ and $J_u(u)$ when $u = u^*$.

So we can get the relationship of traffic volume and trip cost under the condition of competition among many different roads between the same OD pair.

4 Practical Example Analysis

In this paper, the example Tianjian to Qing Huangdao is cited to explain the application of sensitivity analysis measure under the condition of multi-routes choice, namely, it shows how to get the relation between traffic flow of different roads and their toll rate. There are three roads connects Tianjian and Qin Huangdao, they are Jin-Tang freeway, 205 National highway and Yan Hai freeway, as shown in Fig. 1.

Consider that it is hard to quantize the service characteristic and the security characteristic, and we emphasize in analyzing the effects of toll rate to traffic flow, so the toll factor (toll rate) and the time factor are the main factors we consider.

According to (2), the traffic utility functions of the above three roads are:

$$V_n = -\alpha_n t_n - \beta_n u_n, n = 1, 2, 3 \tag{16}$$

in this formula, V_n $(n = 1, 2, 3)$ refers to the trip utility of the three roads; t_n is trip time factor; u_n is toll factor; $\alpha_n, \beta_n (n = 1, 2, 3)$ are undetermined parameters. The unit of t_n is convert into time value, and it can be calculated as average working-day of transport vehicles; time value of truck is 100 yuan (RMB) per hour, and car is 20 yuan (RMB) per hour.

The Generalized Trip Cost of different roads is written in the form of the following power function:

$$f(q_n) = a(q_n)^b - V_n \tag{17}$$

a, b are undetermined parameters, q_n is traffic volume of different roads; V_n is utility of different roads.

The traffic volume (AADT) of Tianjin to Qin Huangdao is given by traffic surveys. And it is 65,000 vehicles per hour shared by the three roads. The formal parameters are showed in Table 1.

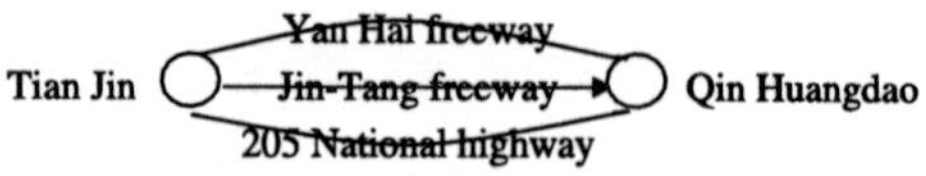

Fig. 1 Three roads of Tianjin to Qin Huangdao

Table 1 Toll and travel time of each route

Number	Route	Toll (yuan)	Travel time (yuan)
1	Jin-Tang Freeway	105	3.5
2	Yan-Hai Freeway	90	4
3	205 National Highway	40	6

After traffic surveys and calculating with (3)–(4), we can get the proportions of the general traffic are: $a_1 = 41.5\%, a_2 = 34.7\%, a_3=23.8\%$ the Average Trip Cost and Average Trip Time can be calculated through the following formula:

$$t = \sum_{n=1}^{3} a_n t_n, \quad u = \sum_{n=1}^{3} a_n u_n \tag{18}$$

from the above, we can get the Average Trip Time of the three roads is $t = 4.01(h)$, the Average Toll is $u = 77.46(yuan)$. Assume the parameters needed in the example are:

$$\beta = 1.0, \alpha_1 = 0.5, \alpha_2 = 0.5, \alpha_3 = 0.5, a = 0.4, b = 0.5$$

According to the total traffic volume between Tianjin and Q in Huangdao and its assignment rate in the three roads, and the derivative of traffic volume to toll rate is $\frac{\partial q}{\partial u} = -268.6$, which can be calculated through sensitivity analysis measure, then solve the planning model (N) to get the assignment result of the three roads: $q_1 = 26650, q_2 = 22555, q_3 = 15755$.

then calculate $J_y(u)$ and $J_u(u)$:

$$J_y(u) = \begin{bmatrix} 0.2(q_1)^{-0.4} & 0 & 0 & -1 \\ 0 & 0.2(q_2)^{-0.4} & 0 & -1 \\ 0 & 0 & 0.2(q_3)^{-0.4} & -1 \\ 1 & 1 & 1 & 0 \end{bmatrix}$$

$$J_u(u) = \begin{bmatrix} 0.4 & 0 & 0 \\ 0 & 0.4 & 0 \\ 0 & 0 & 0.4 \\ \frac{\partial q}{\partial u_1} & \frac{\partial q}{\partial u_2} & \frac{\partial q}{\partial u_3} \end{bmatrix}$$

in the formula, $\frac{\partial q}{\partial u_m} = (\frac{\partial q}{\partial u_1})(\frac{\partial q}{\partial u_m}) = a_m(\frac{\partial q}{\partial u}), m = 1,2,3$ put the datum into matrix $J_y(u)$ and $J_u(u)$, then according to $\nabla_u y = [J_y^*]^{-1}[-J_u]$, we get:

$$\nabla_u y = [J_y{}^*]^{-1}[-J_u] = \begin{bmatrix} -34.3309 & 74.0911 & 58.0611 \\ 78.1223 & -40.9288 & 54.3129 \\ 67.6776 & 60.0419 & -48.4472 \\ 0.2835 & 0.2515 & 0.1971 \end{bmatrix}$$

then we get the approximate relation between traffic volume of the three roads and their toll rates:

$$\begin{bmatrix} q^1{}_1(u_1) \\ q^2{}_1(u_2) \\ q^3{}_1(u_3) \end{bmatrix} = \begin{bmatrix} 26650 \\ 22555 \\ 15755 \end{bmatrix} + \begin{bmatrix} -34.3309 & 74.0911 & 58.0611 \\ 78.1223 & -40.9288 & 54.3129 \\ 67.6776 & 60.0419 & -48.4472 \end{bmatrix} \begin{bmatrix} u^1{}_1 - 105 \\ u^2{}_1 - 90 \\ u^3{}_1 - 40 \end{bmatrix}$$

Now according to the relation between toll rate and traffic volume of the three roads, we can figure out the change of traffic volume of each road, when toll rate range from −20 to 20, as shown in Tables 2–4.

Table 2 Traffic volume change of each route when u_1 changes and u_2, u_3 remain the same

Toll rate change (yuan)	u_1 (yuan)	u_2 (yuan)	u_3 (yuan)	q_1(/h)	u_2(/h)	u_1(/h)
−20	85	90	40	27550.80	21193.00	14575.20
−15	90	90	40	27325.60	21533.50	14870.15
−10	95	90	40	27100.40	21874.00	15165.10
−5	100	90	40	26875.65	22214.40	15460.60
0	105	90	40	26650.00	22555.00	15755.00
5	110	90	40	26424.35	22895.60	16049.40
10	115	90	40	26199.70	23236.20	16344.80
15	120	90	40	25974.40	23576.50	16639.85
20	125	90	40	25749.20	23917.00	16934.80

Table 3 Traffic volume change of each route when u_2 changes and u_1, u_3 remain the same

Toll rate change (yuan)	u_1 (yuan)	u_2 (yuan)	u_3 (yuan)	q_1(/h)	u_2(/h)	u_1(/h)
−20	105	70	40	25347.40	23541.00	14699.40
−15	105	75	40	25673.05	23294.50	14963.30
−10	105	80	40	25998.70	23048.00	15227.20
−5	105	85	40	26324.35	22801.50	15491.10
0	105	90	40	26650.00	22555.00	15755.00
5	105	95	40	26975.65	22308.50	16018.90
10	105	100	40	27301.30	22062.00	16282.80
15	105	105	40	27626.95	21815.50	16546.70
20	105	110	40	27952.60	21569.00	16810.60

Table 4 Traffic volume change of each route when u_3 changes and u_1, u_2 remain the same

Toll rate change (yuan)	u_1 (yuan)	u_2 (yuan)	u_3 (yuan)	q_1 (/h)	u_2 (/h)	u_1 (/h)
−20	105	90	20	25611.80	21583.80	16823.40
−15	105	90	25	25871.35	21826.60	16556.30
−10	105	90	30	26130.90	22069.40	16289.20
−5	105	90	35	26390.45	22312.20	16022.10
0	105	90	40	26650.00	22555.00	15755.00
5	105	90	45	26909.55	22797.80	15512.75
10	105	90	50	27169.10	23040.60	15220.80
15	105	90	55	27428.65	23283.40	14953.70
20	105	90	60	27688.20	23526.20	14686.60

5 Conclusions

As can be seen from the table, among different parallel roads between the same OD pair, when the total traffic demand is relatively stable, if the toll rate of a certain road increases (or decreases), its traffic volume would decrease (or increase), and the traffic volume of its parallel roads would increase (or decrease). The more the toll rate changes, the more obviously the traffic flow changes.

The real relationship between the toll rate of roads and traffic volume assignment can be reflected by using sensitivity analysis measure, and it is helpful for decision-makers to work out a reasonable toll rate level, so that much more economical profit are available. So this measure is effective and feasible in practical engineering problems.

References

1. Li R-M, Tang S-M and Wang F-Y (2006) Research of variational inequality assignment model of dynamic user-optimization. Traffic and Transportation System Engineering and Information, 6(2):83–90
2. Ran B, Boyce DE (1996) A link-based variational inequality formulations of ideal dynamic user-optimal route choice problem. Transportation Research Part C, 4(1):1–12
3. Si B-F, Gao Z-Y (2001) Sensitivity analysis for the relationship between passenger ticket price and passenger volume of different sorting trains. Journal of Northern Jiao Tong University, 4(2), 49–53
4. Gao Z-Y, Ren H-L (2005) Urban dynamic traffic volume assignment model and algorithms. China Communications Press, China

The Application of Dynamic Priority of AHP on Operation Risk Assessment of Metro

Yunhao Gao, Xiuli Du, and Mingju Zhang

Abstract The dynamic priority of analytic hierarchy process is applied in risk assessment and risk prediction of operation metro, and the prediction method of operation risk of metro is established.

Keywords Analytic hierarchy process · Dynamic priority · Operation risk · Risk assessment · Risk prediction

1 Introduction

Chinese rail transportation is very prosperity in recent years, so metro operation safety becomes increasingly prominent, and any failure could lead to significant losses of life and property. Therefore, if the time when the risk occurred can be predicted, precautionary measures could be done. It will effectively reduce the probability of risk occurrence and the losses.

At present, the method of AHP is widely adopted in operation risk assessment of the metro. The process of evaluation aimed mostly at metro current operating condition and did not take the factor of time into account. Metro operation risk changes with time, so the curve of operation risk with time can effectively predict the changeable trend of the risk in the future, which will provide the scientific basis for risk prevention.

Y. Gao (✉), X. Du, and M. Zhang
The College of Architecture and Civil Engineering, Beijing University of Technology, Beijing, People's Republic of China
e-mail: gaoyunhao200704025@emails.bjut.edu.cn; duxiuli@bjut.edu.cn; zhangmj@bjut.edu.cn

D.D. Wu (ed.), *Modeling Risk Management in Sustainable Construction*, Computational Risk Management, DOI 10.1007/978-3-642-15243-6_8,

2 Dynamic Analytic Hierarchy Process

Dynamic analytic hierarchy process is the method considering the factor of time in AHP model, and the judgment matrices are time dependent functions, named dynamic judgment matrices. Saaty [1] gives several normal functions in dynamic judgment matrices and discusses the corresponding solutions, but to find the analytical solution is very difficult. So far, a few methods have been proposed for solving this problem, including least perturbations method [2], least square method [3], and goal programming method [4]. A thorough study of dynamic priority of analytic hierarchy process appears in [5, 6].

The idea suggested by Shubai Xu [7] is adopted to construct judgment matrix in this paper. Set $B(t) = M(t)B_0M^{-1}(t)$, $M(t)$ represents the line affection multiplication matrix, B_0 represents the initial judgment matrix, and $M^{-1}(t)$ row affection multiplication matrix. When W_0 is eigenvectors of B_0 corresponding to the largest eigenvalue $\lambda_{\max}$, eigenvectors $W(t)$ of $B(t)$ corresponding to the largest $\lambda_{\max}$ is as (1).

$$W(t) = M(t)W_0 \tag{1}$$

And, if B_0 is consistent judgment matrix, either does $B(t)$.

3 Operation Risk Assessment of Metro by Dynamic Priority of Analytic Hierarchy Process

3.1 Analyze System and Construct Hierarchy Model

The influencing factors on operation safety of metro can be induced into hierarchy model [8] as Fig. 1.

3.2 Build Initial Judgment Matrices and Dynamic Judgment Matrices

According to the affiliation of upper and lower layers determined by hierarchy model, expert evaluation method is adopted to compare the importance of each factor. Construct the initial judgment matrix according to Saaty's 1–9 scales method. Then the dynamic judgment matrix of certain layers is obtained through analyzing collected datas.

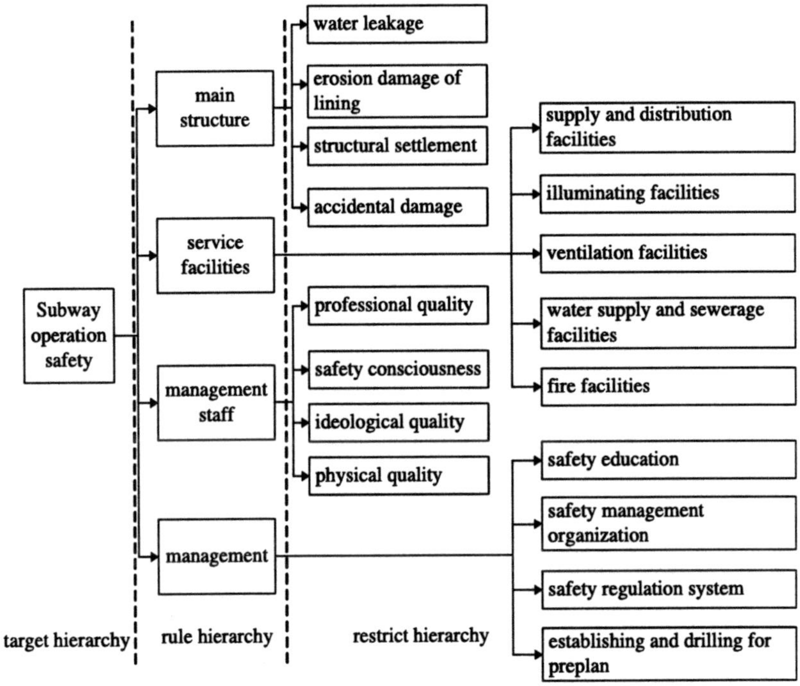

Fig. 1 The hierarchy models

3.3 *Single Taxis of Hierarchy*

To a certain element of upper layer, calculate the weight of importance degree of all correlated elements in self layer. Making use of eigenvalue method, solve out the largest eigenvalue λ_{max} and the corresponding eigenvector of each judgment matrix, then normalize them. In the end, make the consistency check of each judgment matrix.

3.4 *Total Taxis of Hierarchy*

Dynamic matrix of total taxis of hierarchy is established according to all the results of single taxis of hierarchy.

4 Example

Considering all kinds of risk factors, the results of a certain tunnel marked by experts during the past 30 years are as Table 1.

Table 1 The results of a certain tunnel marked by experts

Years	Main structure	Service facilities	Management staff	Management
0	1.0	1.0	0.720	0.740
5	0.972	0.965	0.732	0.786
10	0.947	0.936	0.741	0.823
15	0.925	0.905	0.832	0.854
20	0.904	0.889	0.850	0.878
25	0.886	0.870	0.869	0.898
30	0.869	0.854	0.881	0.914

Based on data on Table 1, the variation functions of main factors can be induced as (2)–(5) using the least square method.

Main structure:

$$b_1(t) = 0.71 + 0.29e^{-0.02t} \tag{2}$$

Service facilities:

$$b_2(t) = 0.76 + 0.24e^{-0.031t} \tag{3}$$

Management staff:

$$b_3(t) = 0.93 - 0.21e^{-0.05t} \tag{4}$$

Management:

$$b_4(t) = 0.98 - 0.24e^{-0.043t} \tag{5}$$

Initial judgment matrix of target hierarchy – rule hierarchy:

$$B_0 = \begin{bmatrix} 1 & 5 & 3 & 3 \\ 1/5 & 1 & 1 & 2 \\ 1/3 & 1 & 1 & 2 \\ 1/3 & 1/2 & 1/2 & 1 \end{bmatrix}$$

Eigenvalue method is adopted to get the largest eigenvalue $\lambda_{\max}$:

$$\lambda_{\max} = 4.139$$

Normalized: $W_0^T = (0.537, 0.165, 0.187, 0.111)$

Inconsistency ratio: $CR = 0.039 < 0.1$

Influence coefficient matrix:

$$M(t) = \begin{bmatrix} 0.781(1 + 0.408e^{-0.02t}) & & & \\ & 4.474(1 + 0.316e^{-0.031t}) & & \\ & & 4.020(1 - 0.226e^{-0.05t}) & \\ & & & 4.464(1 - 0.245e^{-0.43t}) \end{bmatrix}$$

So dynamic judgment matrix is as below:

$$W(t) = M(t)W_0 = \begin{bmatrix} 0.419(1 + 0.41e^{-0.02t}) \\ 0.738(1 + 0.316e^{-0.031t}) \\ 0.752(1 - 0.226e^{-0.05t}) \\ 0.496(1 - 0.245e^{-0.43t}) \end{bmatrix}$$

The reasonable priority vector of each layer could be obtained as below by the same method.

$$W_1^T = (0.286, 0.098, 0.182, 0.434)$$

$$W_2^T = (0.229, 0.229, 0.184, 0.279, 0.078)$$

$$W_3^T = (0.157, 0.157, 0.580, 0.106)$$

$$W_4^T = (0.085, 0.518, 0.180, 0.200)$$

Meanwhile, the consistency of all initial judgment matrices could be accepted. The matrix of total taxis of hierarchy is as follow:

$$W(t) = \begin{bmatrix} 0.286 & & & \\ 0.098 & & & \\ 0.182 & & & \\ 0.434 & & & \\ & 0.229 & & \\ & 0.229 & & \\ & 0.184 & & \\ & 0.279 & & \\ & 0.078 & & \\ & & 0.157 & \\ & & 0.157 & \\ & & 0.580 & \\ & & 0.106 & \\ & & & 0.085 \\ & & & 0.518 \\ & & & 0.180 \\ & & & 0.200 \end{bmatrix} \begin{bmatrix} 0.419(1 + 0.41e^{-0.02t}) \\ 0.738(1 + 0.316e^{-0.031t}) \\ 0.752(1 - 0.226e^{-0.05t}) \\ 0.496(1 - 0.245e^{-0.43t}) \end{bmatrix}.$$

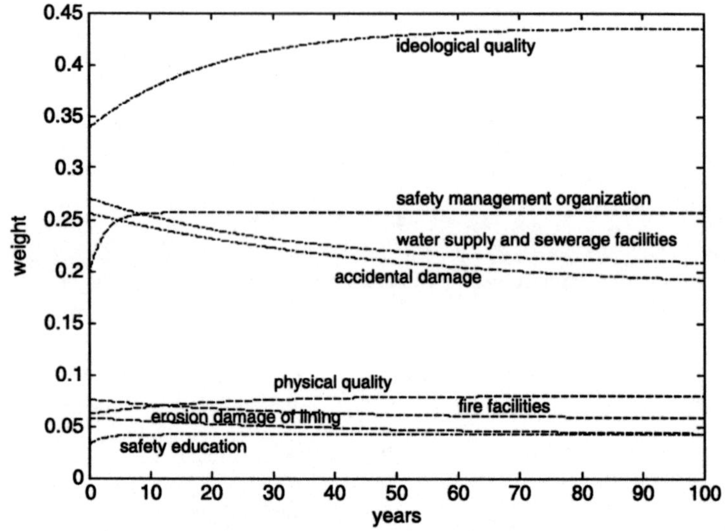

Fig. 2 Variation curves of some risk factors

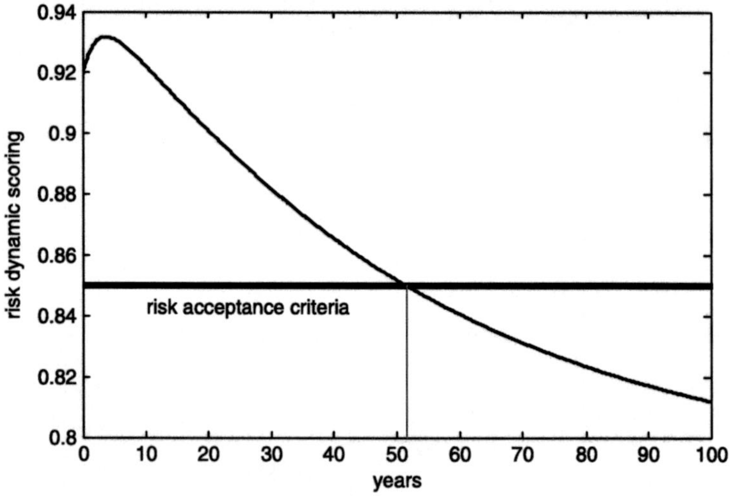

Fig. 3 Dynamic score curves of risk

According to the expression of $W(t)$, the variation curves of risk factors can be draw as Fig. 2.

In the end, the dynamic scoring for operation risk of metro can be calculated according to $B(t)$ and W_0.

$$I(t) = W_0^T \cdot B(t)$$

$$= [0.537\ 0.165\ 0.187\ 0.111] \begin{bmatrix} 0.71(1 + 0.41e^{-0.02t}) \\ 0.76(1 + 0.316e^{-0.031t}) \\ 0.93(1 - 0.226e^{-0.05t}) \\ 0.98(1 - 0.245e^{-0.43t}) \end{bmatrix}$$

Then the variation curves of $I(t)$ can be draw as Fig. 3:

5 Conclusions

Some curves of risk factors are declining and others are increasing in Fig. 2. When the rising curves cross the decline curves, more attention should be paid to these changes.

The dynamic score of risk can be calculated at any time from Fig. 3. Combined with risk acceptance criteria, the time of risk occurring can be predicted. It is about 50 years after operation.

The relative weight of elements in bottom layer can be calculated by the dynamic priority of analytic hierarchy process, while the risk assessment value can be predicted. It expands the use of AHP. This method can be applied to analyze and prediction the operation risk of metro. They also play a guiding role in managing operation risk of metro.

The curve derived from this method is generally determined by the expert evaluation, so its accuracy is affected by the expert experience. It is suggested that data accumulation should be strengthened in daily operation of metro.

Acknowledgements This research was supported by Beijing programs for science and technology (Y0605060000007022).

References

1. Saaty, T.L. (1980) The analytic hierarchy process. McGraw-Hill INC, New York.
2. Xu, Z.S., Wei, C.P. (2004) A new method for priorities in the analytic hierarchy process. Oper. Res. Trans. 4(4):47–54.
3. Jensen, R.E. (1984) An alternative scaling method for priorities in hierarchical structures. J. Math. Psychol. 28:317–332.
4. Bryson, N. (1995) A goal programming method for generating priority vectors. J. Oper. Res. 46: 641–648.
5. Raharjo, H., Xie, M. and Brombacher, A.C. (2009) On modeling dynamic priorities in the analytic hierarchy process using compositional data analysis. Eur. J. Oper. Res. 3(194): 834–846.

6. Xu, R.N. (2000) Fuzzy least-squares priority method in the analytic hierarchy process. Fuzzy Sets Syst. 112(3):395–404.
7. Xu, S.B. (1986) A new model for dynamic priorities in the analytic hierarchy process. J. Syst. Eng.1(2):42–47.
8. Wang, Y., Huang, H.W. (2004) Hierarchy-fuzzy comprehensive judgment for safety evaluation of metro running tunnel. Undergr. Space 3:301–305.

Study on Construction Project Bidding Risk Assessment Model

Guofeng Wen and Liwen Chen

Abstract Project risk assessment is an important basis for construction enterprises to select the right project during the bidding phase. In this paper, a project risk assessment model based on Rough set and TOPSIS is proposed. In this model, the hybrid weight of each index is achieved adopting Rough set theory and Analytical Hierarchy Process (AHP). Then, with the minimized risk as the objective, technique for order performance by similarity to ideal solution (TOPSIS) is applied to determine the ranking order of the bidding projects according to their closeness coefficient. Finally, an example is shown to highlight the procedure of the proposed method and verify its effectiveness.

1 Introduction

Construction project is plagued by risk and often suffers poor performance as a result. Risk evaluation of the bidding project is of great significance for construction enterprises. For the project risk analysis, many scholars have put forward different models and methods. Xu et al. supposed quantities as random variables and proposed a general method of risk evaluation of bidding strategies using risk management procedures and stochastic programming methods [1]. Touran et al. applied Monte Carlo method to conduct a risk analysis of random variables [2]. Tah put forward a Fuzzy logic technique of risk evaluation and applied it to the risk control of Large-scale projects [3]. Some scholars apply Analytical Hierarchy Process (AHP) to analyze the bidding risks [4, 5]. In addition, the projects risk

L.I. Wen
School of Management, Hebei University of Technology, Tianjin, People's Republic of China
and
Shandong Institute of Business and Technology, Yantai, People's Republic of China
e-mail: wengf_sdibt@yahoo.com.cn

L.I. Chen (✉)
School of Management, Hebei University of Technology, Tianjin, People's Republic of China
e-mail: lwchen@hebut.edu.cn

D.D. Wu (ed.), *Modeling Risk Management in Sustainable Construction*,
Computational Risk Management, DOI 10.1007/978-3-642-15243-6_9,

analysis methods include grey theory, artificial neural network approach, case-based reasoning methods, etc. [6–9]. For the models and methods mentioned above, some of them have so strong assumption conditions that it is difficult to obtain the data needed to apply them; some models are too subjective and the evaluation results are affected largely by personal experiences and subjective bias. In order to overcome the two aspects of faults of the existing models, in this study, the Rough set theory and TOPSIS method are hybrid and form a new risk assessment model. In this model, Rough set theory and AHP method are used to calculate the weights of the risk assessment index system, the TOPSIS method is applied for risk assessment and ranking order of multiple projects to be evaluated, and thus provides information for the construction enterprises to support their bidding decision-making.

2 Risk Factors of the Bidding Project

The bidding risks faced by the construction enterprises can be sorted as the following categories based on their origin [10, 11].

2.1 Risks from the Owner

Project risks are mainly reflected in the credit ratings of the owner, its management system, management experience, economic strength and so on. The fairness of the bidding documents and contract conditions and different types of contracts would also be important factors affecting the grade of project risks.

2.2 Risks from Competitors

For the same project, the number and their strength of other companies who attend the bidding affect the risk scale of the project.

2.3 Risks from the External Environment

The external environment risks of the project includes natural environmental conditions, policy and regulation system, the conditions of domestic and foreign markets and the economic environmental factors of the project location. The international project also involves the political stability.

2.4 *Risks from the Construction Enterprise Itself*

The quality of the construction enterprise, including the level of construction technology, equipment conditions, management capacity, corporate qualification grade, quality of personnel and so on, affects the level of the project risk. The risk level differs with the different proficiency to the project type to be bid. Faults in the work during the bidding process would bring risks to the construction enterprise. Construction enterprises with different pricing strategies will also face different risks.

3 Rough Set-TOPSIS Project Risk Assessment Model

The main steps of the Rough Set-TOPSIS project risk assessment model are as follows [12].

3.1 *Determine the Risk Assessment Index System*

Determine the bidding risk assessment index system according to the risk factors affecting the success of the project bidding. Suppose there are n indexes and the index set can be expressed as $C = \{C_1, C_2, \ldots, C_n\}$.

3.2 *Calculate the Weights of the Indexes*

In this study, three kinds of weights of the indexes are proposed: objective weights, subjective weights and synthetic weights.

The weights determined by Rough set are derived from historical projects data, and are objective weights; the weights determined by AHP are derived from the judgment of the field experts and are called subjective weights. In order to make full use of the advantages of the two kinds of weights, an integration of them, the synthetic weights, are more factual.

3.2.1 Determine Objective Weights Based on Rough Set

Let $K = (U, R)$ be an approximation space, where U is a finite and nonempty set of objects which is called the universe; R is a finite set of attributes used to characterize the objects. For any P, $Q \in R$, we will say that Q depends on P if indiscernibility relation $ind(P) \subseteq ind(Q)$. We will say that Q depends on P in a degree k if $k = \gamma_P(Q) = card(pos_P(Q))/card(U)$, where $pos_P(Q) = \cup P\_(X)$, $X \in U/Q$, $P\_(X)$

is the lower approximation of a set X with respect to R; $card(U)$ denotes the cardinality of U [13].

Let $P = \{p_i|i = 1,2,\ldots,m\}$ be set of attributes. According to the Rough set theory, it is possible to define the significance of a conditional attribute p_i from the set of conditional attribute P. The significance of conditional attribute p_i in the equivalence relation is defined by $\gamma_P(Q) - \gamma_{P-\{pi\}}(Q)$, i.e.,

$$Sig_Q(p_i) = (card(pos_p(Q)) - card(pos_{P-\{p_i\}}(Q)))/card(pos_P(Q)) \quad (1)$$

So, the objective weight w_i of p_i can be calculated by the following equation:

$$w_i = Sig_Q(p_i)/\sum_{j=1}^{m} Sig_Q(p_j) \quad (2)$$

3.2.2 Determine the Subjective Weights Based on AHP

AHP method is applied to produce subjective weights of the indexes. Because the application of AHP method has been relatively mature, and there are many literatures describe this method, detailed process will not repeat here.

3.2.3 Determine the Synthetic Weights

Let v_i be subjective weights, w_i be objective weights and g_i be synthetic weights, then

$$g_i = \alpha w_i + (1 - \alpha)v_i,\ i = 1, 2, \ldots, m \quad (3)$$

where α is a coefficient, $0 \leq \alpha \leq 1$. The value of α should be determined according to the credibility of the objective weights. If the data used to determine the objective weights is of high quality and of suitable quantity, α should take a larger value ($\alpha \geq 0.5$); when the data used to determine the objective weights is of low quality and of limited quantity, α should take a smaller value ($\alpha \leq 0.5$) to highlight the advantages of experts.

3.3 Collect Data of Each Project According to the Index System C

Suppose there are m projects to be evaluated. We obtain each index value for every project, namely, the raw data of the projects. It can be marked as x_{ij}. Where x_{ij} express the jth index value of the ith project, $i = 1,2,\ldots,m$; $j = 1,2,\ldots,n$.

3.4 Normalize the Raw Data and Calculate the Weighted Normalized Value

Assessment indexes can be divided into three kinds: benefit type index, cost type index and interval type index. When using TOPSIS to evaluate the project risks, it is required that all the indexes change in the same direction. So the raw data should be processed to satisfy this request. We can turn the cost type and interval type indexes into benefit type indexes. After the change of the raw data x_{ij}, we get y_{ij}, $i = 1,2,\ldots,m$; $j = 1,2,\ldots,n$.

Normalize the raw data y_{ij} we get the normalized value Z_{ij}:

$$Z_{ij} = y_{ij}/\sqrt{\sum_{i=1}^{m} y_{ij}^2},\ i = 1,2,\ldots,m;\ j = 1,2,\ldots,n \tag{4}$$

Using g_j and Z_{ij} we get the weighted normalized value P_{ij}:

$$P_{ij} = g_j \cdot Z_{ij},\ i = 1,2,\ldots,m;\ j = 1,2,\ldots,n \tag{5}$$

3.5 Determine the Ideal and Negative-Ideal Solutions

The ideal solutions vector: $P^+(P_{1\max}, P_{2\max}, \ldots, P_{n\max})$.

The negative-ideal solutions vector: $P^-(P_{1\min}, P_{2\min}, \ldots, P_{n\min})$.

Where $P_{j\max}$ and $P_{j\min}$ denote the best and worst value of the current jth index in the all m projects respectively, $j = 1,2,\ldots,n$.

3.6 Calculate the Euclidean Distances of Each Alternative from the Ideal Solution and the Negative-Ideal Solution

$$D_i^+ = \sqrt{\sum_{j}^{n} (P_{j\max} - P_{ij})^2},\ D_i^- = \sqrt{\sum_{j}^{n} (P_{j\min} - P_{ij})^2},\ i = 1,2,\ldots,m \tag{6}$$

3.7 Calculate the Relative Closeness D_i

Calculate the relative closeness D_i of each project i to the ideal solution, and rank the projects according to the relative closeness to the ideal solution.

$$D_i = \frac{D_i^-}{D_i^- + D_i^+},\ i = 1,2,\ldots,m \tag{7}$$

4 Example

A construction enterprise is facing with a choice of projects to bid. There are four construction projects to choose from. The construction enterprise analyzes the technical and economic situation in detail of each project and regards the grade of the risk and benefit level as the main basis for selection. We apply Rough set-TOPSIS model to evaluate the risks of the four construction projects.

4.1 Determine the Risk Assessment Index System

In consultation with experts' advices, six indexes are selected from a number of risk factors, forming a risk assessment index system, denoted by $C = \{C_1, C_2, \ldots, C_6\}$. Where C_1 is project scale, expressed with the amount of project cost (10,000 Yuan); C_2 is the quantity of start-up capital (10,000 Yuan); C_3 is the usable construction time in a year (months); C_4 is the conditions of contract (Fairness or not); C_5 is competitiveness of the bidding project, which can be measured by the number of competitors participating in the bidding of the same project; C_6 is degree of maturity of the construction technology, which can be measured by whether the construction enterprise has the building experience of the similar project [14].

4.2 Determine the Weights of the Indexes

The construction enterprise selects 15 projects from its previous successful bidding projects. All these projects have been completed and their risk scales have been evaluated. After collecting data from the historical projects according to the risk assessment indexes above mentioned and establishing a decision table, the decision table is discretized and the weights can be calculated.

The objective weights of the indexes: $w_1 = 0.25$, $w_2 = 0$, $w_3 = 0.5$, $w_4 = 0.25$, $w_5 = 0$, $w_6 = 0$.

The subjective weights of each index: $v_1 = 0.17$, $v_2 = 0.1$, $v_3 = 0.2$, $v_4 = 0.2$, $v_5 = 0.23$, $v_6 = 0.1$.

Take α=0.5, the synthetic weights can be calculated: $g_1 = 0.210$, $g_2 = 0.050$, $g_3 = 0.350$, $g_4 = 0.225$, $g_5 = 0.115$, $g_6 = 0.050$.

4.3 Assess the Project Risk

Confirm the index value of each project according to the index system C and fill them into Table 1.

Table 1 The index value of the bidding project

i	C_1	C_2	C_3	C_4	C_5	C_6
1	2,650	1,850	4	Good	7	Y
2	940	1,520	5	Good	8	Y
3	880	750	3	Poor	5	N
4	4,200	1,760	5	Poor	9	Y

Table 2 The distance between the project and the ideal solution

i	D_i^+	D_i^-	D_i	Order
1	0.0349	0.1113	0.7612	2
2	0.0104	0.1222	0.9212	1
3	0.1214	0.0197	0.1398	4
4	0.1085	0.0578	0.3474	3

Quantify the qualitative indexes, and turn the cost-based and interval-based indexes into benefit-based indexes. Then normalize the data and weighted the normalized matrix, we get:

$$\begin{pmatrix} 0.0018 & 0.0009 & 0.0539 & 0.1423 & 0.0079 & 0.0277 \\ 0.0147 & 0.0013 & 0.0842 & 0.1423 & 0.0060 & 0.0277 \\ 0.0167 & 0.0053 & 0.0303 & 0.0356 & 0.0155 & 0.0069 \\ 0.0007 & 0.0010 & 0.0842 & 0.0356 & 0.0048 & 0.0277 \end{pmatrix}$$

The ideal solutions vector:

$P^+(0.0167,0.0053,0.0842,0.1423,0.0155,0.0277)$

The negative-ideal solutions vector:

P^- $(0.0007,0.0010,0.0303,0.0356,0.0048,0.0069)$

Calculate D_i^+, D_i^- and D_i, $i = 1,2,\ldots,4$. The results are shown in Table 2.

From the calculating results we can see that the construction enterprise should select the second project firstly, and then select the first project to bid. This will enable the enterprise to achieve better economic results with lower risk.

5 Conclusions

In this study, the attribute importance measurement methods of Rough set theory and data of historical projects are used to determine risk assessment index weights and the information hidden in the data is mined, so the weights are objective. At the same time, in order to adopt the knowledge and experience of experts in the field effectively, AHP method is applied to determine the subjective weights of assessment indexes. Thus combining both objective and subjective weights to determine the hybrid weights makes full use of the advantages of both, therefore, the weights are scientific and rational, overcoming the weakness of a single one-sided method. TOPSIS method is applied to the risk assessment and ranking order for the bidding project and is beneficial to construction enterprises to make decisions according to their own situation on the project. An example is presented to illustrate the working of the model. It indicates that the model is applicable to multiple-project risk analysis and comparison; it is operable and can, to some extent, overcome the shortcomings in the previous models.

Acknowledgments This study is supported by Natural Science Foundation of Shandong Province (ZR2009HL009); Science and technology plan program of Ministry of housing and urban-rural development of the people's republic of China (2008-k9-51).

References

1. Xu Tianji, Tiong Robert LK (2001) Risk assessment on contractors pricing strategies. Journal of Construction Management and Economics 19:77–84
2. Touran A, Wiser EP (1992) Monte Carlo technique with correlated random variables. Journal of Construction Engineering and Management 118:258–272
3. Tah JHM, Carr V (2000) A proposal for construction project risk assessment using fuzzy logic. Journal of Construction Management and Economics 18:491–500
4. Mohammad A. Mustafa, Jamal F. Al-Bahar (1991) Project risk assessment using the analytic hierarchy process. IEEE Transactions on Engineering Management 38:46–52
5. Yang Lanrong, Zhang Jinlong (2000) The Method of Risk Analysis for Project Bidding. Science Research Management 21:47–49
6. SHI Ke-bin, ZHANG Li-xia, SHI Guo-qing (2005) Study on risk index system and comprehensive evaluation in construction project. Journal of Xinjiang Agriculture University 28:76–80
7. Deng Xidong, Wang Chunyan (2007) the Grey Fuzzy theory appraises the risk of the project. Journal of China Three Gorges University (Natural Sciences) 29:49–53
8. Yasser Hassan and Tazaki Eiichiro (2002) Decision Making Using Hybrid Rough Sets and Neural Networks. International Journal of Neural Systems 12:435–446
9. Chua DKH, Li DZ, Chan WT (2001) Case-based reasoning approach in bid decision making. Journal of Construction Engineering and Management 127:35–45
10. Qi Xijing, Liu Li, Wang Shuwei (1999) The evaluation on tendering risk of construction companies. Journal of Shenyang Architectural and Civil Engineering Institute 15:378–382
11. Li Shun-guo, Li Hui, Huang Qing-ping et al. (2008) Research on Predicting Model of Architectural Engineering Project Bidding Risk. Journal of Wuhan University of Technology 30:165–168
12. Chen Chen-Tung (2000) Extensions of the TOPSIS for group decision-making under fuzzy environment. Fuzzy Sets and Systems 114:1–9
13. Z Pawlak (1982) Rough sets. International Journal of Computer and Information Sciences 11:341–356
14. Sun L (2003) Construction project bidding risk knowledge discovery based on Rough set. PhD Thesis of Huazhong University of Science and Technology

Study on Prophase Risk Management in Informatization of Chinese Construction Enterprises

Luo Fu-zhou and Wang La-Yin

Abstract Information technology, an important means to improve competitiveness, has been adopted by more and more Chinese construction enterprises. Owing to the complexity and high risks, prophase risk management in informatization of Chinese construction enterprises can reduce the possibility of project failure. This paper analyzes the importance of prophase risk management in informatization, investigates prophase risk factors, builds the prophase risk assessment model in informatization, and puts forward some measures to precaution major risk factors.

Keywords Construction enterprises · Informatization · Risk management

1 Introduction

Information technology has been firstly adopted in Chinese construction industry in 1980s, and received great attention and rapid development to enhance the competitiveness of the construction enterprises. The Ministry of Construction of China issued "2004–2010 Compendium of National Construction Industry Informatization Development Plan", which required construction industry to adopt information technology to achieve striding development. In 2007, it explicitly stipulated that the construction contract enterprise with super qualification, should establish local area network (LAN) or management information system (MIS), which can build the network in internal office, information release, data exchange and so on, all of which can further promote the informatization of construction enterprise.

L. Fu-zhou (✉) and W. La-Yin
School of Management, Xi'an University of Architecture & Technology, Xi'an, People's Republic of China
e-mail: luofz@163.com; xjdwanglayin@sina.com

D.D. Wu (ed.), *Modeling Risk Management in Sustainable Construction*,
Computational Risk Management, DOI 10.1007/978-3-642-15243-6_10,

However, with the popularity of information technology, the failure cases in informatization emerged continuously, which aroused general concern in the industry. A case in point is ERP project. According to statistics, among 1,000 enterprises in China who purchased ERP software, those who have achieved the system integration as expected only counted for 10–20%, partial integration counted for 30–40%, and complete failure was as high as 50% [1]. It's proved that the failure in construction enterprise informatization was not due to lack of funds or technology, but lack of awareness of risk management and experiences. It has put forward the problems in risk management of informatization for Chinese construction enterprises. Particularly, prophase risk management in informatization determines the possibility and reliability of the subsequent work. So it is of great significance to apply information technology to improve sustainable competitive advantage of the enterprises.

2 The Importance of Prophase Risk Management in Informatization of Chinese Construction Enterprises

Risks exist in the whole process of informatization of construction enterprises. Different risks may appear in different stages. Therefore, in the study on risk management in enterprise's informatization, risks of every stage in the project life cycle need to be identified, and corresponding risk management should be implemented on different risks in different stages. Based on Life Cycle Theory, informatization includes three circulating stages: the development need, system construction and continuous improvement. Correspondingly, risk management of informatization is divided into three stages: prophase, metaphase and post phase. According to characteristics of construction enterprises and the general law of risk control, their relationship is showed in Fig. 1.

As the value and time of the information project obey the law of diminishing marginal utility, the shape of *OE* shows as curve. In Fig. 1, *OT* represents the whole process of the risk management in informatization of construction enterprises: where *Oa* is the prophase of risk management; *ab* is the metaphase; *bc* is the post phase. The vertical axis represents the effect in different stages of construction enterprises' informatization. As can be seen, the prophase of risk management shows the greatest effect, followed by metaphase, and minimal effect is the post phase.

The greatest prophase risk comes from goal identification. Following the trend blindly and having no or unreasonable goals are dangerous for construction enterprises' informatization; lack of planning or unclear thinking will bring informatization devastating risks; meanwhile, inadequate preparation in personnel, physical and financial resources also lead to dilemma. Thus, though with small investment and short duration, prophase determines the basic framework and blueprint for the future informatization. Ineffective prophase risk control in informatization will bring more difficulties in implementing the project, or identifying and controlling

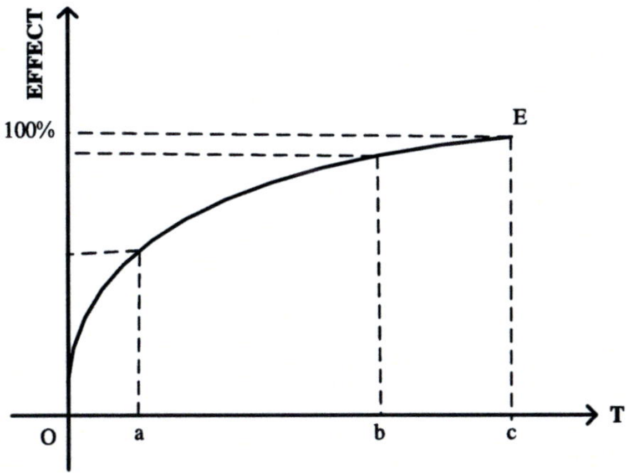

Fig. 1 Risk management process in informatization of construction enterprises

the financial risks, which result in resource dispersion and information silos, subsequently difficult to achieve overall efficiency [2].Therefore, the prophase risk management, concerning the possibility and reliability of informatization, is significant to achieve the goal of informatization.

3 Analysis of Risk Factors in Prophase Informatization of Chinese Construction Enterprises

The risk factors refer to the reasons leading to failure or partial failure in informatization of enterprises. Risk factors involve many aspects: internal factors such as economy, technology, management, and external factors such as market demand, policies and regulations. In recent years, some experts and scholars defined the risk factors and their influence degree in informatization through methods of questionnaires or data analysis. On the basis of predecessors' research, combined with the present situation of construction enterprises, the author conducted a questionnaire survey among a group of implementation consultants from a large software enterprise in China. Thirty questionnaires have been collected. In the questionnaire, implementation consultants rated the influence of each risk factor on the failure of enterprise's informatization, with the score ranges between [0,100]. Higher score indicates greater impact of risk factors. The questionnaire involves a total of 36 risk factors. After sorted out, the top nine risk factors which score highest are as follows (Table 1).

According to the result of the questionnaire survey, this paper divides the nine major prophase risk factors in informatization into four categories: economic risk, technological risk, management risk and personnel risk. Based on the average

Table 1 Major risk factors in prophase informatization of Chinese construction enterprises

Risk categories	Risk factors	Average scores	Sequence
Economic risk	Degree of capital guarantee	77.4	6
	Prospective profit fulfillment rate	70.9	9
Technological risk	Experience of project development group	78.3	5
	Technological complexity	73.7	7
	Follow-up technology of upgrade and maintenance	71.4	8
Management risk	Management level and management system	88.3	2
	Operation flow optimization	82.4	4
Personnel risk	Clarity of project objectives	89.5	1
	Leader's support	85.6	3

scores of various risk factors, influence of risk factors ranked from high to low are as follows: clarity of project objectives, management level and management system, leader's support, operation flow optimization, experience of project development group, degree of capital guarantee, technological complexity, follow-up technology of upgrade and maintenance, prospective profit fulfillment rate.

4 Risk Assessments in Prophase Informatization of Construction Enterprises

When assessing the risks in prophase informatization of construction enterprises, it is necessary to give full consideration to internal and external risk factors; analyze and evaluate each factor, obtain the comprehensive risk coefficient, which could be used to evaluate the risks in prophase informatization. In this paper, risk assessment model is set up on the basis of the nine risk factors which scored high in the questionnaires.

Risk assessment model in Prophase informatization of construction enterprises involves the following indicators:

4.1 Relative Risk: A

Relative risk is defined as

$$A = \sigma/\mu \tag{1}$$

where μ is the prospective value of investment yielded in informatization; σ is the standard deviation of returns, which indicates the dispersion of expected return-on-investment in informatization.

4.2 Relative Loss: B

Loss of the project failure can be obtained as:

$$L = \sum_{i=1}^{n} L_i a_i \tag{2}$$

where L is the potential loss of project failure, including both the visible loss of tangible assets and intangible potential losses like opportunity loss, intangible assets loss, etc. Losses of various degrees caused by project failure are marked as (L1, L2... Ln), and the corresponding probabilities of each loss degree are marked as (a1, a2...an).

Relative loss, which indicates the loss of unit input, is defined as

$$B = L/I \tag{3}$$

where I represents the total input.

4.3 Failure Rate: P

Failure rate P indicates probability of failure in informatization of construction enterprises during a certain period of time. Failure of informatization means the features and the implementing scheme of the project cannot meet the actual management needs; or the enterprises have not received management elevation and value return which they should have, causing the final outcome failed to meet the prospective targets. The probability of project failure can be obtained as:

$$P = P\{g_i < G_i\}, i = 1, 2...m \tag{4}$$

where (G1, G2...Gm) refers to each prospective target before the project started, and (g1, g2...gm) represents each performance index in final result.

4.4 Relative Time Risk: C

According to investigation on the actual performance of informatization of construction enterprises, time factor is one of the elements that need to be considered when evaluating the risk. The project resources are consumed by stages. The longer the project lasts, the greater the losses caused when the project failed. Therefore, time risk needs to be considered in risk assessment model [3]. It is named relative time risk C.

This paper assumes that projects had nine risk factors; k of which would appear during the informatization process. Let ti denote the time duration from the occurrence of risk factor i to the commencement of the project. Let t denote the total time duration of nine risk factors lasts.

$$t = \sum_{i=1}^{9} t_i \tag{5}$$

where T denote total informatization construction time.

Relative time risk is defined as:

$$C = \frac{t}{k} \bullet \frac{1}{T} \tag{6}$$

where C indicates the rate of average time for each risk factor to the total time of the project when k risk factors occurred. This index could be used to adjust the losses when the risks occurred during the construction period.

4.5 Comprehensive Risk Coefficient: r

The occurring possibilities of nine risk factors are marked as (b1, b2...b9). Let (d1, d2...d9) denote the unfavorable consequence when the informatization fails. Comprehensive risk coefficient is:

$$r = \frac{1}{9} \bullet \sum_{i=1}^{9} b_i \bullet d_i \tag{7}$$

4.6 Risk Evaluation Value in Prophase Informatization: R

Risk assessed value in Prophase informatization = Relative risk × Relative loss × Relative time risk × Failure rate × Comprehensive risk coefficient, which is:

$$R = A \times B \times C \times P \times r \tag{8}$$

This is the risk assessment model in prophase informatization. Multiple risk assessed value could be obtained from the risk assessment model. The higher the assessed value is, the greater risks the project will encounter.

5 The Risk Control Strategy in Prophase Informatization of Construction Enterprises

Enterprises need to take some necessary measures to control the risk based on correct analysis and evaluation on the risks, so as to carry out the informatization successfully. Based on the above-mentioned nine risk factors, this paper puts forward some measures to reduce the risks in prophase informatization.

5.1 Measures of Personnel Risk Control

Symposiums should be carried on for the department heads of the company to discuss the specific demand in the informatization, and to form a clear goal including overall objective, short-term objectives and other objectives, which should be polished based on the feedback from the basic level of the company. There must be senior managers in leadership positions to implement the project; In addition, in order to avoid changes caused by senior managers' transfer during the process, the contract or institution should be established at the beginning of the project [4].

5.2 Measures of Management Risk Control

Risk control in operation flow. Before the informatization starts, enterprises should conduct the operation flow regrouping, during which enterprises may follow this principle: first, establish the organizational structure of operation flow regrouping and adjust the objectives in accordance with project goals; second, give regrouping executives decision-making power to eliminate the delay and error in information transmission; finally, select the key processes which could receive periodic profits or have a major impact on achieving the strategic goal of the enterprise as regrouping object.

Risk control in management transformation. The most common and important measure for changing management concept is to offer training program to the personnel of enterprises [5], because it's helpful to reduce the hindrance of the later part of the project implementation by transmitting new management concept to staff in prophase informatization. In addition, enterprises could take advantage of consulting firms to fully consider the enterprise operation flow, organizational structure and other relevant factors, hence to complete the transformation of the enterprise management mode.

5.3 Measures of Technological Risk Control

In the construction process of informatization, enterprises should analyze various possible risks caused by the technology, and appropriately select the management software with successful experience in the industry [6], and then consider whether the software developers are familiar with the basic knowledge of their trades, whether they have ever developed a similar system and what about the quality. It's necessary to make a comprehensive evaluation and comparison on various management functions, software flexibility, the capacity of secondary development, the developer's technical support abilities, after-sale services and so on, to ensure information system to meet the business needs with high quality and reasonable price.

5.4 *Measures of Economic Risk Control*

In fact, how to ensure that financial supply and the funds-allocation in accordance with the project schedule, and how to control the cost within the scheme, are the questions the enterprises need to face seriously. Therefore, when making a budget for the project, the company could study carefully on composition of the cost, funds using plan and auditing approach, then make a detailed utilization scheme in conjunction with the company's financial department, audit department and the advisory body. These measures can ensure funds available timely, and make the information project conducted smoothly.

In addition to above-mentioned four measures, the construction enterprise could select proper consulting and supervision agency to real-time monitor project quality and effectiveness through third party's effort. Enterprises can entrust the management consulting firm to carry out the strategic consultancy and management diagnosis of information. In the light of actual conditions and enterprise development strategy, enterprises make rational plan and operation flow regrouping in prophase of informatization [7]. Large enterprises could also commission a professional risk assessment firm to implement risk assessments reliably and provide comprehensive revision for it.

6 Conclusions

The benefits and risks co-exist during the process of informatization of construction enterprises. The information technology has brought enormous benefits to the enterprises, whereas it is necessary to precaution risks. Carrying out research on informatization of Chinese construction enterprises is helpful to assure the trouble-free construction of the information project, so as to improve integrating capability of internal and external resources in Chinese construction enterprises, strengthen their competitiveness and achieve sustainable development.

Acknowledgements We are grateful to Fan Feng for discussions and Lai Yu for information about format. The study is funded by the Scientific Research Subject Foundation of Education Committee of Shaanxi Province in 2009 (No. 09JZ009).

References

1. Li Shunguo (2008) The theory and method investigation for construction enterprise informatization in our country. Wuhan University of Technology
2. Wu Jiang, Ou Yangfeng (2006) Discussion about risk management of enterprise information. Enterprise Economy 2:34–35
3. Yan Wei, Wang Xiaomei (2007) Multiple-index assessment for informatization risk based on project. Journal of Information 5:77–81
4. Qin Ling, Zhang Zhiqing (2007) Study on ready evaluation system of electronic commerce in construction enterprise. China Management Information 10(8):26–28
5. Peng Hongli (2007) Risk and precaution of enterprise IT application. Modern Management. 12:64–66
6. Joseph Phillips (2003) IT Project Management on Track from Start to Finish. McGraw-Hill Osborne Media, Osborne
7. Reifer D (2006) Ten deadly risks in internet and intranet software development. IEEE Software 19(2):12–14

Managing Construction Risk in SMEs: The Case of Coastal Construction

Hosein Piranfar

Abstract This paper is concerned with risk management in construction SMEs. It argues that risk management is not limited to large companies. Despite financial limitations SMEs can deal with their own risks successfully, though in some cases with a bit of help from experts or members of the supply chain. The paper looks at the case of a small construction company in the UK at reasonable detail hoping that it will show the way to other SMEs. It is shown that managing quality helps with an appropriate approach to risk management where enterprise or company-wide risk management gains a head start.

Keywords Construction · Quality · Risk · SMEs

1 Introduction

Small-and-Medium-Sized Enterprises (SMEs) are continuously exposed to risk in their operations that deters their optimal business performance. Some risk exposures create risks to the organization in terms of production, manufacturing capability, human resources, market share and economic losses (Ariful et al. 2006). SMEs are differently defined in terms of the number of employees or the annual turnover. With EU regulations SMEs employ less than 250 people and or alternatively have a turnover of £4 millions. In the UK a company of 50 or less is regarded as small. SMEs are thought to decline historically. Indeed they did so for a while in the UK during the 1970s, but since they have been growing in size and stature (Sloman and Sutcliffe 2004)

H. Piranfar
Business School (RDBS), University of East London, University Way, London E16 2RD, UK
e-mail: H.Piranfar@uel.ac.uk

D.D. Wu (ed.), *Modeling Risk Management in Sustainable Construction*, Computational Risk Management, DOI 10.1007/978-3-642-15243-6_11,

According to the OECD policy brief June 2000, SMEs form a very important sector as they account for over 95% of firms, 60–70% of employment and generate a large share of new jobs in OECD. However, this same entrepreneurial strength that boosts economies can also be a fatal weakness as almost one-half of SME start-ups fail in the first 5 years. It may appear surprising that the available technological and human resources SMEs should not be able to show a better rate of survival and operate more smoothly. They may not be able to use administrative software such as ERM, but they probably do not need them at smaller size simply because coordination is done personally and probably more efficiently. They have a better relationship with their customers. Customers may prefer their realistic and rough talk to the smooth honeyed voices of the customer services in larger organizations. They may not carry quality badges but are dedicated to quality. Organizationally also they can mimic the large companies by forming networks. However, there are some major reasons that contribute to their demise in particular at lower size. Restlessness and continuous innovation is certainly a cause of higher rate of failure. To survive, they try anything and naturally fail. Whatever their advantages in quality small and medium enterprises do have an added disadvantage in the area of risk management as the subject is ill-defined thus causing difficulty especially to such companies. It is recognized that SMEs have a lower risk threshold than larger companies, while 5m pounds loss may drive a SME out of business larger companies are able to absorb such risks much better and continue to survive. To deal with risk exposures effectively, SMEs need a systematic approach along with an appropriate set of tools to identify and treat their potential effects. The main objective of this report is to develop a risk management framework for SMEs in construction so as to avoid a loss in reputation or a plunge in share value. In particular, it illustrates how managing risk in Dimpy Construction LTD can be used as a model case to tackle risks in other SMEs in general.

2 Business Risks and Risk Appetite for SMEs

2.1 Business Risk

Many businesses are focused on maximizing profit without an appropriate risk plan to cope with the downsides of their operations. Businesses ought to consider identifying and assessing their risk exposure in order to be in a better position to organize a proactive response strategy. According to KPMG's Global Construction Survey, 2005 carried out on 1,000 directors, only 11% had an understanding of current risks and only 8% had understanding of long-term risk exposures.

Economic downturns generally affect businesses of all sizes; the economic slump of 2008–2009 has considerably affected the operations of the SMEs. Weak demand, tight credit and reduced orders from the larger companies are the main concerns for these enterprises. Despite the government lowering interest rates, access to credit is limited as a result of banks becoming more risk averse in such economic atmosphere and also because of the difficulty of screening even the creditworthiness of good clients in a downturn. The Basel II Accord requirement that banks should align their capital allocation with the risk characteristics of bank lending resulted in higher cost of borrowing and the imposition of more stringent criteria on SME borrowing (Basel Committee on Banking Supervision 2005).

2.2 Risk Appetite

What is risk appetite? It's the level of risk that a company chooses to take based on the company-specific capability and assets available to absorb the risk. The Turnbull requirement on risk appetite advises companies to consider what risks are acceptable to company and to uphold a suitable guidance to be followed throughout the organization (Turnbull 1999). There is no one correct way to fix the level of risk appetite or risk tolerance of a company. Small and medium sized enterprises for instance would have a lesser risk appetite than the larger entities that are more able to absorb the downside consequences of taking additional risks. The level of Risk appetite for an SME will depend on the industry it operates, the selected strategy and the organizational culture: all inter-linked (Russell 2008).

A certain level of business risk is inherent in a company's operations and thus they need to be accepted, otherwise operations in that environment will be limited to the extent of balancing costs and revenues deterring the business profitability and growth objectives. On the other hand, a business may choose to take a high level of risk as part of their strategy, which can easily cripple sound operations. The judgment, however, should not be based on the company's own performance alone. The risk management function, or better yet, the company as a whole, should be aware of the relative risk appetite of other companies in the industry and carry out a benchmark. Moreover, it is important for firms to understand that it is not enough to take a moderate level of risk based on self-assessment and benchmarking. Risk appetite is not all encompassing but is relative to the specific type of risk exposure, for instance, tax risk, where a company may want to pursue, perhaps, a tax avoidance strategy to lower costs and thus take extra risks, but not so much that it might damage reputation (Independent director, FTSE 100) (Fig. 1).

2.3 The Challenge of Risk Management in Construction SMEs

Risk issues that concern larger construction firms will apply to SMEs too with some exceptions. KPMG's Global Construction Survey, 2005, found that the greatest challenge for construction firms was the management of risks. This was followed by skills shortages and securing forward workload. Management of contract risk and pricing were also of great concern. A worrying discovery was that 75% of

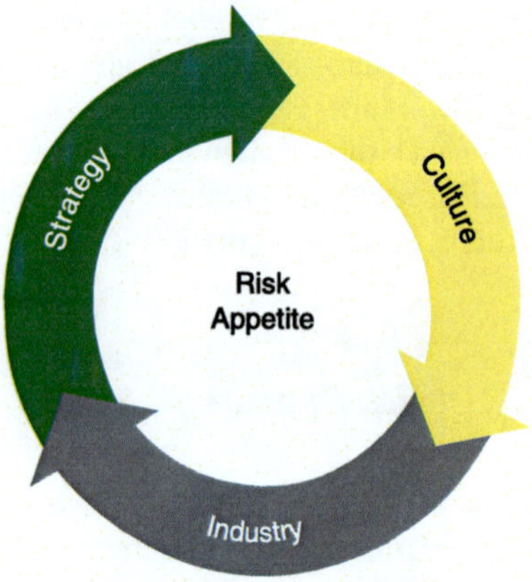

Fig. 1 Adapted from: Russell (2008), Ernst and Young research report

construction companies were found to be willing to take calculated risks in order to secure profitable projects by overriding their risk management policies. Whittington head of building and construction at KPMG LLP expressed his concern that such a risk appetite might end up damaging the firms' reputation and management culture. Since then KPMG have moved increasingly towards the exploration of litigations, tax issues and of course towards sustainability. Hopefully their post recession findings will stress the importance of risk and sustainability as against untrammelled greed and exuberance.

The tendency of SMEs to take such risks is if anything, greater. This is partly because they are on knife edge and have to take proportionally greater risk to survive. For smaller firms, the fact that they can reemerge under a different name may act as an additional propeller to take irrational risks.

3 Case Study: Coastal Construction (Building) LTD

The following section presents the risk management system of Coastal Construction (Building) LTD as a case study to demonstrate the importance of managing risk in SMEs and how firms of such size can effectively manage their own risk exposures.

3.1 Background

Coastal Construction (Building) LTD is one of the largest privately owned construction specialists in the UK by turnover, portfolio and experience. The business falls in the SMEs' category. It currently has 180 employees, and, has increased its turnover from 670 k in 2002 to over £5 million over the last few years. Coastal Construction started as a brick worker partnership in the late 1950s and as turnover and employee numbers steadily increased over the years the company restructured into a limited company in year 2000 with the family members as the directors. Since becoming a limited company the company now provides scaffolding services, joinery packages as well as their core business of subcontracting.

3.2 *Coastal Construction LTD Approach to Risk Management*

In the past few years Coastal Construction LTD has developed a more sophisticated approach to its risk management practice. The company has experienced considerable improvements as a result in their core business activities. They have taken a company-wide approach to risk management that involves not only the directors/owners of the business but also their employees. This is a great step forward compared to many who are still confined to the old ways of insurance-oriented risk management. The modern approach to risk management tends to relate to quality management both in terms of company-wide approach (Piranfar and Combstock 2008) and in terms of mimicking the concept of quality cost (Cavignac (2009). CC's risk management is part of their overall management philosophy. Their management objectives are of business continuity, maintaining growth prospects, minimization of risk exposure in their projects and insurance costs. Commitment to business continuity is certainly commitment to quality as without a company-wide approach and people involvement neither would be possible. Most small companies avoid business continuity are yet to take interest in business continuity despite encouragement from local authorities. Only progressive SMEs take it seriously. Their commitment to growth similarly is an important strategy. Without growth it is difficult to have quality which is also true of innovation and risk. Project base facilitates growth and growth provides for innovation, minimization of risks and insurance coverage for the risks that cannot be economically controlled without insurance. Here, the challenges faced by CC, is one of matching the estimation of the overall company risks and the estimation for individual project risks. The existing literature identifies the main characteristic of risk management in a project-based company as the duality of risk management levels (Guserl 1999, p. 426; Tah and Carr 2000). CC's approach to risk management is based on linking overall company planning with individual projects planning. It systematically deals with this by taking the following steps: risk identification, risk analysis, risk management (risk transfer or avoidance of those risks that the company is not able to manage), risk monitoring and risk refinement. These are the fundamental stages of risk management that apply to both projects and the company, to small and large companies.

3.3 Risk Identification

This is a very important stage in risk management when the company uses all possible sources to identify its risks and list them in a file known as risk register. Some companies may regard analysis and implementation as more important. It is likely that large construction companies would be torn between giving higher weight to identification and implementation stages. Depending on the clients and the power structure within the company construction companies can be swayed between emphasizing implementation due to continuous response to clients' scope change and the risk managers' focus on getting the identification right. In CC, identification stage is of strategic importance.

Initially, Coastal Construction identifies its risk exposure through a self assessment exercise which involves use of checklist of potential risk available. In addition, the company make used of other methods to identify their risks such as simulation modeling (Monte Carlo) to analyze different scenarios and committee brainstorming sessions enhanced by the use of previous risk experiences and risks identified in the past. With less familiar projects sometimes facilitators are invited to workshops where all the involved team members are present. Interviewing of experts is recommended by the leadership of the company but risk managers often avoid it just in case it belittles their authority. Table 1 is the summary of a larger list.

3.4 Risk Analysis

The risk analysis process involves the following activities: determining risk impacts, the probability of occurrence, and, prioritizing in order of importance.

The most effective way to map those risks is by illustrating them in a simple likelihood-impact grid as shown below with probability and risk impact in simple scale of low, medium, and high (Fig. 2).

Probabilities are accompanied by confidence levels and bands for p values. These are usually worked out by in-house experts, but the impact is a thorny issue. Sometimes the directors and external experts are involved. The insurance concern is the main reason.

Once the risks have been identified and their potential impact on the company assessed, these are then allocated in order of priority.

3.5 Risk Response

The third step in Coastal Construction LTD for managing risk is called Risk Response, which includes risk treatment strategies given the identified risks and their associated potential impact on company's operations. The company employs

Table 1 Risk exposure checklist (recognized risks are ticked)

Environment	Third party	Damage to surrounding elements	/
		Obstruction to surrounding businesses or others	/
		Other claims	
		Violation of legal requirements	/
		Provisions	
	Accessibility of the construction site	Accidents	/
		Vandalism	
		Weather delay	/
		Risk related to the accessibility	/
	Pollution	Pollution	
		Archaeological finds	
		Soil quality	/
	Plan	Supply of plan	/
Organisation		Changes in plan	/
		Changes of requirement	/
		Claims related to not keeping promises	
	Task	Extra work	/
		Errors in executions	/
		Inaccurate estimation of duration	/
		Indistinctness on who will perform the task	/
	Permits	Lack of formalities/documents/permits	
Consumer goods	General	Price increase/decrease	/
		Material supply	/
		Availability	/
		Theft	
Workforce	Expertise	Lack of expertise	/
		Absence of key persons	/
	Social	Difficulties within teams	/
	Availability	Absenteeism	
Machines	Availability	Machine breakdown	/
		Supply	/
		Availability	/
		Damage	/
		Theft	
Subcontractor	General	Price increases/decrease	/
		Failure of company	/
		Respecting lead time	/
		Error in execution	/

various methods to deal with risk, it features a combination of risk control and risk transfers techniques.

For its risk control activity Coastal Construction implements strategies to lower the frequency or severity of potential risk, for instance, the provision of back-up equipment and emergency planning procedure. In addition, it manipulates ways to reduce the probability of occurrence by providing training and education to its personnel in the use of specialized equipment.

Once all the steps up to this point have been achieved, the company transfers its remaining risk. Risk transfer includes retention, contractual risk transfer and insurance risk transfer.

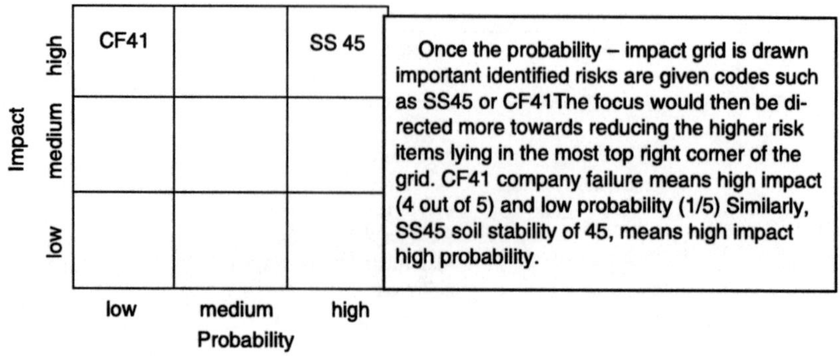

Fig. 2 Likelihood – impact grid

Contractual risk transfer is a big issue for company such as Coastal Construction whose core business is subcontracting. Whenever a contract is signed by the company, risk is automatically transferred, generally, through an indemnity agreement. Insurance risk transfers are the most costly measure to manage risk: Hence its prominent place in the company's risk management process. Only after identifying its potential risk, assessing their likely impact on the company's operation and business and setting up effective risk control techniques, can Coastal Construction determine what they need to insure and thus better able to approach the insurance market and negotiate lower rates.

3.6 Risk Monitoring and Follow Up

The last stage in the company's risk management process is Risk monitoring. The company strongly believes in the importance of continually reviewing and updating its risk management processes as its industry environment presents it with a dynamic and ever changing environment especially when considering individual projects and their different needs. Regular monitoring provides management and directors with an assurance that its risk management system is working properly in reducing risks and helping to keep track of the identified risks, including watch list (that is minor risks exposures). Its main purpose is a retrospective view to enable proactive corrective actions to be taken. According to the company's experience constantly reviewing and monitoring its risk process put the company in a better position to deal with unforeseen events causing the project falling behind schedule. Change in the companies environment can impact existing risks and also give rise to new risks, thus the company carries out this step in its risk management process to also identify new risks arising at a later time. Tools such as variance and trend analysis to monitor over project costs help to indicate when risk identification and performance should be performed by highlighting significant variances. The technique used in the monitoring process is a close loop feedback system, characteristic of most monitoring systems utilizing feedback. Table 2 can be a good representation of the risk management process in Coastal Construction.

Table 2 Adapted from Henschel (2009) Implementing a holistic risk management in SMEs

Project milestone	Process steps	Responsible personnel
Conceptualization	Kick-off the risk management project (initiation of the project)	Board of Directors
	Formulation of risk strategies	Board of Directors
	Organisation of risk mgt responsibilities and project team	Board of Directors
Risk identification	Planning of project (tasks and durations)	Responsible employee for risk mgt and project team
	Definition of risk categories	Responsible employee for risk mgt and project team (board of directors)
	Organisation of risk assessment workshop	Responsible employee for risk mgt and project team, heads of functions
	Execution of risk identification	Responsible employee for risk mgt
Risk evaluation	Preparation of risk catalogue	Responsible employee for risk mgt
	Risk evaluation and risk monitoring	Responsible employee for risk mgt and project team, heads of functions
Risk reporting and evaluation	Risk reporting	Responsible employee for risk mgt and project team, heads of functions
	Risk mgt documentation	Responsible employee for risk mgt and project team

4 Concluding Discussion

Most SMEs are reluctant to think about their risk. There are certain areas that they cannot close their eyes and ears when the Government warns about the risk, the supplier or customer reminds them or a subcontractor refuses to shoulder the risks. According to interviews carried out on SME Thomas Henschel found that most SME interviewed seek help from tax advisor and accountant. They think the accountants should be involved in managing the risk by acting as knowledge stewards. Table 2 depicts a generic list of personnel being responsible in managing risk in SME. In the case of Coastal Construction the situation is not as desperate. The finance director is responsible for risk management as well as other core responsibilities of managing the company's finance. Being aware of the limited role an individual can have, the enlightened directors in Coastal Construction have developed a more efficient way to manage risk by promoting the idea of company-wide risk management through company culture and by involving all the employees in one way or another. This is probably the only way risk management in SMEs can be practicable and effective.

Short Biography

Hosein Piranfar (PhD, MSc, BSc) is a Senior Lecturer in Operations Management, and Programme Leader of MSc Risk Management, Docklands Business School, University of East London. Prior to UEL, he worked as a researcher on Complexity and Organisational Learning in Kingston Business School. He has published widely in the fields of Foreign Direct Investment, Finance, Marketing & Operations Management, Networking (Social Capital), Risk Management, and Organisational Learning.

References

Ariful, I., Tedford, J.D., and Haemmerle, E. (2006) Strategic Risk Management Approach for Small and Medium-Sized Manufacturing Enterprises (SMEs). A Theoretical Framework

Basel Committee on Banking Supervision (2005), Overview of the New Basel Capital Accord. Basel: Bank for International Settlements

Cavignac, J. (2009) Managing Risk In a Construction Company, Construction business Owners, http://www.constructionbusinessowner.com/topics/insurance/ (viewed March 15, 2010)

Guserl, R. (1999). Management Accounting and risk management in project-based enterprises. *Controlling*, 11 (8/9):425–430

Henschel, T. (2009), Implementing a holistic risk management in Small and Medium Sized Enterprises (SMEs). Edinburgh Napier University School of Accounting, Economics & Statistics. Nov/Dec 2008

Piranfar, H. and Combstock, L. (2008), Risk and quality management: the symbiosis. i-manager's Journal on Management. 2(4): March–May, 2008

Russell, G. (2008). Risk management: What do the independent directors do? Research Report, Ernst and Young

Sloman, J. and Sutcliffe, M., (2004) *Economics for Business*, 2nd ed., Prentice Hall (Pearson Education), Harlow

Tah, J.H.M. and Carr, V. (2000). Information modeling for a construction project risk management system. Engineering, *Construction and Architectural Management*, 7(2):107–110

Turnbull (1999) ICAEW, Internal Control: Guidance for Directors on the Combined Code, The Combined Code of Corporate Governance (Turnbull Report) – UK. England and Wales's (ICAEW) Internal Control Working Party chaired by Nigel Turnbull

A Study on Management Risk Evaluation System of Large-Scale Complex Construction Projects

Linlin Xie and Yu Yang

Abstract A large-scale complex construction project is a gigantic system integrated with multiple factors, participants, management levels and relations. Complicated and varying management risks arise in such projects due to the diversity of project targets, the limitation of resources, the variation of environments and conflicts of multiple interests. Traditional risk management methods may be improper and inadaptable for large complex projects. Based on the characteristics and laws in management risks of such projects, a study was conducted on the feasible methods and related steps of management risk analysis. A system of management risk evaluation for large complex projects based on Grey Evaluation was brought forward, with a case study of Nanning International Convention and Exhibition Center presented as a demonstration. The result indicates that this method can reflect the randomicity, fuzziness and grayness of risk information in the management of large complex projects, and make the risk evaluation more scientific and reasonable.

Keywords Grey · Risk

1 Introduction

Since 1980s, construction projects all over the world tend to be increasingly large-scale and complex. The project management is facing growing challenges due to more and more risk factors concerned and the complexity and interaction of

L. Xie (✉)
School of Civil Engineering and Transportation, South China University of Technology, Guangzhou, People's Republic of China
e-mail: llxie@scut.edu.cn

Y. I. Yang
Faculty of Construction Management and Real Estate, Chongqing University, Chongqing, People's Republic of China
e-mail: cquyangyu@163.com

D.D. Wu (ed.), *Modeling Risk Management in Sustainable Construction*, Computational Risk Management, DOI 10.1007/978-3-642-15243-6_12,

multiple risk factors [1]. Traditional project management theories and methods show their limitation and inadaptability when applied to large complex construction projects [2]. It is well acknowledged in academic and practical circles that new theories and methods should be built for the management of large complex projects.

A large complex construction project is a gigantic system integrated with multiple factors, participants concerned, management levels and relations. This kind of projects has significant effects on the society and attracts great concern from the public. Once the management of such projects was out of control, not only the projects would suffer huge economic loss, but also it would cause a series of adverse and detrimental effects on the politics, society and environment. Therefore, it is imperative to raise the practitioners' awareness of project management risks, and more important, take steps to conduct effective risk analysis and prediction for large complex projects. Due to the diversity of project targets, limitation of resources, variation of environments and conflicts of multiple interests, there exist diverse, various and nonlinear management risk of large complex projects. Accordingly, it is needed to extensively investigate every step of risk analysis and then design a risk evaluation system suitable for the management of large complex projects.

2 Risk Identification

Risk identification is the first step and the basis of the entire risk analysis. The commonly used methods generally include the Delphi Method, Flow-Chart Method, Trouble-tree Method and Incident-tree-and-branch Chart Method, etc. In practice, a combination of several methods is usually applied in order for a more complete and objective risk identification. By collecting and analyzing the results of risk identification, the hierarchy structure of multi-layer risk factors can be set up, including the objective layer, the criterion layer and the sub-criterion layer. More details about the structure of risk factors are demonstrated in the following section of Case Study.

3 Risk Estimation

The probability of risk occurrence and corresponding loss should be taken into account in risk estimation. The probability of risk occurrence can be gained through expert interviews. The loss induced by risks may be figured out through some calculation models or obtained through expert interviews as well.

It is found that many non-technical risk factors influenced the management quality of large complex projects. And the function mechanisms of different risks are very complicated. The history information and statistical data about risk factors are usually hard to be obtained. Moreover, it is usually impossible to conduct long-span observation on certain risks of large complex projects. Therefore, the obtained

Table 1 The classification of risk levels

Classification	Catastrophic level	Serious level	High level	Moderate level	Mild level
Score	9	7	5	3	1

risk information usually is incomplete, non-representative or with low accuracy. So the risk information is random, grey and fuzzy to a great degree, and it is difficult to analyze related problems with determinate quantified models. In general, risk estimation depends on subjective judgment from experienced experts. Interviews with experts and questionnaire are more suitable methods for evaluating the risk factors of large complex projects.

According to these characteristics of risk factors in large complex projects, a practical risk estimation method is used here. Management risks of large projects are classified into five levels after conducting an overall evaluation on the occurrence likelihood and consequence of the risks. The risk in each level is estimated and given an appropriate score. A higher score indicates that a greater or more serious consequence may be caused by the risk, as shown in Table 1.

4 Risk Evaluation

After risk identification and risk estimation are conducted, risk evaluation should be made. The methods of risk evaluation include expert-scoring methods, AHP Method, CIM Method, fuzzy analysis methods, Monte Carlo Method, and so on. To overcome the deficiency of traditional risk evaluation methods and make evaluation results more objective and realistic, a comprehensive evaluation method for management risks of large complex projects is presented here based on Multiple-Layer Grey Theory.

After identifying and estimating the management risks of large complex projects, multiple-layer grey evaluation can be conducted as following [2, 3].

1. Building risk level judging matrix *D* of sub-criterion risk factors

The matrix can be gained by summarizing the scores of every risk factor in sub-criterion layer assessed by ‘*s*’ experts in the stage of risk estimation:

$$d_{\mathrm{ijk}}, (i = 1, 2, \cdots, m; j = 1, 2, \cdots n_i; k = 1, 2, ..., s).$$

2. Determining the weights of risk factors

The weights of different risk factors were determined using subjective weighing method according to the actual situation. Vector *W* denotes the weights of risk factors in the criterion layer:

$$W = (w_1, w_2, \cdots, w_m), w_i \geq 0, \sum_{i=1}^{m} w_i = 1\,(i = 1, 2, \cdots, m).$$

Vector W_i denotes the weights of risk factors in the sub-criterion layer:

$$W_{\mathrm{i}} = (w_{i1}, w_{i2}, \cdots, w_{in_i}), \quad w_{ij} \geq 0, \sum_{j=1}^{n_i} w_{ij} = 1, (i = 1, 2, \cdots, m; j = 1, 2, \cdots n_i).$$

3. Building definite weighted functions of risk factors

Definite weighted functions of risk factors in different grey categories are established based on five levels of risk factors in Table 1. The grey levels are determined as five grey categories for evaluation. Assuming that the serial number of evaluation grey categories as e, e = 1, 2,..., 5, the corresponding definite weighted functions f^{e} are as following:

(a) $e = 1$, suppose grey number $\otimes 1 \in [9, \infty]$ (Figs. 1 and 2)
(b) $e = 2$

In the same manner, f^3, f^4 and f^5 can be worked out.

4. Calculating the gray evaluation index

Label the evaluation index of risk factor X_{ij} in the sub-criterion layer which belongs to the e evaluation gray category as x_{ij}^e, so

$$x_{ij}^e = \sum_{k=1}^{s} f^e(d_{ijk}) \quad e = 1, 2, \cdots 5. \tag{1}$$

a $e=1$, suppose grey number $\otimes 1 \in [9, \infty]$;

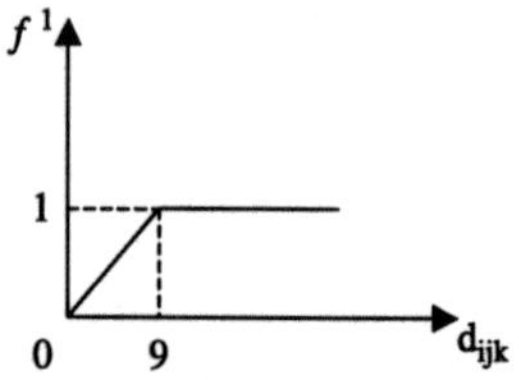

$$f^1(d_{ijk}) = \begin{cases} 0 & d_{ijk} \leq 0 \\ \dfrac{d_{ijk}}{9} & 0 < d_{ijk} \leq 9 \\ 1 & d_{ijk} \geq 9 \end{cases}$$

Fig. 1 The definite weighted function of f^1

b $e=2$

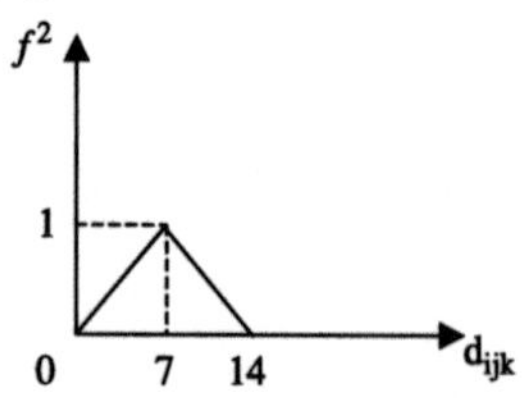

$$f^2(d_{ijk}) = \begin{cases} 0 & d_{ijk} < 0 \\ \dfrac{d_{ijk}}{7} & 0 \leq d_{ijk} \leq 7 \\ \dfrac{14 - d_{ijk}}{14 - 7} & 7 \leq d_{ijk} \leq 14 \\ 0 & d_{ijk} > 14 \end{cases}$$

Fig. 2 The definite weighted function of f^2

The sum of gray evaluation indices of the risk factor that belong to each evaluation gray category is marked as x_{ij}, so

$$x_{ij} = \sum_{e=1}^{5} x_{ij}^{e}. \tag{2}$$

5. Calculating the gray evaluation weight vector

All the experts' evaluation on the risk factor X_{ij} that belong to the e gray evaluation category is marked as r_{ij}^{e}, so

$$r_{ij}^{e} = x_{ij}^{e}/x_{ij}. \tag{3}$$

There are five evaluation gray categories, so the gray evaluation weight vector of the risk factor X_{ij} to every gray category can be obtained as r_{ij}:

$$r_{ij} = (r_{ij}^{1}, r_{ij}^{2}, \ldots, r_{ij}^{5}). \tag{4}$$

For every evaluation gray category, the gray evaluation weigh vectors of all risk factors X_{ij} in the sub-criterion layer which belong to the risk factor X_i in the criterion layer are synthesized, then the gray evaluation weight matrix R_i of X_i can be obtained:

$$R_i = \left[r_{i1}, r_{i2,\cdots,} r_{in_i}\right]^{T}. \tag{5}$$

6. Making a comprehensive evaluation on risk factors in the criterion layer

For the risk factor X_i, the evaluation result is marked as B_i:

$$B_i = W_i \times R_i = (b_i^1, b_i^2, \cdots b_i^5). \tag{6}$$

7. Making a comprehensive evaluation in the objective layer

From B_i, the evaluation result of X_i, we get the gray evaluation weigh matrix R of risk factor X_i in every criterion layer for every evaluation gray category under the comprehensive risk F:

$$R = [B_1, B_2, \cdots, B_m]^{T}. \tag{7}$$

Mark the comprehensive evaluation result of standard comprehensive risk F as B, so

$$B = W \times R = (b^1, b^2, \cdots, b^5). \tag{8}$$

8. Calculating the comprehensive evaluation value of the risk

Take the value vector of each evaluation gray category as $C = (9, 7, 5, 3, 1)$, and the comprehensive evaluation value of management risks of large complex projects will be

$$F = B \times C^T. \tag{9}$$

Compare F with the values in Table 1, the risk level of project management can be worked out.

9. Risk prevention

According to the risk evaluation result, risk prevention measures may be figured out to control the risks effectively and to reduce the loss resulted from the risks.

5 Case Study

Nanning International Convention and Exhibition Center (NICEC), as the permanent convention site of China-Asian Expo, combining conferences, exhibitions, visits, tours and other functions into one, is a landmark of Nanning, Guangxi, China. In its construction process of entire life cycle, there exists eight aspects of management risks from project management system, society, market, environment, and organization, etc. In order to effectively control risks, risk management personnel performed quantitative evaluation analysis of management risks.

1. Management risk identification of NICEC

With flow-chart method, following the logical sequence of project management, the whole management process was subdivided into a number of sub-processes, and the risks at all stages of the project management were identified. Meanwhile, the key links of management process and related weakness were analyzed, and main risk factors were caught. With environment analysis method, from the viewpoint of link and development, the dynamics and varying management risks of the NICEC project were figured out. The hierarchy structures of management risk factors of the NICEC project are shown in Table 2.

2. Risk estimation in sub-criterion layer

In this project, ten experts were selected to score on the risks in the sub-criterion layer in Table 2. Then the estimated values from the experts were synthesized and the risk estimation sample matrix D was figured out (omitted here).

3. Weight determination

The weight of every index in the Table 2 was drawn out with AHP method. The weight vectors are as following:

$$W = (0.13,\ 0.09,\ 0.03,\ 0.06,\ 0.20,\ 0.15,\ 0.18,\ 0.16)$$

Table 2 The hierarchy structures of multi-layer management risk factors of NICEC

Objective layer	Criterion layer	Sub-criterion layer
Comprehensive risks of management of NICEC, F	System risk X_1	System and regulation X_{11}
		Responsibility system X_{12}
		Management models X_{13}
		Supervision system X_{14}
	Social risks X_2	Legal environment X_{21}
		Culture cooperation X_{22}
		Interests groups X_{23}
		Public opinion X_{24}
	Market risks X_3	Macro-economic situation X_{31}
		Regional economic conditions X_{32}
	Environment Risks X_4	Natural environment X_{41}
		Social environment X_{42}
		Engineering environment X_{43}
	Organization risks X_5	Organizational structure X_{51}
		Personnel quality X_{52}
		Work flow X_{53}
	Technology risks X_6	Technology innovation X_{61}
		Tools and software X_{62}
		Research investment X_{63}
	Control risks X_7	Schedule control X_{71}
		Investment control X_{72}
		Quality control X_{73}
	Communication risks X_8	Contract restrictions X_{81}
		Knowledge management X_{82}
		Information interactive X_{83}

$$W_1 = (0.2,\ 0.4,\ 0.3,\ 0.1),\quad W_2 = (0.3, 0.1, 0.3, 0.3),\quad W_3 = (0.5,\ 0.5),$$
$$W_4 = (0.3,\ 0.3,\ 0.4)\quad W_5 = (0.5,\ 0.1,\ 0.4),\quad W_6 = (0.4,\ 0.4,\ 0.2),$$
$$W_7 = (0.4, 0.3, 0.3),\quad W_8 = (0.4,\ 0.3,\ 0.3)$$

4. Grey estimation coefficient calculation

For the factor x_{11}, with (1), the gray evaluation index x_{11}^e which belong the e evaluation gray category can be worked out as following:

$$x_{11}^1 = 1.5472; x_{11}^2 = 2.3011; x_{11}^3 = 3.2541; x_{11}^4 = 5.3298; x_{11}^5 = 6.9856$$

For the factor of system and regulation risks, with (2), the total gray evaluation index x_{11} of the risk corresponding to each evaluation gray category was worked out: $x_{11} = 19.4178$.

5. Gray evaluation weight vector and matrix calculation

Then with (3) and (4), the gray evaluation weight vector r_{11} from the evaluation of the ten experts based on the evaluation gray category e was gained: $r_{11} = (0.0797,\ 0.1185,\ 0.1676,\ 0.2745,\ 0.3598)$.

In the same way, the gray evaluation weight vectors of other risk factors with regard to each evaluation gray category were figured out. With (5), the evaluation weight matrix R_i (i = 1, 2, ..., 8) of each risk in the criterion layer was worked out.

6. Evaluation on risk factors X_i in the criterion layer

With (6), the evaluation result B_i can be figured out (the process was omitted).

7. Comprehensive evaluation on management risks of NICEC

With (7), the total gray evaluation weight matrix R of management risks of NICEC was drawn out as following:

$$R = \begin{bmatrix} B_1 \\ B_2 \\ B_3 \\ B_4 \\ B_5 \\ B_6 \\ B_7 \\ B_8 \end{bmatrix} = \begin{bmatrix} 0.1054 & 0.1497 & 0.2204 & 0.2503 & 0.2683 \\ 0.0910 & 0.1078 & 0.1598 & 0.2712 & 0.3678 \\ 0.1189 & 0.1446 & 0.2159 & 0.3076 & 0.2034 \\ 0.1286 & 0.1723 & 0.2148 & 0.2499 & 0.2104 \\ 0.1500 & 0.1895 & 0.2711 & 0.3062 & 0.0941 \\ 0.3101 & 0.3278 & 0.2916 & 0.0910 & 0 \\ 0.2411 & 0.2901 & 0.2732 & 0.1329 & 0.0529 \\ 0.2002 & 0.2451 & 0.2731 & 0.2111 & 0.0972 \end{bmatrix}$$

Then with (8), the comprehensive evaluation result of management risks resulted as $B = (0.1851, 0.2223, 0.2532, 0.2138, 0.1306)$. According to the valued vector of evaluation gray categories $C = (9, 7, 5, 3, 1)$, with (9), the comprehensive evaluation value of management risks of NICEC was worked out as $F = 5.260$.

Comparing this value with the values in Table 1, it is indicated that according to the evaluation results of the ten experts, the risk level of management of NICEC is between the 'serious level' and 'high level', and is more close to the "serious" level. Based on the above calculation results, a further exploration and investigation were conducted on the risk factors in the criterion layer and the sub-criterion layer to find out the origins of main risk factors. Then corresponding risk management measures were made and early warning system and prevention system were designed for the management of NICEC. Hence, through comprehensive evaluation on management risks of NICEC, the risks were controlled effectively and received a good result [4].

6 Summary

In this paper, main steps and applicable methods of risk analysis for management of large and complex projects were discussed in accordance with the characteristics of management risk of this kind of projects. A risk analysis method was presented based on Grey Evaluation Theory. This method overcomes the deficiency of traditional methods in evaluation of gray degree of various types of risk information. The results of a case study indicate that this method can reflect the characteristics of randomicity, fuzziness and grayness of risk information in the management of large and complex projects, thus can make the risk evaluation more scientific and reasonable and the risk management of such projects better.

References

1. Alan R. Bowman (2006). Developing activity duration specification limits for effective project control. European Journal of Operational Research 174(2): 1191–1204.
2. Kara S and Kayis B (2001). Concurrent resource allocation (CRA): A heuristic for multi-project scheduling with resource constraints in concurrent engineering. Concurrent Engineering 9(1): 64–73.
3. Deng J (2002). Basis of grey theory. The Publication of Central China University of Technology, Wuhan, China.
4. He W, Xie L, He Q (2008). Studies on life cycle integrated management system of large-scale convention and exhibition venues. Journal of Central China University of Technology 25(2): 59–64.

Risk-Based Determination of the Prenium Rate of Construction Work Safety Liability Insurance

Hongxia Wang, Gui Ye, and Chuanjing Ju

Abstract Work Safety Liability Insurance (WSLI) will develop rapidly in the Chinese construction industry as a way combining liability insurance and work safety. The establishment of the premium rate is haunting insurance and construction industry, and having hindered its development. By combining quantitative and qualitative analysis, a multi-criteria comprehensive evaluation model based on fuzzy mathematic is proposed in this paper to calculate the risk coefficient for adjusting basic premium rate of Construction Work Safety Liability Insurance (CWSLI). By following this method, different risk grades of construct project can be appropriately reflected through different premium rate, which can let the leverage of price be exerted adequately.

Keywords Adjusting coefficient · Construction work safety · Safety risk · Work Safety Liability Insurance

1 Introduction

The safety situation in China has became better in recent years, but safety accidents are still frequently occur, which caused great danger to the human life and wealth security. In order to alleviate safety accidents risks, the government has formulated some Proposals for the Reformation and Development of the Insurance Industry of the

H. Wang (✉)
Faculty of Construction Management and Real Estate, Chongqing University, Chongqing, People's Republic of China
and
Department of Economic and Trade, Chongqing Education College, Chongqing, China
e-mail: whx1255@tom.com

G. Ye, and C. Ju
Faculty of Construction Management and Real Estate, Chongqing University, Chongqing, People's Republic of China
e-mail: yegui760404@126.com; jcjandjcf@yahoo.com.cn

D.D. Wu (ed.), *Modeling Risk Management in Sustainable Construction*, Computational Risk Management, DOI 10.1007/978-3-642-15243-6_13,

State Council, Principle of Developing Work Safety Liability Insurance (WSLI) in High-risk Industries of State Administration of Work Safety and so on. The measures can, to a large extent, promote the role of insurance mechanism in work safety [1–3].

WSLI has been also developed in the construction industry, within which the accident rate is ranked third among all national sectors. Through developing the WSLI, an effective incentive mechanism can be constructed to effectively prevent and deal with safety accidents through the industry, and thus interests of the masses can be protected. Furthermore, it can also serve as a strategy to settle society contradictions and lighten the burden of addressing post-accident issues. In this sense, it can help transfer and enhance government function.

Construction Work Safety Liability Insurance (CWSLI) means that when safety accidents occur in the insured construction project, causing employees or a third party to suffer casualties or property losses, the legal liability that should assume by insurant to pay compensation for the victim, turn to be sure by insurance company basis a kind of assurance that the contract gives compensation inside insurance liability limit, and also pay compensation to the loose of rescue and self-reproduction [4].

Currently CWSLI has not been used in wide-spread throughout China, since most insurance companies and construction enterprises are still taking "wait-and-see" attitudes toward the "new" system. One main reason is that the premium rate of CWSLI is, to some extent, difficult to price precisely, because the scales and characters of construction projects vary a lot. In addition, there is lacking of statistical data in related to the construction work safety accident rate and related loses. Therefore, insurance companies have to set procrustean rate, which greatly hinders the development of CWSLI.

The primary determinant of whether a new insurance product can be developed in future is decided by the question whether there is a rational premium rate or not. In this regard, a method for confirming the rational premium is in pressing need, so that the WSLI can be greatly developed in the construction industry. There are solidified rate of Non-coal mine WSLI in Chongqing [5]. The methods of Probability, the Fuzzy Analysis Hierarchy Process Comprehensive Evaluation, Set Pair Analysis, Combined Algorithms, and so on are used to evaluate the state of construction safety [6–9]. Zhang et al. have done game analysis between the construction contractor and the insurance company based on the construction safety [10]. Monte Carlo techniques is used to establish the model of risk losses in simulated breakwaters building period by Zhou Handong et al. [11].

In this paper, fuzzy comprehensive evaluation (FCE) model is proposed to determine a risk coefficient for adjusting basic premium rate of CWSLI, thereby realizing different rate based on the quantification.

2 Fuzzy Comprehensive Evaluation

It is generally known that construction projects are complicated and changeful, and the safety liability risks vary greatly across different projects. Therefore, the premium rates of CWSLI for different construction projects should be determined individually. Nevertheless, it is difficult to put into effect given the facts that technologies for safety risk assessment are backward and the record of frequency and losses caused by safety accidents is lacking. It is more effective to adopt the variance-correcting method. By using this method, firstly basic rate reflecting the average risks of similar projects is determined. The basic rate can refer to the past prenium rate of building insurance or the experience-rate of international projects. Then insurance companies assess the safety risks of the project need to be insured based on FCE and take a coefficient to adjust the basic rate. The calculating formula for FCE is as follows:

$$\mathrm{i} = \mathrm{q} \times \mathrm{a} \tag{1}$$

where i is prenium rate after adjustment, q is the basic rate and a is the risk coefficient. By using this method, insurance companies only need to calculate the coefficient when they determine the CWSLI premium rate.

FCE is a method to quantify and evaluate some factors which are ill-defined and difficult to be quantified, based on the application of fuzzy mathematics method and the fuzzy relation synthetic. It is a very effective multi-criteria decision-making method. Considering that most of the safety liability risks in CWSLI are fuzzy variables, it is impossible to find a precise mathematical model to measure their impacts on CWSLI premium rates. Therefore, it is reasonable and feasible to calculate a project risk coefficient to adjust the basic rate by establishing a corresponding index system, which is useful to evaluate the safety liability risk by using fuzzy mathematics method. The different premium rates reflect the different risk grades of construction projects, which can let the leverage of price be adequately exerted.

3 Procedures for Calculating the Coefficient [12]

3.1 Establishing Index System

The calculation of the coefficient should be considered in line with the project and its building contractors to acquire factors influencing the work safety. All the risk factors as listed in Table 1 are determined finally by using the factor analysis after s series of pilot study and interviews conducted among construction safety experts.

3.2 Determining Risk Grade and Establishing Evaluation Sets

According to the requirements of calculating the coefficient, five grades are set for assessment, namely, set $V = \{V_1, V_2, V_3, V_4, V_5\}$. The alphabet of V_1, V_2, V_3, V_4 and V_5 denote "very inferior risk", "lower risk", "average risk", "more risk" and

Table 1 Index system for assessing safety risk in CWSLI

	First-grade indexes	Second-grade indexes
State of safety liability risk X	Safety management of construction enterprise (X_1)	Qualification of the construction enterprise (X_{11})
		Security system of the work safety funds (X_{12})
		Education and training programmes in safety (X_{13})
		System of safety supervision and examination (X_{14})
		System of check-up, rewards and penalties (X_{15})
		Number of safety accidents happened in the enterprise (X_{16})
		Safety culture construction of the enterprise (X_{17})
	Characteristic of the construction project (X_2)	Project scale (X_{21})
		Complex degree of engineering technique (X_{22})
		Construction conditions (X_{23})
		Construction period (X_{24})
		Project subcontracting (X_{25})
	Safety management in construction site (X_3)	Responsibility and level of the safety management of the client and supervision (X_{31})
		Number and responsibility of safety managers (X_{32})
		Funds input work safety (X_{33})
		Safety inspection for project (X_{34})
		Hazardous sources identified and control measures (X_{35})
		Safety construction-organizing design and technical clarification (X_{36})
		Safety management of construction plant and equipment (X_{37})
		Emergency preplan (X_{38})

$X = \{X1, X2, X3\}$
$X1 = \{X_{11}, X_{12}, X_{13}, X_{14}, X_{15}, X_{16}, X_{17}\}, X2 = \{X_{21}, X_{22}, X_{23}, X_{24}, X_{25}\}, X3 = \{X_{31}, X_{32}, X_{33}, X_{34}, X_{35}, X_{36}, X_{37}, X_{38}\}$
Where X is the set of factors influencing construction project safety liability risks

"highest risk" respectively. The level of each risk is corresponded with the risk coefficient, which would be indicated by a_m. When the risk of the project is higher than the average level, the value for variable a_m should be larger than 1. The higher risk an insurance company assumes for a policyholder, the higher the value for variable a_m, as well as the higher the premium rate. Similarly, when the risk is lower than the average level, the value for a_m should be less than 1. The lower the risk, the smaller the value for variable a_m.

3.3 Determining the Single-Factor Fuzzy Judgment Matrix

According to the standard of evaluation defined, all members of qualified experts selected from construction and insurance companies need to appraise the project risk grade of each factor in second-grade index one-by-one, through which the single-factor judgment matrix (Ri) of individual subset of X_1, X_2, X_3 can be obtained. Then the membership grade of each factor is got by the weight coefficient vector of each single-factor (X_i), and finally the membership function matrix of evaluation index can be confirmed. Supposed that r_{ij} represents the membership grade of X_{ij} on V_j. The value of r_{ij} is obtained by expert marking method. That is to say, if the remarks of one factor for class V_1, V_2, V_3, V_4, V_5 are S_1, S_2, S_3, S_4, S_5 respectively, among the S experts attending project safety risk evaluation, the membership grade can be calculated as follow:

$$r_{ij} = Sm \Big/ \sum_{j=1}^{5} Sj \text{或} r_{ij} = Sm/S \ (m = 1, 2, ..., 5) \tag{2}$$

There are ten experts evaluating the risks of a construction project work safety. Two of the experts marked the X_{11} factor to class V_1, five to class V_2, two to class V_3, and one to class V_4. According to (2), $R_{11} = (0.2, 0.5, 0.2, 0.1, 0)$. In the same way, we can have calculated other factors' membership grades. They take the single-factor fuzzy judgment matrix (R_i), which is the membership function matrix of first-grade indexes. The membership function matrix of the project is as follows:

$$R_1 = \begin{bmatrix} R_{11} \\ R_{12} \\ \cdot \\ \cdot \\ \cdot \\ R_{17} \end{bmatrix} = \begin{bmatrix} 0.2 & 0.5 & 0.2 & 0.1 & 0 \\ 0.1 & 0.2 & 0.4 & 0.2 & 0.1 \\ 0.2 & 0.2 & 0.3 & 0.2 & 0.1 \\ 0.1 & 0.4 & 0.2 & 0.2 & 0.1 \\ 0.4 & 0.2 & 0.2 & 0.1 & 0.1 \\ 0 & 0.4 & 0.3 & 0.2 & 0.1 \\ 0.1 & 0.1 & 0.5 & 0.2 & 0.1 \end{bmatrix}$$

$$R_2 = \begin{bmatrix} R_{21} \\ R_{22} \\ \cdot \\ \cdot \\ R_{25} \end{bmatrix} = \begin{bmatrix} 0.2 & 0.2 & 0.4 & 0.1 & 0 \\ 0.3 & 0.3 & 0.2 & 0.2 & 0 \\ 0.2 & 0.2 & 0.3 & 0.2 & 0.1 \\ 0.2 & 0.2 & 0.4 & 0.1 & 0 \\ 0.1 & 0.2 & 0.3 & 0.2 & 0.2 \end{bmatrix}$$

$$R_3 = \begin{bmatrix} R_{31} \\ R_{32} \\ \cdot \\ \cdot \\ R_{39} \end{bmatrix} = \begin{bmatrix} 0.2 & 0.2 & 0.3 & 0.1 & 0.1 \\ 0.1 & 0.1 & 0.2 & 0.3 & 0.3 \\ 0.1 & 0.2 & 0.2 & 0.4 & 0.1 \\ 0.1 & 0.2 & 0.3 & 0.3 & 0.1 \\ 0.1 & 0.2 & 0.2 & 0.4 & 0.1 \\ 0 & 0.1 & 0.2 & 0.5 & 0.2 \\ 0.1 & 0.2 & 0.4 & 0.2 & 0.1 \\ 0 & 0.1 & 0.3 & 0.5 & 0.1 \end{bmatrix}$$

3.4 Calculating the Weight of Indicators

Risk assessment on construction project work safety is a process of multi-criteria fuzzy comprehensive evaluation. The weight should be meaningful to explain the importance of each factor. Various methods, such as the Analytic Hierarchy Process (AHP), Delphi method, etc have been used to calculate the weight. In this paper, ten experts were invited to study some factors influencing the premium rate of CWSLI and give them scores on a scale ranging from 0 to 100. After three rounds of experts' opinions were collected, the weighted average scores have been calculated and normalized as follow:

The weighting function of the first-level indexes $W = \{W_1, W_2, W_3\} = \{0.25, 0.3, 0.45\}$.

The weighting functions of the second-level indexes $W_i = \{w_{i1}, w_{i2}, \ldots, w_{ij}\}$. After calculation, $W_1 = \{w_{11}, w_{12}, \ldots, w_{17}\} = \{0.15, 0.1, 0.25, 0.05, 0.1, 0.25, 0.1\}$,

$$W_2 = \{w_{21}, w_{22}, \ldots, w_{25}\} = \{0.1, 0.3, 0.2, 0.1, 0.3\},$$

$$W_3 = \{w_{31}, w_{32}, \ldots, w_{38}\} = \{0.15, 0.1, 0.15, 0.12, 0.1, 0.1, 0.2, 0.08\}.$$

3.5 Establishing a Fuzzy Comprehensive Evaluation Model

Supposing that first-level fuzzy comprehensive evaluation model can be expressed as:

$$Bi = W_i \bullet R = (b_{i1}, b_{i2}, \cdots, b_{ik}) \tag{3}$$

where " $\bullet$ "is a fuzzy operator, which used "M(∨∧)" composition operation of X_i subsets and R subsets. That is to say, firstly the single-factor membership grade is modified to minimum value of W_i and r_{ij}, then the maximum value is taken as the evaluation grade, and other factors are not taken into consideration. So the operator is called as decision under main factors. The operator "∨" means "taking maximum" and "∧" means "taking minimum". The formula is shown as follows:

$$\begin{aligned} bj &= \vee(Wi \wedge rij) \\ &= \max\{\min(W1, r1j), \min(W2, r2j), \cdots\cdots, \min(Wm, r2j) \end{aligned} \tag{4}$$

$$R = (B1, B2, B3)^T \tag{5}$$

The fuzzy comprehensive evaluation matrix of the project is:

$$B1 = W_1 \cdot R_1 = (0.15,0.1,0.25,0.05,0.1,0.25,0.1) \bullet \begin{bmatrix} 0.2 & 0.5 & 0.2 & 0.1 & 0 \\ 0.1 & 0.2 & 0.4 & 0.2 & 0.1 \\ 0.2 & 0.2 & 0.3 & 0.2 & 0.1 \\ 0.1 & 0.4 & 0.2 & 0.2 & 0.1 \\ 0.4 & 0.2 & 0.2 & 0.1 & 0.1 \\ 0 & 0.4 & 0.3 & 0.2 & 0.1 \\ 0.1 & 0.1 & 0.5 & 0.2 & 0.1 \end{bmatrix}$$

$$\begin{aligned} b_{11} &= (W_{11} \wedge r_{11}) \vee (W_{12} \wedge r_{21}) \vee (W_{13} \wedge r_{31}) \vee (W_{14} \wedge r_{41}) \vee (W_{15} \wedge r_{51}) \\ &\quad \vee (W_{16} \wedge r_{61}) \vee (W_{17} \wedge r_{71}) \\ &= 0.15 \end{aligned}$$

Similarly, $b_{12} = 0.25$, $b_{13} = 0.25$, $b_{14} = 0.2$, $b_{15} = 0.1$.

$$B2 = (0.3,0.3,0.3,0.2,0.2), B3 = (0.15,0.2,0.2,0.2,0.1)$$

$$\begin{aligned} B &= W \cdot R \\ &= (0.25,0.3,0.45) \bullet \begin{bmatrix} 0.15 & 0.25 & 0.25 & 0.2 & 0.1 \\ 0.3 & 0.3 & 0.3 & 0.2 & 0.2 \\ 0.15 & 0.2 & 0.2 & 0.2 & 0.1 \end{bmatrix} \\ &= (0.3,0.3,0.3,0.2,0.2) \end{aligned}$$

The result is normalized to B = (0.23, 0.23, 0.23, 0.155, 0.155).

3.6 Determinating the Risk Coefficient of the Project

The premium rate of CWSLI should be reasonable because both parties in insurance are rational economic human beings. In order to let the leverage of price be exerted adequately, the above result should be processed to a risk coefficient of the project. We can use the method of weighted average, which the contributions of all indexes in evaluation sets are considered comprehensively. When the risk is higher than the average level, the coefficient is larger than 1. So the final result should be $C = B * F$, where F is the weight vector of evaluation grade. C is the risk coefficient of the project. The safety risk should not only be accepted by insurance enterprises but also make construction enterprise be willing to buy CWSLI. There set $F = (0.4, 0.7, 1, 1.3, 1.6)^T$. The coefficient of the project is:

$$C = (0.23,0.23,0.23,0.155,0.155) * (0.4,0.7,1,1.3,1.6)^T = 0.9325$$

Therefore, the prenium rate of CWSLI is the product of basic premium and 0.9325. The result indicates that the risk of the project is a bit lower than the average level.

4 Conclusion

With the increasing importance of construction safety related problems, it is anticipated that WSLI would develop rapidly in the construction industry. The findings of this paper show that by combining quantitative and qualitative analysis, the multi-criteria comprehensive evaluation model based on fuzzy mathematic proposed serves as a useful and practical vehicle for determining the premium rate of CWSLI.

References

1. Some Proposals for the Reformation and Development of the Insurance Industry of the State Council (The Document (2006) No. 23).
2. Principle of Developing Work Safety Liability Insurance (WSLI) in High-risk Industries of State Administration of Work Safety (The Document (2009) No. 137).
3. Suggestion on Improving the Security System and Pressing Ahead with Liability Insurance in Work Safety of State Administration of Work Safety (The Document (2006) No. 207).
4. Qiao Weibin, Chen Guang. Research on Work Safety Liability Insurance for High-risk Industries[M]. China Fiscal and Economic Publishing. Beijing. (2009), p. 139–147.
5. Notice of Opinions on Work Safety Liability Insurance in Non-coal Mine of Chongqing State Administration of Work Safety (The Document (2008) No. 2).
6. Ma Yingju. Reference Probability of Death and Injure Relation in Industrial Accidents. Journal of Dalian Railway Institute, Vol. 24: 62–64 (2003).
7. Lv Kang, Zheng Hong-bo, Zhang Yun. Application of the Model of Improved Fuzzy AHP Synthetic Evaluation in Major Risk Sources Assessment. Liaoning Chemical Industry, January, Vol. 38, No. 1 (2009).
8. Xizhong Wang, Jin Zhu, Yuhong Dong, et al. Safety evaluation management on the construction based on set pair analysis. Third International Symposium on Intelligent Information Technology Application, Shanghai China, Proceedings, (2009) p. 653–655.
9. Li Yancang, Suo Juanjuan. Safety Assessment of Construction Engineering Based on Combined Algorithms. International Conference on Intelligent Human–Machine Systems and Cybernetics. Hangzhou, Zhejiang China, (2009) p. 47–50.
10. Zhang FL, Lai CY, Zhang YJ. Game Analysis Between the Construction Contractor and the Insurance Company Based on the Construction Safety. 2006 Xi'an International Conference of Architecture and Technology, Proceedings, (2006), p. 1015–1019.
11. Zhou Handong, Jiang Xuelian, Li yanbao. "Study on the Risk-Based Determination of the Premium Rate in Breakwater Construction". The Ocean Engineering, Vol. 25, No. 3: 40–45 (2007, 8).
12. Peng Zhuzeng, Sun Weiyu. The Fuzzy Mathematics and Its Applications. Cambridge University Press, Cambridge, 2002:1–47.

Part III
Enterprise Risk Management in Projects

Multi-criteria Decision Model for BOT Project Selection

Min-Ren Yan

Abstract Due to many disadvantages resulting from limited government budget and time, the increasing infrastructure projects via build-operate-transfer (BOT) model has been a significant factor affecting the economic developments in many countries. However, as BOT projects are usually risky businesses which induce huge capital investments, the project feasibility should be comprehensively evaluated and an appropriate project selection model is needed to reduce the risk of project failure. By incorporating Analytical Hierarchy Process and Utility Theory, this paper proposes a multi-criteria decision model for supporting the selection of BOT projects. The proposed model enables decision makers to evaluate BOT projects and handle the project risk systematically. A case study of the national sewerage system plan in Taiwan is provided to demonstrate that the implementation of the proposed model can effectively help decision-making teams participate in economical evaluations so that the feasibility of as-planed BOT projects can be systematically determined and project priority can be set efficiently.

Keywords AHP · BOT · Decision support · Evaluation · Multi-criteria decision making · Utility

1 Introduction

Due to many restrictions and limitations resulting from limited government budget and time, the governments of many countries introduced the concept of Public Private Partnership (PPP) to launch infrastructure projects for Private Financial Initiatives, which are collective terms for build-operate-transfer (BOT), build-operate-own

M.-R. Yan
Department of Business Administration, Chinese Culture University, No. 231, Sec. 2, Jianguo S. Rd., Da-an Dist., Taipei City, Taiwan, ROC
e-mail: mjyen@sce.pccu.edu.tw

D.D. Wu (ed.), *Modeling Risk Management in Sustainable Construction*, Computational Risk Management, DOI 10.1007/978-3-642-15243-6_14,

(BOO), build-own-operate-transfer (BOOT), build-transfer-operate (BTO), built and transfer (BT), and operate and transfer (OT), etc. [1].

A successful BOT project requires more favorable conditions than projects procured by the traditional way. The project promoters should ascertain that the project be politically, socially, legally, economically, and financially viable [2]. Before implementing BOT projects, the government must effectively evaluate the feasibility of each project to eliminate unqualified projects and execute the selected project progressively according to its capabilities. In the past BOT practice, governments depended upon project feasibility studies prepared by private consultants. Usually, decision makers responsible for determining the feasibility of the project before proceeding with its implementation concentrate mainly on the quantitative decision factors, and used sometimes misinformed subjective evaluation or neglect of potentially viable project opportunities [3]. Previous studies have indicated that many BOT projects failed to be completed or suspended, and a prior feasibility study was insufficient to be concluded the entire undertaking [4]. Therefore, how to establish an objective BOT project evaluation model to comprehensively assess the quality of each project and determine the priority of implementation has become an important issue. Since the allocation of BOT projects induces significant capital investments and impacts on the country's economy, factors including economics and social developments should be broadly considered [5]. In addition, multi-criteria analysis method enables broad perspectives for the assessment and risk valuation is essential during the decision-making process [6, 7]. Thus, this paper aims to develop a multi-criteria decision model by incorporating Analytical Hierarchy Process (AHP) and Utility Theory to manage the visible, invisible or unquantifiable factors that affect the effectiveness of BOT projects. Through this research, the feasibility and priority of each planned BOT projects can be evaluated objectively. A real case of BOT sewerage system projects in Taiwan will be used to demonstrate the usefulness of the proposed decision model. The result is expected to be a valuable reference for both administrators and legislators to manage future BOT projects.

The multi-criteria decision model and the whole process of BOT projects evaluation comprises of three main parts: (a) developing the criteria and measurement, (b) determining the weight and utility function of each criterion, and (c) applying the model to real cases. Each part will be presented accordingly in the following sections.

2 The Criteria and Measurements

The US Environmental Protection Agency and International Development Institute have provided a list of criteria for state government to follow in the introduction of civil participation into construction of sewerage systems [8, 9]. These criteria are classified into financial and nonfinancial groups, with eight criteria identified as follows:

2.1 *Financial Criteria*

1. Initial construction cost of the sewerage treatment plant = construction cost of the first phase sewerage treatment plant ($)/designed capacity of wastewater to be processed (ton)
2. Cost of construction per household = total construction cost ($)/number of households to be served (household)
3. Cost of prevalence rate improvement = sum of discounted construction costs in all years ($)/ratio of households to be served to the total households around the nation (1%)
4. Wastewater treatment rates = wastewater treatment rates of each phase × planned treatment capacity in each phase ($)/planned total treatment capacity (ton)

2.2 *Non-financial Criteria*

1. Construction efficiency: the duration that a sewerage system requires to be connected to 10,000 households after contracting is used as a parameter to evaluate the construction efficiency of a sewerage system; this parameter reveals the investment efficiency to be presented by a civil contractor. If the sewerage system can serve fewer than 10,000, this duration is estimated according to the proportion of the total household number of 10,000. When ranking the sewerage systems, those with a shorter duration have a higher priority.
2. Pipeline service efficiency = total pipeline length (meter)/total number of households.
3. Operation and maintenance cost ratio = operation and maintenance cost/ weighted average treatment rates per unit
4. Local government's financial ability = weighted average wastewater treatment cost × annual volume of wastewater treated in the first phase/the average current account revenue budget of the most recent years

3 The Weighting and Utility Function of Each Criterion

The AHP framework organizes logic and personal feelings or intuitive judgments so that researchers can map out complex situations as what they perceived. Today, AHP has been proved as a reliable method to provide problem solutions for multi-factors decision-making situations.

Table 1 Weight value, threshold, most preferred point, and utility function for criteria

Criteria	W_i	y_T	y_m	Utility function
Initial construction cost of the treatment plant	0.150	19323.6	29.8	$u_i(y_i) = -0.0000518y_i + 1.00154631$
Cost of construction per household	0.140	58599.2	62.6	$u_i(y_i) = -0.0000171y_i + 1.00106893$
Cost of prevalence rate improvement	0.155	685.6	464.0	$u_i(y_i) = -0.0045118y_i + 3.09330446$
Wastewater treatment rates	0.175	31.2	26.1	$u_i(y_i) = -0.1959824y_i + 6.10926017$
Construction efficiency	0.113	5.25	5	$u_i(y_i) = -4y_i + 21$
Pipeline service efficiency	0.088	1.56	0.93	$u_i(y_i) = -1.59y_i + 2.47$
Operation and maintenance cost ratio	0.079	0.3	0.24	$u_i(y_i) = -18.666746y_i + 5.52527164$
Local government's financial ability	0.100	0.02	0.01	$u_i(y_i) = -98.2604796y_i + 1.7728483$

AHP-based questionnaires are mailed to 31 experts and scholars for collecting the consensus of opinions, including (1) members of the sewerage system promotion committee in Construction and Planning Agency of Ministry of the Interior, (2) construction consulting firms involved in the design and execution of the sewerage systems in Taiwan, and (3) central government officials in charge of BOT sewerage systems business. Fourteen experts have completed and returned the questionnaire.

Utility theory is an accepted approach used to provide an objective decision based on subjective, qualitative data [10]. Based on the historic records of sewerage systems constructed using the public funds provided by central and local governments, utility functions shown in Table 1 are developed with the threshold (y_T) and the most preferred point (y_m) [11]. The utility functions, which represent individual preference and attitude towards risk by decision makers, can be used to convert the evaluation score of each criterion into comparable relative ratings.

The expected utility value equals to the sum of relative ratings × weighting value of each criterion as shown in (1):

$$\text{Expected Utility Value (EUV)} = \sum_{i=1}^{n} (u_{ri} \times W_i) \tag{1}$$

4 The Case Study

In Taiwan, the Executive Yuan has approved 36 BOT sewerage system projects and also preliminarily reviewed the feasibility of adopting BOT model for another 53 projects [12, 13]. All these projects, 89 in total, are large in scale with a total cost over 100 billion US dollars. In this section, 36 BOT projects all around Taiwan area and outlying islands listed in the third-phase national construction plan are used to illustrate how the proposed model can be applied to objectively select feasible projects and determine the implementation priority. Each BOT project is evaluated using the proposed model to derive the utility value of each criterion and the overall utility value.

As shown in Table 2, the original BOT plans are arranged sequentially by locations. Although the government has gathered the concerned information regarding financial and non-financial perspectives, the original BOT plans can't be evaluated and compared objectively. Thus, the government should heavily rely on the group decision making mechanism based on invited experts' opinions, despite each expert's decision is subjectively made. Since the decision mechanism doesn't incorporate supportive quantitative models and numerical analysis, the mechanism would be a descriptive decision model and the decision rationale and consistency can't be properly justified.

Different from the conventional descriptive decision model, the proposed decision model enables decision makers to implement a normative decision method.

Table 2 Model applications on BOT project selection

Original BOT plans (based on locations)		Reorganized plans (based on EUV)		Implications for decision supports	
Region	Name	Name	EUV	Priority	Feasible?
North Taiwan	Luodung	Lugang	1.821	1	Yes
	Rueifang	Taichung	1.001	2	Yes
	Sanying	Fengyuan	0.658	3	Yes
	Puding	Changhua	0.591	4	Yes
	Taoyuan	Tainan	0.531	5	Yes
	Jungli	Sanying	0.472	6	Yes
	Junan-Toufen	Yungkang	0.399	7	Yes
Central Taiwan	Taichung	Taoyuan	0.142	8	Yes
	Fengyuan	Junan-Toufen	0.071	9	Yes
	Nantou	Jungli	−0.068	10	No
	Puli	Gangshan	−0.229	11	No
	Tsautuen	Taitung	−0.273	12	No
	Jushan	Yanshuei	−0.291	13	No
	Changhua	Chiai City	−0.309	14	No
	Hemei	Luodung	−0.333	15	No
	Lugang	Shihlong river	−0.334	16	No
	Dounan	Tsautuen	−0.549	17	No
	Beigang	Magung	−0.616	18	No
	Chiai City	Nantou	−1.033	19	No
	Taibau	Gueiren	−1.316	20	No
South Taiwan	Tainan	Jushan	−1.429	21	No
	Yanshuei	Puli	−1.597	22	No
	Yungkang	Rueifang	−1.806	23	No
	Gueiren	Jiali	−1.926	24	No
	Jiali	Taibau	−1.969	25	No
	Shihlong river	Puding	−2.289	26	No
	Gangshan	Neipu	−2.457	27	No
	Neipu	Hemei	−2.885	28	No
East Taiwan	Yuli	Beigang	−3.535	29	No
	Taitung	Dounan	−4.100	30	No
Outlying island	Magung	Yuli	−4.879	31	No

The expected performance of each system for each aspect and the overall project are listed in Table 2. Based on the calculated EUV of BOT projects, the project feasibility and utility can be evaluated objectively. Since the proposed model is developed by benchmarking previous public-fund projects, a project with positive EUV represents a feasible BOT plan which is expected to generate more benefits than using public-fund method. On the contrary, a project with negative EUV represents that the project is not favor BOT approach and might generate worse performance than using public-fund method. According to the aforementioned decision rules, 9 feasible BOT projects are identified, while 22 projects are not considered beneficial for the government by implementing BOT approach. Clearly, the proposed decision model generates a useful signal for the government to re-evaluate unfavorable BOT plans in advance of implementation.

In addition to support the evaluation of BOT project feasibility, the evaluated EUVs of BOT projects can be used to support the decision of priority setting. A project with higher EUV represents prior order to be implemented. According to the decision rule, the priority of all BOT plans can be objectively and efficiently reordered based on their EUVs.

As shown in Table 2, Lugang sewerage system project has the highest expected utility by BOT approach (EUV = 1.821). This BOT project should have the first priority to be implemented. The project that has the second priority for implementation is Taichung sewerage system project (EUV = 1.001). For other projects, the government can easily set their sequences for implementation based on their EUV ranking.

The EUVs derived from the proposed model can reveal the advantages and shortcomings of each BOT project as a basis. It will reduce errors and mistakes and improve the effectiveness and efficiency of decision-making. Although some projects having negative EUVs would not be expected as effective via BOT, those projects still can be ranked and properly arrange a sequence for other considerations, such as promotion on specific region development, whether the BOT project is feasible or needs further evaluations.

5 Conclusions

To improve the selection process of the BOT projects, AHP and utility theory are successfully incorporated and a multi-criteria decision model is developed. The proposed model using the utility function shows the advantages that it can overcome the difficulties of building a multi-criteria model and support decision-makers to adjust decisions according to their preference and considerations. Thus, inconsistent decisions influenced by various factors can be eliminated.

The utilization of AHP method allows for the incorporation into the decision-making process of subjective judgments and user intuition by producing a common formal and numeric solution. Besides, importance weights are quantified and the utilities of attributes are measured in the project selection process. Finally, individual attribute utilities are combined to develop one single aggregate utility index for each alternative. With the aid of the proposed model, decision-makers can improve the quality and efficiency of their decisions because of full participation by all involved in the evaluation process and the integration of their opinions. The case study demonstrates the practical values of the proposed decision model, which is expected to be a valuable reference for both administrators and legislators to manage future BOT projects.

References

1. Kumaraswamy M.M., and Morris D.A. (2002) Build-operate-transfer-type procurement in Asian Maga projects. Journal of Construction Engineering and Management 128: 93–102.
2. Abdel Aziz (2007) Successful delivery of public-private partnerships for infrastructure development. Journal of Performance of Constructed Facilities 21: 918–931.
3. United Nations Industrial Development Organization (UNIDO) (1996) Guideline for infrastructure development through build-operate-transfer (BOT) projects. Vienna, UNIDO.
4. CRANA Corporation (2002) Privatization in Egypt. Privatization Coordination Support Unit.
5. Ginevicius R., and Podvezko V. (2009) Evaluating the changes in economic and social development of Lithuanian counties by multiple criteria methods. Technological and Economic Development of Economy 15: 418–436.
6. Sliogeriene J., Kaklauskas A., Zavadskas E.K., Bivainis J., and Seniut M. (2009) Environment factors of energy companies and their effect on value: analysis model and applied method. Technological and Economic Development of Economy 15: 490–521.
7. Shevchenko G., Ustinovichius L., and Andruskevicius A. (2008) Multi-attribute analysis of investments risk alternatives in construction. Technological and Economic Development of Economy 14: 428–443.
8. United States Environmental Protection Agency (USEPA) (2000) Guidance on the privatization of federally funded wastewater treatment works. USEPA, USA.
9. International Development Institute (IDI) (2002) Guidelines for Management of Sewerage Facilities in Developing Countries. IDI Water Series.
10. Cheung S.O., and Suen H.C.H. (2002) A multi-attribute utility model for dispute resolution strategy selection. Construction Management and Economics 20: 557–568.
11. Dozzi S.P., AbouRizk S.M., and Schroeder S.L. (1996) Utility-theory model for bid markup decisions. Journal of Construction Engineering and Management 122: 119–124.
12. Construction and Planning Agency of Ministry of Interior (CPAMI) (2007) A study on priority evaluation of sewerage rehabilitation Taipei Taiwan. CPAMI, Taiwan (in Chinese).
13. Construction and Planning Agency of Ministry of Interior (CPAMI) (2003) The third phase of sewerage system construction. CPAMI, Taiwan (in Chinese).

Equitable Risk Allocation in Chinese Public–Private Partnership Power Projects

Yongjian Ke, ShouQing Wang, and Albert P. C. Chan

Abstract It is important for the public and private sectors to establish effective risk allocation strategies for PPP projects in order to achieve a more efficient process of contract negotiation. This paper has studied the equitable allocation of risks in China's PPP power projects based on a comparative analysis of preferred and actual risk allocations. According to the analysis, three risks, namely, "Change in law", "Competition (Exclusive right)" and "Organization and coordination risk" had different allocations. Reasons behind the differences were analyzed and more appropriate allocations for the three risks were also discussed. The preferred and actual allocation for other risks would also be reported in this paper.

Keywords Power projects · Public–private partnership · Risk allocation

1 Introduction

Public–Private Partnership (PPP) financing modality, as an innovative tool for attracting foreign and private capital in the development of infrastructure, has the ability of alleviating the budgetary pressure to the government, fulfilling the need of infrastructure development, and improving the efficiency of investment and operation [1]. In China, the tremendous economic growth has resulted in an immense demand for basic infrastructure like roads, ports and power facilities. Since most of

Y. Ke (✉) and S. Wang
Department of Construction Management, Tsinghua University, Beijing 100084, People's Republic of China
e-mail: kyj05@mails.tsinghua.edu.cn; sqwang@tsinghua.edu.cn

A.P.C. Chan
Department of Building and Real Estate, The Hong Kong Polytechnic University, Kowloon, Hong Kong, SAR, China
e-mail: bsachan@polyu.edu.hk

D.D. Wu (ed.), *Modeling Risk Management in Sustainable Construction*,
Computational Risk Management, DOI 10.1007/978-3-642-15243-6_15,

the local governments are still subject to severe budgetary pressure, there is a heavy reliance on the private sector investment. This might provide a great opportunity for private investors to get more involved in infrastructure development via PPP mode. However, only a few PPP projects in China could perform successfully and disputes often arise during concession period because of changes in various risks or non-performance of its obligations, especially when one party was forced to accept the requirements by the other due to the project urgency or other reasons [1]. Therefore, it is worth examining the application of PPP in the past and deriving lessons learnt for future references. Given that private participation in infrastructure development in China was first seen in the power sector in the 1980s in the form of Build-Operate-Transfer (BOT), this paper thus focuses on the power sector.

2 PPP in Chinese Power Sector

Shajiao B power plant in Shenzhen, which came to operation in 1988, is regarded as the first BOT project in China. However, government took over too many risks in Shajiao B project due to the lack of BOT experience [2]. Thereafter, several state-approved pilot BOT projects have been awarded in order to introduce BOT on a larger scale since late 1996, such as Laibin B power project etc. Since then, the involvement of private investors in infrastructural development of public utilities has improved greatly. However, at the end of last decade, the central government invested huge amounts of treasury bonds in infrastructure, and was determined to clean up the unregulated or illegal projects, which led to a gradual fade out of the first round of private investment in infrastructure [3].

Taking a closer look at the PPP history, it could be found that the government only encouraged foreign investment in the power sector initially. Followed by corporatization and decentralization of the industry, domestic investors gradually came into the sector and nowadays domestic investors become major investors in the Chinese power industry [4]. After nearly two decades of utilization of private funds to mainly build and renovate power plants, China is still facing a number of fundamental issues that are critical to the success of attracting private capital. An imperfect legal framework, underdeveloped local financial markets, transitional accounting systems and a yet to be developed institutional capability for implementation are major areas that need to be carefully studied and addressed [5, 6]. Excessive layers of approvals required for launching a power project adds more development costs, and is time consuming. The rigid approval process does not provide investors with enough flexibility to amend the project structure according to the latest market developments [5]. Tariffs have also been an issue that frustrates investors and puts them in a weaker position [7]. Given the above existing issues, it is thus essential for public clients and private bidders to place particular attention on the procurement process while negotiating contracts for PPP to ensure a fair risk allocation between them.

3 Research Aim and Methodology

The aim of this research is to develop an equitable risk allocation scheme between the public and private sectors. As part of a previous research into PPP implementation by the authors, a two-round Delphi survey was conducted in China from December 2008 to February 2009 with experienced practitioners to identify the preference of risk allocation in China's PPP projects, which has been reported in the authors' other publication [8]. However, the preferred risk allocation based on the perception and understandings of experts may not be appropriate for all sectors. A round of face-to-face interviews was subsequently carried out from March 2009 to May 2009 to collect actual risk allocation in the past PPP power projects. By comparing the preferred and actual allocations and discovering the reasons behind the differences, an equitable risk allocation scheme which is more appropriate for the power sector could be obtained.

Instead of collecting pieces of project information and analyzing the risk allocation, the authors requested the experienced experts to provide their understandings on the actual risk allocation in one of their successful PPP power projects. In order to improve the interview efficiency, an invitation letter was accompanied by a structured questionnaire and sent to the selected experts. The letter explained the purpose of the research and the interview process. The definition of each risk as presented in the authors' previous paper [8] was also provided at the beginning of the questionnaire, to ensure that experts have the same understanding of these risks. These respondents were requested to evaluate the success degree of the selected case based on eight criteria indexes and allocate the described risk according to a five-point Likert scale (1 – Government takes sole responsibility, 2 – Government takes the majority of responsibility, 3 – Both parties take equal responsibility, 4 – Private sector takes the majority of responsibility, and 5 – Private sector takes sole responsibility). A comparative analysis of the actual and preferred allocations was conducted once the responses from the experts were returned. Reasons behind the actual allocation of those risks which have different preferred allocation as well as the commercial principles and contract terms for the allocation were also collected from the interviews. Experts from eight different PPP power projects were interviewed. Table 1 shows the respondents' information and their roles in the power projects that the survey respondents reported as their PPP case studies.

4 Discussion of Survey Results

The survey feedback concerning the preferred and actual risk allocations is presented in Table 2 (where D.M. means mean values from Delphi survey, P.A. means preferred allocation, I.M. means mean values from Interviews taking into account the success degree, A.A. means actual allocation, T. and Sig. are the results from the T-test between actual and preferred allocations, Diff. means differences).

Table 1 Information of the respondents and selected projects

No.	Title	Year of PPP experience	No. of PPP involved	Investment of the case project (RMB)	Role in the case project
1	Director	More than 20	More than 6	5.6 billion	Stakeholder of project company
2	Vice general manger	4	30	0.3 billion	Government agency
3	Investment manager	3	6	–	Stakeholder of project company
4	Deputy dean	5	2	0.07 billion	Stakeholder of project company
5	Director	More than 20	More than 6	0.8 billion	Stakeholder of project company
6	Division chief	Less than 5	1–3	0.65 billion	Stakeholder of project company
7	Consulting manager	Less than 5	1–3	0.14 billion	Consultant
8	Consulting manager	Less than 5	1–3	0.14 billion	Consultant

The preferred allocation as presented in Table 2 shows that the public sector would take the majority of responsibility for 13 risks related to government or government officials and their actions. Fourteen risks which neither the public nor private sector could be able to deal with them alone are preferred to be shared equally. The private sector would take the majority of responsibility for ten risks that are at the project level. However, this paper focuses on the reasons behind the differences and discusses whether the actual allocation would be more appropriate for the power sector. As mentioned above, differences in allocations would only be considered if the T-test returns a significant result in mean values between two sets of allocations. There are five risks which had different actual allocations, i.e. "Corruption", "Change in law", "Competition (Exclusive right)", "Uncompetitive tender" and "Organization and coordination risk". It is worth noting that the number of eight PPP power projects is still regarded as a small sample, and a closer look at the allocation in every case would be necessary to check whether the difference is common in the power sector.

4.1 Corruption

This risk is preferred to be allocated to the public sector. The mean value of the actual allocation fell in the category of shared between the public and private sector. But a closer look at the allocation in every case shows that the allocation score in 6 out of 8 projects was two (Government takes the majority of responsibility). Only experts from 2 projects thought it was taken by the private sector and provided a high score of 4 and 5 respectively. This observation suggests that the allocation difference is not common in the sector. The equitable allocation for the risk of corruption is therefore to be assigned to the public sector.

Table 2 Comparative analysis of preferred and actual risk allocations

No	Risk factor	D.M.	P.A.	I.M.	A.A.	T.	Sig.	Diff.
1	Corruption	2.11	Public	2.58	Share	−3.381	0.002*	√
2	Government's intervention	1.70	Public	1.47	Public	1.794	0.079	
3	Expropriation and nationalization	1.28	Public	1.51	Public	−2.464	0.018*	
4	Government's reliability	1.65	Public	1.46	Public	1.394	0.170	
5	Third party reliability	3.39	Share	3.26	Share	1.416	0.164	
6	Public/Political opposition	2.54	Share	2.50	Public	0.569	0.572	
7	Immature juristic system	2.43	Public	2.50	Share	−0.517	0.607	
8	Change in law	2.33	Public	2.66	Share	−2.713	0.009*	√
9	Interest rate	3.39	Share	3.51	Private	−0.903	0.371	
10	Foreign exchange and convertibility	3.26	Share	3.51	Private	−1.857	0.070	
11	Inflation	3.22	Share	3.38	Share	−1.930	0.060	
12	Poor political decision-making	1.83	Public	2.38	Public	−4.398	0.000*	
13	Land acquisition	2.00	Public	1.85	Public	1.467	0.149	
14	Approval and permit	2.11	Public	2.25	Public	−1.201	0.236	
15	Improper contracts	3.15	Share	3.23	Share	−1.128	0.265	
16	Financial risk	4.07	Private	4.25	Private	−1.603	0.116	
17	Construction/operation changes	3.52	Private	3.50	Share	0.238	0.813	
18	Construction completion	4.02	Private	4.02	Private	−0.023	0.982	
19	Delay in supply	3.96	Private	4.14	Private	−1.557	0.127	
20	Technology risk	4.37	Private	4.77	Private	−3.397	0.001*	
21	Ground/weather conditions	3.33	Share	3.23	Share	0.984	0.330	
22	Operation cost overrun	4.20	Private	4.49	Private	−2.583	0.013*	
23	Competition (exclusive right)	2.30	Public	2.87	Share	−3.958	0.000*	√
24	Market demand change	3.37	Share	2.98	Share	3.212	0.002*	
25	Tariff change	2.87	Share	3.14	Share	−2.599	0.013*	
26	Payment risk	3.00	Share	3.08	Share	−0.656	0.515	
27	Supporting utilities risk	2.26	Public	2.34	Public	−0.637	0.528	
28	Residual assets risk	3.52	Private	3.54	Private	−0.157	0.876	
29	Uncompetitive tender	2.28	Public	2.59	Share	−2.413	0.020*	√
30	Consortium inability	3.78	Private	4.63	Private	−5.252	0.0008	
31	Force majeure	2.91	Share	2.89	Share	0.538	0.593	
32	Organization and coordination risk	3.65	Private	3.15	Share	4.442	0.000*	√
33	Tax regulation changes	2.35	Public	2.24	Public	0.979	0.333	
34	Environmental protection	3.02	Share	2.88	Share	1.218	0.229	
35	Private investor change	3.85	Private	4.41	Private	−5.187	0.000*	
36	Subjective evaluation	3.13	Share	3.39	Share	−2.246	0.030*	
37	Insufficient financial audit	3.04	Share	3.14	Share	−0.816	0.419	

4.2 Change in Law

Experts in five power projects agreed that this risk was shared in the past PPP projects. This actual allocation would be considered as common. The change history in law in the power sector includes three stages, i.e. first stage reform to raise capital (1986–1996), second stage reform to change the role of government (1997–2001), and third stage reform to introduce competition (2002–present) [9]. Taking case 8 for example, in December 2002, China announced its intent to implement the standard global model of deregulation toward competitive utility markets, including the separation of electricity generation and transmission. The wholesale market price for electricity thereafter turned out less than the price in the concession agreement of case 8. Private investors thus failed to earn expected investment return. However, the change in law is out of authority of the local government, which does not have the ability to cover all the additional costs and helps private partner be restored to the same economics position. Actually, in recent cases, an agreed threshold of tariff is usually set. The government only covers the additional costs above the threshold. In addition, since 2002, the reform of power sector has been a hot topic and some regulations related to the tariff reform were promulgated one after the other. In October 2009, the National Development and Reform Commission, State Electricity Regulatory Commission, and National Energy Administration together released the announcement about standardizing power transaction price. This paper therefore suggests that special attention should be paid to the risk of change in law for both public and private sectors. Under current system, this risk shall be assigned to the government when the concession agreement is signed by the provincial government, but be shared when the agreement is signed by the municipal (city) government.

4.3 Competition (Exclusive Right)

The risk of exclusive right was actually shared by the public and private sectors in 7 out of 8 projects, which is clearly regarded as a common allocation. There are many types of power projects such as coal-fired power, hydropower, wind power, solar, hydrogen, etc. If the exclusive right is fulfilled, the governmental authorities shall not permit the development projects of new competitive projects in any type or the alteration and expansion projects of any existing power projects during the term of the concession agreement. This guarantee would be against the long-term policy by the central government to encourage the development of new energy. In addition, the policy support to the new energy projects actually caused great competitive pressure to those regular PPP power projects, such as control of emission reduction target, purchase priority to new energy projects, subsidy to new energy project companies, etc. Since the local government actually does not have the authority to fulfill the requirement of exclusive right, none of the selected case projects provided specific clauses to deal with this risk. It is worth noting that private investors from all projects signed a take or pay electricity purchase contract with the government, which is believed to be able to mitigate the negative influence by the risk of exclusive right. In light of the above, this paper thus suggested that the equitable allocation for the risk of competition (exclusive right) is to be shared on the premise that a take or pay electricity purchase contract is set.

4.4 Uncompetitive Tender

The allocation difference of this risk is not common in the sector, because the allocation score in 6 out of 8 projects was 2 and only experts from 2 projects provided a high score of 4 and 5 respectively. The equitable allocation for the risk of uncompetitive tender is therefore to be assigned to the public sector as the preferred allocation.

4.5 Organization and Coordination

Six out of eight power projects had the actual allocation score smaller than 4. It means that instead of being allocated to the private sector in the perspectives of experts, the risk of organization and coordination was usually shared by both the public and private partners. For instance, as case 6 is a pilot project, the government paid special attention to it, and undertook most coordination tasks for the project company. Similarly in other projects, the partners as the fuel supplier, electricity purchaser, dispatching station and some other process were the government's subsidiary department or companies. It is therefore unavoidable for the involvement of the government in the organization and coordination task. In light of this, this paper thus recommends a better allocation for the risk of organization and coordination in the power sector to be shared. However, the private sector is also suggested that the timing and process of the government's involvement should be clearly defined so as to avoid the risk of government's unreasonable intervention.

5 Conclusions

This paper has studied the equitable allocation of risks in China's PPP power projects. According to the analysis, there are three risks which had different actual allocation from the preferred allocation, i.e. "Change in law", "Competition (Exclusive right)" and "Organization and coordination risk". The equitable allocation for other risks would be the preferred allocation reported in Table 2. The risk of change in law shall be assigned to the government when the concession agreement is signed by the province government, but be shared when the agreement is signed by the city government. The equitable allocation for the risk of competition (exclusive right) is to be shared on the premise that a take or pay electricity purchase contract is set. The risk of organization and coordination shall be shared but the private sector needs to define the timing and process of the government's involvement so as to avoid the risk of government's unreasonable intervention.

Acknowledgments The work described in this paper was fully supported by a joint grant from the National Natural Science Foundation of China (Project No. 70731160634) and the Research

Grants Council of the Hong Kong Special Administrative Region, China (RGC Project N_PolyU514/07). Special gratitude is extended to those industrial practitioners, who have kindly participated in the interviews reported in this paper from March to May 2009.

References

1. Ke YJ, Wang SQ, Chan APC (2009) Public-Private Partnerships in China's Infrastructure Development: Lessons Learnt. In: Proceedings of International Conference on Changing Roles: New Roles and New Challenges, Noordwijk aan Zee, The Netherlands, p. 177–188
2. Feng LJ, Luo ZS (1999) Laibin Model – Application of BOT Financing Modality in China (in Chinese). Guangxi People Press, Nanning
3. Shen JY, Wang SQ, Qiang MS (2005) Political and Sovereign Risks in Chinese BOT/PPP projects: A Case Study (in Chinese). Chinese Businessman: Investment and Finance, 1: 50–54
4. Zhang L (2009) Development of Infrastructure Sectors in China: Status Quo and Trends (Seminar speech). Revamping PPPs: From 'Revisiting and Rethinking' to 'Revamping and Revitalising' PPPs, The University of Hong Kong, Hong Kong, China
5. Cunningham EA (2007) Chinese Power: Reform and Development in China's Electricity Industry. China Public Administration Review, 6: 1–23
6. Williams JH, Kahrl F (2008) Electricity Reform and Sustainable Development in China. Environmental Research Letters, 3: 1–14
7. Asian Development Bank (2003) Power Pricing Strategy – Tariff Setting and Regulation. Technical Assistance 4117-PRC
8. Ke YJ, Wang SQ, Chan APC, Lam PTI (2010) Preferred Risk Allocation in China's Public–Private Partnership Projects. International Journal of Project Management, 28(5): 482–492
9. Zhang C, Heller TC (2004) Reform of the Chinese Electric Power Market – Economics and Institutions. Program on Energy and Sustainable Development, Working paper #3

Developing a Construction Safety Management System

Jian Zhang and Weng Tat Chan

Abstract Various safety management systems (SMS) have been introduced to the construction industry as a formal means of managing site safety. There are several shortcomings with the current perspective of SMS which is implemented among construction projects. Firstly, the focus is exclusively on contractors and their performance on safety related factors. However, safety is not only the contractors' responsibility but should involve owners as well. Secondly, current SMS presents a fixed set of safety related factors and activities which does not account for the diversity of projects and organizations in construction industry. Lastly, current methods of SMS auditing take a check-and-verify approach and miss customization and development opportunities. This paper proposes an alternative view of SMS based on the well-established Capability Maturity Model Integration (CMMI) framework. The proposal includes owners as active participants/stakeholders during the development of SMS, and allows flexibility during the implementation of SMS. The framework encourages a shift perspective from SMS factor and activity auditing to system development in terms of capability and maturity. This promotes a long term view of SMS development beyond a single project and fosters development of safety management capability within the construction industry.

Keywords Capability · Construction safety · Maturity · Safety management system

---

J. Zhang (✉)
Department of Civil Engineering, National University of Singapore, 1 Engineering Drive 2, E1 08-20 Singapore, Singapore 117576,
e-mail: g0800227@nus.edu.sg

W. T. Chan
Department of Civil Engineering, National University of Singapore, 1 Engineering Drive 2, E1A 07-03 Singapore, Singapore 117576,
e-mail: cvecwt@nus.edu.sg

D.D. Wu (ed.), *Modeling Risk Management in Sustainable Construction*,
Computational Risk Management, DOI 10.1007/978-3-642-15243-6_16,

1 Introduction

Construction is a key industry in many countries both in terms of employment and economic output. Construction work is also dangerous because the broad range of tasks, required skills, climatic conditions and work environments result in challenges to stakeholders' ability of managing safety issues. Construction organizations are increasingly more aware that merely controlling the physical aspects and technical hazards of a project are not sufficient to reduce the occurrence of accidents. A more holistic and proactive approach is required to increase the effectiveness of SMS.

Essential components of a SMS whose implementation and operation are mainly considered the sole responsibility of the contractor. The introduction of the Construction, Design, and Management (CDM) regulations in the UK has emphasized that safety on construction projects must involve more key stakeholders beyond the actual construction period. More specifically, owners have a key role to play in the conception and successful operation of the project SMS since they are the ones who specify key requirements and budgets for the projects. During construction, the owner also needs an effective means to ensure that the SMS is adequate for the project and is operating as intended. Owners may make the adequacy of contractor's SMS as a criterion for selecting a contractor. Contractors also need a means to actively integrate safety and health issues into project planning. An activity based SMS is inadequate since work activities and physical site conditions vary from project to project, and the capability and experience of contractors also varies.

The aim of this study is to introduce a new perspective to develop SMS which includes not only contractors but also owners as parties responsible for safety. The new proposal is organized around processes and goals rather than activities. This increases the flexibility of designing a SMS that meets the project requirements.

2 Literature Review

Various types of SMSs have been introduced into the construction industry as a formal means of managing site safety, by targeting the safety policies, procedures, and practices within companies [1]. Compared with Occupational Health and Safety Management System (OHSMS)-based standards, guidelines, and audits established in other industries, a construction SMS includes the physical work environment and focuses more on preventing serious injuries related to the loss of control of processes. Contractors are expected to manage site safety through a formal SMS, evaluate the effectiveness of their SMS implementation and correct any deficiencies found [2].

The Construction Safety Audit Scoring System (ConSASS) is an audit tool which provides an independent assessment of the SMS at a worksite. Central to

ConSASS is a standardized checklist and scoring system which could enhance audit consistency and offer comparison of SMS performance across different worksites. The checklist encompasses approximately 300 questions which are organized around Deming's Plan-Do-Check-Act (PDCA) cycle. ConSASS is derived from OHSAS 18001 and follows concept of quality and environmental system models based on ISO standards. The audit questions for each element of the SMS are banded in levels (I–IV) to reflect the increasing development extent of the element. The score card is a 'final report card' which tabulates the audit results of different SMS elements [3].

The ConSASS checklist, whilst comprehensive, may not be suitable for small or medium sized projects and contractors. This is recognized by the safety legislation which imposes such audit only on projects with contract sum S$30 million or more. Furthermore, some of the audit questions are similar in nature but are repeated for each safety element. The attainment of a particular band level depends on the answers to the audit questions but this is somewhat inconsistent since the same audit question appears at different band levels for different system elements.

CMMI (Capability Maturity Model Integration) uses a more advanced framework to assess the adequacy and capability of a system. CMMI follows a two-dimensional model structure rather than the one-dimensional one used in ConSASS. It defines the essential elements of effective processes for one or more disciplines and describes an evolutionary improvement path from ad hoc, immature processes to disciplined, mature processes with improved quality and effectiveness [4]. CMMI is an application of the principles introduced almost a century ago and whose value has been confirmed over time. Organizations using the CMMI to improve their system processes have experienced increased productivity and quality, improved cycle time, and more accurate and predictable schedules and budgets [5]. SMS could benefit from the CMMI framework to improve its effectiveness.

3 Developing a Construction Safety Management System

In this section, we describe a two-dimensional framework based on CMMI. In this framework, a system is characterized by maturity as well as capabilities of process areas. The framework provides a richer set of possibilities for system development based on alternative development paths, and moves beyond the one-dimensional audit/checklist approach.

We conceptualize a construction SMS as being made up of a number of key process areas. This differs from the view espoused in ConSASS that the safety system comprises system elements and activities. A process area is a cluster of related practices when implemented collectively, satisfies a set of goals considered important for making improvement in that area [4]. Based on an extensive review of the construction safety management literature, we provide 15 process areas which intends to contain the essential elements of construction SMS (see Fig. 1). We call this model ConSASS-2D to emphasize its two-dimensional nature.

Process Areas	ML	CL 1	CL 2	CL 3	CL 4	CL 5
Safety Policy	2					
Safety Plan	2	Target Profile 2				
Responsibility and Authority Definition	2					
Construction Safety Monitoring and Control	2					
Safety Training	2					
Safety Performance Measurement	2					
Accident and Incident Management	2					
Near miss and First aid management	3					
Objective and Goal management	3		Target Profile 3			
Communication management	3					
Risk and Hazard Management	3					
Safety Audits	4					
Safety Data Management	4		Target Profile 4			
Causal Analysis and Resolution	5		Target Profile 5			
Organizational Innovation and Deployment	5					

Fig. 1 An example of ConSASS-2D

ConSASS-2D enables safety parties to improve their SMS along two possible dimensions – capability and maturity. The capability dimension emphasizes incremental improvement corresponding to an individual process area selected by the organization. The capability of each of the 15 process areas is graded into five band levels reflecting their ability to satisfy generic goals. The maturity dimension advances system maturity level through the addition of process areas. These process areas enable the system to design, plan, benchmark and improve the effectiveness of the overall system.

Based on this framework, owners and contractors could select appropriate process areas and how much they would like to mature associate with each process area which depends on the characteristics of their projects and the resources they have. As the organization reaches a particular development extent, it can set its sights on the next capability level for one of these existing process areas or decide to widen the scope of concern by increasing the number of process areas. This combination of process areas and capability levels is typically described as a "system profile".

For target profile, specific goals and generic goals are used to measure the capability level of each process area and maturity level of the SMS. A specific goal describes the unique characteristics that must be present to satisfy the process area. A generic goal which could be used in multiple process areas describes the characteristics that must be present to institutionalize a process area [4]. With these two goal settings, we could appraise how institutionalized and consistent a process areas is, as well as how mature the SMS is.

4 Advantages of the ConSASS-2D

A comparison of ConSASS and ConSASS-2D across several dimensions is shown in Table 1. The current system-in-use is ConSASS according to which SMS is audited by absence/presence of particular system elements/activities. The results are mainly used to determine adequacy of the SMS. In contrast, ConSASS-2D takes

Table 1 A comparison of ConSASS and ConSASS-2D

	ConSASS	ConSASS-2D	Remarks
Approach	Check-and-verify	Proactively design appropriate process areas and development paths	Approach shifts from simply checking for adequacy of system elements and conformance to rules towards determining requirements, system design and development of processes.
Stakeholders	Contractor	Owner and contractor	The owner is now involved in a collaborative effort with the contractor to create a project specific SMS to satisfy their common target safety goals and requirements rather than being a passive recipient of audit results.
System components	Project environment factors and safety related activities	Process areas, goals	The points of interest shift from a list of pre-determined factors and activities to a set of process areas and goals to improve the system consistency and suitability.
Methodology	Focus on auditing factors and activities	Focus on identifying requirements, goals, and development paths	Audit entity shifts from activities to goals with the aims of providing greater flexibility to design the SMS across a wide diversity of projects.

a step beyond auditing. With the use of current and target system profiles, the emphasis shifts to determine system requirements, gaps and deficiencies and development pathways to move to a desired profile. This two dimensional model structure also offers organizations and projects the flexibility to proactively select and plan their appropriate process areas and development extent.

Another benefit of ConSASS-2D is that under a two dimensional framework comprised of process areas, it is possible to focus on particular process area development or decide to add new process areas to improve system maturity. This is especially beneficial for small and medium-sized companies and projects since they may not have enough resources or there's no need for them to address all the elements or activities of the SMS.

For ConSASS, the owner impose a general requirement on the audit results that is improve the system performance when most system elements falls in low band levels. In ConSASS-2D, both owner and contractor work in a collaboration to design and develop an effective SMS. This is done using a methodology that involves determining a definite target requirements, designing and planning, evaluating gaps/deficiencies, and development.

In ConSASS, the audit focuses on traditional SMS components such as safety-related factors and activities. In ConSASS-2D, the main concepts are process areas which intends to include essential areas of SMS, as well as goals associated with these process areas. In moving away from a fixed checklist towards a goal-centered approach, this model brings more potential users and promotes long-term development. Because although activities or practices are different among construction sites, projects and organizations have similar goals to satisfy in key process areas. In ConSASS 2D, specific goals for each process area are fixed rather than system factors and activities which permits diverse activities to attain these goals.

References

1. Tam, C.M., Tong, T.K.L., Chiu, G.C.W., and Fung, I.W.H. (2002). "Non-structural fuzzy decision support system for evaluation of construction safety management system." International Journal of Project Management, 20(4), 303–313.
2. Teo, E.A.L., and Ling, F.Y.Y. (2006). "Developing a model to measure the effectiveness of safety management systems of construction sites." Building and Environment, 41(11), 1584–1592.
3. Huat, G.H., Meng, Y.C. (2007). "A guide to the construction safety audit scoring system (ConSASS)." Singapore.
4. CMMI. (2009). CMMI for Service, Version 1.2, Carnegie Mellon University, US.
5. Gibson, D.L.G., Dennis R.; and Kost, Keith. (2006). Performance Results of CMMI-Based Process Improvement, Carnegie Mellon University.

Analysis of the Equipment's Maintenance Period Under Different Operation Stages

Jie Chi and Miao Chi

Abstract To improve the equipment' operation efficiency, this paper discusses the various maintenance strategies in different employ stages by analyzing the rules of devices faults and the maintenance methods. Results shown, when the faults take place in chance fault stage, i.e., fault rate $\lambda'(t) = 0$, it is impossible to improve the operation efficiency of the devices when preventive maintenances are made. When the faults take place in wear out fault stage and initial fault stage, i.e., fault rate $\lambda'(t) \neq 0$, the best time for maintenance T should satisfy $\int_0^T t\lambda'(t)dt = t_p/t_f$. Meanwhile, on the basis of the broken-down data of Series Air Compressors (ZW-17/29) in using, we find the suitable time for maintenance T in wearing stage and bring the relevant maintenance plans.

Keywords Distributing function · Equipment management · Fault rate · Preventive maintenances · The best maintenance period

1 Introduction

Failure diagnosis of mechanical equipment and gasping the laws of equipment failure and its variations can improve both technological and managerial level of mechanical equipment and its service efficiency. Equipment maintenance runs through equipment's whole life circle, i.e., programming, design, testing, manufacture, marketing, installation, manipulation and retirement. Experimentalism is very likely to cause a considerable discrepancy between maintenance of equipment and its actual condition in terms of maintenance for devices. Both excessive and insufficient maintenance still exist today. There are three factors that contribute to

J. Chi (✉) and M. Chi
School of Management, Chongqing Jiaotong University, Chongqing Municipality 400074, People's Republic of China
e-mail: cjwcjcmcj@126.com; miachi871012@gmail.com

D.D. Wu (ed.), *Modeling Risk Management in Sustainable Construction*, Computational Risk Management, DOI 10.1007/978-3-642-15243-6_17,

good equipment maintenance: the maintainability of equipment, the quality and technique of maintenance personnel and the safeguards system. Therefore making a good maintenance project, according to actual condition of equipment, is the priority of equipment management. Although the authors of references [1–7] have carried on researches in general laws of equipment failure and failure management problem under various conditions. They have done little research on problems such as, which maintenance method should be adopted, how to determine the best maintenance period, how to make maintenance projects, etc. Aiming at boosting the efficiency of mechanical equipment, this paper dissects those problems mentioned above by analyzing laws of equipment failure and maintenance methods.

2 Maintenance Policy

A piece of equipment has its certain service life if being used properly. During its service life, it might malfunction more than once. Many malfunctions, however, could be mended. As a general rule, failure rate for equipment is relevant to how long a piece of equipment has being used. Failure rate usually depends on time, with the rate varying over the life circle of the equipment. Figure 1 show the Bathtub Curve (the name is derived from the cross-sectional shape of the eponymous device) that describes particular form of hazard function which comprises three parts.

Maintenance method (also called maintenance simulation) means to control the timing of maintenance including following methods [1–3].

2.1 *Corrective Maintenance*

Corrective Maintenance is also known as Breakdown Maintenance or damage maintenance. It is any maintenance activity which is required to correct a failure that is has already occurred so that the failed equipment can be restored to its normal operable state. Corrective Maintenance requires sufficient human resources, abundant number of tools and spare parts, etc, in order to deal with malfunctions effectively. It not only leads to downtime but also interrupts production plan.

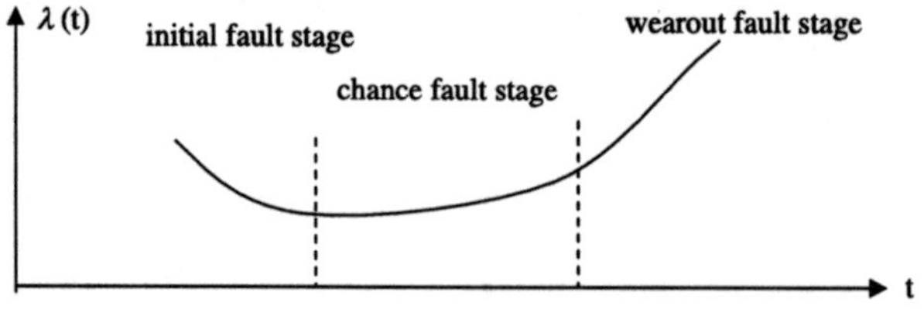

Fig. 1 Bathtub curve

Besides, maintenance content, time cost and arrangement are too random. So, by all means, this is a backward maintenance method, a settlement needs minimum requirements. Figure 2 shows situations of corrective maintenance.

2.2 Preventive Maintenance

Preventive Maintenance, also known as Scheduled Maintenance or Periodical Maintenance, is maintenance which is carried out to prevent sudden failure before it actually occurs regardless of what kind of technological state equipment is under. This maintenance method subjects to mandatory requirement and is preventative. Its maintenance activities are scheduled to perform at intervals of production so that maintenance resource could be sufficiently prepared beforehand. Basing on the theory of mechanical wear, Preventive Maintenance emphasizes on finding out exact maintenance time. The advantages of Preventive Maintenance are that easily manageable maintenance time, plane and organizing. Preventive Maintenance could prevent failure form occurring. Figure 3 tells us that Preventive Maintenance could decrease maintenance load and shorten downtime.

2.3 On-Condition Maintenance

On-condition Maintenance is also called Condition-based Maintenance or Condition Monitoring Maintenance. Such a maintenance activity uses real-time data acquired from on-line monitoring, rather than fault signature, to prioritize and

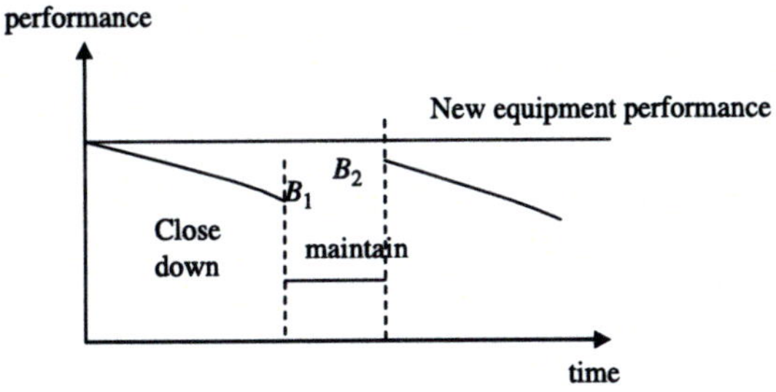

Fig. 2 Correction maintenance

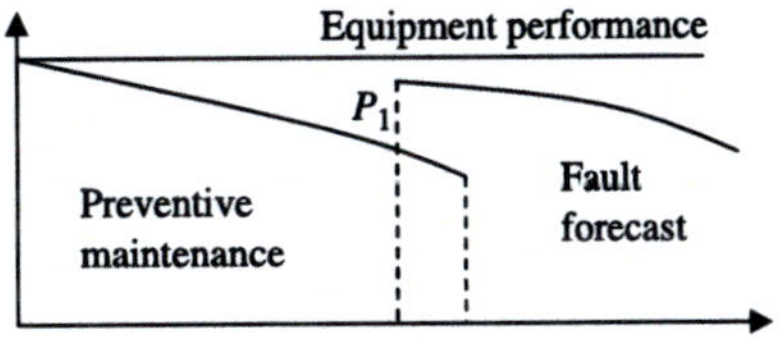

Fig. 3 Scheduled maintenance

optimize maintenance resources. On-line monitoring includes status checking and tendency monitoring etc. These are carried out on-line according to project at regular intervals. It is the most effective maintenance policy which requires investment and current expenditure.

2.4 Opportunistic Maintenance

Opportunistic Maintenance is an effective maintenance policy being carried out along with On-condition Maintenance or Preventive Maintenance while causing no production loss. Opportunity occurs during Preventive Maintenance or troubleshooting. Effectiveness could be acquired by using it.

2.5 Revising Design

When failure occurs frequently, which means mean time to failure is short, and cost of maintenance or replacement is high, which means the cost of manpower, components and spare parts and loss on work stoppage are high, redesign will be the best way to deal with the problem. Doing it in the right way, people can solve all the problems at once. In the practice of equipment management, the adoption of strategies and maintenance policy is based on running state of a piece of equipment.

3 The Relation Between Failure Rate $\lambda(t)$ and the Best Maintenance Time

People can find out economical maintenance means by researching equipment dependability. Preventive Maintenance is often used to maintain important equipment in order to avoid loss caused by machine halt. Nowadays there isn't enough monitor means for most equipment to make sure that equipment could be repaired right before failure symptom appears, because of the lack of monitoring techniques. Maintenance interval is determined by statistic information and practical situation. Repair plan should be made according to maintenance interval. Components and parts of equipment should be either replaced or fixed at regular intervals.

A reasonable Maintenance cycle requires the maximization of equipment availability and the minimization of maintenance cost. If maintenance cost is in direct proportion to maintenance time, then they have same the same maintenance cycle. The analysis of the best maintenance cycle of Fig. 4, which stands for Preventive Maintenance, is as follows.

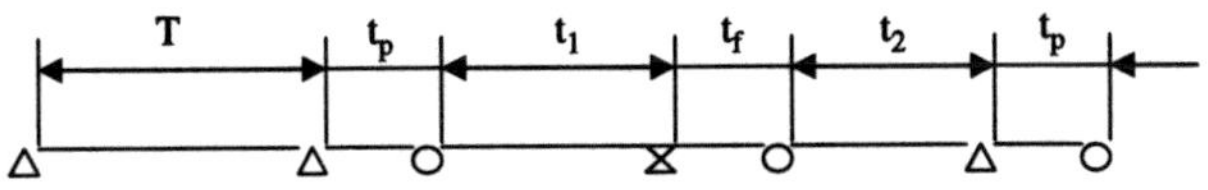

Fig. 4 Maintenance cycle

In Fig. 4, t_p is mean preventive maintenance time. t_f is mean time to repair. Means occurrence of one failure, means carrying out preventive maintenance for one time. Preventive maintenance is carried out every other maintenance cycleT (and $t_1 + t_2 = T$). In maintenance cycle T, if the failure rate is $\lambda(t)$, the down time scale is $\int_0^T \lambda(t)dt$. Mean time to repair (MTTR) is $MTTR = t_p + t_f \int_0^T \lambda(t)dt$, Mean operate time is MTBF = T_o

Capacity utilization rate is

$$A = \frac{MTBF}{MTBF + MTTR} = \frac{T}{t_p + t_f \int_0^T \lambda(t)dt + T}$$

$$A[t_p + t_f \int_0^T \lambda(t)dt + T] = T$$

$$\frac{dA}{dT}[t_p + t_f \int_0^T \lambda(t)dt + T] + A[t_f\lambda(T) + 1] = 1$$

$$\frac{dA}{dT} = \{1 - A[t_f\lambda(T) + 1]\}/\{t_p + t_f \int_0^T \lambda(t)dt + T\} = 0,$$

$$t_p + t_f \int_0^T \lambda(t)dt + T)0$$

$$1 - A[t_f\lambda(T) + 1] = 0$$

$$T[t_f\lambda(T) + 1] - [t_p + t_f \int_0^T \lambda(t)dt + T] = 0$$

So

$$T\lambda(T) - \int_0^T \lambda(t)dt = \frac{t_p}{t_f} \quad (1)$$

Suppose $\lambda'(t) = \frac{d\lambda(t)}{dt}$

To perform integration on (1)

$$\int_0^T t\lambda'(t)dt = \frac{t_p}{t_f} \tag{2}$$

In (2),When $\lambda(t) = \lambda$ is constant, maximal value of A can't be found for $\lambda'(t) = 0$. When $\lambda'(t) = 0$, $\int_0^T t\lambda'(t)dt = 0$, $\frac{t_p}{t_f} \neq 0$. So the equation is incorrect. T cannot be found, maximal value of A cannot be found either. $\lambda(t) = \lambda$ is constant, that is to say the function of failure rate is a constant without t. The failure rate is always a fixed value regardless of time. Under the circumstance of random failure, there is no close causal relation between failure rate and time. Approximately, random failure can be seen as the case under which $\lambda(t) = \lambda$ is constant. So there is no preventive maintenance that can increase time availability rate of equipment. In this case, preventive maintenance is meaningless.

Theoretically, when $\lambda'(t) \neq 0$, the maximal value of A can be found in the light of (2). Preventive Maintenance can prolong working time of equipment when failure rate increases as time goes by, this period is called Wearing Malfunction Period. When Maintenance Cycle is short, implementation of Preventive Maintenance during Random Failure period is excess and unnecessary. Time availability rate can't be increased by doing so. On the contrary maintenance time and costs will be increased.

4 Case Study

Air compressors are widely used in engineering construction. Suppose there are ten air compressors ZW-17/29 with the same type and durable years. Before Preventive Maintenance plan being carried out, record the time points as zero. Under the same operant level, the mean time of failure occurrence are 70, 150, 190, 220, 310, 100, 160, 230, 280, 180 (see Table 1), mean breakdown maintenance time is $t_f = 6$ h, mean preventive maintenance time is $t_p = 2$ h.

Acquire the plot position by median classification, calculate the median MR [8]:

$$MR\% = \frac{i - 0.3}{N + 0.4} \times 100 \tag{3}$$

i represents the series number of failure occurrence, N represents total sample number. Failure times and their corresponding medians are in Table 2.

Table 1 The time series table of failure occurrence

Failure time	70	100	150	160	180	190	220	230	280	310
Failure series	1	2	3	4	5	6	7	8	9	10

Table 2 Medians

Failure time	70	100	150	160	180
MR%	6.73	16.35	25.96	35.58	45.19
Failure time	190	220	230	280	310
MR%	54.81	64.42	74.04	83.65	93.27

Failure rate, reliability, cumulative failure rate and step-density function could be calculated by using Weibull probability paper.

$$F(t) = 1 - e^{-(t/119)^3}$$

$$f(t) = \frac{3}{119}\left(\frac{t}{119}\right)^{3-1} \cdot e^{-(t/119)^3} = \frac{3}{119}\left(\frac{t}{119}\right)^{2} .e^{-(t/119)^3}$$

$$R(t) = 1 - F(t) = e^{-(t/\eta)^\beta} = e^{-(t/119)^3}$$

$$\lambda(t) = f(t)/R(t) = \frac{\beta}{\eta}\left(\frac{t}{\eta}\right)^{\beta-1} = \frac{3}{119}\left(\frac{t}{119}\right)^{3-1} = \frac{3}{119}\left(\frac{t}{119}\right)^{2}$$

$$\int_0^T t\lambda'(t)dt = \frac{t_p}{t_f} = 6/2 = 3 \tag{4}$$

See reference [8] for more details.

T =136.6 h can be calculated.

No matter which maintenance is carried out, corrective maintenance or preventive maintenance, equipment has the same serviceable condition once it has been repaired. According to the calculation, the mean preventive maintenance time of this equipment is about 130 h. The maintenance project based on the calculation effectively prevents failures from occurring. After preventive maintenance project has been carried out, rate of occurrence of failure has reduced by 37% and utilization efficiency has increased by 8%.

5 Conclusion

Theoretically equipment has nothing to do with temporal change when it is under random failure period. Preventive maintenance is not useful because it is unlikely to increase time availability. Preventive maintenance can prolong equipment's operating time and increase equipment's time availability only when it is under wear out failure time, i.e. when failure rate increases as time goes by. However it is hard to make sure whether equipment is under wear out failure time. Equipment has to be in observation for a long time and statistic data need to be analyzed. Besides a accurate failure rate function is hard to get. Equipment's service performance, failure rate, function etc. are required when above method is adopted.

References

1. Wu Shi-jing (2005) Equipment management engineering. 1st edition. China Electric Power press, Beijing
2. Li De-yuan, Yang Shi-hua (2006) Mordern Equipment Economics Management. 1st edition. China Communications Press, Beijing
3. Heinz P. Bloch (1998) Improving Machinery Reliability. Gulf Publishing Company Houston, USA TX
4. Peng Yong, Tian Peng, Jiang Fu (2004) A Study on Multiple Fleet Maintenance Problem with Deterioration Homogenous Assets. Systems Engineering Theory·Methodology·Applications, 13: 172–176
5. Peng Yong, Tian Peng, Jiang Fu (2004) On Optimal Policies for Multiple Fleet Maintenance. Systems Engineering-Theory and Practice. (1):46–50
6. Marvin Rausand (1998) Reliability-Centered Maintenance. Reliability Engineering and System Safety. Vol. 60, No. 2: pp. 121–132
7. Dekker R (1996) Applications of Maintenance Optimization Models: a Review and Analysis. Reliability Engineering and System Safety. 51(3), 229–240.
8. Chi Jie (2006) Study on the Failure Distribution and Reliability Variation of the Equipment in Use. Journal of Chongqing Jianzhu University (5):34–37

An Evolutionary Game Model for the Risk Management Cooperation Among the Project Participants

Guo-jun Zhang and Yun-li Gao

Abstract An evolutionary game model for the risk management cooperation of owner and contractor is presented. Using this model, the parameters of the evolutionary system are analyzed. The rule of the cooperation between owner and contractor is illustrated. The results indicate that cooperation cost and distributing mechanism for loss or profit are the key factors influencing cooperation among the project participants.

Keywords Cooperation · Evolutionary game · Risk management

1 Introduction

Recently with the economic development of China, the great projects such as housing construction, highway and bridge etc. are increasing. However, some factors will influence these projects, for example, long project time, technical complicacy and changeful environment. There exist a lot of risks during the process of constructing these projects. As the result, it is most important to identify these risks of projects and to manage them. Tang Wenzhe et al. researched the status of risk management in China construction industry, and they found 28 project risks was similar for owners and contractors. Among them, quality, site accident and safety were the three most important risks. If any of the three risks happened, all participants would be responsible for the consequence [1]. The research result shows that all participants need to cooperate to management project risks.

G.-j. Zhang (✉)
Faculty of Infrastructure Engineering, Dalian University of Technology, Liaoning Dalian, People's Republic of China
e-mail: zhanggj8686@163.com

Y.-l. Gao
Department of Civil Engineering and Architecture, Dalian Nationalities University, Liaoning Dalian, People's Republic of China
e-mail: yunligao@163.com

D.D. Wu (ed.), *Modeling Risk Management in Sustainable Construction*, Computational Risk Management, DOI 10.1007/978-3-642-15243-6_18,

The project objectives can be better achieved through the cooperation of project participants. This idea of win–win origins from the United States decades ago and it is practiced in many projects in Europe and USA [2]. The scholars also realize that the cooperation idea can help all participants to acquire information faster than before. The project information can make the decision-maker learn the project process in time and give a right decision [3]. In literature [4], we know that the key risk factors of projects are mainly associated with owners and contractors. In order to make the research simpler, the article only discussed the cooperation between owner and contractor during the process of project construction.

At present, there are a lot of scholars to research the morality risk and adverse selection problem of contractors by the principal-agent method of non-cooperative game. The main bodies of game are demanded to be high rational in those research. However, the owners and the contractors are finite rational in the process of risk cooperation. Their information is incomplete. Furthermore, the equilibrium and evolution of the game is complex. The main bodies who are finite rational couldn't find the optimal strategy at the beginning of game. Both the owners and contractors are not able to find the optimal choice. They will study in the process of game and find the better strategy through the way of trial [5]. In this paper, the non-symmetric evolutionary game theory is used to research the cooperation strategy between the owners and the contractors in the process of risk management. The main factors that affect cooperation are further identified.

2 The Evolutionary Game Model Between the Owners and Contractors for the Risk Management Cooperation

2.1 *Hypotheses of the Model*

In the process of project construction, the cooperation of owners and contractors can help to realize the project objective. On the contrary, the project risk will appear owing to non-cooperation of any participant and the loss will be happened. In order to make the research simpler, we give the following assumption:

- The project risks bring loss only, no profit.
- After the project is accomplished, the normal profit of the owners and the contractors respectively is R_1 and R_2. The normal profit can be gained when the owners and the contractors choose cooperation strategy in the process of risk management.
- Whether the cooperation can achieve or not, any participant who chooses cooperation strategy need to afford cost for information collection and risk pre-controlling and other necessary management. The cost of owners is C_1. Similarly the cost of contractors is C_2. Certainly, $C_1 \geq 0, C_2 \geq 0$.

Contactors

Owners	Cooperation B_1 (q)	Non-cooperation B_2 (1−q)
Cooperation A_1 (p)	$R_1 - C_1$; $R_2 - C_2$	$R_1 - C_1 - \beta\Delta L$; $R_2 - (1-\beta)\Delta L$
Non-cooperation A_2 (1−p)	$R_1 - \beta\Delta L$; $R_2 - C_2 - (1-\beta)\Delta L$	$R_1 - \beta\Delta L$; $R_2 - (1-\beta)\Delta L$

Fig. 1 The payment matrix of the owners and the contractors taking different strategy

- The non-cooperation strategy of any participant will bring the project loss. The loss is expressed by ΔL, and it can be shared by the owners and contractors according appropriate proportion. The proportion is expressed by β. Thus the loss of owners is $\beta\Delta L$ and the loss of contractors is $(1-\beta)\Delta L$.

Based on these above hypotheses, the payment matrix can be given when the owners and the contractors take cooperation strategy or non-cooperation strategy in the process of risk management. The result is shown in Fig. 1. The probability that the owners take cooperation strategy is expressed by p, and the probability of taking non-cooperation is expressed by (1 − p). Similarly the probability of taking co-operation for the contractors is expressed by q and the probability of taking non-cooperation is expressed by (1 − q).

2.2 *Analysis of the Evolutionary Game Model*

Based on the payment matrix in Fig. 1, the owners' imitator dynamic equation of taking cooperation strategy is

$$\frac{dp}{dt} = p\left[E(A1) - \bar{E}(A)\right] = p(1-p)(q\beta\Delta L - C_1) \tag{1}$$

The contractors' imitator dynamic equation of taking cooperation strategy is

$$\frac{dq}{dt} = q\left[E(B1) - \bar{E}(B)\right] = q(1-q)(p(1-\beta)\Delta L - C_2) \tag{2}$$

The differential (1) and (2) can be calculated by the Jacbian matrix. There are four equilibrium points $E_1(0,0)$, $E_2(1,0)$, $E_3(0,1)$ and $E_4(1,1)$ in the plane S, where $S = \{(p,q); 0 \le p, q \le 1\}$. There exists another equilibrium point $E_5\left(\frac{C_2}{(1-\beta)\Delta L}, \frac{C_1}{\beta\Delta L}\right)$ when the following condition is satisfied:

Fig. 2 The phase diagram of the game dynamic process

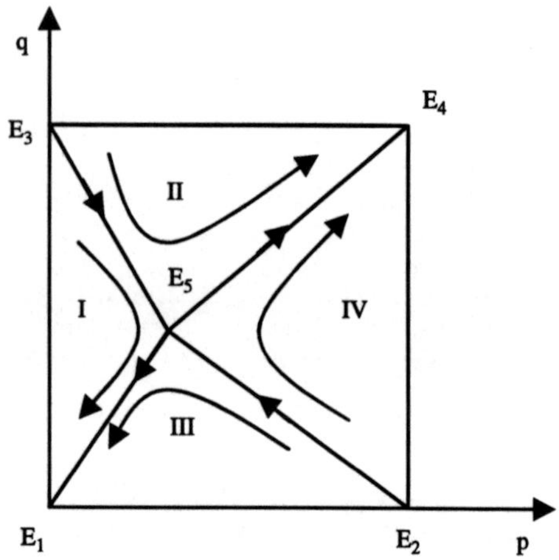

$$0 \leq \frac{C_2}{(1-\beta)\Delta L} \leq 1, \quad 0 \leq \frac{C_1}{\beta \Delta L} \leq 1$$

Having an analysis of these five equilibrium points, we find that only two equilibrium points $E_1(0,0)$ and $E_4(1,1)$ are asymptotical stable points. The equilibrium points $E_2(1,0)$ and $E_3(0,1)$ are instable points. The equilibrium point $E_5\left(\frac{C_2}{(1-\beta)\Delta L}, \frac{C_1}{\beta \Delta L}\right)$ is a saddle point. In this game model, we can give the result that the owners and contractors both take the cooperation strategy or both take the non-cooperation strategy at the same time. The phase diagram of the game dynamic process is shown in Fig. 2. The connection line of the equilibrium point E_5 and any apex denotes the path from the saddle point to apex. Because the path is unknown, we can replace it by beeline.

In Fig. 2, the plane S is divided four regions and these regions are expressed by I, II, III and IV. When the initial state of p and q satisfies the condition: $(p,q) \in I, III$, the system will be convergence to the stable equilibrium $E_1(0,0)$. Namely the owners and contractors will choose non-cooperation strategy. When the initial state of p and q satisfies the condition: $(p,q) \in II, IV$, the system will be convergence to the other stable equilibrium $E_4(1,1)$. Namely the owners and contractors will choose cooperation strategy. So I and III are named non-cooperation regions and II and IV are named cooperation regions.

2.3 Analysis of Parameter

Based on the above evolutionary game model, the evolutionary direction of the owners and contractors depends on the point (p, q) dropping in which region. At the same time the area of cooperation region also indicates the probability of taking cooperation strategy and vice versa.

2.3.1 Risk Management Cost Parameter C_1, C_2

Whether the cooperation between owners and contractors succeed or not, it depends on the risk management cost. When $0 \le \frac{C_2}{(1-\beta)\Delta L} \le 1, \quad 0 \le \frac{C_1}{\beta \Delta L} \le 1$, we have:

$$\beta \Delta L - C_1 \ge 0, \quad (1 - \beta)\Delta L - C_2 \ge 0$$

Namely, the risk management cost of owners and contractors is less than the loss that risk brings. In this condition it is necessary to cooperate to manage risk. Supposed the loss is certain and the risk management cost C_1 and C_2 is reduced, the saddle point $E_5\left(\frac{C_2}{(1-\beta)\Delta L}, \frac{C_1}{\beta \Delta L}\right)$ tends towards left lower. We find the area of cooperation in Fig. 2 being bigger than before. Then the owners and contractors will be more likely to avoid risk by cooperation. We also find that the evolutionary behavior of the participants will be affected as the risk management cost of the other participant being reduced. As the risk management cost C_1 of owners reduce, the owners will take cooperation strategy in risk management. The owners will take many measures to promote the cooperative relation with contractors and these friendly behaviors will affect the contractors to take cooperative strategy. The game system will evolve to the equilibrium point $E_4(1, 1)$.

2.3.2 Proportion Coefficient β of Risk Loss

The proportion coefficient of risk loss is fully reflected the idea of risk share. Considering the three conditions:

- As the proportion coefficient $\beta \to 0$

In this condition the full risk loss is afforded by contractors. We can see the cooperation region being enclosed by E_2, E_4 and E_5 in Fig. 3. The non-cooperation

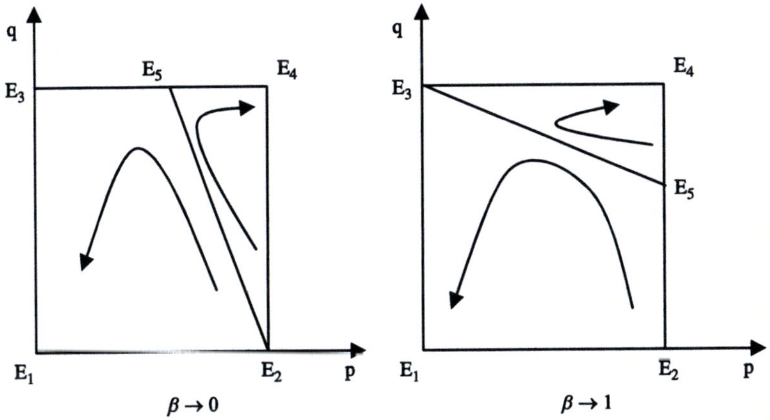

Fig. 3 The evolutionary phase diagram as $\beta \to 0$ and $\beta \to 1$

region is bigger than cooperation region. Then the owners and contractors tend to choose non-cooperation strategy.

- As the proportion coefficient $\beta \to 1$

In this condition the full risk loss is afforded by owners. In Fig. 3, the non-cooperation region is enclosed by E_1, E_3, E_2 and E_5. The area is bigger than cooperation region. Then the owners and contractors tend to choose non-cooperative strategy.

Namely, as the full risk loss is afforded by one participant, the other participant will not want to take any measure to cooperate in risk management. At last the cooperation will not be achieved.

- As the proportion coefficient $\beta \in (0, 1)$

The proportion coefficient β can be calculated by the solution of bargaining problem [6]. Supposed δ_1 and δ_2 to be respectively discount factors of owners and contractors and they satisfy the condition: $0 \le \delta_1, \delta_2 \le 1$, owners first bid, then the solution of bargaining of owners and contractors is:

$$\beta = \frac{(1-\delta_1)}{1-\delta_1\delta_2}, \quad 1-\beta = \frac{\delta_2(1-\delta_1)}{1-\delta_1\delta_2}$$

If δ_1 and δ_2 are respectively thought as the expectation of owners and contractors for risk management cooperation effect, the utility of owners and contractors increases with the discount factors δ_1 and δ_2. We can see the area of cooperation region increasing and the area of non-cooperative decreasing in Fig. 2. The probability of cooperation increases. However, as the discount factors δ_1 and δ_2 decreasing, owners and contractors pay more attention to the immediate profit and easy take opportunism action. The probability of non-cooperation increases. As the discount factor being quite great, the probability of tending average distribution is greater. The tendency helps the stable evolution of cooperation system.

3 Conclusion

The cooperation between owners and contractors by the evolution game theory are discussed in the paper. Actually there are many participants in the project such as designers, supervisors and material providers etc. The discussion result between owners and contractors can extend to the other participants.

From the above analysis, we can result the risk management cost and the proportion coefficient are the main factors that affect cooperation. Firstly, the strategy will evolve towards cooperation when the risk management cost is less than the loss that risk brings. Secondly, the distribution of the loss should be fair and be equivalent to their effort in risk management. Only when the two conditions are satisfied, the cooperation can be formed and the stable evolution happens.

The calculation of risk management cost and the mechanism of risk loss distribution are based on risk evaluation. Namely the owners and contractors need to discuss on risk identification, risk influence and risk effect together and keep consensus. So the owners and contractors should exchange and communicate each other fully, analyze the probable risk and its effect, definite their responsibility in the project risk management before their cooperation. To assure the cooperation, owners and contractors should negotiate about the loss or the profit and contract.

References

1. Tang WZ, Qiang MS, Lu YM, Chen YH (2006) Partnering-based risk management research. Water Power 32:1–4
2. Cheng E, Li, H (2002) Construction partnering process and associated critical success factors: quantitative investigation. Journal of Engineering Management 18:194–202
3. Tang WZ, Colin F. Duffield, David M. Young (2006) Partnering mechanism in construction: an empirical study on the Chinese construction industry. Journal of Construction Engineering and Management 132:217–228
4. Zou Patrick X.W., Zhang Guomin, Wang Jiayuan (2007) Understanding the key risks in construction projects in China. International Journal Project Management 25:601–614
5. Xie Shiyu (2006) *Economic Game Theory*. Shanghai: Fudan University Press
6. Zhang Weiying (2004) *Game Theory and Information Economics*. Shanghai: Shanghai People Press

Application of Industrialized Housing System in China: A Chongqing Study

Yuhong Pan, Francis K.W. Wong, and Eddie C.M. Hui

Abstract Various industrialized housing technologies were introduced to developing countries in the early 1950–1970s, volumetric (i.e. box), panelized units and tunnel-form are typical examples. These technologies lead to improvements in housing production, such as high turnover, improved productivity of both machines and labour, quick assembly and better quality of industrialized products. However, there are limitations for these technologies such as high production costs, application of heavy and large components, lack of standardization in design, and lack of consideration given to the local environment in choosing materials. Owing to the surging demands for housing, industrialization seems to be an inevitable trend in housing construction particularly for those densely populated cities like Chongqing. Thus, this paper aims to evaluate different innovative systems and determine the most suitable system(s) for the construction of industrialized housing in China, by using Chongqing as a case study. Six innovative housing systems have been considered in this study. These systems have been successfully adopted in major cities in the Chinese Mainland, using prefabrication of standardized components, which provide valuable reference to the undertaking of this study. An analytical hierarchy process (AHP) was adopted as a tool to determine the preferences of Chongqing practitioners in relation to the use of selected innovative housing systems. The finding has highlighted a practical and logical approach to identify the most appropriate industrialized housing system to be adopted in densely populated cities such as Chongqing, as well as promoting the implementation of industrialized housing system in other major cities in China.

Keywords AHP · Chongqing · Industrialized housing system

Y. Pan (✉)
School of Management, Chongqing Jiaotong University, Chongqing, People's Republic of China
e-mail: panyuhong3@hotmail.com

F.K.W. Wong and E.C.M. Hui
Department of Building and Real Estate, The Hong Kong Polytechnic University, Hong Kong, China
e-mail: bskwwong@inet.polyu.edu.hk; bscmhui@inet.polyu.edu.hk

D.D. Wu (ed.), *Modeling Risk Management in Sustainable Construction*,
Computational Risk Management, DOI 10.1007/978-3-642-15243-6_19,

1 Introduction

Chongqing is an ancient city, as well as the largest city in South-Western China. It has the largest population and occupies the largest area as one of the four municipalities in China. Covering an area of approximately 82,400 km^2 and with a population of approximately 31 million, it is also the only municipality in western China that falls under the direct control of the Central Government. Chongqing has been identified as a strategically important city for opening up the development of Western China. Its economy has grown on average about 10% per annum in recent years. And the local construction industry is considered as one of the major contributors to this development. The Chongqing construction industry is still rather traditional and the deficiencies exist across many areas in the local industry. The typical outstanding problems include lower skill labour-intensiveness, substantial use of wet trades, excessive time-consumption; poor workmanship, a mismatch between design and supply chains and inability to meet the housing demand.

Housing not only concerns with construction, but also associates with social development, with economic development, and with the development of reform programs in China. Therefore, housing is positioned as one of the most important issues in the Government's agenda. This importance is further emphasized in those densely populated large cities such as Chongqing where the demand for housing has been surged. Because of increasing urbanism and mass reconstruction of old towns in Chongqing, more affordable housing needs to be built by the government for resettlement purposes. This puts Chongqing in a favorable situation to develop industrialized housing because of its strong demand for housing. It is also more advantageous to develop industrialized housing when the project is of larger scale and repetitive in nature, with tight project duration and high quality of work is required. In line with this background, both the central Government and local governments such as the Chongqing Government have been seeking for more effective solutions for implementing housing development, and industrialized housing is identified as an alternative approach.

Housing industrialization has become a new construction method which applies new technologies and new materials. By adopting this new construction methodology, construction activities happen both on and off site, and the principles developed from factory production are used to prefabricate off-site building components, elements or modules. These building components and modules will form part of the completed building more efficiently when they are fixed in position on site.

There are good lessons to be learned from developed countries over the past decades in terms of industrialized housing development. But, there are some problems regarding directly imported industrialized housing systems to developing countries. The imported industrialized housing systems are too expensive and therefore impractical for developing countries. Moreover, there are certain industrialized housing systems such as volumetric and tunnel-form systems, which are not suitable for application in developing countries such as China, either because of environmental issues or because of economic and social benefits directly relating to

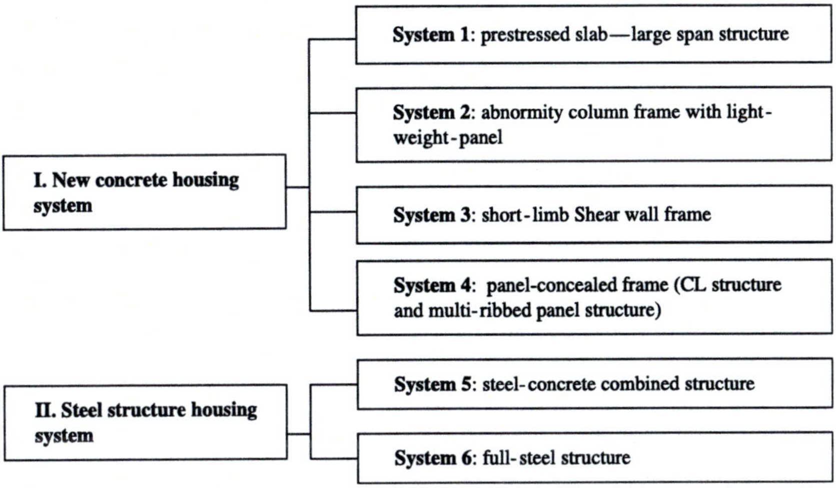

Fig. 1 Classification of innovative housing systems available in the Chinese mainland

the local conditions. While these approaches to industrialized housing production resulted in expensive and inappropriate dwellings, the thrust of technology development is geared towards two streams, i.e., prefabrication of small components and partial prefabrication. Hence, the innovative housing systems that relate to the technological characteristics have been developed in the Chinese Mainland. The systems are used local resources for feasible application of industrialized housing. Six innovative housing systems are summarized from those that have been successfully adopted in large cities in the Chinese Mainland, using prefabrication of standardized components [1–5]. The six innovative housing systems are divided into two categories: (1) New concrete housing system and (2) Steel structure housing system. The new concrete housing system has four sub-systems, and the steel structure housing system has two sub-systems (see Fig. 1).

2 Research Methodology

Firstly, the Analytical Hierarchy Process structure and hierarchy is created. Secondly, the interview of ten experts from the construction industry is completed by AHP pairwise comparison to determine priority vectors at levels 1 and 2. Thirdly, a statistical comparison and normalization based on the test of degree of significance is needed to elicit the finalization of priorities. Fourthly, a questionnaire survey is carried out by interviewing 30 practitioners from the Chongqing construction industry. The survey respondents indicated that the suitability of each of the six housing systems on a scale of 1–10 applied to each of level 2 factors. Fifthly, the results are analyzed and the six housing systems are subsequently evaluated, then, the top two most suitable housing system(s) for application in Chongqing are selected.

These systems selected are ranked according to the relevant key factors to enable judgments to be made by questionnaire surveys. These relevant key factors laid out in Table 1 are determined base on a literature review conducted at the outset of this study [6–9].

2.1 Analytical Hierarchy Process

AHP is a technique for decision making to deal with complex technological, economic, and sociopolitical issues [10]. The AHP's systematic approach to soliciting an expert's judgment and a consistency check have made it a reliable way to determine the priorities of a set of factors, which may then be incorporated into other evaluation systems. For example, Paek et al. [11] adopted the AHP method to determine the relative weights of the criteria in a fuzzy-logic system for the selection of design/build proposals. The work by Dozzi et al. [12], Pocock et al. [13] and Feng et al. [14] also employed the method in a similar fashion.

This study exploits AHP to weigh the relative importance of relevant factors in order to identify the most suitable system among the six selected industrialized housing systems for application in Chongqing. A strategic decision model for the most suitable industrialized housing systems for application in Chongqing was produced, based on an analysis of the present conditions. The decision model is divided into four levels: (a) objective, (b) level 1 factors, (c) level 2 sub-factors and (d) alternative systems. The objective is at the top; followed by level 1 factors which comprises six main criteria to achieve the objective; level 2 sub-factors consists of 31 factors with an increasing degree of detail. These relevant factors are grouped within the six criteria for evaluation. The bottom level of the hierarchy consists of six alternative housing systems. The hierarchical model for the most suitable housing system is presented in Fig. 2.

2.2 Prioritization of the Six Industrialized Housing Systems

$Si = \overline{LI} \times PV$, where: Si is the score of System i; and $\overline{LI}$ is the mean of the level of importance based on 30 Chongqing respondents to indicate the suitability of each of the six industrialized systems on a scale of 1–10 applied to each of the level 2 factors; PV is the normalized level 1 and level 2 priority vectors. The result of ranking of the six industrialized housing systems is shown in Table 2.

Table 1 The relevant key factors of industrialized housing systems

Level 1 factors	Construction industry	Supply chain	Infrastructure	Environment	Customer needs	Socio-political
Level 2 sub-factors	Manpower	Raw material	Transport	Climate	Floor area	Public expectation
	Skills	Components	Power	Pollution	No. of storeys	Amenity
	Knowledge	Equipment	Water	Exposure condition	Quality	Vested interests
	Procurement	Manufacturing capacity	Communication	Topography	Affordability	Communication
	Quality	Innovation	Sewerage	Urban dev. policy	Location	Change culture
			Waste disposal			

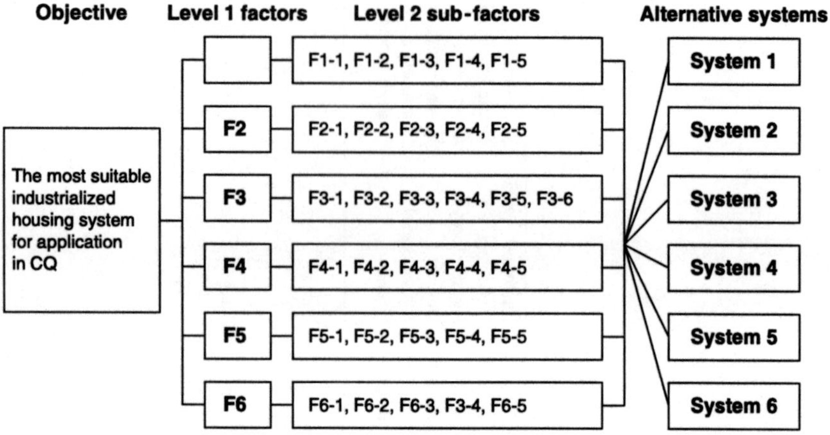

Fig. 2 AHP structure and hierarchy

Table 2 Ranking of six innovative housing systems

System	Score	Priority ranking
Prestressed slab-large span structure (S1)	5.84	6
Abnormity column frame with lightweight-panel (S2)	7.25	1
Short-limb shear wall frame (S3)	6.85	3
Panel-concealed frame (S4) (CL structure and multi-ribbed panel structure)	6.56	4
Steel-concrete structure (S5)	6.95	2
Full-steel structure (S6)	6.08	5

3 Analysis of the Results

The ranking of the six innovative housing systems shows that the top two systems [(i.e. Abnormity column frame with lightweight-panel (ACF) and Steel-concrete structure (SCS))] are the two industrialized housing systems best suited for Chongqing (see Table 2).

ACF and SCS systems are important because they embody economic and social benefits directly relating to the present conditions in Chongqing. These systems involve traditional components constructed or combined in innovative ways using specialized techniques; and with components produced in factories and assembled on-site. In this context, the product of components should be small, simple, economically competitive, lightweight and easy to handle. The housing system is an open system, i.e., compatible with conventional and other building methods. The production process involves minimal capital, use of local materials, require small and affordable equipment or machinery, and demand simple skill specialization. According to the requirements of industrialized housing development, wall materials of the two systems adopted is higher-efficient, multi-functional, lightweight, heat insulated and energy-saving. The use of local materials and industrial bi-products should be considered. Such materials can be, for example, coal gangue, pumice and perlite or flyash and slag.

The usable area of the ACF system is about 8–10% higher than that of the conventional housing systems. The dead load reduction is about 1/2–1/3 higher than the traditional housing systems. In addition, because of mass production, materials can be better utilized and wastage kept to a minimum. The use of formwork can also be reduced by the use of precast concrete units.

The SCS system is a composite type based on steels and concrete. Due to successful application in high-rise residential buildings in Tianjin, the SCS system possesses credible technological support, and also accords with national industrialized policy. Consequently the SCS system has great development potential.

However, there are some shortcomings of using either ACF or SCS systems. The first problem is that if precast components are only of a small quantity, the construction cost per unit will be high. Another problem is the joint between the precast components and frame columns need to be continuously improved in order to prevent crack. The storage and transportation of precast components could also be a problem for construction sites located in congested urban areas, and the transportation of precast components entails high construction costs. Finally, there is an incomplete supply chain for the local construction industry in Chongqing and poor manufacture capability of local manufacturers. In a word, the top two housing systems are characterized by the use of local materials and resources, involving simple techniques and open systems that make them more viable and affordable.

4 Conclusion

This study adopted the Analytical Hierarchy Process (AHP) as a decision making tool to analyze multi-layer factors from the six selected industrialized housing systems to rank their suitability for application in Chongqing. The six selected industrialized systems have been evaluated, and the most suitable system(s) for application in Chongqing have been determined.

The findings suggest that the AFC and SCS systems were ranked top. From the practitioners' perspectives, the two systems are most suitable for application in Chongqing. However, these systems have a number of shortcomings such as lack of design standardization, higher cost as compared to conventional construction systems, low skill level, shortage of building materials, low manufacturing capacity, and problems with transportation of precast components. To overcome these problems, the Chongqing government should take measures in order to encourage developers to adopt these systems in terms of design, production and erection on-site. The findings also show that customer needs, supply chain and construction industry are strongly interrelated and should be viewed as part of an integrated process which requires advance planning and coordination to develop industrialized housing in Chongqing.

It is anticipated that this study will provide an essential catalyst for the realization of industrialized housing in Chongqing and the use of precast concrete systems would play an important part in delivering affordable housing in the region.

Acknowledgements This study was founded by the Chongqing Science & Technology Commission (Project No. CSTC, 2008BB0067) and Chongqing Jiaotong University.

References

1. Chen, Z.H., Wang, X.D. and Li, S.H. (2004). "Techno-Economic Analysis and Configuration of Steel Houses", *Steel Construction*, (3), Vol. 19, No.72.
2. Li, Q.Y. (2004). "System of composite heated board and housing energy-saving", *Building Energy-Saving*, (3).
3. Shen, J.Z. (2002) Present state and Prospects of China housing industry development, *Housing Science (Chinese)*, Vol. 11, 4–5.
4. Wang, M.G. and Zhang, L.R. (2004). "Study on Technology of Steel Houses", *Steel Construction*, Vol. 19, No.72, (3).
5. Yao, Q.F. and Huang, W., (2003). "Summary of Development and Application Study on New Types of Residential Building Structure System," *Journal of Construction Technology*, Vol. 32, No. 10, 6–9.
6. Arditi, D., Ergin, U. and Gunhan, S. (2000), Factors Affecting the Use of Precast Concrete Systems, *Journal of Architectural Engineering*, September, Vol. 6, No. 3, 79–86.
7. Gann,D. M., (1996) Construction as a manufacturing process? Similarities and differences between industrialized housing and car production in Japan, *Construction Management and Economics*, 14, 437–450 (N/A).
8. Wong, K.W., Hui, C.M., Yeung, C.W., Li, S.R., Howes, R. and Wu, M. (2001) *Research monograph*: A study of Manufactured Affordable Housing in Chongqing, Department of Building and Real Estate, The Hong Kong Polytechnic University.
9. Wong, K.W., Hui, C.M., Howes, R. and Pan Y.H. (2005) *Research monograph*: Industrialized Housing Development in Chongqing China. Department of Building and Real Estate, The Hong Kong Polytechnic University.
10. Saaty, T.L., and Vargas, L.G. (1991) *Prediction, projection and fore-casting*, Kluwer Academic, Boston.
11. Paek, J.H., Lee, Y.W., and Napier, T.R. (1992) Selection of design/build proposal using fuzzy-logic system. *Journal of Construction Engineering and Management*, ASCE, 118(2), 303–317.
12. Dozzi, S.P., AbouRizk, S.M., and Schroeder, S.L. (1996) Utility-theory model for bid markup decisions. *Journal of Construction Engineering and Management*, ASCE, 122(2), 119–124.
13. Pocock, J.B., Hyun, C.T., Liu, L.Y., and Kim, M.K. (1996) Relationship between project interaction and performance indicators, *Journal of Construction Engineering and Management*, ASCE, 122(2), 165–176.
14. Feng, C.C. and Edwin H. W. Chan (2004) Application of AHP in Decision-Making on Urban Land Use: A Case Study of Chao-Hu City Development in China, *The International Journal of Construction Management*, 101–108.

Part IV
Energy Risk Management

The Study on Energy Consumption and Pollutant Emission of Civil Vehicles in Beijing

Li-xiang Zhao, Yi-long Xiong, and Fei Ye

Abstract This study models for the energy consumption and pollution emission by civil vehicles in Beijing during the period from 2008 to 2020 associated with Leap software. The energy consumption and pollutant emission respectively in the context of current and future standards of fuel consumption and pollutant emission by civil vehicles are estimated with the assumption that the number of civil vehicles will increase from 3.14 million in 2008 to 7 million in 2020. The estimations show that the fuel consumption and pollutant emission by civil vehicles in 2020 will be 240% of that in 2008 under the new policies, and the emission of major air pollutant will increase significantly.

Keywords Energy · Emission

1 Introduction

One of the greatest challenges faced by a metropolis like Beijing is to control local pollution during fast economic development. One of the major factors that affect the air quality of Beijing is the heavy smog emitted from motor vehicles, which accounts for as much as 50% of the total air pollution [1]. However, with the increasing support from government's economic policies, the number of motor vehicles registered in Beijing will increase dramatically in the next decade. The purpose of this paper is to raise the awareness of the potential of air quality deterioration caused by pollution emission by motor vehicles in Beijing in the coming years.

L.-x. Zhao (✉), Y.-l. Xiong, and F. Ye
School of Economics and Management, Beijing University of Technology, Beijing, People's Republic of China
e-mail: zhaolixiang@bjut.edu.cn; yilong7826@emails.bjut.edu.cn; yefei@bjut.edu.cn

D.D. Wu (ed.), *Modeling Risk Management in Sustainable Construction*, Computational Risk Management, DOI 10.1007/978-3-642-15243-6_20,

2 Methodology

LEAP, Long-range Energy Alternatives Planning System, is a widely used software tool for energy policy analysis and climate change mitigation assessment developed at the Stockholm Environment Institute [2]. This study employs the transportation analysis methodology of LEAP to estimate the energy consumption and emissions from civil vehicles. The estimation is made in two different scenarios. One is Same Old Scenario (SOS), the continuation of current policies on fuel consumption and pollutant emission. The other is New Standard Scenario (NSS), which introduces the new and stricter fuel consumption standard and pollution emission regulations.

3 Model of Energy Consumption and Pollution Emission

3.1 Research Model

As shown in Fig. 1, energy consumption is calculated as the multiplication of number of motor vehicles, mileage, and fuel economy. Based on the function of survival rate of vehicles, the number of motor vehicles is calculated by the number of motor vehicles in 2008, the composition of vehicle age, the number of vehicles sold in 2008 and the estimated number of vehicles sold from 2009 to 2019. Two methods will be used to calculate pollution emission: distance-based and energy-based. The distance-based method is used to calculate the emission of CO_2 as well as the emission of CO, NO_X, HC, PM from light-duty vehicles. The emission rate of CO_2 is calculated as the fuel economy multiplied by a transformation factor. The total pollution emission is the product of the mileage, the number of vehicles and the emission factor which specifies per unit of distance traveled by a vehicle. The energy-based method is used to calculate the emission of CO, NO_X, HC, and PM by heavy-duty vehicles. Total pollution emission is calculated as the emission rate which specifies per unit of energy consumed multiplied by the total energy consumption.

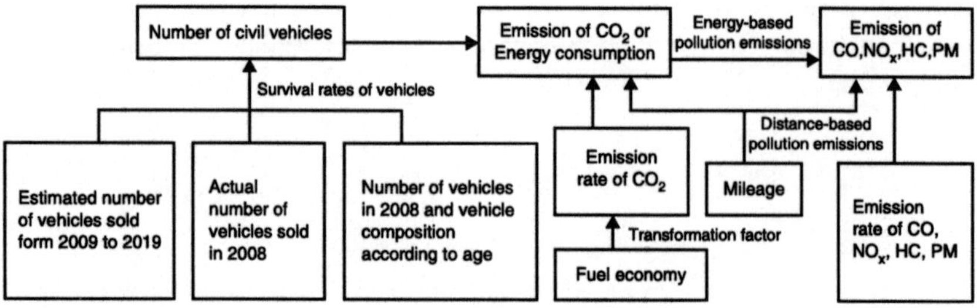

Fig. 1 Model of energy consumption and pollution emission

3.2 Mathematical Modeling

According to the research model specified above, the following mathematical models [3] are developed.

3.2.1 Energy Consumption

$$\text{Energy Consumption}_{t,y,v} = \text{Stock}_{t,y,v} \times \text{Mileage}_{t,y,v} \times \text{Fuel Economy}_{t,y,v} \quad (1)$$

Here, t is the type of vehicle, y is the calendar year, v is the vintage, Stock is the number of vehicle existing in a particular year, Mileage is the annual distance traveled per vehicle and Fuel Economy is the fuel use per unit of vehicle distance traveled.

$$\text{Stock}_{t,y,v} = \text{Sales}_{t,v} \times \text{Survival}_{t,y-v} \quad (2)$$

$$\text{Stock}_{t,y} = \sum\nolimits_{v-0.V} \text{Stock}_{y,v,t} \quad (3)$$

Here, Sales is the number of vehicles added in a particular year, Survival is the fraction of vehicles surviving after a number of years. Note that, $S_{t'} = S_{t'-1} \times e^{a \cdot t'}$ [4], where S is the fraction of surviving vehicles, t is the age in years of the vehicle, and a is the constant parameter of the survival exponential curve. In order to estimate a, $S_{t'} = S_{t'-1} \times e^{a \cdot t'}$ is transformed into $a = \ln\frac{S_{t'}}{S_{t'-1}} / t'$ and a is calculated as historical survival data of Beijing civil vehicles. This paper assume that there are two types of vehicles – passenger vehicles and trucks, and therefore two sets of constant parameters are utilized. For passenger vehicles the "a" is −0.02, and for trucks the "a" is −0.005, where v is the maximum number of vintage years which is determined automatically from the survival exponential curve with a maximum of 30 years.

3.2.2 Pollution Emissions

Distance-Based Pollution Emissions

$$\text{Emission}_{t,y,v,p} = \text{Stock}_{t,y,v} \times \text{Mileage}_{t,y,v} \times \text{Emission Factor}_{t,v,p} \quad (4)$$

Here, p is the pollutant (CO_2, CO, NO_X, HC, PM). Emission Factor is the emissions rate for pollutant p, and the units used are grams of pollutant per vehicle-kilometer of distance traveled.

Energy-Based Pollution Emissions

$$\text{Emission}_{t,y,v,p} = \text{Energy Consumption}_{t,y,v} \times \text{Emission Factor}_{t,v,p} \quad (5)$$

Here, Emission Factor is the emissions rate for pollutant p, and the units used are grams of pollutant per kilowatt-hour of energy consumed.

The stock of vehicles in 2008 and the composition of vehicle age, and the number of vehicles sold in 2008 are all taken from the China Statistical Yearbook [5]. According to the historical sales data with consideration of the survival rates of vehicles, this paper estimate the number of vehicles sold from 2009 to 2019 is 0.8 million annually based on the projection that stock turnover will be 7 million [1] in 2020. The mileage data is from research. In both SOS and NSS the fuel economy data is the fuel standard [6–9] used in different period which are taken from Standardization Administration of the People's Republic of China and Ministry of Transport of the People's Republic of China. The emission factor of pollutant (CO, NO_X, HC, PM) is the emissions standard [10, 11] in different period which is taken from General Administration of Quality Supervision, Inspection and Quarantine of the People's Republic of China. The emission rate of CO_2 is calculated as the transformed fuel economy multiplied by a transformation factor 23.2 [12].

4 Research Findings

As shown in Fig. 2, the energy consumption in SOS in 2020 will be 37.08 million tons and that in NSS will be 34.17 million tons with a decrease of 7.85%. In NSS, the energy consumption will increase from 14.23 million tons in 2008 to 34.17 million tons in 2020 with an increase of 140%.

Figure 3 shows, the emission of CO_2 in SOS in 2020 will be 76.05 million tons and that in NSS will be 70.08 million tons with a reduce of 7.85%. In NSS, the emission of CO_2 will rise from 29.18 million tons in 2008 to 70.08 million tons in 2020 with a growth of 140%.

The emission of CO is summarized in Fig. 4. In 2020, the CO emission will be 994.88 thousand tons in SOS while it will be 498.45 thousand tons in NSS with a drop of 49.9%. In NSS, the emission of CO will evolve from 318.29 thousand tons in 2008 to 498.45 thousand tons in 2020 with an increase of 56.6%.

Figure 5 shows that the emission of NO_X in 2020 will be 237.31 thousand tons in SOS and 99.52 thousand tons in NSS with a decrease of 58.06%. In NSS, the emission of NO_X will come down from 223.24 thousand tons in 2008 to 99.52 thousand tons in 2020 with a decrease of 55.42%.

In 2020, the emission of HC will be 82.98 thousand tons in SOS and 50.25 thousand tons in NSS with a decrease of 39.44%. In NSS, the emission of HC will grow from 43.7 thousand tons in 2008 to 50.25 thousand tons in 2020 with an increase of 15%, as shown in Fig. 6.

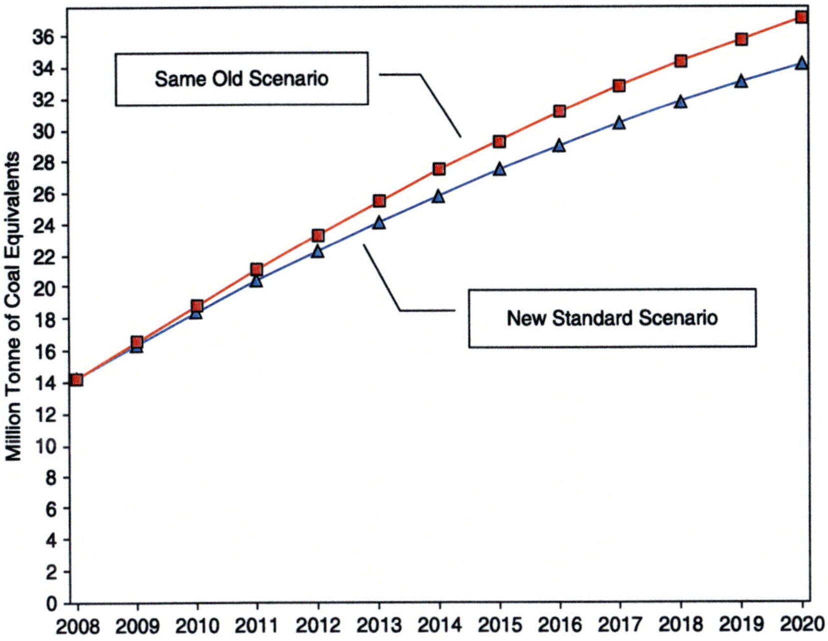

Fig. 2 The energy consumption of Beijing civil vehicles in 2008–2020

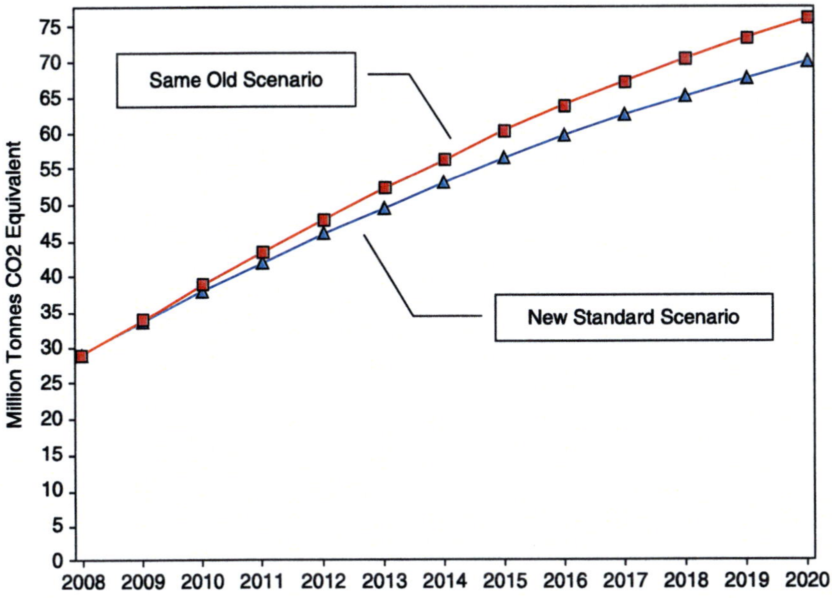

Fig. 3 CO_2 emission of Beijing civil vehicles in 2008–2020

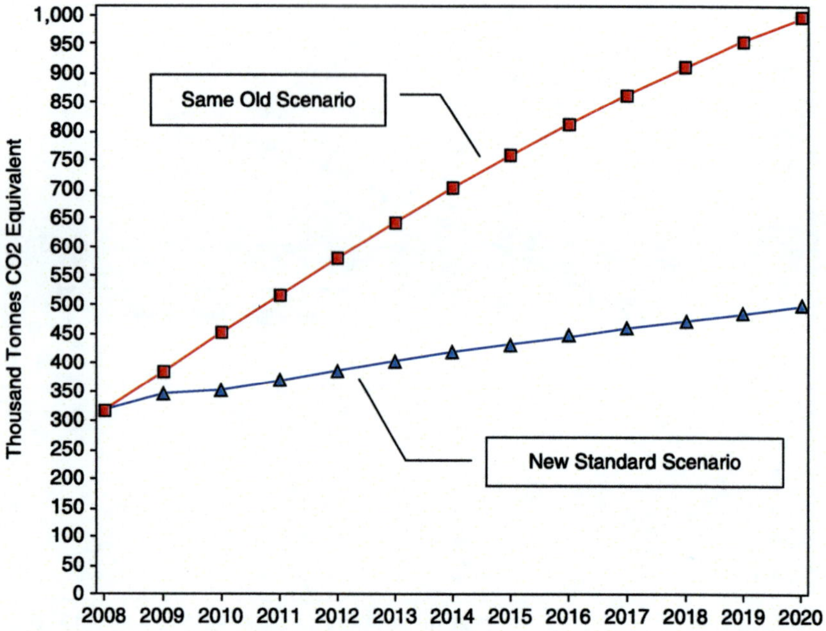

Fig. 4 CO emission of Beijing civil vehicles in 2008–2020

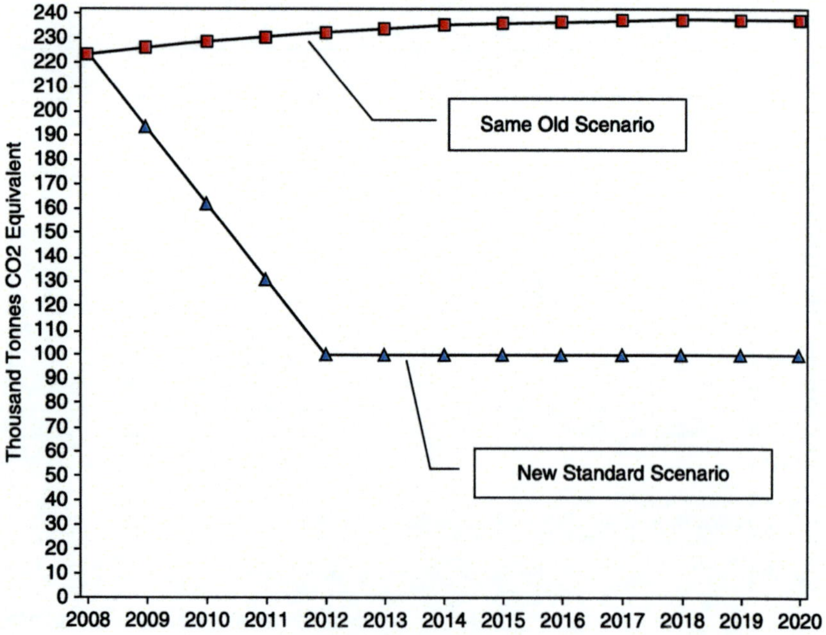

Fig. 5 NO_X emission of Beijing civil vehicles in 2008–2020

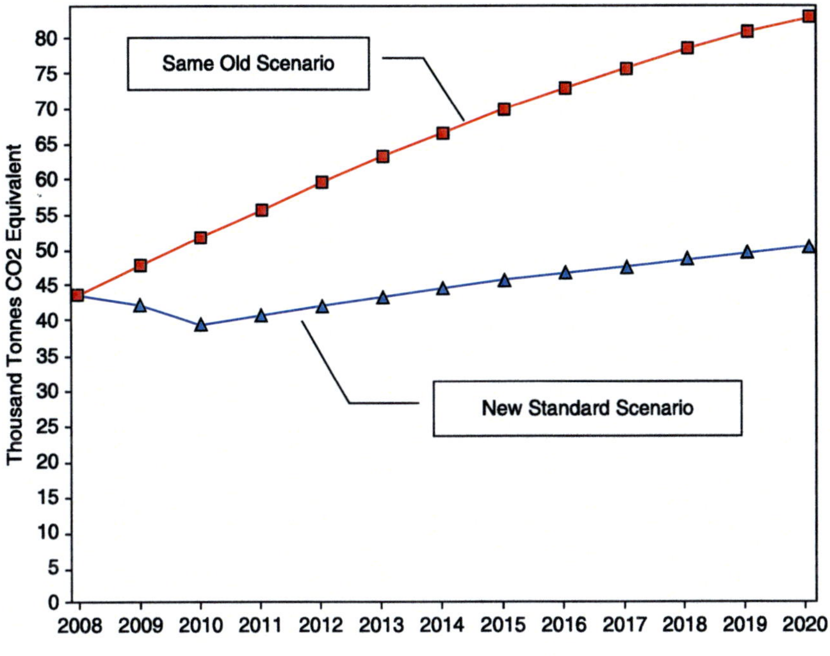

Fig. 6 HC emission of Beijing civil vehicles in 2008–2020

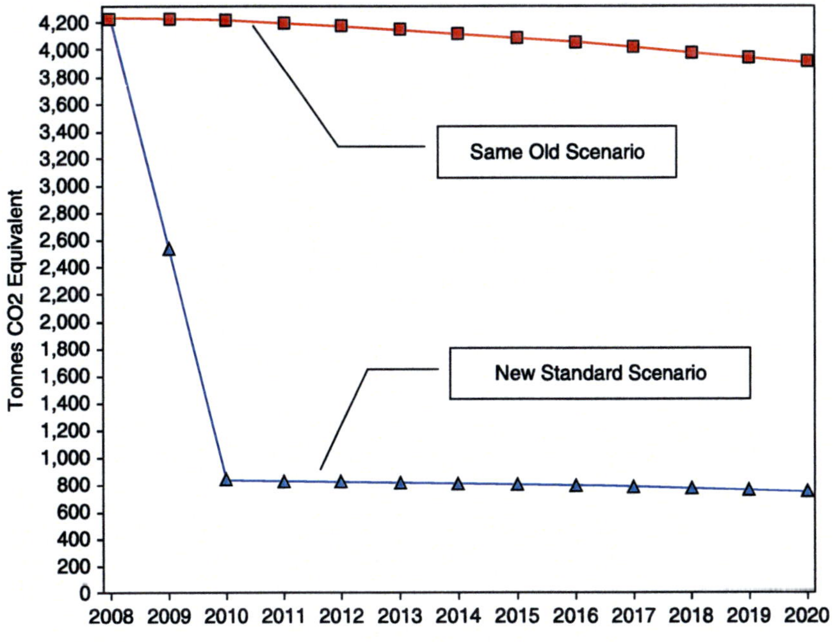

Fig. 7 PM emission of Beijing civil vehicles in 2008–2020

Based on the data in Fig. 7, the emission of PM will range from 3908.79 tons in SOS to 758.04 tons in NSS with a fall of 80.6% in 2020. In NSS, the emission of PM will decline from 4232.05 tons in 2008 to 758.04 tons in 2020 with a decrease of 82%.

5 Summary

The energy consumption and pollution emission in NSS will decrease. By examining the data from 2008 to 2020, the research finding indicates that in the NSS, the energy consumption and emission of CO_2, CO and HC will increase by 140%, 140%, 56.6% and 15%, respectively. Only the emission of NO_X and PM will decrease by 55.42 and 82%.

Acknowledgments This study is part of the research project " (SZ201010005003) A Study of the performance of mitigation from modern manufacturing in Beijing" funded by Beijing Municipal Commission of Education.

References

1. Yan Xiaoming, Wang Jianxin (2009) Beijing amount of motor vehicle break 4 million mark. People's Daily. http://gd.people.com.cn/GB/123946/10620617.html. Accessed 30 December 2009
2. Charles Heaps (2008) An Introduction to LEAP. Stockholm Environment Institute – US Center. http://www.energycommunity.org/documents/LEAPIntro.pdf. Accessed 15 October 2009
3. Charles Heaps (2006) LEAP User Guide. Stockholm Environment Institute – U.S. Center. http://www.energycommunity.org/documents/Leap2008UserGuideEnglish.pdf. pp. 87–88. Accessed 15 October 2009
4. Stockholm Environment Institute (2008) Training Exercises for LEAP. Stockholm Environment Institute – US Center. http://www.energycommunity.org/documents/LEAPTrainingExercisesEnglish2008.pdf. p. 52. Accessed 15 October 2009
5. National Bureau of Statistics of China (1991–2009) China Statistical Yearbook. China Statistics Press, Beijing
6. China Automotive Technology and Research Center (2004) GB 19578-2004 Limits of fuel consumption for passenger cars. Standardization Administration of the People's Republic of China. http://www.fueleconomy.cn/doc_pdf/chych-bzh.pdf. Accessed 29 December 2009
7. China Automotive Technology and Research Center (2007) GB 20997–2007 Limits of fuel consumption for light duty commercial vehicles. Standardization Administration of the People's Republic of China. http://www.autoinfo.gov.cn/autoinfo_cn/rootfiles/zfwj/zfwj-060420-fj1.pdf. Accessed 29 December 2009
8. Research Institute of Highway (2008) JT 711-2008 Limits and measurement methods of fuel consumption for commercial vehicle for passenger transportation. Ministry of Transport of the People's Republic of China. http://www.zsda.gov.cn/uploads/soft/091203/4-091203095120.pdf. Accessed 29 December 2009
9. Wang Wei, Liu Li, Li Yongfu et al. (2009) Study on "Operating Vehicle Fuel Consumption Limit and Measurement Method". Transport Standardization 2009-Z2-010

10. China Automotive Technology and Research Center (2005) GB 18352.3-2005 Limits and measurement methods for emissions from light-duty vehicles (III, IV). General Administration of Quality Supervision, Inspection and Quarantine of the People's Republic of China. http://www.sepa.gov.cn/image20010518/4569.pdf. Accessed 29 December 2009
11. Chinese Research Academy of Environmental Sciences (2005) GB 17691-2005 Limits and measurement methods for exhaust pollutants from compression ignition and gas fuelled positive ignition engines of vehicles (III IV V). General Administration of Quality Supervision, Inspection and Quarantine of the People's Republic of China. http://www.zhb.gov.cn/image20010518/3882.pdf. Accessed 29 December 2009
12. Feng An, Sauer Amanda (2004) Comparison of Passenger Vehicle Fuel Economy and GHG Emission Standards around the World. iCET. http://www.autoproject.org.cn/english/new_advance_en/Fuel%20Economy%20and%20GHG%20Standards.pdf. p. 20. Accessed 25 December 2009

An Investigation of the Coal Demand in China Based on Variable Weight Combination Forecasting Model

Guohao Zhao, Shufen Guo, Jing Shentu, and Yongguang Wang

Abstract Variable weight combination forecasting combines the individual forecasting models after giving them proper weights at each time point. Weight is the kind of function which changes with the forecast time. A relatively rational description of objective fact of the system can be proposed with the forecasting method which is a higher precision and a better stability. Two individual forecasting models, the Grey system forecasting and the multiple regression forecasting, are constituted based on the historical data and the influencing factors of the coal demand in China from 1981 to 2008 in this paper. And based on the theory of combination forecasting, the variable weight combination forecasting model is formulated for the coal demand to forecast the coal demand of China in the coming 12 years.

Keywords Coal demand · Energy resources · Variable weight combination forecasting model

1 Introduction

Many experts and research institutes have forecasted the coal demand of China through different methods. But because they adopted different methods and essential data, the results differed greatly and had a lower precision.

Based on the analysis and experience of previous forecasting methods and their results, we make a thorough study of the coal market demand in China. After analyzing systematically the correlative factors which can influence coal market demand and adopts individually the multiple regressions model and the grey model, we make a combination forecasting through variable weight combination forecasting (Guntao 2004; Shiying 2000).

G. Zhao (✉), S. Guo, J. Shentu, and Y. Wang
School of Management Science and Engineering, Shanxi University of Finance and Economics, Taiyuan 030006, People's Republic of China
e-mail: gzhao1958@yahoo.com.cn

D.D. Wu (ed.), *Modeling Risk Management in Sustainable Construction*,
Computational Risk Management, DOI 10.1007/978-3-642-15243-6_21,

Since Bates and Granger proposed the combination forecasting model for the first time in 1960s, the studies and applications of the combination forecasting method have developed rapidly. Combination forecasting combines properly different forecasting methods in a certain way and sums up the information given by each of them, so it can overcome the limitations of the individual models and can gather more information effectively (Lu and Peiliang 2003). Thus the random of forecast decreases and the forecast precision increases. Therefore, combination forecasting method can be applied particularly in complex economic systems with uncompleted information (Xie and Zhou 2003; Tang et al. 1993).

In light of the current research findings at home and abroad, combinational weight falls into two categories: permanent weight and time-variant weight (Wang et al. 1997; Chen 2001). The former one has a longer history and a more mature determination technique. While the latter one starts later and its determination technique is still at exploratory stage. However, it is obvious that the latter one's precision is much higher than the former one. So the combination forecasting attracts the wide interests of the forecasting circles (Zhao et al. 2001; Weigen 1996). Because variable weight function is the function of time, and is difficult to determine, so the paper determines the variable weight coefficient of the combination forecasting through linear program method. According to its historical stimulated value, it can be seen that variable weight combination forecasting has a higher precision, so its results is thought to be more credible.

2 Individual Model Forecasting of the Coal Demand in China

2.1 Multiple Linear Regression Model Forecasting

2.1.1 The Construction of Multiple Linear Regression Model

Through the analysis of the correlative factors of the coal consumption of China, it is thought that the explaining variable of coal demand should reflect economic development's demand for coal and the major energy-consuming industries' demand for coal (Lu 2005; Kouris 1998). Therefore, the thesis makes the coal demand index (Coal) as the explained variable, and the explaining variables are industrial GDP index, coal price index (Pcoal), oil price index (Poil), the index of generated electrical energy from thermal power (Elec), pig iron output index (Iron), crude-steel output index (Crude-steel), steel output index (Steel) and mate output index (Mate), etc. Because both the explaining and explained variables are the indexes of correlative factors (the index of 1981 is 100), so the great differences in the order of magnitude can be avoided. Meanwhile, the indexes can reflect the growth trend better and meet the need of the demand forecasting better.

Suppose that the coal demand index shows a linear relation with each explaining variables, we can build a following model:

$$Coal_t = \beta_0 + \beta_1 \times GDP_{\mathrm{Indus}_t} + \beta_2 \times P_{\mathrm{Coal}_t} + \beta_3 \times P_{\mathrm{Oil}_t} + \beta_4 \times Elec_t \\ + \beta_5 \times Iron_t + \beta_6 \times Crude\_steel + \beta_7 \times Steel + \beta_8 \times Mate_t + u_t \quad (1)$$

In this equation: β_0 – eversporting variable; $\beta_1, \beta_2..., \beta_8$ – coefficient, representing the influence of the explaining variables on the explained variables; u_t – random error.

We choose the data of each variables from 1981 to 2008 as the sample observed values, and then work out the observed values of each variables through using the correlative data of Chinese Economics Internet industrial data base. Then we make a linear regression analysis on the obtained 28 groups of sample observed values through SPSS statistical software. From the corresponding statistical results, it can be known that because the t test values of some indexes are smaller than the critical value, including pig iron output index, oil price index, coal price index and crude-steel output index, so they cannot pass the t test, which means that these independent variables have no remarkable influence on these dependent variables.

And the test value of crude-steel output raise remarkably and can pass the t test after we cast out three variables, pig iron output index, oil price index and coal price index, whose t test values are smaller. Then the new statistical results of regression equation which has only five explaining variables are obtained.

Through calculation we get the multiple regression forecasting model as (2):

$$Coal_t = 44.749 - 0.314 \times GDP_{Indus_t} + 0.448 \times Elec_t \\ + 0.432 \times Crude\_steel - 0.297 \times Steel + 0.321 \times Mate_t \quad (2)$$

From statistical results we can know that coefficient R^2 and adjusted coefficient $\bar{R}^2$ are close to 1, which means the equation has a good fitting as a whole; since the multiple correlation coefficient R = 0.993, so there is a good relativity between the independent variables and the dependent variables. $F = 307.838 > F_{0.05}(5, 22) = 2.661$, so the regression equation is remarkable and has a pretty good regression effect generally. The absolute values of the t test values of the left five independent variables in the model all can be put as $|t| > t_{0.025}(22) = 2.074$, so they can pass the t test, which means the independent variables have a remarkable influence on the dependent variables. And $1.03 = d_l < DW = 1.147 < d_u = 1.85$, so the model cannot decides whether there is lag correlation; because both the two stimulations have a high degree of fitting, neither the quality nor the quantity of the explaining variable in the model need to be changed.

2.1.2 Independent Variable Forecasting

We suppose the variable indexes of 2008 as the base number, the forecasted growth speed of each independent variables are in Table 1. According to the growth speed, the forecasted values of each independent variables can be worked out.

Table 1 The forecasted growth speed of each indexes (2009–2020)

Time	Index					
	Industrial GDP index	Elec index	Crude-steel index	Steel index	Mate index	Remarks
2008	2109.5	1111.93	1330.23	2144.30	1893.01	Base number
2009–2010	7.50%	6.50%	7.00%	7.50%	6.50%	
2011–2015	7.00%	6.00%	6.50%	7.00%	6.00%	
2016–2020	6.50%	5.50%	6.00%	6.50%	5.50%	

According to the growth speed, the forecasted values of each independent variables can be worked out.

2.1.3 Coal Demand Forecasting

Putting the historical data of independent variables into the obtained regression equation, the fitted value of coal demand will be obtained. And we check the fitting precision of the model by the error between fitted value and actual value. The average value of the relative error between fitted value and actual value of the coal demand index is 3.46%, the error sum squares is 1948.9, the forecast precision = 1–3.46% = 96.54%; So we can say the model has a high fitting precision and it can be used to forecast the future demand. Put the forecasted future data of the independent variables into the obtained regression equation, we can get the forecasted value of coal demand index.

2.2 *Grey System Forecasting Model*

2.2.1 Construction of Coal Demand GM (1, 1)

If the coal demand indexes of 1981–2008 are the initial data sequence, that is,

$$X^{(0)} = \left(x^{(0)}(1), x^{(0)}(2), \ldots, x^{(0)}(28)\right)$$

Then the $X^{(1)}$ can be generated through one accumulation,

$$X^{(1)} = \left(x^{(1)}(1), x^{(1)}(2), \ldots, x^{(1)}(28)\right)$$

in this sequence, $x^{(1)}(k) = \sum_{i=1}^{k} x^{(0)}(i)$, $k = 1, 2, \ldots, 28$

In order to decrease the work load of human and to increase the calculation efficiency, the calculation work of the grey system GM (1, 1) is carried out by the

DPS data processing system software, into which we input the initial data sequence of coal demand index. We can obtain the corresponding parameter, fitted value and forecasted value after the software's analysis and calculation (Jin and Zhang 2004).

The model parameter worked out by the software:

a = −0.041310, b = 105.787249, in which $-a < 0.3$, GM (1, 1) model can be applied in medium-term and long-term forecasting. The determined model is

$$\frac{dx^{(1)}}{dt} - 0.04131x^{(1)} = 105.787249 \tag{3}$$

The time response sequence is

$$\hat{x}^{(1)}(t+1) = \left[x^{(0)}(1) - \frac{b}{a}\right]e^{-at} + \frac{b}{a} = 2660.808559e^{0.041310t} - 2560.808559 \tag{4}$$

2.2.2 Test of the Model

Residual Error Test

The average value of relative error of model's simulated value $\bar{\Delta} = \frac{1}{n}\sum_{k=1}^{n} \Delta_k = 8.512\% < 10\%$, so the relative precision is $1 - \bar{\Delta} = 91.49\%$, error sum squares is 15231.7.

Association Degree Test

According to the calculated residual error sequence $\varepsilon^{(0)}$, the association degree coefficient

$$\eta(k) = \frac{\min\left(\left|\varepsilon^{(0)}(k)\right|\right) + \rho \times \max\left(\left|\varepsilon^{(0)}(k)\right|\right)}{\varepsilon^{(0)}(k) + \rho \times \max(|\varepsilon^{(0)}(k)|)}, k = 1, 2, ..., n, \text{ let } \rho = 0.5$$

The coefficient will be $\gamma = \frac{1}{n}\sum_{k=1}^{n} \eta(k) = 0.6602 > 0.6$, so it is an association degree acceptable model.

Mean Variance Ratio Value Test and Small Probable Error Test

Mean variance ratio value $C = \frac{S_2}{S_1} = 0.3379 < 0.35$, in the extra fine grade, so the model is a mean variable ratio acceptable model.

Small probable error $p = (|\varepsilon(k) - \bar{\varepsilon}| < 0.6745S_1) = 0.8889 > 0.80$, in the fine grade, so the model is a small probable error acceptable model.

The above three tests show that GM (1, 1) model has a better fitting effect for the coal demand index, it can be used to forecast the future coal demand index.

2.2.3 Coal Demand Forecasting

If we put time t into (4), we can work out the stimulated value and the forecasted value $X^{(1)}$ of sequence $\hat{X}^{(1)}$, after restoring, the stimulated and the corresponding forecasted value of $\hat{X}^{(0)}$ will be obtained.

3 Variable Weight Combination Forecasting of Coal Demand in China

3.1 *Construction and Solving of the Model*

Suppose there are n forecasting methods (or forecasting models) for one certain forecasted problem, and

Y_t – the tth period's actual observed value, $t = 1, 2, ..., M$;

f_{it} – the ith method's forecasted value at the tth period, $i = 1, 2, ..., n$;

k_{it} – the ith forecasting method's weighting coefficient at tth period, it meets $\sum_{i=1}^{n} k_{it} = 1, k_{it} \geq 0\ (i = 1, 2, ..., n)$;

$e_{it} = Y_t - f_{it}$ – the ith forecasting method's forecasted error at the tth period;

$f_t = \sum_{i=1}^{n} k_{it} \times f_{it}$ is the variable weight combination forecasting's forecasted value at the tth period;

$e_t = Y_t - f_t$ – variable weight combination forecasting's forecasted value at tth period,

so we have: $e_t = Y_t - f_t = \sum_{i=1}^{n} k_{it} e_{it}$

The fundamental principle to obtain weight coefficient of combination forecasting is to make its error the smallest at the sample point. Here we use the method whose error's absolute value is the smallest by the combination forecasting, taking the need of weight coefficient itself into account, we get the following optimum model of combination forecasting:

$$\begin{cases} Min\ J_t = |e_t| = \left| \sum_{t=1}^{n} k_{it}\ e_{it} \right| \\ s.t. \sum_{i=1}^{n} k_{it} = 1, k_{it} \geq 0, (t = 1, 2, ..., M) \end{cases} \tag{5}$$

There are two situations for the solving of the above model:

At the sample point t, for all the i, $e_{it} \geq 0$ (or $e_{it} \leq 0$), that is, at a certain point, the forecasted errors of all the forecasting modals are in the same direction, thus the modal can be changed as following:

$$\begin{cases} Min\ J_t = \left|\sum_{t=1}^{n} k_{it}\ e_{it}\right| = \sum_{t=1}^{n} k_{it} \times |e_{it}| \\ s.t. \sum_{i=1}^{n} k_{it} = 1,\ k_{it} \geq 0, (t = 1, 2, \ldots, M) \end{cases} \tag{6}$$

Here, the model is a linear programming problem with only one linear restriction, suppose $e_{pt} = \min\{e_{it}\}$, the solution of the model must be:

$$\begin{cases} k_{it} = 1 (i = 1, 2, \ldots n,\ i = p) \\ k_{it} = 0 (i = 1, 2, \ldots n,\ i \neq p) \end{cases} \tag{7}$$

At the sample point t, for some i, $e_{it} > 0$; while for other i, $e_{it} < 0$.

If $I_1 = \{Ie_{it} > 0\}$, $I_2 = \{Ie_{it} < 0\}$, and $I = I_1 + I_2$, that is, at a certain point, the forecasted errors of some forecasting models are bigger than zero, while those of other forecasting models are smaller than zero, so model (5) can be changed into:

$$\begin{cases} \min\ J_t = |e_t| = \left|\sum_{i=1}^{n} k_{it} \times e_{it}\right| = \left|\sum_{i \in I_1} k_{it} \times e_{it} + \sum_{i \in I_2} k_{it} \times e_{it}\right| \\ s.t. \sum_{i \in I_1} k_{it} + \sum_{i \in I_2} k_{it} = 1,\ k_{it} \geq 0 (i = 1, 2, \ldots, n) \end{cases} \tag{8}$$

This model has multiple optimum solutions. If $U_t = |e_t| + e_t, V_t = |e_t| - e_t$, then $|e_t| = (U_t + V_t)/2$, $e_t = (U_t - V_t)/2$, thus the model changes as:

$$\begin{cases} \min\ J_t = \left|\sum_{i \in I_1} k_{it} \times e_{it} + \sum_{i \in I_2} k_{it} \times e_{it}\right| = (U_t + V_t)/2 \\ s.t. \sum_{i \in I_1} k_{it} \times e_{it} + \sum_{i \in I_2} k_{it} \times e_{it} - (U_t - V_t)/2 = 0, \\ \sum_{i \in I_1} k_{it} + \sum_{i \in I_2} k_{it} = 1,\ k_{it} \geq 0,\ U_t \geq 0,\ V_t \geq 0 (i = 1, 2, \ldots, n,\ t = 1, 2, \ldots, M) \end{cases} \tag{9}$$

It is obvious that (9) has infinite solution sets. Suppose in the previous I_1 models, if $p_1 \in I_1$, then $e_{p_1 t} \leq e_{p_i t}$ ($i \in I_1$ and $i \neq p_1$), so $f_{p_1 t}$ is the optimum point forecasting method of the previous I_1 forecasting methods at sample point t; and it is the same case for the left $n - I_1$ forecasting methods, there must be a $p_2 \in I_2$, which made

$|e_{p_2t}| \leq |e_{p_1t}|$ ($i \in I_2$ and $i \neq p_2$), and f_{p_2t} is the optimum point forecasting method of the left $n - I_1$ forecasting methods at sample point t. Here if we make $k_{it} = 0$ ($i \in I$ and $i \neq p_1$, $i \neq p_2$), model (9) changes as following:

$$\begin{cases} k_{p_1t}e_{p_1t} - k_{p_2t}|e_{p_2t}| = 0 \\ k_{p_1t} + k_{p_2t} = 1 \end{cases} \tag{10}$$

Its solution is:

$$\begin{cases} k_{p_1t} = \dfrac{|e_{p_2t}|}{|e_{p_1t}| + |e_{p_2t}|} \\ k_{p_2t} = \dfrac{|e_{p_1t}|}{|e_{p_1t}| + |e_{p_2t}|} \end{cases} \tag{11}$$

Based on the above two situations, the optimum combined weight coefficient, k_{it}, can be worked out through (6) and (11).

Because the purpose of constructing the combination forecasting model is to forecast, so we need to determine the combined weight coefficient of the forecasted time point, which is $k_{i,\,M+j}(i = 1, 2, \ldots, n;\ j = 1, 2, \ldots)$, and one method can determine $k_{i,\,M+j}$:

$$k_{i,\,M+1} = \frac{1}{M}\sum_{t=1}^{M} k_{it},\ k_{i,M+2} = \frac{1}{M}\sum_{t=2}^{M+1} k_{it}, \ldots,\ k_{i,\,M+j} = \frac{1}{M}\sum_{t=j}^{M+j-1} k_{it} \tag{12}$$

It is easy to prove that the $k_{i,\,M+j}$ obtained in this way meets $\sum_{i=1}^{n} k_{i,\,M+j} = 1$ and $k_{i,\,M+j} \geq 0$

3.2 *Variable Weight Combination Forecasting of Coal Demand*

Suppose multiple linear regression model is f_1, grey model is f_2.

In the former part, we work out the errors of these two individual forecasting models at each time point, based on which we construct the linear program model and from (6) and (11), we get its solution, that is, the optimum combined weight coefficient k_{it} of the two forecasting methods. And the combined weight coefficient of the future forecasted time point $k_{i,\,M+j}(i = 1, 2, \ldots, n;\ j = 1, 2, \ldots)$ can also be determined by (12). The forecasted value of variable weight combination forecasting at the tth period is $f_t = \sum_{i=1}^{n} k_{it} \times f_{it} = k_{1t} \times f_{1t} + k_{2t} \times f_{2t}$, from which we can get the average value of relative error and the relative error of the fitted value, the value of the relative error of the fitted value, $\bar{\Delta} = \frac{1}{n}\sum_{k=1}^{n} \Delta_k = 2.04\% < 3.46\% < 8.512\%$,

Table 2 Coal demand's forecasted values of each model

Year	2008	2009	2010	2011	2012	2013	2014
Forecasted value of multiple linear regression model	258,313	266,818	275,369	282,679	289,879	296,923	303,759
Forecasted value of grey model	210,597	219,479	228,735	238,382	248,436	258,914	269,833
Forecasted value of variable weight combination	248,325	256,555	264,897	272,377	279,897	288,013	296,734
Year	2015	2016	2017	2018	2019	2020	
Forecasted value of multiple linear regression model	310,331	315,149	319,511	323,345	326,572	329,103	
Forecasted value of grey modal	281,214	293,074	305,434	318,316	331,741	345,732	
Forecasted value of variable weight combination	304,086	310,245	316,273	322,147	327,848	333,254	

average value of the relative precision, $1-\bar{\Delta}=97.96\%$. The forecasted error sum squares of the combination forecasting, $\sum_{t=1}^{M}(e_t^2)=1088.5<1948.9<15233.1$. All of these prove that the fitting effect of combination forecasting is better than the two individual forecasting models, the multiple linear regression model and the grey model. What's more, the former one has a higher precision than the latter two. The forecasted values of these three models are in Table 2.

The forecasted coal demand of combination forecasting in 2020 is 3.33 billion, so during 2007–2020, the number of coal demand increases year after year, but the growth speed decreases yearly, the average growth speed is 2.92%.

4 Conclusions

The forecasted results show that with the development of China's economy, the demand of coal will also increase. And the coal demand will be up to 3.33 billion tons by 2020. The forecasted demand is given in light of current economic growth rate and development pattern. But the demand for coal will decrease if we take other things into account, such as the readjustment of industrial structure, the decrease of the proportion of high energy-consuming industries; the progress of science and technology, the improvement of production technology, the vigorous development of recycling economy, the build of a conservation-minded society, the decrease of unit consumption of GDP; the utility of alternative energy sources and energy restructuring. Therefore, the coal demand in the future should be smaller than the forecasted one.

Variable weight can make good use of the information source of each individual forecasting model. It can improve the fitting effect and raise remarkably the forecasting precision. Moreover, it can eliminate the influence of some random factors and increase the stability of forecasting. And also it can give a rational description of the system's objective fact. All of these show that this model can become the effective method to forecast the future coal demand of China. However, the calculation of time-variant weight is relatively complicated; we can get different results through different optimized models. Thus, this forecasting method also needs some further study and improvement. It is our hope that the paper will draw attentions from those who are involved in the field.

Acknowledgements The research was supported by National Natural Science Foundation in China (No. 70873079) and (No. 70941022), Shanxi Natural Science Foundation (No. 2009011021-1) and Shanxi international science and technology cooperation foundation (2008081014).

References

Lu Erpo. 2005. A study of the forecasting modal of Chinese energy demand. *Statistics and Decision*, 20: 31–33. (in Chinese).

Guo Guntao. 2004. Analysis and prediction of medium and long term coal supply and demand in China. *China Coal*, 10: 22–25. (in Chinese)

Chen Huayou. 2001. Research on combination forecasting model with non negative and time-variant weights based on effective measure of forecasting methods. *Operations Research and Management Science*, 1: 50–54.

Kouris, George. 1998. Energy consumption and economic activity in industrialized countries: a note. *Energy Economics*, 5: 207–212.

Lu Qi, Gu Peiliang, Qiu Shiming. 2003. The construction and application of combination forecasting model in Chinese energy consumption system. *Systems Engineering-Theory & Practice*, 3: 25–31. (in Chinese).

Jin Quanzhong, Zhang Jian. 2004. GM (1, 1) Application of the modal in the forecasting of the coal demand. *China Coal*, 1: 17–19. (in Chinese)

Shiying Dong. 2000. Energy demand projections based on an uncertain dynamic system modeling approach. *Energy Sources*, 7: 443–451.

Wang Jing, Liu Liangdong, Wang Zuoyi. 1997. Current situation and development of combination forecasting model. *Forecasting*, 6: 7–38. (in Chinese).

Weigen, Andress S. 1996. Time series and prediction using gated experts with application to energy demand forecasts. *Applied Artificial Intelligence*, 11–12: 583–624.

Tang Xiaowo, Zeng Yong, Cao Changxiu. 1993. Study of time-variant weight combination forecasts. *Forecasting*, 3: 48–50. (in Chinese).

Xie Kaigui, Zhou Jiaqi. 2003. Combination forecasting models using regression analysis method. *Journal of Chongqing University (Natural Science Edition)*, 1: 64–67. (in Chinese).

Zhao Liming, Qian Weirong, Shen Yanfeng. 2001. Combination of forecasts for demand of dwelling market. *Journal of Systems Engineering*, 3: 66–69. (in Chinese).

Investment Cost Analysis for Key Industries of New Energy Based on Boston Experience Curve

Yuanying Chi, Benkun Chi, Xiangyang Li, and Dongxiao Niu

Abstract Based on the Boston Experience Curve model, the article analyzes China's new energy key industry – wind power industry investment and find that wind power industry has greater development potentiality in China, and the learning rate of China's wind power is less than the developed countries learning scope, the cost and price of wind power will turn down with the rising of China's learning rate and integrate with the thermal power ultimately.

Keywords Boston learning curve model · Learning rate · New energy key industry · Wind power

1 Introduction

Energy structure adjustment, the requirements of energy saving strategies, and socio-economic development lead to the construction of the new energy development in full swing. With the promulgation of "New Energy Law" in 2006, China's new energy industry, particularly wind power industry has made rapid development and achieved the national planning objectives in 2008, 2 years ahead to the planning. In the future, the China's wind power market may become the second largest wind power market just after the U.S. in the world.

Y. Chi (✉)
North China Electric Power University, Beijing 102206, People's Republic of China
and
Changchun University of Technology, Changchun 130012, People's Republic of China

B. Chi
School of Management, Jilin University, Changchun 130025, People's Republic of China

X. Li
China's Power Investment Group Company, Beijing 100053, People's Republic of China

D. Niu
North China Electric Power University, Beijing 102206, People's Republic of China

D.D. Wu (ed.), *Modeling Risk Management in Sustainable Construction*,
Computational Risk Management, DOI 10.1007/978-3-642-15243-6_22,

Although the investment on China's wind power industry doubled over the same period, the wind power costs are far higher than the thermal power and hydropower compared to the strong wind power countries'. Based on the data known, our investment per kW of wind power is as high as 9,000 yuan, 5,000 yuan more than the thermal power, 3,000 yuan more than the hydropower. This shows that wind power's high investment and high cost will prevent the development of the wind power industry, but with the industrial scale expansion, technological innovation and development of large units, the wind power costs will show a decreasing trend [1]. This article will use reasonable data model – Boston Experience Curve to forecast the cost of wind power investment so as to provide a reference for government and business investment decision.

2 Boston Experience Curve and New Energy Industry

2.1 Experience Learning Curve

It is also known as Boston Experience Curve. In 1960, Mr. Bruce, Henderson in Boston Consulting Group first proposed the Experience Curve Effect. The basic idea of the model is that the reduction of production costs is caused by the accumulated experience results.

1. Model of experience learning curve is generally expressed as: $Y_x = AX^{-b}$

Y_x is the average production cost per unit of product X; A is the cost of the first unit in theory; X is continuous quantity of the last unit that required calculation of the average cost; bis the learning index, I.E. the slope of the Logarithm lines;

2. Learning rate (LR): $LR = 1-2^{-b}$;

The investment costs decline rate I.E. technological;

3. Progress rate (PR):. $PR = 2^{-b}$

Learning rate is an indicator used to describe the learning curve. The experience effect is much better, the learning costs decline much faster and the learning rate is much higher [2].

2.2 The Experience Curve Model and the New Energy Wind Power Industry [3–7]

In most literature, the development of new energy industry including solar power, wind power and other new power energies complies with the experience learning curve model [2]; the downward trend in the investment cost is often described by the learning curve. This article will be in line with the basic idea of the learning curve and the relevant conclusions. The experience accumulated leads to the cumulative wind power capacity growth and wind power costs declining gradually.

Changes in the wind power cost can be described by the learning curve model. We regard the wind power investment cost as a function of cumulative wind power capacity, and the learning curve model is:

$$C(k) = C_1 N(k)^{\varphi} e^{u(k)} \quad (1)$$

In the function, C(k) shows the unit investment cost of wind fans at the time of k, which is a function of cumulative installed capacity – N(k); φ is elasticity between cumulative installed capacity and the unit investment cost; u(k) is random factor; the investment cost reduction rate, I.E. the technological progress rate (PR) is decided by φ, expressed as:

$$PR = 2^{\varphi} \quad (2)$$

Wind power learning rate is:

$$LR = 1-2^{\varphi} \quad (3)$$

3 Investment Cost Analysis for Wind Power Industries Based on Boston Experience Curve

3.1 *The Calculation Process*

Investment per kilowatt is an important economic indicator in wind farm construction and also an important basis for confirming the purchase price. This article will use relevant data from 1998 to 2007 to calculate the weighted average of installed capacity, so as to get the average investment per kW (see Table 1) each year from 1998 to 2007. It can be seen from the table that the wind farm construction unit investment shows a declining trend from 1998 to 2006, while prices of wind fans declined rapidly too.

According to relevant data in 1998–2006, using non-linear modules in STATLSTICAL software and curve fitting toolbox in MATLAB software for parameter estimation and mutual validation, parameter estimation and statistical test results are shows in Table 2.

3.2 *Computational Model and Investment Forecast*

From above we can get the learning curve model for investment changes per kW

$$C(k) = 1.787292 \times N(k)^{-0.21356} \quad (4)$$

Table 1 1998–2007. Wind generator investment per kW

Year	The accumulative installed capacity (10,000 kW)	Investment/kW (10,000 yuan)	The wind generator unit kW (10,000 yuan)	The wind generator price of investment proportion (%)
1998	22.4	1.0022	0.7837	78.20
1999	26.8	0.9842	0.7559	76.81
2000	34.43	0.9414	0.7123	75.67
2001	39.98	0.8831	0.6526	73.90
2002	46.8	0.8600	0.6136	71.36
2003	56.7	0.8413	0.5827	69.27
2004	76.14	0.8393	0.5691	67.81
2005	126.0	0.8100	0.5226	64.52
2006	260.4	0.7931	0.4780	60.27
2007	605.0	0.7789	0.4229	56.47

Source: Based on data consolidation SERC

Table 2 Parameter estimates and statistical test values

Parameter and statistical test values	Investment changes (kW)	Wind generator price changes (kW)
C_0	1.787292	1.523105
$t-ratio$	17.346	5.182
$p-level$	≈ 0	≈ 0
φ	−0.21356	−0.29322
$t-ratio$	−10.502	−4.253
$p-level$	≈ 0	≈ 0
$Adj\, R^2$	0.965	0.810
F	110.291	18.088
$D \cdot W \cdot$	1.955	1.418

Technological progress rate of investment per kW PR = 86.2%, learning rate is 13.6%. It means that when the cumulative installed capacity doubled, the investment per kW is down to 86.2% of the original investment.

The learning curve model for wind fans price changes per kW:

$$\mathrm{P(k)} = 1.523105 \times \mathrm{N(k)}^{-0.29322} \tag{5}$$

Technological progress rate of wind fans price per kW PR = 81.6%, learning rate is 18.4%. It means that when the cumulative installed capacity doubled, the wind fans price per kW is down to 81.6% of the original.

According to the above data of China's wind power capacity, we can predict the change situation in wind power investment in the next few years, shown in Table 3.

4 Results and Conclusions

1. **China's wind power learning rate is less than developed countries' learning scope, there is greater potentiality for wind power development.**

Table 3 Change situation in the next few years of wind power investment

Item/year	2008	2010	2015	2020
Cumulative installed capacity (kW)	778.52	1456.10	4172.34	10021.83
Investment per kW (10,000 yuan)	0.7022	0.6021	0.5298	0.4626
Wind fans price per kW (10,000 yuan)	0.3887	0.3167	0.2614	0.2141
Wind fans price ratio to total investment (%)	55.36	52.61	49.34	46.29

First of all, the learning rate of wind power investment by the World Economic Development and Cooperation Organization in 1981–1994 is 17%. In this paper, through the learning curve model the authors calculated and got the learning rate for the wind power industry per kW investment declining in China is 13.6%, which is less than 17% in 1990s of OECD, indicating that China's wind power industry is near the same level of early 90s in Europe and other countries, there is very large development potentiality and the next few years will be China's wind power industry investment peak.

Secondly, it can be seen from the above calculation that our fans per kW price of wind power learning rate is 18.4%, compared to the other developed countries' fans price learning rate of 8–31%, China's learning rate is within the developed countries' range, showing that our rapid development of fans manufacturing industry in recent years is inevitable.

2. **Wind power cost and price will decrease as learning rate increase in China, ultimately will integrate with thermal power.**
   The calculations indicate that the learning rate of China per kW fans price remain at around 18%, which is still lagging behind the high learning rate of 31% in developed countries. This is because that the fans manufacturers in China mainly depend on introduction of foreign technology and have not done a real absorption and innovation.
3. **The expected price difference among wind power, thermal power and hydropower will become smaller and smaller.**
   Relevant data shows that the hydropower investment per kW will stabilize at around 5,000 yuan, 4,000 yuan in thermal power. Based on our investment cost prediction of wind power, we can see that by 2015 wind power can compete with hydropower and by 2020 wind power investment costs are near thermal power's. Therefore, we can expect in the next few years, wind power, thermal power, hydropower electricity price spreads will be diminishing gradually.

Acknowledgments Chi Yuanying, Associate Professor Doctoral, Main Research in the low carbon economy and new energy.
This article is supported by Chinese post-doctoral science fund (20090460262).

References

1. Chi Y., Zhang S., Li J. Development of Wind Power at Home and Abroad [J], Productivity Research, 2008, 19
2. Holttinen, H., Tuhkanen, S. The Effect of Wind Power on CO_2 Abatement in the Nordic Countries[J], Energy Policy, 2004, 32 (14):1639–1652

3. McDonald A, Schrattenholzer L. Learning Rate for Energy Technologies [J], Energy Policy, 2001, 29 255–261
4. Munksgaard J., Larsen, A. Socio-economic Assessment of Wind Power Lessons from Denmark [J], Fuel and Energy Abstracts, 1998, 39 (3): 202
5. Patrik S Derholm. Thomas Sundqvist Learning Curve Analysis for Energy Technologies, Theoretical and Econometric Issues, 2002 (5)
6. Xu Liping, Lin Li. Study on the Cost Trends of Wind Power in China Based on the Learning Curve, Electric Power Science and Engineering, 2008, 03
7. Zheng Zhaoning, Liu Deshun. The Learning Curve Model of China PV Module Price Changes and Policy Recommendations, Solar Energy, 2005 (2) 93–96

Part V
Environmental Risk Management

Green Adaptive Reuse: Issues and Strategies for the Built Environment

Craig Langston

Abstract Adaptive reuse is a powerful alternative to building demolition or destruction and can deliver a range of economic, social and environmental benefits to society that represent good value for money. It can extend the useful life of a facility through a change in function or purpose from that which previously applied and take advantage of the remaining physical life embedded in its materials and systems. When done well, the resultant projects are very successful, and much admired. This paper explores the issues that surround adaptive reuse intervention and proposes a number of strategies that can enhance the possible benefits that flow from adoption of this approach. Adaptive reuse is important to our future in an era of climate change where maximizing wealth and utility must be tempered against minimizing resources and environmental impact. It is argued that the concept of 'green adaptive reuse' is a valid strategy to both extend a facility's life and reduce its carbon footprint, while helping to preserve important heritage values that define our cultural development over time. Coordinating adaptive reuse intervention with 'greening' initiatives can deliver opportunities for cost efficiency.

Keywords Adaptive reuse · Existing buildings · Intervention · Property management · Sustainability

1 Introduction

It has been said that the greenest buildings are the ones we already have (Jacobs 1993). This is a reference to the embodied energy within materials and systems that would be largely wasted through traditional demolition paradigms that may be invoked to make way for new construction and progress. Even adopting reuse and recycling approaches would rarely be as effective as leaving components in-situ

C. Langston
Mirvac School of Sustainable Development, Bond University, Gold Coast, Australia
e-mail: clangsto@bond.edu.au

D.D. Wu (ed.), *Modeling Risk Management in Sustainable Construction*,
Computational Risk Management, DOI 10.1007/978-3-642-15243-6_23,

where possible (Douglas 2002). Refurbishment is considered a more appropriate strategy compared to new build provided the quality of the existing facility is consistent with the aims of the revitalization (e.g. Bromley et al. (2005), Pearce (2004)). Achieving lower operating energy performance through implementation of green design principles and technologies may enhance the benefits of refurbishment further.

In many cases refurbishment also entails a change of function, as the original purpose of the facility may be obsolete or close to it. Known as adaptive reuse, such type of refurbishment would be appropriate for facilities that would otherwise be destroyed to make way for a different type of activity. Similarly, adaptive reuse offers opportunity to improve operating performance, and the term 'green adaptive reuse' is sometimes applied to highlight this outcome[1]. So, given the alternatives, adaptive reuse is already able to better deliver sustainable outcomes for society by avoiding unnecessary waste, and green adaptive reuse is likely to be a further advantage provided a convincing value for money proposition is mounted.

The objectives of this paper are: (1) to discuss the issues that affect adaptive reuse implementation in practice, and (2) to propose a series of strategies that are capable of delivering economic, social and environmental advantage. Adaptive reuse has the additional complication of timing, as to undertake significant functional change too early or too late invites resource inefficiency. This paper begins by looking at recent research into adaptive reuse intervention, before moving onto a detailed examination of issues and strategies, and concludes with some practical recommendations for building owners and developers.

2 Adaptive Reuse

Adaptive reuse is not appropriate in all cases. It can be defined as a subset of refurbishment where a change in a facility's primary function is involved. The timing of adaptive reuse intervention is critical, and requires an understanding of a range of obsolescence drivers that might conspire to make a particular facility of no further use to its owner, or prospective owners operating in a similar domain, despite displaying inherent capacity as a property asset. This position can be complicated by heritage control and constraints that may prohibit demolition, and owners may have no option but to seek a buyer through creative redesign of the facility for a different market (Rovers 2004).

Modeling of adaptive reuse potential (ARP) is necessary to identify opportunities for strategic intervention where appropriate. Suitable facilities are ones that were originally built using principles of 'long life, loose fit and low energy', with

[1]For example, the Whitehead-Elniski Residence in Chicago (see story available at http://www.jetsongreen.com/2008/03/whitehead-elnis.html).

considerable remaining (embedded) physical life and structural integrity, but where their current functional purpose is waning.

Initial work by Langston and others (e.g. Langston et al. (2008), Langston and Shen (2007)) has led to a means of identifying ARP in buildings through estimating useful life. A model was developed to predict useful life as a function of physical life and obsolescence. Through application of traditional discounting techniques, expected physical life (itself an outcome of a separate model) was reduced by a derived annual obsolescence rate to arrive at expected useful life. The potential for adaptive reuse could then be calculated at any particular date in the facility's life cycle, so the timing of the intervention could be optimized. The concept behind this research is summarized in Fig. 1.

Obsolescence was hypothesized to be a combination of physical, economic, functional, technological, social, legal and political criteria. Each criterion was shown to be capable of evaluation using surrogate estimation techniques. The calculated annual rate of obsolescence (akin to a discount rate) has lead to a range of useful lives arising between 25 (maximum obsolescence) and 100% (no obsolescence) of the expected physical life of the facility. Using this model, buildings can be compared and ranked according to their potential for adaptive reuse given their current age. High ARP scores mean more potential for adaptive reuse intervention.

Models, by definition, are intended to simulate reality. To do this they make assumptions that simplify the complexity of the final product while maintaining

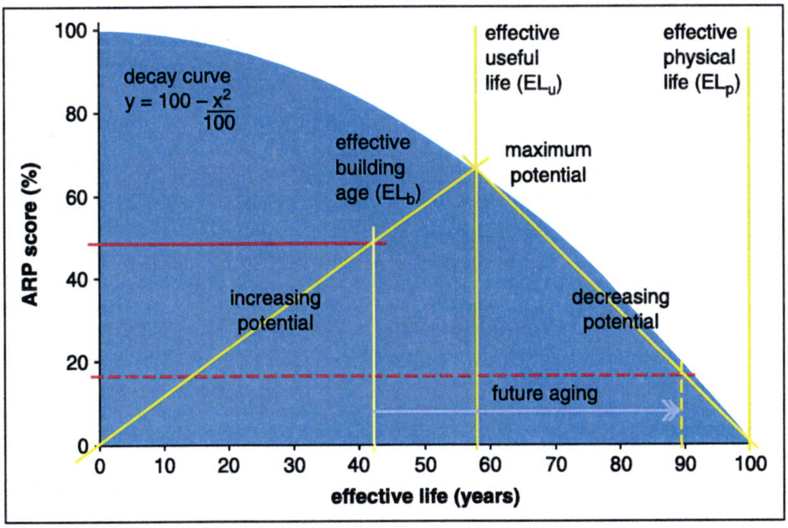

$$\text{ARP (increasing)} = \frac{100 - \frac{EL_u^2}{100}}{EL_u} \cdot EL_b \qquad \text{ARP (decreasing)} = \frac{100 - \frac{ELu^2}{100}}{100 - EL_u} \cdot (100 - EL_b)$$

Fig. 1 Adaptive reuse potential model

reasonable forecasting accuracy. Langston (2008) has tested his model in hindsight against 64 adaptive reuse projects sourced from around the world. He found there was a strong correlation between predicted useful life and actual useful life, as shown in Fig. 2. The accuracy of the model is therefore judged by its forecast of the outcome, and provided this is robust, the inner workings of the model are validated. Such is the case here. When the regression line was modified to $y = x$, the value of r^2 fell only to 0.69971, which confirmed the model's integrity.

Work by Bullen (2007) has tested attitudes towards adaptive reuse, although admittedly on a very small sample of building owners and managers in Western Australia. The sample in fact was drawn from 30 members of the Western Australian Sustainability Industry Group (WASIG) with 14 respondents. Nevertheless, as you would expect, the majority considered adaptive reuse to be preferable over new build provided the economics of the approach could be justified.

The top five drivers identified to support adaptive reuse were environmental sustainability (87% agreed), heritage significance (83%), effectiveness in meeting sustainability benchmarks (79%), technical ability of building to adapt (74%), and economic sustainability (70%). The top five barriers to implementation were constraint on creativity compared to redevelopment (85% agreed), estimating social viability (84%), compliance with building codes (67%), increasing urban density (65%), and estimating economic viability (61%). The top five opportunities for adaptive reuse were opportunity for technical innovation (89% agreed), expected

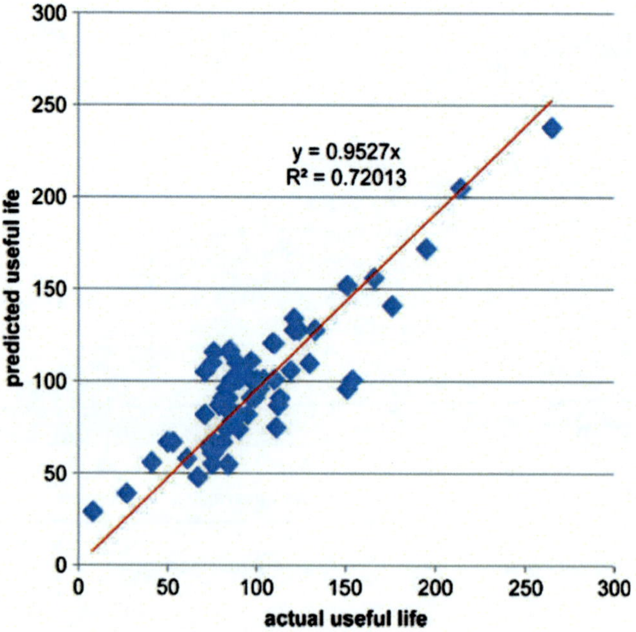

Fig. 2 Validation of useful life forecast

benefits of reusing (83%), enhancing community values (82%), visual amenity and cultural heritage (81%), and increased demand after revitalization (69%).

Despite the obvious limitations, the above will be used as a basis to explore issues of adaptive reuse implementation. Rather than rely on further opinion, this discussion takes the form of reasoned argument. In particular, further discussion is required on the proposition that "*older buildings may be unable to meet current sustainability standards*" (p. 29). This is critical to the notion of green adaptive reuse. Furthermore, a multi-criteria approach is needed to blend economic, social and environmental considerations into a single decision tool, as adaptive reuse includes intangible benefits (Bell and Morse 1999; Lutzkendorf and Lorenz 2005).

3 Issues

Adaptive reuse implementation demands an appropriate context. It is generally regarded that the following conditions must be met:

- The existing function or purpose of the facility has become inappropriate due to changing social expectations and/or market demand
- The facility has significant embedded physical life (or residual value) and structural integrity
- There is some compelling cultural, heritage or environmental value in the facility to support its retention
- An argument can be mounted to show that the proposed new use delivers a higher value for money ratio than alternative new build or sale options

The first point is relevant to adaptive reuse while the remainder apply to refurbishment more generally. Additional value can be achieved if the intervention enables the facility to improve its green performance. To some extent this is a given, as material reuse and avoidance of unnecessary waste generation is integral to an adaptive reuse strategy. Adaptive reuse will usually outperform other refurbishment strategies due to the increased in-situ reuse involved (Chusid 1993; Poon 2001). Operational performance, however, may have been poor, and intervention represents an opportunity to improve on this as part of the adaption where feasible.

It is also important that design consultants are able to show creativity and sensitivity to the project (Latham 2000). This is not always easy, and demands experience and skill. Creativity extends to finding imaginative new uses for the facility that can be demonstrated to be viable. Adaptive reuse differs from restoration as it provides greater 'license' for change, such as extension and integration of new build components, or even selected demolition.

Further to Bullen's findings, political agenda can be a key driver. Revitalization of dilapidated areas of our urban environment and the desire to blend progress with heritage conservation goals are often the purview of government and local planning authorities. Linked to this is the opportunity for government funding to support projects that are seen as culturally significant. Such funding can make the difference between feasible and non-feasible projects.

A key issue is cost. The economics of adaptive reuse are not necessarily clear. Benefits can include social and environmental contributions that are not easily translated into financial terms, either for the facility owner, developer or other stakeholders (Maggs 1999). The identification of adaptive reuse potential is one thing, but realizing it is another. A sophisticated evaluation process is needed to express benefits (both tangible and intangible) against costs (capital and operating) within the context of an acceptable risk profile and time horizon. If the ratio of benefits to costs is less than 1, the project is unlikely to advance any further. If higher ratios can be achieved for new build solutions, then an adaptive reuse strategy will be hard to justify. So this analysis is critical to success.

Benefits may be related to maximizing wealth and utility. Costs may be related to minimizing resources and environmental impact. Hence adaptive reuse demands consideration of a wider range of issues outside of traditional return on investment. Nevertheless, adaptive reuse can be cost effective as a result of the reuse of expensive building elements and time for completion can be shorter (Saleh and Chin 2009), particularly where heritage constraints are not overwhelming. Use of a greening strategy as part of the adaptation provides opportunity to introduce future operational savings into the analysis and reduce the facility's carbon footprint.

Compliance with building regulations can be more difficult for adaptive reuse projects compared to new build, and can lead to increased costs. Compliance could relate to fire safety and egress, insulation and energy performance, disabled access, asbestos removal, occupational health and safety, car parking and the like. Planning controls may prohibit some alternative new uses or require time and effort in negotiation (Ball 1999). Many new developments also have these problems, but with adaptive reuse any discovered (latent) conditions during construction can introduce additional problems, and therefore it may be concluded that adaptive reuse increases the risk of time and cost overruns.

Sustainability is an interesting question in the context of compliance. Existing facilities usually possess both positive and negative attributes in regard to sustainability. They clearly perform well in regard to material reuse and embodied energy savings (Brandt 2006). They often have low technology solutions that lend themselves well to natural ventilation, natural light and thermal mass objectives. But their orientation may be sub-optimal, solar access may be limited, insulation may be problematic to add, and there may be problems with dampness and weatherproofing that are expensive to overcome. However, sustainability standards recognize these limitations and provide some flexibility to achieve compliance. While some projects may have difficult challenges, this should not be considered as a significant issue, and in many cases adaptive reuse solutions will achieve higher operational performance than their new build counterparts. Green adaptive reuse is an area that warrants further investigation. It is likely that the costs of greening existing buildings during adaptive reuse are lower then the costs of greening existing buildings independently, and so a value proposition should be easier to mount.

Most adaptive reuse projects are in the older parts of cities and surrounding communities and therefore tend to have more central locations with good access to transport and markets (Myers and Wyatt 2004). While increased urban density may be an outcome, this is not necessarily a bad thing, compared to urban sprawl and disused or unsafe city precincts, and may actually be an opportunity for revitalization through preservation of cultural values that would otherwise be lost or diluted. From a sustainability perspective, greater urban density offers advantage over development of new land and the resultant loss of biodiversity that usually follows (Sustainable Construction Task Group 2004).

Heritage conservation and the celebration of cultural values attached to a facility or precinct are a prime motivation for restoration, refurbishment and adaptive reuse. However, the latter usually offers the most advantage in this regard, as it is able to blend preservation and revitalization to create interesting places for people to inhabit. Adaptive reuse offers potential to introduce new business opportunities, particularly where the historical context of the facility is sympathetic with commercial goals, as may be the case in tourism, hospitality, education and retail ventures. Reused materials add character to the architecture of the adaptation and provide connections with history that can attract visitors and clients alike.

So the key benefits of adaptive reuse centre round engagement of the community and a celebration of the past. This mix of old and new can be quite compelling. Many completed adaptively reused facilities are national landmarks and much beloved. Yet most of them are not recognized as leading environmental exemplars. Despite their contribution to sustainability in terms of material reuse and waste minimization, they have generally not introduced green principles and technologies over and above those that were part of the original design or accepted contemporary practice. To some extent this is because they don't need to, as they already may have comfortable internal conditions, a low reliance on energy for heating, ventilation and air conditioning, and ample natural light. But an opportunity may have been missed to introduce solar power and hot water, building management systems that can regulate the internal environment more efficiently, water catchment and stormwater run-off solutions, cogeneration, and waste recycling, to name just a few.

It seems odd that Bullen's results indicate the main opportunity for adaptive reuse is technical innovation, yet there is little evidence to suggest that this has occurred in relation to green building performance. The notion of green adaptive reuse appears still to be embryonic, and perhaps for reasons of economic viability have been left out or cut out of past projects. The problem may not be one of principle but rather one of evaluation. The sophistication of our triple bottom line assessment tools may be inadequate to account for the complexities of adaptive reuse, or the risks may just be too high for most clients.

It is generally regarded that high performance environmental buildings cost more than traditional solutions. Hopefully this premium will reduce over time. Nevertheless, it is also held that most adaptive reuse projects cost less than new build solutions of the same size. So it may be possible, therefore, to introduce green solutions with adaptive reuse intervention provided the two can be coordinated. This is an area that needs to be developed more seriously and be supported by government via incentives and successful case examples.

4 Strategies

Green adaptive reuse needs to become a priority. More concentration needs to be directed to refurbishment over new construction as time passes, and where appropriate adaptive reuse should be seen as preferable to demolition for facilities that are becoming obsolete. Green adaptive reuse is then an optimal strategy as it combines embodied and operational benefits in a coordinated fashion. It should be obvious that reuse and greening, if done separately, will cost more and involve greater disruption then if done simultaneously. Greening of our existing building stock is a contemporary imperative to help reduce greenhouse gas emissions and carbon footprints (Balaras et al. 2004). The cost efficiency of adaptive reuse for most projects can be used to offset the (often) higher capital costs of sustainable development, even though the level of greening is not likely to be as high as might be expected with more modern design solutions.

To some extent the blame for lack of green adaptive reuse examples lies with building designers. There are two quite different skill sets involved. Adaptive reuse requires engagement and understanding of historical connections and cultural sensitivities. Green building requires technical expertise in environmental modeling, comfort and energy performance. Combining these two pursuits demands multi-skilled designers or multi-disciplinary design teams who can integrate preservation and sustainability with creativity and flair. But when achieved successfully, the outcomes can be extraordinary (e.g. Holyoake and Watt 2002; Department of Environment and Heritage 2004).

Using the US Green Building Council LEED Platinum certification as a method for identifying high performance green buildings, it appears that several adaptive reuse projects have made the list. These are real examples of green adaptive reuse, but they represent less than 5% of the LEED Platinum list. They provide evidence that existing buildings are capable of meeting the highest current sustainability standards within acceptable budget constraints. Examples sourced from the Internet comprise:

- *Franklin Environmental Center* at Hillcrest, Vermont (information available at http://www.middlebury.edu/administration/enviro/initiatives/design/hillcrest/)
- *Boora Studio* at Portland, Oregon (information available at http://www.boora.com/projects/boora_leed_platinum_studio)
- *The Christman Building* at Lansing, Minneapolis (information available at http://www.smithgroup.com/?id=1323)
- *Alberici Corporate Headquarters* at St. Louis, Missouri (information available at http://www.alberici.com/index.cfm/Projects/Alberici Corporate Headquarters)
- *Blackstone Station* at Cambridge, Massachusetts (information available at http://www.edcmag.com/CDA/Articles/Web_Exclusive/BNP_GUID_9-5-2006_A_10000000000000214697)
- *Center for Neighborhood Technology* at Chicago, Illinois (information available at http://building.cnt.org/)

- *First Regiment Armory Annex* at Portland, Oregon (information available at http://www.archiplanet.org/wiki/First_Regiment_Armory_Annex)
- *William A. Kerr Foundation Office* at St. Louis, Missouri (information available at http://stlouis.bizjournals.com/stlouis/stories/2008/10/27/focus17.html)

An appropriate strategy in a climate-challenged future is to make better use of the facilities we already have. This translates to a general shift towards refurbishment. But where obsolete facilities still have residual value, adaptive reuse is likely to be appropriate. Intervention techniques such as those described earlier in this paper can help to identify which facilities offer the most potential for adaptive reuse and hence tell us where design time and effort should be concentrated. When this intervention occurs, an opportunity is provided to incorporate a greening campaign to ensure that future operational performance is maximized. The combined effect of substantial reuse and ongoing operational efficiencies can make a difference to the overall impact of the constructed environment provided such efforts have widespread adoption.

Adaptive reuse is an international topic and is relevant particularly to those countries with a rich heritage of built assets. Projects may have heritage-focused or opportunistic characteristics, but in both cases respond well to sustainability ideals and strategies. Green adaptive reuse does not appear to be limited to specific building typologies or client classifications (such as public or private sector) but may attract stakeholders and financiers with more altruistic attributes.

Adaptive reuse potential needs to be justified and demonstrated through appropriate analysis. A multi-criteria framework comprising economic, social and environmental considerations is essential. A value for money proposition must be made, but not one restricted to financial return and short payback periods. The quantification of benefits that are intangible might sound like an oxymoron, but some objective analysis is necessary to ensure that vital social and environmental advantage are not undervalued or ignored. Such tools are now beginning to emerge.

Put simply, the ratio of benefit (wealth and utility) to cost (resources and environmental impact) gives an indication of value for money. The higher this ratio, the better the social outcome. This assumes that benefits and costs are considered broadly, not to specific interest groups, and are assessed over the full life cycle of the facility, not just the period of ownership of the initial investor. Such thinking needs to be embedded in the planning approval process so that society has some confidence that future facilities will be in line with international climate change adaptation principles and targets.

5 Conclusion

Green adaptive reuse needs to be at the forefront of our thinking about existing building stock. In most countries new construction represents around 1% of the total value of property assets per annum. On this basis it may take a century to upgrade their performance, even if from tomorrow every new intervention delivered high environmental performance outcomes. A shift in focus to refurbishment of existing facilities in preference to premature destruction and new build is necessary from a sustainability perspective, and some evidence this shift is already happening is now becoming available, such as the recent decline in the proportion of expenditure on new construction compared to refurbishment in some western countries.

Adaptive reuse offers advantage over normal refurbishment where an existing functional purpose has become obsolete. Green adaptive reuse, defined as a merge of adaptation to a new purpose and the integration of green principles and technologies, is an opportunity to improve the performance of our existing building stock. Through this strategy a faster process of upgrade to higher standards of compliance can be achieved, while simultaneously preserving important heritage and cultural values. The assessment of such opportunities must take account of multiple criteria to demonstrate that value for money has been achieved and is higher than alternative new build options. This is the challenge for building owners and developers into the future. Positive action in this regard will help mitigate the damaging effects of climate change and assist governments in fulfilling international agreements on greenhouse gas emissions.

Facilities within a portfolio can be ranked and prioritized according to their potential for adaptive reuse. In fact, entire cities can be analyzed to identify which properties have reuse merit. By matching suitable cases with creative solutions, incorporating sustainable design and environmental certification, a quantum shift in the performance of existing building stock can be achieved. A practical recommendation for contractors is to increasingly seek out and pursue green adaptive reuse opportunities, as the frequency of such projects is anticipated to be on the rise.

Acknowledgements This research is funded by the Hong Kong Polytechnic University, Hong Kong Special Administration Region, China. Thanks also to the Australian Research Council for their funding of a Linkage Project investigating the strategic opportunities of building adaptive reuse, and collaborative research partners Bond University, Deakin University, Williams Boag Architects, and The Uniting Church in Australia.

References

Balaras, C.A., Dascalaki, E. and Kontoyiannidis, S. (2004) Decision support software for sustainable building refurbishment, *ASHRAE Transactions*, 110[1], 592–601.

Ball, R. (1999) Developers, regeneration and sustainability issues in the reuse of vacant industrial buildings, *Building Research and Information*, 27[3], 140–148.

Bell, S. and Morse, S. (1999) *Sustainability Indicators: Measuring the immeasurable?*, Earthscan Publications.

Brandt, M. (2006) How to adaptively reuse a community asset? *Heritage: The magazine of the Heritage Canada Foundation*, 9[2], 21–22.

Bromley, R.D.F., Tallon, A.R. and Thomas, C.J. (2005) City centre regeneration through residential development: Contributing to sustainability, *Urban Studies*, 42[13], 2407–2429.

Bullen, P. (2007) Adaptive reuse and sustainability of commercial buildings, *Facilities*, 25[1/2], 20–31.

Chusid, M. (1993) Once is never enough, *Building Renovation*, Mar–Apr, 17–20.
Department of Environment and Heritage (2004), *Adaptive Reuse*, Commonwealth of Australia, Canberra.
Douglas, J. (2002), *Building Adaptation*, Butterworth-Heinemann.
Holyoake, K. and Watt, D. (2002) The sustainable re-use of historic urban industrial buildings: Interim results and discussion, in proceedings of COBRA 2002, available at: http://www.rics-foundation.org/index.html.
Jacobs, J. (1993) *The death and life of great American cities*, Random House.
Langston, C. (2008) The sustainability implications of building adaptive reuse (keynote paper), in proceedings of CRIOCM2008, Beijing, Oct/Nov, 1–10.
Langston, C. and Shen, L.Y. (2007) Application of the adaptive reuse potential model in Hong Kong: A case study of Lui Seng Chun, *The International Journal of Strategic Property Management*, 11[4], 193–207.
Langston, C., Wong, F., Hui, E and Shen L.Y. (2008) Strategic assessment of building adaptive reuse opportunities in Hong Kong, *Building and Environment*, 43[10], 1709–1718.
Latham, D. (2000) *Creative re-use of buildings*, Donhead Publishing Ltd., Shaftesbury.
Lutzkendorf, T. and Lorenz, D. (2005) Sustainable property investment: Valuing sustainable buildings through property performance assessment, *Building Research and Information*, 33[3], 212–234.
Maggs, A. (1999) Adaptive reuse, *In place*, 1[4], 33–34.
Myers, D. and Wyatt, P. (2004) Rethinking urban capacity: Identifying and appraising vacant buildings, *Building Research and Information*, 32[4], 285–292.
Pearce, A.R. (2004) Rehabilitation as a strategy to increase the sustainability of the built environment, available at http://maven.gtri.gatech.edu/sfi/resources/pdf.
Poon, B.H.S. (2001) Buildings recycled: City refurbished, *Journal of Architectural Education*, 54[3], 191–194.
Rovers, R. (2004) Existing buildings: A hidden resource ready for mining, available at http://www.sustainbalebuilding.info.
Saleh, T. and Chin, A. (2009) Building green via design for deconstruction and adaptive reuse, in proceedings of CIB W115 Lifecycle Design of Buildings, Systems and Materials, Enschede, The Netherlands, 12–15 June, 29–34.
Sustainable Construction Task Group (2004) Making the most of our built environment, DTI, available at http://www.dti.gov.uk/index.html.

Risk Assessment of Regional Industrial Clusters

Take the Baoji Titanium Industrial Clusters as an Example in Baoji City

Yongheng Fang and Zhouping Jia

Abstract This article, on the basis of analyzing the risk types of industrial clusters, puts forward a kind of evaluation method of risk assessment of industrial clusters based on the Fuzzy Analytic Hierarchy Process. Combined with investigating findings, a system of risk assessment has been set up applying the Fuzzy Analytic Hierarchy Process; the risk of the Baoji Titanium industrial clusters in Baoji City has been well evaluated. The result of the evaluation shows that the network risk and environmental risk of Baoji Titanium industrial cluster in Baoji City are medium; however, the structural risk and innovation risk are comparatively high. The cluster stakeholders could take this result as a basis of avoiding risk.

Keywords Assessment · Fuzzy analytic hierarchy process · Industrial cluster · Risk

1 Introduction

Risk assessment of industrial clusters aims at taking the corresponding countermeasure for the risk of industrial clusters, the application of management science and technology, using a combination of qualitative and quantitative methods. Quantitative methods can estimate the size of the risk of industrial clusters and evaluate the possible impact of the industrial clusters' risk. Domestic and international scholars have undertaken extensive research about the risk of industrial clusters; these researches mostly use qualitative methods to analyze the causes of risk, the risk performance and the measures to defuse the risk of the industrial clusters, etc. However, the risk factors of industrial clusters are of fuzzy characteristics, a simple qualitative analysis method cannot accurately grasp the quantitative characteristics and cannot make the quantitative assessment for the strength of risk

Y. Fang (✉) and Z. Jia
School of Management, Xi'an University of Architecture and Technology, Xi'an 710055, People's Republic of China
e-mail: yhfang@xauat.edu.cn; jiazhoupingping@163.com

D.D. Wu (ed.), *Modeling Risk Management in Sustainable Construction*, Computational Risk Management, DOI 10.1007/978-3-642-15243-6_24,

and the capacity of risk resistance of industrial clusters. Therefore, the risk assessment of industrial cluster should be done by a method of combining qualitative analysis and quantitative analysis together. Through qualitative analysis, the causes and regularity of the risks are quite known and correctly understand; through quantitative assessment, the size of the risk is quantified and provides a basis for risk management of the industrial clusters. The biggest advantage of Fuzzy Analytic Hierarchy Process is to achieve a combination of qualitative analysis and quantitative analysis. And it can accurately determine the risk assessment index and its weights; therefore it can reasonably reflect the relative importance among the indicators of risk assessment and lay foundation for the objective and scientific way to conduct performance evaluation for industrial clusters (Markusen 1996). Overall, the article applies Fuzzy Analytic Hierarchy Process method to assess the risk of industrial clusters, and it can provide a theoretical basis and supporting data to the risk management of industrial clusters.

2 Set Up the Risk Evaluation System for Industrial Clusters

According to sources of risk, the risks of industrial clusters can be divided into two categories: endogenous risk and exogenous risk (Fei et al. 2008). Endogenous risks arise from the internal industrial clusters, and shown in the process forming, development and evolution; it is the fundamental risk and unavoidable. The endogenous risks include structural risk, network risk, ecological risk, organizational risk, and products life-span risk, etc. Exogenous risks are caused by external factors of industry clusters, and include the cyclical economic risk, political risk, natural disaster risk, etc. (Yin et al. 2009). Risk evaluation index system of regional industrial clusters is shown in Fig. 1.

Based on the above analysis, the article introduces the concept of hierarchy, that is, various factors will be divided into different levels according to their relationship and affiliation which influence the performance of industrial clusters (Cai et al. 2003). We will dominate the relationship between indicators and express the association with lower layers by the line segments, and then according to the associated attribute of indicators, make the indicators into a sequential hierarchy through decomposition-aggregation. As shown in Fig. 1, the entire structure has a total of three layers: First layer: target layer – risk of regional industrial clusters (A); Second layer: Guidelines Layer – network risk (B1), structural risk (B2), innovation risk (B3) and the environmental risk (B4); Third layer: target layer (C1–C20).

Baoji City, Shaanxi Province is China's largest production base of titanium and titanium alloy, it has formed an axle-type industrial cluster after years of development. Baoji Titanium industrial cluster attracted scientific research, production, processing, trade and circulation, etc. more than 400 business sectors; it has a supporting platform and management organizations, and the production capacity is 70% of the total gross domestic; it is known as the "China Titanium Valley".

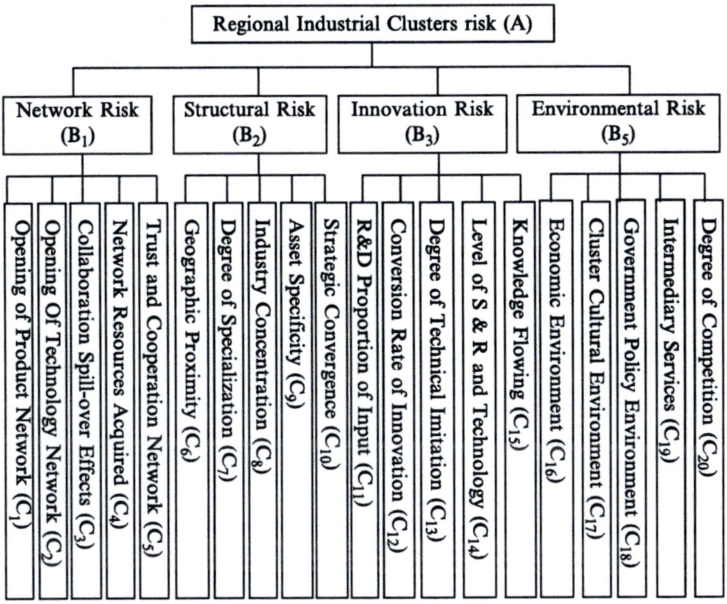

Fig. 1 Risk evaluation index system chart of regional industrial clusters

2.1 The Steps for Risk Assessment of Industrial Clusters of AHP Method

The first step is to set up the determination matrix. Determination matrix represents the relative importance comparison between the proper layers with the upper layer. These judgments can be quantified through the introduction of an appropriate scale to write down the determination matrix with values, generally to be quantified with 1–9 scale matrix method. The formation of determination matrix's cluster characteristics needs to be analyzed by many experts (Wang 2004).

The second step is to calculate the matrix to determine the largest Eigen value λmax, and its corresponding eigenvector, this feature vector will be normalized by processing $\left(\text{formula}: W_i = \frac{1}{n}\sum_{j=1}^{n} \frac{\alpha_{ij}}{\sum_{k=1}^{n}\alpha_{ki}}\right)$ and getting the factors in the order of importance, that is, weights allocation. The third step is the consistency testing of the determination matrix. In order to carry out the consistency tests of the determination matrix, it is required to calculate consistency ratio and average random index; the value can be looked up in the table. When the random consistency ratio is < 0.10, it is believed that the result of analytic hierarchy sequencing has satisfactory consistency, i.e., the weight index is distributed reasonably; when the random consistency ratio is ≥ 0.10, it means the determination matrix should be revised and the weight index value redistributed.

2.2 Setting Up the Determination Matrix

Using experts' scoring method and combining it with the survey data from the Baoji Titanium industrial cluster, the determination matrix will be set up as follows: the determination matrix target A to the first class indicator; determination matrix for the second class indicator (C1–C5) to the first class (B1); determination matrix for the second class indicator (C6–C10) to the first class (B2); determination matrix for the second class indicator (C11–C15) to the first class (B3); determination matrix for the second class indicator (C16–C20) to the first class (B4), as shown in the following matrix.

$$A = \begin{bmatrix} 1 & 1 & 3 & 5 \\ 1 & 1 & 4 & 3 \\ 1/3 & 1/4 & 1 & 2 \\ 1/5 & 1/3 & 1/2 & 1 \end{bmatrix} \quad B_1 = \begin{bmatrix} 1 & 2 & 3 & 2 & 1/3 \\ 1/2 & 1 & 1/2 & 1/2 & 1/6 \\ 1/3 & 2 & 1 & 2 & 1/4 \\ 1/2 & 2 & 1/2 & 1 & 1/5 \\ 3 & 6 & 4 & 5 & 1 \end{bmatrix}$$

$$B_2 = \begin{bmatrix} 1 & 1 & 3 & 5 & 7 \\ 1 & 1 & 5 & 4 & 4 \\ 1/3 & 1/5 & 1 & 2 & 3 \\ 1/5 & 1/4 & 1/2 & 1 & 2 \\ 1/7 & 1/4 & 1/3 & 1/2 & 1 \end{bmatrix} \quad B_3 = \begin{bmatrix} 1 & 3 & 7 & 1 & 5 \\ 1/3 & 1 & 3 & 1/2 & 2 \\ 1/7 & 1/3 & 1 & 1/5 & 1/3 \\ 1 & 2 & 5 & 1 & 7 \\ 1/5 & 1/2 & 3 & 1/7 & 1 \end{bmatrix}$$

$$B_4 = \begin{bmatrix} 1 & 5 & 3 & 7 & 5 \\ 1/5 & 1 & 1/3 & 2 & 1 \\ 1/3 & 3 & 1 & 3 & 4 \\ 1/7 & 1/2 & 1/3 & 1 & 1 \\ 1/5 & 1 & 1/4 & 1 & 1 \end{bmatrix}$$

2.3 Calculation to Determine Matrix

Taking use of Matlab software to calculate the largest eigenvalue of the determination matrix A and its corresponding eigenvector, it equals to 4.0843, the weight vector of B1–B4 to $A : W = (0.4020, 0.3802, 0.1305, 0.0873)$. Similarly, to calculate the largest eigenvalue of the determination matrix $B1 = 5.1888$, the weight vector of C1–C5 to $B1 : W1 = (0.2043, 0.0714, 0.1243, 0.0977, 0.5024)$; to calculate the largest eigenvalue of the determination matrix $B2 = 5.1632$, the weight vector of C6–C10 to $B2 : W2 = (0.3797, 0.3596, 0.1246, 0.0822, 0.0537)$; to calculate the largest eigenvalue of the determination matrix $B3 = 5.1612$, the weight vector of C11–C15 to $B3 : W3 = (0.3772, 0.1487, 0.0471, 0.3478, 0.0792)$;

to calculate the largest eigenvalue of the determination matrix B4 = 5.1024, the weight vector of C15–C19 to B4 : W4 = (0.5121, 0.0978, 0.2405, 0.0693, 0.0804).

2.4 Consistency Test

Calculating the consistency ratio for the determination matrix A : $\text{C.I.} = \frac{\lambda_{max} - n}{n - 1} =$ 0.0281.

The average random index from the table is R.I.= 0.89, and the random consistency ratio is $\text{C.R.} = \frac{\text{C.I.}}{\text{R.I.}} = 0.0316 < 0.1$. Therefore, the result after analytic hierarchy processing is satisfactory consistency, that is, the weight is very reasonable. Similarly, testing the consistency of matrix B_1 is C.I. = 0.0472, C.R.= 0.0421 < 0.1, through the consistency test; testing the consistency of matrix B_2 is C.I. = 0.0408, C.R. = 0.0364 < 0.1, through the consistency test; testing the consistency of matrix B_3 is C.I. = 0.0403, C.R. = 0.0360 < 0.1, through the consistency test; testing the consistency of matrix is C.I. = 0.0256, C.R. = 0.0229 < 0.1, through the consistency test.

3 Fuzzy Comprehensive Evaluation of Each Index

This article uses fuzzy comprehensive evaluation method to quantify the evaluation of index, and to obtain the total score of the risk evaluation of Baoji Titanium industrial cluster in Shaanxi Province.

3.1 Determining the Evaluation Set and Remark Rating

First, according to research findings and given evaluation set of each index, if the research data shows that 40% of the research object was evaluated as "Smaller," 20% of the research object was evaluated as "Moderate," 30% of the research object was evaluated as "Large," and 10% of the research object was evaluated as "Great," then the target is [0.4, 0.2, 0.3, 0.1]. The evaluation set for each index and index weight's value can be seen in Table 1 below.

Taking use of semantics, it can be divided into four scales (Smaller, Moderate, Large and Great). In order to facilitate the calculation, the subjective evaluation of the semantic scale must be quantified, and in turn, they are assigned a value of 40, 60, 80 and 100, respectively. If the final evaluation value is greater than or equal to 80, it believed as great, if less than 60, it is considered as small (shown in Table 2 below).

Table 1 Index weight and evaluation set

Target (A)	The first indicator (B_i)	Weight	The second indicator (C_i)	Weight	Evaluation set			
Risk assessment of Baoji titanium industrial cluster (A)	Network risk (B_1)	0.4020	Opening of product network (C_1)	0.2043	0.3	0.4	0.2	0.1
			Opening of technology network (C_2)	0.0714	0.2	0.5	0.2	0.1
			Collaboration with the spill-over effects (C_3)	0.1243	0.5	0.3	0.1	0.1
			Network resources acquired (C_4)	0.0977	0.2	0.5	0.2	0.1
			Trust and cooperation network (C_5)	0.5024	0.1	0.2	0.5	0.2
	Structural risk (B_2)	0.3802	Geographic proximity (C_6)	0.3797	0.1	0.3	0.5	0.1
			Degree of specialization (C_7)	0.3596	0.2	0.3	0.4	0.1
			Industry concentration (C_8)	0.1246	0.1	0.2	0.5	0.2
			Asset specificity (C_9)	0.0822	0.1	0.3	0.4	0.2
			Strategic convergence (C_{10})	0.0537	0.2	0.2	0.4	0.2
	Innovation risk (B_3)	0.1305	R&D proportion of input (C_{11})	0.3772	0.4	0.3	0.2	0.1
			Conversion rate of innovation (C_{12})	0.1487	0.3	0.4	0.2	0.1
			Degree of technical imitation (C_{13})	0.0471	0.6	0.2	0.1	0.1
			Level of S & R and technology (C_{14})	0.3478	0.6	0.2	0.1	0.1
			Knowledge flowing (C_{15})	0.0792	0.5	0.3	0.1	0.1
	Environmental risk (B_4)	0.0873	Regional economic environment (C_{16})	0.5121	0.4	0.4	0.1	0.1
			Cluster cultural environment (C_{17})	0.0978	0.1	0.2	0.5	0.2
			Government policy environment (C_{18})	0.2405	0.3	0.2	0.4	0.1
			Intermediary services (C_{19})	0.0693	0.1	0.1	0.6	0.2
			Degree of competition (C_{20})	0.0804	0.4	0.4	0.1	0.1

Table 2 Classification criteria for quantitative evaluation

Evaluative values	Comment	Grading
$Xi \geq 80$	Great	E1
$70 \leq Xi < 80$	Large	E2
$60 \leq Xi < 70$	Moderate	E3
$Xi < 60$	Smaller	E4

3.2 Determining the Weight Vector of Evaluation Index

Let weight vector of B1–B4 to A be W, let weight vector of C1–C5 to B1 be W1, let weight vector of C6–C10 to B2 be W2, let weight vector of C11–C15 to B3 be W3, and let weight vector of C16–C20 to B4 be W4. The above has been obtained by using Analytic Hierarchy Process:

$$W = (0.4020, 0.3802, 0.1305, 0.0873)$$

$$W1 = (0.2043, 0.0714, 0.1243, 0.0977, 0.5024)$$

$$W2 = (0.3797, 0.3596, 0.1246, 0.0822, 0.0537)$$

$$W3 = (0.3772, 0.1487, 0.0471, 0.3478, 0.0792)$$

$$W4 = (0.5121, 0.0978, 0.2405, 0.0693, 0.0804)$$

3.3 Determining the Evaluation Matrix of Index

The determination matrix of risk assessment for the network risk of Baoji Titanium industrial cluster in Shaanxi Province is: S1 = W1R1 = (0.208, 0.304, 0.338, 0.150). Similarly, the determination matrix of Structural Risk assessment for the Baoji Titanium industrial cluster in Shaanxi Province is: S2 = W2R2 = (0.141, 0.282, 0.451, 0.126); the determination matrix of innovation risk assessment for the Baoji Titanium industrial cluster in Shaanxi Province is: S3 = W3R3 = (0.472, 0.275, 0.153, 0.100); the determination matrix of environmental risk assessment for the Baoji Titanium industrial cluster in Shaanxi Province is: S4 = W4R4 = (0.326, 0.312, 0.246, 0.116). Let the matrix: M = (S1,S2,S3,S4)T. So, the determination matrix of evaluation for the Baoji Titanium industrial cluster in Shaanxi Province is:

$$S = WM = (0.338, 0.298, 0.229, 0.135)$$

3.4 The Index Rating

The score of network risk assessment for the Baoji Titanium industrial cluster in Shaanxi Province is: VB1 = S1[40, 60, 80, 100]T = 69, which is considered as E3 grade, meaning that it is moderate; the score of structural risk assessment f is: VB2 = S2[40, 60, 80, 100]T = 71, which is considered as E2 grade, implying that it is large; the score of innovation risk assessment: VB3 = S3[40, 60, 80, 100] T = 58, which is considered as E4 grade, meaning that it is smaller; the score of environmental risk assessment: VB4 = S4[40, 60, 80, 100]T = 63, which is considered as E3 grade, indicating that it is moderate; the score of the risk assessment of Baoji Titanium industrial clusters in Baoji City, Shaanxi Province is: VA = S [40, 60, 80, 100]T = 68, which is considered as E3 level, which also means it is moderate.

4 Conclusion

The assessment results of Baoji Titanium Industrial Cluster risk shows that the network risk is “moderate,” indicating the network structure of cluster is normal, and it will not bring about a greater risk for cluster. The structural risk is “large,” indicating cluster structure is lacking flexibility, and the ability to cope with external market changes is weak. The grade of innovative risk is “large,” this shows that there exists the imitation phenomenon in the cluster, and the low proportion of R & D investment. The grade of environmental risk is “moderate,” showing that the external environment of cluster is superior; the government’s policies are well supported, intermediary services are available, and the availability of external technology is strong. Overall, the comprehensive evaluation result of Baoji Titanium Industrial Cluster is “moderate.” Evaluation results can help the industry and government to understand the development of clusters, and take corresponding countermeasures based on the risk’s size of the cluster.

Acknowledgements This paper is funded by Key Project in Shaanxi province, China: Characteristic & preponderant discipline project of philosophy and social sciences in Shaanxi Province, China. The title of the project is Research on Real Estate Economy and Management in Shaanxi Province, China.

References

Cai Ning, Yang Shuanzhu, Wu Jiebing. (2003). Research on risk of industrial clusters. China Industrial Economy, 4, 59–64.

Gao Fei, Li Kai, Liu Rui. (2008). Risk-Oriented Evaluation Based on Fuzzy Proximity for Clusters. Journal of Northeastern University (Natural Science), 12, 1787–1802.

Markusen A. (1996). Sticky places in slippery spaces: a typology of industrial districts .Economic Geography, 72(3), 293–313.

Wang Yingluo (2004). Systems Engineering. Beijing: China Machine Press.

Yin Jianhua, Xu Erpeng, Wang Zhaohua. (2009). Research on the Risk of Industrial Clusters Based on the Fuzzy Evaluation. Science & Technology Progress and Policy, 6, 122–125.

Subway System Safety Risk Analysis Based on Bayesian Network

Ying Lu, Qiming Li, and Jimmie Hinze

Abstract Subway system is associated with a high level of uncertainty because it usually operates in a dynamic environment in which technical and human and organizational malfunctions may cause possible accidents. This paper proposed a Bayesian network approach to model causal relationships among risk factors. This model explicitly represented cause and effect assumptions between variables. The method allows for multiple forms of information to be used to quantify model relationships, including formally assessed expert opinions whe quantitative data are lacking. This makes the risk and safety analysis of subway systems more functional and easier. A case study of the fire risk due to human errors during operation was used to illustrate the application of the proposed model.

Keywords Bayesian networks · Risk analysis · Safety assessment · Subway systems

1 Introduction

Characterized by large transit volume, low pollution and swiftness, subway transit can effectively bring out the overall benefit of urban transit. However, subway is a public gathering place with dense passenger flows. Some parts of the subway system are in the underground spaces where closed environments are formulated. Once accident occurs, the injuries and fatalities will be overwhelmingly disastrous. Therefore, safety risk analysis is vital to the effective operation of the subway system.

Y. Lu (✉) and Q. Li
Department of Construction Management and Real Estate, Southeast University, Nanjing, People's Republic of China
e-mail: luying_happy@126.com, njlqming@163.com

J. Hinze
M.E. Rinker, Sr. School of Building Construction, University of Florida, Gainesville, FL, USA
e-mail: hinze@ufl.edu

D.D. Wu (ed.), *Modeling Risk Management in Sustainable Construction*, Computational Risk Management, DOI 10.1007/978-3-642-15243-6_25,

Current analytical risk methods, such as fault trees, event trees, often lack the refinement to result in meaningful and relevant recommendations. Multiple causalities of known and sometimes unknown risk factors need to be analyzed in an integrated system. A Bayesian network is a random m-dimensional variable for which a structure of relationships that are frequently causal has been specified between its components. This approach is useful to complement existing methods such as Fault Tree Analysis or Probabilistic Risk Analysis.

2 Subway System Safety Analysis

The Federal Transit Administration (FTA), Office of Safety and Security formally defines a subway as follows.

"Subway is a transit mode with rail cars powered by electricity that is usually drawn from a third rail and the capacity for a heavy volume of traffic. It is characterized by high speed and rapid acceleration passenger rail cars operating singly or in multi-car trains on fixed rails; separate rights-of-way from which all other vehicular and foot traffic are excluded; sophisticated signaling; and high platform loading. It generally uses longer trains and has longer spacing between stations than light rail" [1]. Other commonly used terms for subway are Heavy Rail (HR), Rapid Rail (RR), Mass Transit Railway (MTR), and Metropolitan Railways.

According to subway incidents ever happened at U.S. from 2002 to 2008, FTA's NTD (National Transit Database) Reporting System divides the incidents into four parts, including Collisions, Derailments/Vehicles leaving roadway, Not Otherwise Classified (Personal Casualties), and Fires. In the subway incidents, the number of fire incidents is really higher than the collisions and derailments. Following, Fig. 1 shows the safety hazard occurred in subway system.

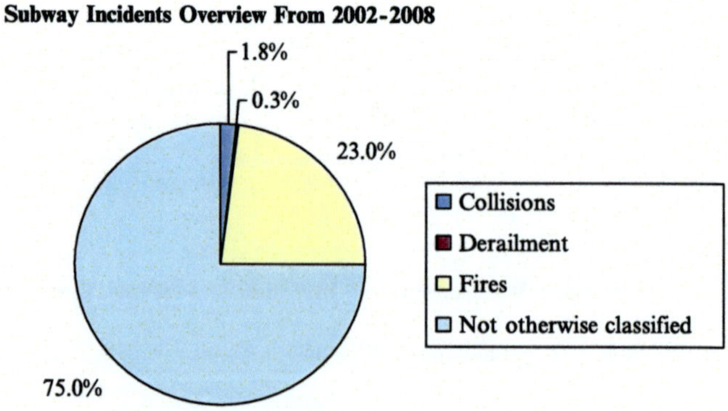

Fig. 1 The percent of safety hazard occurred in subway system

3 Bayesian Network Model

Bayesian network is a pair N = {(V, E), P}, where V and E are the nodes and the edges of a directed acyclic graph (DAG), and P is a probability distribution over V. Discrete random variables V = (X1, X2, ..., Xn) are assigned to the nodes while the edges E represent the causal probabilistic relationship among the nodes. Each node in the network is annotated with a conditional probability table (CPT) that represents the conditional probability of the variable given the values of its parents in the graph. For nodes that have no parents, the corresponding table will simply contain the prior probabilities for that variable. The principles behind Bayesian network are Bayesian statistics and concentrate on how probabilities are affected by both prior and posterior knowledge.

Conditional independence:

$$P(X_1, X_2, \dots X_n) = \prod_{i=1}^{n} P(X_i | parents(X_i)) \tag{1}$$

Joint probability:

$$P(Y = y_j, X = x_i) = P(X = x_i) \times P(Y = y_j | X = x_i) \tag{2}$$

Marginalization rule:

$$P(Y = y_j) = \sum_i P(X = x_i) \times P(Y = y_j | X = x_i) \tag{3}$$

Bayesian rule:

$$P(X = x_i | Y = y_j) = \frac{P(X = x_i) \times P(Y = y_j | X = x_i)}{P(Y = y_j)} \tag{4}$$

Using the above equations, Bayesian network inference can be conducted.

Bayesian networks have been applied in several fields, including risk analysis of military vehicles [2], modeling the operational accident causation in railway industry [3], and the reliability of search and rescue operations [4]. They have been used in modeling nuclear power plant operators' situation assessment [5]. In Aviation System Risk Model (ASRM) presented by Luxhøj [6], human factors in aviation accidents were assessed using Bayesian networks and HFACS human error framework. In 2006, utilization of Bayesian network at step 3 of Formal Safety Assessment was suggested in a document [7] submitted by the Japan body of maritime safety to the IMO Maritime Safety Committee.

4 Case Study: Fire Risk of Subway System

4.1 General Description and Bayesian Network Model Establishment

Subway system is with high risk due to the electrical fires, discarded cigarettes, igniting of stored materials and arson. In a generic scenario, subway system can fire with these reasons. The consequence of the fire varies from minor incidents to accidents that may cause personnel injury, environment pollution, and damage to the system. For demonstration purposes, this case study considers six factors: discarded cigarettes, high temperature, igniting of stuff, failure to discover, fire with subway system, and personnel injury. The causal relationships among those six factors are addressed in a way that discarded cigarettes or high temperature may cause the igniting of stuff. The igniting of stuff may cause fire with subway system and thus may cause personnel injury. The causal relationships are demonstrated in Fig. 2. The six nodes are organized by the acyclic arrows that represent the causal relationships among them. One of the most interesting questions is to find out that if there is a personnel injury observed, then in what possibility it is caused by discarded cigarettes.

4.2 Prior and Conditional Probabilities

Domain experts were asked to give judgments about the probabilities regarding all the nodes. Table 1 gives the prior probabilities of nodes X, Y, and V, respectively.

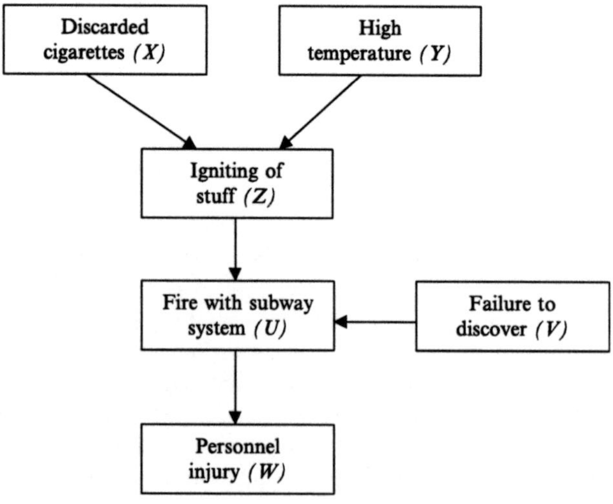

Fig. 2 A Bayesian network structure of fire risk of subway system

Table 1 The prior probabilities of node X, Y and V

X	P(X)	Y	P(Y)	V	P(V)
True	0.10	True	0.25	True	0.05
False	0.90	False	0.75	False	0.95

Table 2 The conditional occurrence probabilities of node Z and U

X	Y	P(Z = true|X,Y)	P(Z = false|X,Y)	Z	V	P (U = true|Z,V)	P(U = false|Z,V)
True	True	0.80	0.20	True	True	0.99	0.01
	False	0.50	0.50		False	0.60	0.40
False	True	0.20	0.80	False	True	0.20	0.80
	False	0.05	0.95		False	0.01	0.99

Table 3 The conditional occurrence probabilities of node W

U	P(W = true|U)	P(W = false|U)
True	0.99	0.01
False	0.20	0.80

Table 4 Sensitivity analysis results between $P(W = true)$ and $P(X = true)$, $P(Y = true)$, $P(V = true)$

No	P(X = true) P(W = true)	P(Y = true) P(W = true)	P(V = true) P(W = true)
2	0.2 **0.28768**	0.275 **0.28142**	0.055 **0.28130**

Tables 2 and 3 give conditional probabilities of nodes Z, U, and W, respectively. As shown in Table 4, there are two possible states (true or false). If X is true, it means that the errors caused by discarded cigarettes take place.

4.3 Bayesian Inference and Sensitivity Analysis

The starting point of the inference is to calculate all the marginal probabilities. The marginal probabilities of all the linguistic variables can be computed using (3). For node Z,

$$\begin{aligned} P(Z = true) &= P(X = true; Y = true; Z = true) + P(X = false; Y = true; Z = true) \\ &\quad + P(X = true; Y = false; Z = true) + P(X = false; Y = false; Z = true). \end{aligned}$$

The joint probabilities of the nodes in the Bayesian network structure are calculated through the conditional independence rule of probability using (2):

$$P(X;Y;Z) = P(X) \times P(Y|X) \times P(Z|X;Y).$$

Using conditional independence relationships as (1), the following is obtained:

$$P(X;Y;Z) = P(X) \times P(Y) \times P(Z|X;Y).$$

Hence,

$$\begin{aligned}P(Z = true) &= P(X = true) \times P(Y = true) \times P(Z = true|X = true; Y = true)\\&\quad + P(X = false) \times P(Y = true) \times P(Z = true|X = false; Y = true)\\&\quad + P(X = true) \times P(Y = false) \times P(Z = true|X = true; Y = false)\\&\quad + P(X = false) \times P(Y = false) \times P(Z = true|X = false; Y = false)\\&= 0.10 \times 0.25 \times 0.80 + 0.90 \times 0.25 \times 0.2 + 0.10 \times 0.75 \times 0.5\\&\quad + 0.90 \times 0.75 \times 0.05 = 0.13625.\end{aligned}$$

Similarly, $P(Z = false)$ can be calculated as:

$$P(Z = false) = 0.86375.$$

For node U,

$$P(U = true) = 0.10125; P(U = false) = 0.89875.$$

For node W,

$$P(W = true) = 0.27999; P(W = false) = 0.72001.$$

Bayesian network analysis can be conducted using software package HUGIN. Using HUGIN, it is possible to view the status of any given number of observations and "run" to obtain posterior probabilities (see Fig. 3).

What is really of interest, however, is how the prior probabilities change when new observations are added into the Bayesian network for a particular node. Suppose it is observed that there is personnel injury, and it is required to inference to what degree this personnel injury was caused by discarded cigarettes. This needs to calculate posterior probability $P(X = true|W = true)$. Using Bayesian rule (4), the relevant calculation is

$$P(X = true|W = true) = P(X = true; W = true)/P(W = true).$$

From Fig. 4, it can be calculated as:

$$P(X = true|W = true) = 0.17428.$$

Comparing the posterior probability $P(X = true|W = true) = 0.17428$ with prior probability $P(X = true) = 0.10$, it can be seen that there is a significant change in the occurrence likelihood of discarded cigarettes when a personnel injury accident has been observed. This might imply that node personnel injury is quite sensitive to node discarded cigarettes. To further justify the conclusion, sensitivity analysis must be conducted.

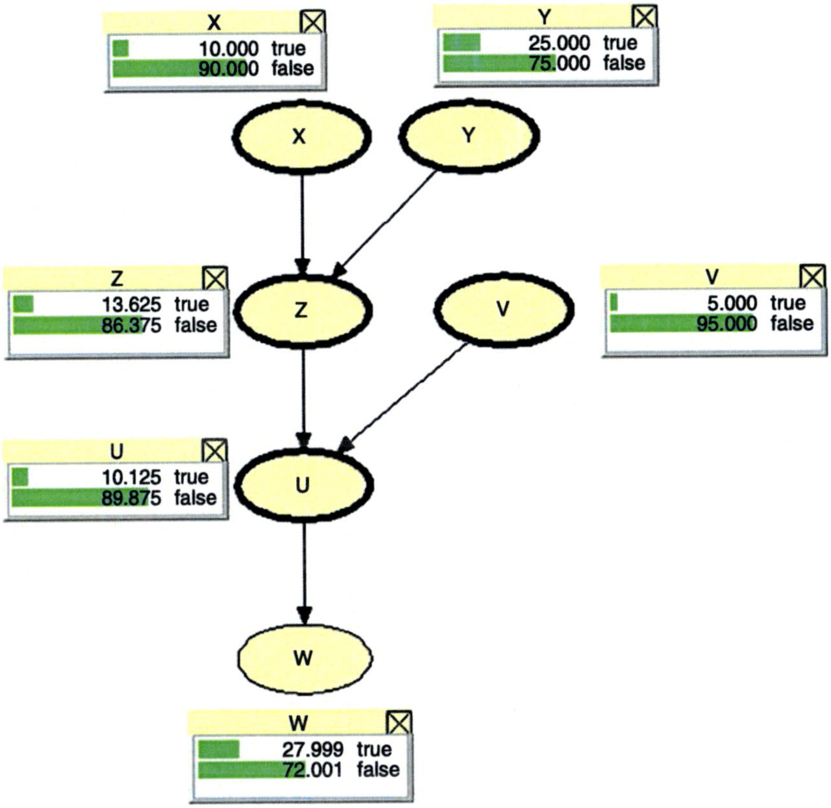

Fig. 3 Marginal probabilities

Sensitivity refers to how sensitive a model's performance is to minor changes in the input parameters. Sensitivity analysis is particularly useful in investigating the effects of inaccuracies or incompleteness in the parameters of a Bayesian network model on the model's output. The most natural way of performing sensitivity analysis is to change the values of the parameters and then, using an evidence propagation method, monitor the effects of these changes. Thus one of the most important sensitivity analysis aspects is to analyze how they change when prior probabilities take different values. The results in Table 4 were generated. As can be seen in Table 4, the values indicate that $P(W = true)$ clearly changes with $P(X = true)$. Therefore there is a reason to believe that the above conclusion is reliable.

$$P(X = true) \times (1 + 10\%) = 0.11$$

$$P(Y = true) \times (1 + 10\%) = 0.275$$

$$P(V = true) \times (1 + 10\%) = 0.055$$

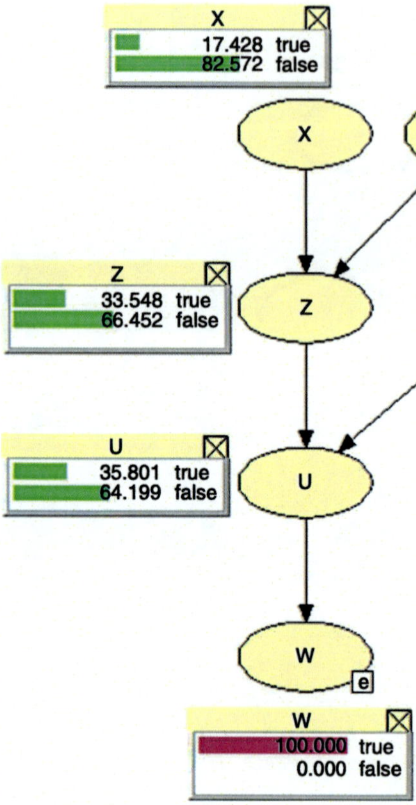

Fig. 4 Posterior probabilities

5 Conclusions

Bayesian network is a technology with huge potential for application across many domains. This paper discusses its application in subway safety risk analysis. The proposed approach uses probabilities to conduct Bayesian inference, which includes risk factor inter-relationship identification, Bayesian network model establishment, prior probability and likelihood calculation, and inference and interpretation. Based on the case study of the fire risk, it implies that node personnel injury is quite sensitive to node discarded cigarettes. So the safety managers should pay more attention to discarded cigarettes. In conclusion, the Bayesian network methodology appears to be an effective tool for explicitly addressing uncertainty and utilizing data from multiple sources.

Acknowledgments This research was supported by National Natural Science Foundation of China (50878049) and Postgraduates' Science and Innovation Foundation of Jiangsu Province.

References

1. FTA (2005) Transit Safety and Security Statistics and Analysis 2003 Annual Report (Formerly SAMIS)
2. M Neil, N Fenton, S Forey et al. (2001) Using Bayesian belief networks to predict the reliability of military vehicles. Comput Contr Eng J 12:11–20
3. W Marsh (2004) Using Bayesian Networks to Model Accident Causation in the UK Railway Industry. http://www.eecs.qmul.ac.uk/~william/PSAM7/accident_causation_PSAM7.pdf. Accessed. 4 June 2008
4. L Norrington, J Quigley, A Russell et al. (2008) Modelling the reliability of search and rescue operations with Bayesian Belief Networks. Reliab Eng Syst Saf 93:940–949
5. MC Kim, PH Seong (2006) An analytic model for situation assessment of nuclear power plant operators based on Bayesian inference. Reliab Eng Syst Saf 91:270–282
6. JT Luxhøj (2003) Probabilistic Causal Analysis for System Safety Risk Assessments in Commercial Air Transport. Proceedings of the Workshop on Investigating and Reporting of Incidents and Accidents, Williamsburg:16–19, Hampton NASA:17–38
7. International Maritime Organization (2006) Formal Safety Assessment. Consideration on utilization of Bayesian network at step 3 of FSA. Maritime Safety Committee 81st Session. IMO, London

Eco-Efficiency Assessment for the Eco-Industrial Park Based on the Emergy Analysis

Hua Shang and Jiabo Li

Abstract This paper is to evaluate the economic performance and the environmental performance of an industrial park in China based on the concept and measurement methods of "Eco-efficiency" by using Emergy analysis. And the methodology is applied to a case study of an industrial park located in Dalian. The results show that Emergy analysis is practical in evaluating the Eco-Industrial Park.

Keywords Eco-efficiency · Eco-industrial park · Emergy analysis

1 Introduction

Eco-efficiency (EE) is an important way to study sustainable development of environmental-economic system. It is a concept that stresses on the balance of economic growth, environmental protection and social equity. In the past 20 years, Eco-industrial parks (EIPs) have played an important role in Chinese economy development, however, there are few effective measures yet put in practice to evaluate and improve the Eco-performance of the industrial parks.

H. Shang (✉)
School of Management, Dalian University of Technology, Dalian 116024, People's Republic of China
e-mail: dlutshanghua@163.com

J. Li
91439 Army Unit, PLA, Dalian 116041, People's Republic of China
e-mail: lijb@163.com

D.D. Wu (ed.), *Modeling Risk Management in Sustainable Construction*, Computational Risk Management, DOI 10.1007/978-3-642-15243-6_26,

2 Issues Brought Forward

According to the traditional PDCA cycle the industrial ecologists require quantitative methods to measure and evaluate the benefits of the eco-industrial ecology [1, 2]. Many people are interested and had made some dedication to the study of performance evaluation of EIP, while most of the studies mainly focus on the setting up of the index system by the qualitative methods. And the most puzzles are: how to get the quantitative results? How to unify the different kinds of index? How to reflect the whole eco-performance of EIPs? A deficiency of industrial ecology is the lack of numerical data to support the existing theories. While Eco-efficiency is the right qualitative method by calculating a series of indicators to measure the performance from the aspects of both environment and economics.

3 Methodology

This paper focuses on the concept and measurement methods of "Eco-efficiency" to evaluate both the economic performance and the environmental performance of EIP by using Emergy analysis.

Emergy analysis, a method of system analysis, is a powerful tool to evaluate the sustainability [3], and is used for natural ecological system initially, then for agriculture, forestry, regional economical system, etc. [4]. It provides a universal measure for different kinds of energy flows in a system. It considers the historical accumulation of all the energy. Some indices based on emergy analysis are introduced to describe a system and to evaluate the sustainability of a process [5, 6].

By setting up an index system first, the index of EE are measured by the method of Emergy, and based on it, the eco-performance of the whole park can be evaluated. In this paper, normative research is combined with case study, dealing with the application of emergy analysis in EIPs, as a result, a new emergy indices system for EIPs is established, finally, the EE of Dalian Development Zone (DDZ) is measured and analyzed as a case study.

4 Emergy Flow of EIPs

Eco-Industrial Park is built as a network co-operation between processing companies, waste handling company and heat consumer, etc., where is recycling water, exchanging energy at different levels, recycling waste. And all members carry out cleaner production; treated the exhaust gas of all members can discharge to meet the national standard level [7]. In a word, the Eco-Industrial Park is an Eco-industrial system, where material is circulating, energy is cascade utilizing and waste is being minimized.

5 Emergy Analysis of EIPs

The Emergy indices system includes six indices subsystems: Emergy flow, Emergy sources, social subsystem, economical subsystem, and natural environment subsystem and sustainability indices. Compared with the industrial system, Eco-Industrial Park is an Eco-Industrial System. Emergy analysis of Eco-Industrial Park is different. An improved emergy analyzing method is introduced that can effectively consider both material circulation and energy cascade utilization in Eco-Industrial Park [7].

Emergy flow system diagram for Eco-Industrial Park is shown in Fig. 1. The diagram shows the flow of emergy among the renewable and nonrenewable resources and economy and the studied Eco-Industrial Park.

In Eco-Industrial Park, there are many energy forms including renewable such as water and air, nonrenewable such as coal, oil, metal and nonmetal mineral, commodity, services, industrial facility, labor, information, etc. and among which nonrenewable inputs are principle. The amount and scale of material circulation and energy cascade and water circulation are considerable.

Because all enterprises are operating on cleaner production in Eco-Industrial Park, the total emergy, input of the system will be increased. But the all wastes are reused for new products, both nonrenewable and renewable resources are saved,

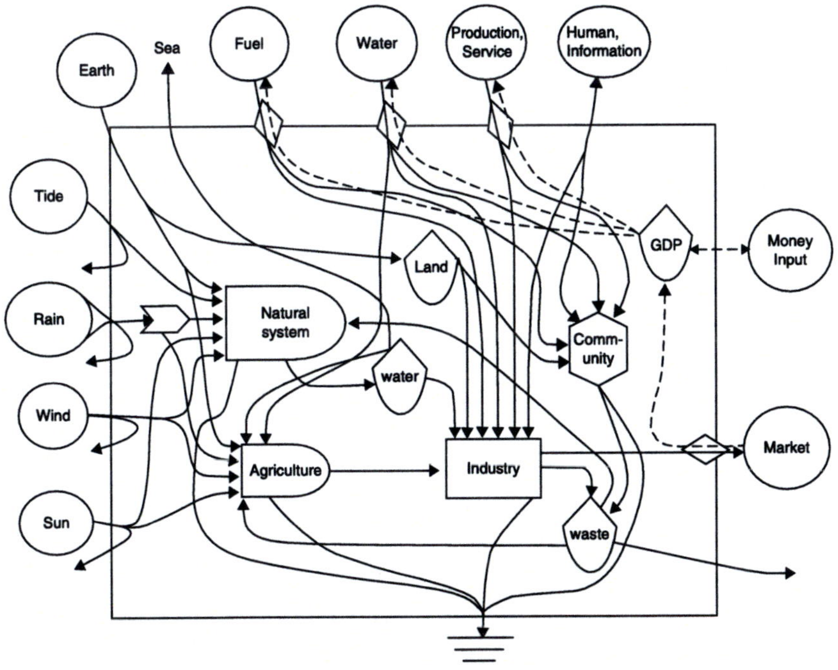

Fig. 1 Emergy flow system diagram of EIPs

and accessorial emergy will be distributed to new products. Thus, the emergy-based indices do not use for Eco-Industrial Park directly. The common contribution of members in Eco-Industrial Park should be accounted for emergy yield ratio (PEYR) and emergy investment ratio (PEIR). The following relationships can be established as (1) and (2):

$$\text{PEYR} = \frac{\sum_{i=1}^{6} Y_i}{\sum_{i=1}^{6} F_i} = \frac{\sum_{i=1}^{6} (F_i + R_i + N_i)}{\sum_{i=1}^{6} F_i} \tag{1}$$

$$\text{PEIR} = \frac{\sum_{i=1}^{6} F_i}{\sum_{i=1}^{6} (N_i + R_i)} \tag{2}$$

As renewable and nonrenewable resources are saved, emissions are reduced, and environmental loads are reduced in Eco-Industrial Park by material circulation utilization, the efficiency of energy resources utilization is raised, and energy resources are saved by energy cascade utilization. The proportion of nonrenewable resources in all inputs of EIPs is principal. Note that a traditional sustainability index is defined as (3) and (4):

$$\text{ESI} = \frac{\text{EYR}}{\text{ELR}} \tag{3}$$

$$\text{ELR} = \frac{F + N}{R} \tag{4}$$

Determining ELR and ESI, the emergy flow from renewable and nonrenewable resources must be available. However, in Eco-Industrial Park, the inputs are mostly nonrenewable, R is nearly zero. Hence, the ELR is very large. For these reason, an improved emergy environment load ratio for Eco-Industrial Park (PELR) is presented as (5) and (6):

$$\text{PELR} = \sum_{i=1}^{6} \frac{F_i}{F'} \tag{5}$$

$$\text{F}' = \text{F}'1 + \text{F}'2 + \text{F}'3 + \text{N}'4 + \text{F}'5 + \text{R}'6 \tag{6}$$

We define:

- F′1 is the improved economic benefit by electricity load stability.
- F′2 is the saved energy of high consumption energy user is power supplied lower cost.
- F′3 is the improved benefit of economy, environment and society by energy cascade utilization.
- N′4 is the saved nonrenewable and its treatment fee by utilizing the by-production.
- F′5 is the saved energy resources.

- R′6 is the saved renewable resources and punish fee of reusing waste water treated by waste water plant.

The above items show that the inputs of Eco-Industrial Park are decreased by material circulation and energy cascade utilization. The PELR is lower if F′ is bigger, and it is because the efficiency of material circulation and energy cascade utilization are advanced.

But also, F′ in index PELR to a general industrial system with waste reuse and recycle only, it is (7):

$$\mathrm{F}' = \mathrm{N}'4 + \mathrm{R}'6 \tag{7}$$

Accordingly, a new index of sustainability for Eco-Industrial Park (PESI) is defined as (8):

$$\mathrm{PESI} = \frac{\mathrm{PEYR}}{\mathrm{PELR}} \tag{8}$$

6 Case Study

Dalian Development Zone (DDZ) is a state-level Economic and Technological Development Area, an Eco-industrial park, located on the perimeter of Dalian's urban core, sitting on a 220-square kilometer land. It was the first such zone to be authorized by the State Council of China in 1984, and it has provided an excellent base to many overseas investors [8]. The basic data for DDZ in 2006 are shown in Table 1.

The emergy of DDZ was calculated by using formula (3) and (4) and (6). The results are shown in Table 2, showing that the PESI are higher, and the PELR are lower in DDZ, mainly due to the material circulation and energy cascade utilization.

7 Summary

An indices system of emergy analysis are presented in this paper, to deal with the application of emergy analysis of EIPs for Eco-efficiency evaluation The sustainability of Eco-Industrial Park may be improved by increasing the PEYR and decreasing the PELR. According to the study, we can conclude that the environmental load is high in DDZ, and the sustainability is relatively low. Meanwhile the emergy analysis of DDZ shows that new emergy indices we set up are practical in evaluating the Eco-system. Based on it, advice should be given separately at three level: corporations, inter-corporation (the whole park) and the government.

Table 1 Data of emergy transfering for DDZ (2006)

Item	Basic data	Transformity ratio (sej/unit)	Solar transformity (sej)
Emergy of the renewable resource			
1. Sunlight (J)	2.93E + 17	1.00E + 00/J	2.93E + 17
2. Wind energy (J)	3.88E + 14	6.63E + 02/J	2.57E + 17
3. Rain potential energy (J)	1.18E + 12	8.88E + 02/J	1.05E + 15
4. Rainwater chemical energy (J)	1.70E + 14	1.54E + 04/J	2.62E + 18
5. Tidal energy (J)	8.66E + 14	2.36E + 04/J	2.04E + 19
6. Wave energy (J)	6.06E + 16	2.59E + 04/J	1.57E + 21
7. Earth cycle energy (J)	7.25E + 13	2.90E + 04/J	2.10E + 18
Subtotal			1.60E + 21
Emergy of renewable resources of local products			
1. Food (J)	9.37E + 13	8.30E + 04/J	7.78E + 18
2. Fruit (J)	1.01E + 13	5.30E + 04/J	5.35E + 17
3. Vegetable (J)	8.02E + 13	2.70E + 04/J	2.16E + 17
4. Seafood (J)	6.70E + 14	1.71E + 06/J	1.15E + 21
5. Meat (J)	7.14E + 12	1.71E + 06/J	1.22E + 19
Subtotal			1.17E + 21
Emergy of non-renewable resources	0		0
Input emergy			
1. Non-renewable resource input			
①. Water (J)	1.14E + 14	4.10E + 04/J	4.67E + 18
②. Electric (J)	6.04E + 15	1.60E + 05/J	9.66E + 20
③. Coal (J)	1.64E + 16	3.98E + 04/J	6.53E + 20
④. Fuel oil (J)	4.72E + 15	6.60E + 04/J	3.11E + 20
⑤. Fuel gas (J)	2.09E + 16	6.60E + 04/J	1.38E + 21
Subtotal			33.15E + 20
2. Money flow ($)			
①.Other commodities, raw material inputs ($)	4.84E + 09	8.67E + 12/J	4.20E + 22
②. Fixed investment ($)	7.01E + 08	8.67E + 12/J	6.08E + 21
③.The actual use of foreign investment ($)	5.98E + 08	8.67E + 12/J	5.18E + 21
3. Labor input (person)	7.00E + 04	1.55E + 17/p	1.09E + 22
Subtotal			6.75E + 22
Emergy of non-renewable output			
Gross industrial output value ($)	7.23E + 09	8.67E + 12/$	6.27E + 22
Emergy of waste			
1. Wastewater (J)	8.30E + 13	6.60E + 05/J	5.45E + 19
2. Solid waste (g)	2.08E + 11	1.50E + 08/g	3.12E + 19
Subtotal			8.57E + 19
Comprehensive utilization of waste product value ($)	9.07E + 06	8.67E + 12/$	7.86E + 19
Emergy of imports and exports			
1. Import ($)	3.00E + 09	8.67E + 12/$	2.60E + 22
2. Exports ($)	3.60E + 09	1.45E + 13/$	5.22E + 22

Table 2 Results of the emergy analysis of DDZ

Indices	PEYR	PEIR	PELR	PESI
Data	2.78	0.61	3.67	0.76

Acknowledgements Supported by the Young Scientists Fund of the National Natural Science Foundation of China (Grant No. 70903010), the Specialized Research Fund for the Doctoral Program of Higher Education (Grant No. 20090041120048), and the Doctoral Research Starting Foundation of Liao Ning Province (Grant No. 20081094).

References

1. Pekka, J. Korhonen, Mikulas, Luptacik. Eco-efficiency Analysis of Power Plants: An Extension of Data Envelopment Analysis[J]. European Journal of Operational Research, Vol. 154 (2004): 437–446
2. Morales, M.A., Herrero, V.M., Martinez, S.A., Rodriguez, M.G., Valdivieso, Cleaner Production and Methodological Proposal of Eco-efficiency Measurement in a Mexican Petrochemical Complex[J]. Water Science and Technology, Vol. 153(11) (2006): 11–16
3. Helminen, R. Developing Tangible Measures for Eco-efficiency: The Case of the Finnish and Swedish Pulp and Paper Industry[J]. Business Strategy and Environment, Vol. 9 (2000): 196–210
4. Park, J., Haemyung, Ok., Kyounghoon, Cha., Tak, Hur. Tackling Challenges in Measuring and Communicating Eco-efficiency[C]. Proceedings of the 2006 IEEE International Symposium on Electronics and the Environment, Vol. 8 (2006): 58–72
5. Cote, R., Aaron, Booth., Bertha, Louis. Eco-efficiency and SMEs in Nova Scotia, Canada[J]. Journal of Cleaner Production, Vol. 14 (2006): 542–550
6. Paul, Ekins. Eco-efficiency: Motives, Drivers, and Economic Implications[J]. Journal of Industrial Ecology, Vol. 9(4) (2005): 12–14
7. Shang Hua. 2005, Ecological Performance Assessment of Industrial Parks based on the Measurement of Eco-efficiency, Leipzig Annual Civil Engineering Report., Vol. 10 (2005), 437–443
8. Tian L., Wu C.Y., Geng. The Study on the Eco-efficiency of Industrial Park, Journal of Dalian University of Technology (2006), 36–39

The Study of Green Risk Assessment for Construction Project Based on "AHP–FCE" Method

Danfeng Xie, Shurong Guo, and Sulei Li

Abstract This article presents the concept of the green risk assessment for construction project. Combined with "Green Construction Guidelines" issued by quondam Ministry of Construction (MOC), a green risk evaluation index system is established. Besides, a "AHP–FCE" model is made. First, the index weight of ordering in single level is determined with the use of Analytic Hierarchy Process (AHP). Second, the green risk rank of construction project is assessed with the use of Fuzzy Comprehensive Evaluation (FCE) method. A case-study proves that the evaluation model has a certain practical application worth, and aims at promoting the theoretical research of green risk evaluation for construction project.

Keywords Analytic hierarchy process (AHP) · Construction project · Fuzzy comprehensive evaluation (FCE) · Green risk · Ordering in single level

1 Introduction

In recent years, with the implement of the Sustainable Development Strategy and green construction, the concept of green risk is attracting more and more attention from the construction industry. However, the research on this aspect is still at its elementary stage. Moreover, most of the study is qualitative analysis rather than quantitative analysis. Combined with the document No. 223 of "Green Construction Guidelines" issued by quondam Ministry of Construction (MOC) in 2007, the concept of green risk is proposed. It aims to establish the green risk evaluation system and seek a more appropriate method of assessing risk.

D. Xie (✉), S. Guo, and S. Li
Shandong University of Technology, Zibo, Shandong 255049, People's Republic of China
e-mail: xiedanfeng2001@126.com, zbshur@sina.com, lsulei@163.com

D.D. Wu (ed.), *Modeling Risk Management in Sustainable Construction*, Computational Risk Management, DOI 10.1007/978-3-642-15243-6_27,

2 The Concept of Green Risk in Construction Project

Risk is the uncertainty of some losses. For the construction project, it refers to the negative impact on construction engineering. Compared with other risks, the distinctive feature of green risk concept lies in the word "green". This concept is closely related to the ultimate goal of sustainable development of humankind. That is to say, to reduce environment pollution, reduce the consumption of resources and reduce consumption of energy (3R goals) [1]. Thus, the green risk in construction project is defined like this: it is the uncertainty of various factors contributing to the goal (3R goals) of sustainable development of human being.

3 The Establishment of the Green Risk Evaluation System for Construction Project

Combined with the "General Framework of Green Construction" in the document No. 223 of "Green Construction Guidelines" issued by quondam Ministry of Construction (MOC) in 2007 and based on the "3R" concept, the green risk evaluation system for construction project is established, which takes the construction of ZiBo Century Garden Residential District in Shan Dong as a case. The system is shown in Fig. 1, it contains Destination level, Principle level, Sub-principle level.

4 "AHP–FCE" Model of Green Risk

4.1 Index Weight of Ordering in Single Level is Determined with the Use of AHP Model

AHP, that is Analytic Hierarchy Process, it is a decision-making method which can combine qualitative analysis with quantitative analysis together. Its theory can be referenced at literature [2]. Based on a case of construction engineering, index weight of ordering in single level is determined with the use of AHP method, calculation steps go like this:

1. Establish hierarchical structure, destination level, principle level and sub-principle level both are shown in Fig. 1.
2. Set up judgment matrix with the adoption of "nineth level method", calculate the maximum eigenvalue (λ_{max}) and its eigenvector (W) with the use of square root method, W_i is each index weight. They are shown in Table 1. In Table 1, the row of judgment matrix is n, it is the number of index in each level of sub-hierarchy; the judgment matrix is A, AW is the vector obtained as multiplying A by W.

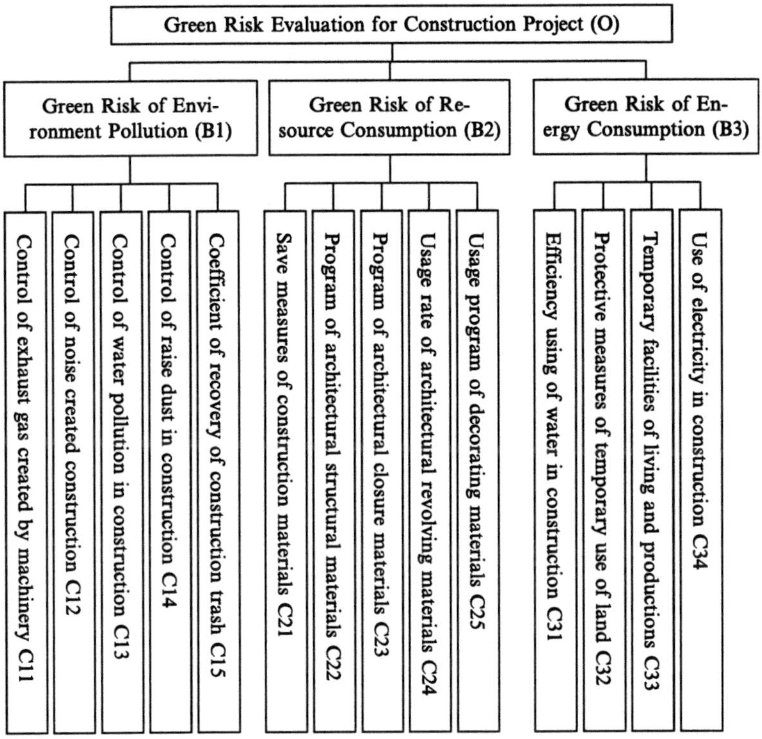

Fig. 1 Green risk evaluation system of construction project

Table 1 O–B index weight with the use of square root method

O	B1	B2	B3	$M=\prod M_{ij}$	$W_i' = \sqrt[n]{M}$	$W_i=W_i'/\sum W_i'$	$(AW)_i$	$(AW)_i/W_i$
B1	1	2	4	8.000	2.000	0.558	1.686	3.019
B2	1/2	1	3	1.500	1.145	0.320	0.965	3.018
B3	1/4	1/3	1	0.083	0.437	0.122	0.368	3.018
–	–	–	–	Total $\sum$	3.582	1.000	–	9.055

From Table 1, as to green risk assessment for construction project, in principle level, the index weight of green risk of environment pollution (B1), resource consumption (B2) and energy consumption (B3) respectively go like this: $W^{O-B} = (0.558, 0.320, 0.122)$.

3. Consistency test of ordering in single level.

By using of square root method, the maximum eigenvalue is obtained, that is:

$$\lambda_{\max} = \frac{1}{n}\sum_{i=1}^{n}\frac{(AW)_i}{W_i} = \frac{1}{3} \times 9.055 = 3.018 \tag{1}$$

Consistency index is:

$$CI = \frac{\lambda_{max} - n}{n - 1} = \frac{3.018 - 3}{3 - 1} = 0.009 \quad (2)$$

Random consistency rate is:

$$CR = \frac{CI}{RI} = \frac{0.009}{0.58} = 0.015771 \quad (3)$$

RI is average random consistency index, when n is taken as 3, 4, 5, RI is taken 0.58, 0.89, 1.15 correspondingly. The judgment matrix is satisfactory when CR $\leq$ 0.1.

Similarly, each index in sub-principle can be ordering in single level, index weight can be determined, random consistency rate can also be confirmed. Calculating process is omitted. Results are shown in Table 2.

From Table 2, the index weight belonged to B1 are: W^{B1-C1} = (0.039, 0.202, 0.069, 0.155, 0.535), belonged to B2 are: W^{B2-C2} = (0.042, 0.277, 0.440, 0.161, 0.080), belonged to B3 are: W^{B3-C3} = (0.212, 0.099, 0.638, 0.050). Due to all the random consistency rates are less than 0.1, so all the judgment matrix are satisfactory.

4.2 *Green Risk Rank is Confirmed with the Use of FCE Model*

Due to the accumulation of inconsistencies of various levels, the disorder will arise when they are ordered. Therefore, the overall ordering will not be done. Instead, based on the ordering in single level, the membership grade of risks at various levels will be confirmed with the adoption of Fuzzy Comprehensive Evaluation model. Furthermore, the green risk rank will be confirmed through fuzzy transformation. Definite steps go like this:

1. Determine factors set (U). They are shown in Fig. 1.
2. Establish evaluation set (V). According to green construction measures, in the green risk evaluation system, all factors' green risk can be evaluated. The better the green construction measures are, the lower the green risk is. Green construction measures can be divided into five grades, evaluation set is defined as V′, V′ = {worse, bad, general, good, better}. Correspondingly, green risk evaluation set is defined as V, V = {higher, high, general, low, lower}, the five grades is assigned as V = {5, 4, 3, 2, 1}.

Table 2 B–C index weight of ordering in single level and consistency check

B1–C1	C11	C12	C13	C14	C15	λ_{max} = 5.332; CI = 0.083; CR=0.074
	0.039	0.202	0.069	0.155	0.535	
B2–C2	C21	C22	C23	C24	C25	λ_{max} = 5.333; CI=0.083; CR = 0.074
	0.042	0.277	0.440	0.161	0.080	
B3–C3	C31	C32	C33	C34		$\lambda_{ma}x$ = 4.240; CI = 0.080; CR=0.090
	0.212	0.099	0.638	0.050		

3. Confirm weight set (W). It is shown in Tables 1 and 2.
4. Create single-factor fuzzy evaluation matrix. According to the practical experience in construction or expert evaluation, a fuzzy mapping can be obtained from factors set to evaluation set, it expresses the membership grade of a factor to a risk evaluation rank [3], it is shown in Table 3.

   From Table 3, a membership grade matrix is obtained as a fuzzy matrix for evaluating green risk.
5. First degree of fuzzy evaluation for green risk ("×" expresses matrix multiplication).

   According to experts' judgment for the construction of ZiBo Century Garden Residential District in Shan Dong, as to these index belonged to green risk of environment pollution, their measures of green construction are judged in Table 4.

   From Table 4, a fuzzy evaluation matrix is obtained, it is defined as $R^{B1\text{–}C1}$:

$$R^{B1-C1} = \begin{bmatrix} R_3 \\ R_1 \\ R_4 \\ R_2 \\ R_3 \end{bmatrix} = \begin{bmatrix} 0 & 0.25 & 0.5 & 0.25 & 0 \\ 0 & 0 & 0 & 0.3 & 0.7 \\ 0.25 & 0.5 & 0.25 & 0 & 0 \\ 0 & 0 & 0.25 & 0.5 & 0.25 \\ 0 & 0.25 & 0.5 & 0.25 & 0 \end{bmatrix} \tag{4}$$

Table 3 Table of fuzzy mapping

Evaluation (measures of green construction)	Fuzzy mapping (membership grade of green risk rank)					Expressions for membership grade of green risk rank	Transform (R_i)
	Higher (5)	High (4)	General (3)	Low (2)	Lower (1)		
Worse	0.7	0.3	0	0	0	Mostly belongs to higher green risk Rank 5	R_5
Bad	0.25	0.5	0.25	0	0	Mostly belongs to high green risk Rank 4	R_4
General	0	0.25	0.5	0.25	0	Mostly belongs to general green risk Rank 3	R_3
Good	0	0	0.25	0.5	0.25	Mostly belongs to low green risk Rank 2	R_2
Better	0	0	0	0.3	0.7	Mostly belongs to lower green risk Rank 1	R_1

Table 4 Fuzzy mapping of green risk for environment pollution

B1–C1		W^{B1-C1}	Evaluation	Higher	High	General	Low	Lower	Transform (R_i)
Green risk of environment pollution (B1)	C11	0.039	General	0	0.25	0.5	0.25	0	R_3
	C12	0.202	Better	0	0	0	0.3	0.7	R_1
	C13	0.069	Bad	0.25	0.5	0.25	0	0	R_4
	C14	0.155	Good	0	0	0.25	0.5	0.25	R_2
	C15	0.535	General	0	0.25	0.5	0.25	0	R_3

Define P^{B1-C1} as the fuzzy evaluation set of green risk rank of environment pollution (B1)

$$P^{B1-C1} = W^{B1-C1} \times R^{B1-C1}$$

$$= [0.039 \quad 0.202 \quad 0.069 \quad 0.155 \quad 0.535] \times \begin{bmatrix} 0 & 0.25 & 0.5 & 0.25 & 0 \\ 0 & 0 & 0 & 0.3 & 0.7 \\ 0.25 & 0.5 & 0.25 & 0 & 0 \\ 0 & 0 & 0.25 & 0.5 & 0.25 \\ 0 & 0.25 & 0.5 & 0.25 & 0 \end{bmatrix}$$

$$= [0.017 \quad 0.178 \quad 0.343 \quad 0.282 \quad 0.180] \tag{5}$$

Implications are: the membership grade of green risk of environment pollution (B1) to higher green risk Rank 5 is 1.7%, while it is 17.8% to high green risk Rank 4, 34.3% to general green risk Rank 3, 28.2% to low green risk Rank 2 and 18.0% to lower green risk Rank 1.

Similarly, the fuzzy evaluation set of green risk rank of resource consumption (B2) is obtained, defined as P^{B2-C2}, and the fuzzy evaluation set of green risk rank of energy consumption (B3) is also obtained, defined as P^{B3-C3}, they are shown in formula (6), formula (7).

$$P^{B2-C2} = W^{B2-C2} \times R^{B2-C2}$$

$$= [0.042 \quad 0.277 \quad 0.440 \quad 0.161 \quad 0.080] \times \begin{bmatrix} 0.25 & 0.5 & 0.25 & 0 & 0 \\ 0 & 0.25 & 0.5 & 0.25 & 0 \\ 0 & 0 & 0.25 & 0.5 & 0.25 \\ 0 & 0 & 0 & 0.3 & 0.7 \\ 0 & 0.25 & 0.5 & 0.25 & 0 \end{bmatrix}$$

$$= [0.010 \quad 0.110 \quad 0.299 \quad 0.358 \quad 0.223] \tag{6}$$

$$P^{B3-C3} = W^{B3-C3} \times R^{B3-C3}$$

$$= [0.212 \quad 0.099 \quad 0.638 \quad 0.050] \times \begin{bmatrix} 0.25 & 0.5 & 0.25 & 0 & 0 \\ 0 & 0 & 0.25 & 0.5 & 0.25 \\ 0 & 0.25 & 0.5 & 0.25 & 0 \\ 0 & 0 & 0 & 0.3 & 0.7 \end{bmatrix}$$

$$= [0.053 \quad 0.266 \quad 0.397 \quad 0.224 \quad 0.060] \tag{7}$$

6. Second degree of fuzzy evaluation for green risk
   The above $P^{B1\text{–}C1}$, $P^{B2\text{–}C2}$, $P^{B3\text{–}C3}$ compose the fuzzy complex evaluation matrix (R):

$$R = \left[P^{B1-C1} \quad P^{B2-C2} \quad P^{B3-C3}\right]^T = \begin{bmatrix} 0.017 & 0.178 & 0.343 & 0.282 & 0.180 \\ 0.010 & 0.110 & 0.299 & 0.358 & 0.223 \\ 0.053 & 0.266 & 0.397 & 0.224 & 0.060 \end{bmatrix} \tag{8}$$

Thus, fuzzy evaluation for green risk of the construction of ZiBo Century Garden Residential District can be done. Define $P^{O\text{–}B}$ as fuzzy evaluation set of green risk rank in Destination Level.

$$P^{O-B} = W^{O-B} \times R = [0.558 \ \ 0.320 \ \ 0.122] \times \begin{bmatrix} 0.017 & 0.178 & 0.343 & 0.282 & 0.180 \\ 0.010 & 0.110 & 0.299 & 0.358 & 0.223 \\ 0.053 & 0.266 & 0.397 & 0.224 & 0.060 \end{bmatrix}$$

$$= [0.019 \ \ 0.167 \ \ 0.336 \ \ 0.299 \ \ 0.179] \tag{6}$$

Implications are: in the construction of ZiBo Century Garden Residential District, the membership grade to higher green risk Rank 5 is 1.9%, while to high green risk Rank 4 is 16.7%, to general green risk Rank 3 is 33.6%, to low green risk Rank 2 is 29.9%, to lower green risk Rank 1 is 17.9%.

According to the principle of maximum membership degree, green risk rank can be confirmed. Take the maximum index, its corresponding evaluation set is the result. Due to max {0.019, 0.167, 0.336, 0.299, 0.179} = 0.336, the maximum value is the membership grade of general green risk Rank 3, so in the construction of ZiBo Century Garden Residential District, its green risk rank is general green risk Rank 3.

7. Calculate green risk degree.

Define v as green risk degree; It is the quantitative expression of green risk rank. It is shown in formula (10)

$$\begin{aligned} v &= P^{O-B} \times V^T = [p_1 \quad p_2 \quad p_3 \quad p_4 \quad p_5] \times [5 \quad 4 \quad 3 \quad 2 \quad 1]^T \\ &= [0.019 \quad 0.167 \quad 0.336 \quad 0.299 \quad 0.179] \times [5 \quad 4 \quad 3 \quad 2 \quad 1]^T = 2.548 \end{aligned} \tag{10}$$

The green risk degree is 2.548, it implies that in the construction of ZiBo Century Garden Residential District, its green risk rank is Degree 2.548.

5 Conclusions

AHP is an evaluation system combined qualitative and quantitative method under the guidance of many principles. Because the overall ordering of all levels will be blurred with the accumulation of inconsistencies of various levels, the Analytic Hierarchy Process (AHP) method and Fuzzy Comprehensive Evaluation (FCE) method is combined, then the index weight of order in single level is determined with the use of AHP. On the basis of the analysis, every factor will be evaluated and the green risk level in construction business will be determined with the use of fuzzy transformation. This evaluation system overcomes the inconsistencies of overall ordering with the use of AHP method and can get a more practical green risk grade. The data will be useful for the analysis and assessment of green risk. But the selection of the index of green risk for the construction business leaves much room for improvement.

References

1. Zhou Fang et al. (2009), The Management of the Green Risk of Construction Project [J]. Construction and Design for Project: p. 136 (in Chinese)
2. Du Nan (2006). Study on Green Building Assessment and Green Construction Assessment [D]. Wuhan: Huazhong University of Science and Technology (in Chinese)
3. Hong Feng (2009) Green Construction Assessment of Pile Foundation Based on Fuzzy Comprehensive Evaluation [J], Journal of Kunming University of Science and Technology (Science and Technology), 34(4): p. 50 (in Chinese)

Intensive Land Use Evaluation of Urban Development Zones: A Case Study of Xi'an National Hi-Tech Industrial Development Zone in China

Wei Xiao and Qingqi Wei

Abstract The degree of intensive land use is of great significance to urban planning and urban development. In order to evaluate the intensive land use level of Xi'an National Hi-tech Industrial Development Zone in China, this paper chooses 16 indexes according to Intensive Land Use Evaluation Protocols of Development Zones. The 16 indexes are divided into 3 categories: (1) land use condition; (2) land output efficiency; (3) land management performance. The weights of indexes are determined by using Delphi method. On the basis of calculation of indexes' actual value, ideal value, and the degree of realization, the score of the intensive land use level of Xi'an National Hi-tech Industrial Development Zone is obtained, which is 96.44%, and the scores of the three objectives are as follows: land use condition is 96.41%, land output efficiency is 96.90%, land management performance is 95.73%. The scores of the three objectives are higher and balanced, which indicates a significant intensive land use level of Xi'an National Hi-tech Industrial Development Zone in China.

1 Introduction

Currently, the shortage of land resources has become a major constraint factor to the development of Chinese economy [1]. With the rapid development of Chinese urbanization, utilization of urban land increases rapidly [2, 3]. So, the development mode of Chinese economy should turn from extensive to intensive. Urban development zone is an important part of the city, and the efficiency of land resources development and utilization is the basis of the development zone [4, 5]. Urban

W. Xiao (✉)
Chongqing Jiaotong University, Chongqing, People's Republic of China
e-mail: xiao98612343@163.com
Q. Wei
Chongqing Jiaotong University, Chongqing, People's Republic of China
Northwestern Polytechnical University, Xi'an, People's Republic of China
e-mail: weiqingqi@163.com

D.D. Wu (ed.), *Modeling Risk Management in Sustainable Construction*,
Computational Risk Management, DOI 10.1007/978-3-642-15243-6_28,

development zone can promote the growth of regional economy; however, there are also a waste of land, capital precipitation and range of social and ecological problems. Researches on intensive land use potential of development zone has important theoretical and practical significance on urban planning and urban development [6].

In order to evaluate the intensive land use level of Xi'an National Hi-tech Industrial Development Zone in China, this paper chooses 16 indexes according to *Intensive Land Use Evaluation Protocols of Development Zones*. The 16 indexes are divided into 3 categories: (1) land use condition; (2) land output efficiency; (3) land management performance. The weights of indexes are determined by using Delphi method. On the basis of calculation of indexes' actual value, ideal value, and the degree of realization, we get the score of the intensive land use level of Xi'an National Hi-tech Industrial Development Zone in China, and present an objective assessment to the development zone.

2 Evaluation Index System

In this paper, intensive land use evaluation index system comes from *Intensive Land Use Evaluation Protocols of Development Zones* established by Ministry of Land and Resources of the People's Republic of China. The evaluation index system contains three levels, which are objective, sub-objective, and index. The level of objective includes three items: land use condition, land output efficiency, and land management performance. The level of sub-objective includes six items: degree of land development, structural condition of land use, land use intensity, input–output efficiency of industrial land, regulation performance of land use, and the degree of marketization of land supply. The level of index includes 16 items, such as the rate of land development, the rate of industrial land, general floor-area ratio, the intensity of industrial investment in fixed assets, the rate of land disposal for maturity project, the rate of compensative land use, etc.

Delphi method is adopted to determine the weights of objectives, sub-objectives, and indexes. Based on scale construction and questionnaire investigation, 12 corporations and institutions are surveyed, including Department of Land and Resources of Shaanxi Province, Bureau of Land and Resources of Xi'an National Hi-tech Industrial Development Zone, Xi'an National Hi-tech Industrial Development Zone Administration, Domestic Investment Promotion Agency of Xi'an National Hi-tech Industrial Development Zone, Asia-Pacific Investment Promotion Agency of Xi'an National Hi-tech Industrial Development Zone, Investment Service Agency of Xi'an National Hi-tech Industrial Development Zone, Bureau of Finance of Xi'an National Hi-tech Industrial Development Zone Administration, Shaanxi Huadi Real Estate Appraisal and Consulting Co., Ltd., Zhenghe Real Estate Appraisal Co., Ltd., etc. In the survey, 30 questionnaires are sent out, and 27 pieces of effective data are received, response rate is 90%.

Table 1 Evaluation index system and the weights

Objectives (weight)	Sub-objectives (weight)	Indexes (weight)
Land use condition (0.42)	Degree of land development (0.29)	The rate of land development (0.39)
		The rate of land supply (0.30)
		The rate of land construction completed (0.31)
	Structural condition of land use (0.29)	The rate of industrial land (0.49)
		The rate of Hi-tech industrial land (0.51)
	Land use intensity (0.42)	General floor-area ratio (0.27)
		Building density (0.25)
		General floor-area ratio of industrial land (0.26)
		Building density of industrial land (0.22)
Land output efficiency (0.37)	Input–output efficiency of industrial land (1.00)	The intensity of industrial investment in fixed assets (0.31)
		Output intensity of industrial land (0.32)
		Output intensity of Hi-tech industrial land (0.37)
Land management performance (0.21)	Regulation performance of land use (0.57)	The rate of land disposal for maturity project (0.42)
		The rate of idle land disposal (0.58)
	The degree of marketization of land supply (0.43)	The rate of compensative land use (0.53)
		The rate of land transfer by using bidding, auction and listing (0.47)

According to the sample data, the weights of objectives, sub-objectives and indexes are calculated. Evaluation index system and the weights are shown in Table 1.

3 Data and Calculation Results

3.1 Actual Value of Indexes

With the help of several related institutions in Xi'an National Hi-tech Industrial Development Zone, the initial data of indexes are collected, and the actual values of indexes are computed after compiling. The results are shown in Table 2.

3.2 Ideal Value of Indexes

There are two steps to determine the ideal values of indexes:

1. The initial ideal values are obtained from expert survey. By using questionnaire investigation, 27 pieces of effective data are gained, and the average values are considered as the initial ideal values.
2. For the significant difference between the initial ideal values and the actual values, it is obviously unreasonable. So, on the basis of the initial ideal values,

Table 2 Actual value, ideal value, and degree of realization

Index	Actual value	Ideal value	Degree of realization
The rate of land development	86.48%	89.89%	96.21%
The rate of land supply	99.61%	100%	99.61%
The rate of land construction completed	98.90%	100%	98.90%
The rate of industrial land	29.61%	32.00%	92.53%
The rate of Hi-tech industrial land	18.07%	19.53%	92.52%
General floor-area ratio	1.75	1.78	98.31%
Building density	38.27%	39%	98.13%
General floor-area ratio of industrial land	1.12	1.15	97.39%
Building density of industrial land	36.50%	37%	98.65%
The intensity of industrial investment in fixed assets	5144.54 [10^4Yuan/ha]	5398.83 [10^4Yuan/ha]	95.29%
Output intensity of industrial land	23292.34 [10^4Yuan/ha]	24559.97 [10^4Yuan/ha]	94.84%
Output intensity of Hi-tech industrial land	35721.39 [10^4Yuan/ha]	32197.48 [10^4Yuan/ha]	100%
The rate of land disposal for maturity project	100%	100%	100%
The rate of idle land disposal	100%	100%	100%
The rate of compensative land use	61.55%	65.00%	94.69%
The rate of land transfer by using bidding, auction and listing	27.94%	32.71%	85.42%

some forecasting models, including Auto-Regressive Model, Moving Average Model, ARIMA Model, are adopted to forecast the ideal values.

Finally, a set of reasonable ideal values are achieved. The results are shown in Table 2.

3.3 Degree of Realization

The standardized values of indexes are calculated by using ratio estimation method, the measurement indicator is the score of degree of realization. The calculation method is shown in (1).

$$S_{ijk} = \frac{X_{ijk}}{T_{ijk}} \times 100\% \tag{1}$$

where S_{ijk} is the score of objective i, sub-objective j and index k; $X_{ijk}$is the actual value of objective i, sub-objective j and index k; T_{ijk} is the ideal value of objective i, sub-objective j and index k.

According to *Intensive Land Use Evaluation Protocols of Development Zones*, the score of degree of realization should be between 0 and 100%. If the score is more than 100%, it should be recorded as 100%. The score of each index is shown in Table 2.

3.4 Intensive Land Use Evaluation and Analysis

By using above methods, the score of degree of realization for the three levels (objectives, sub-objectives, indexes) can be calculated, and the general score of intensive land use in Xi'an National Hi-tech Industrial Development Zone can also be obtained. The results are shown in Table 3.

Table 3 shows that the general score of intensive land use in Xi'an National Hi-tech Industrial Development Zone is 96.44%, and the scores of the three objectives are higher and balanced, which indicates a significant intensive land use level of the development zone.

In particular, the second objective, land output efficiency, shows an outstanding performance with a score of 96.90%. Especially for the index of output intensity of Hi-tech industrial land, whose actual value exceeds the ideal value under the "Eleventh 5-Year Plan" of Xi'an National Hi-tech Industrial Development Zone. The score of the intensity of industrial investment in fixed assets is 95.29%, the actual value is 51.4454 million yuan/ha, the ideal value is 53.9883 million yuan/ha, and the difference is 2.5429 million yuan/ha. The score of output intensity of industrial land is 94.84%, the actual value is 232.9234 million yuan/ha, the ideal value is 245.5997 million yuan/ha, and the difference is 12.6763 million yuan/ha.

The first objective, land use condition, is also better, which get a score of 96.41%. The scores of its two sub-objectives, degree of land development and land use intensity, are greater than 98%. In its nine indexes, the two lowest scores are the rate of industrial land and the rate of Hi-tech industrial land. The rate of land

Table 3 The score of degree of realization (objectives, sub-objectives, indexes)

Objectives (score)	Sub-objectives (score)	Indexes (score)
Land use condition (96.41%)	Degree of land development (98.04%)	The rate of land development (96.21%)
		The rate of land supply (99.61%)
		The rate of land construction completed (98.90%)
	Structural condition of land use (92.52%)	The rate of industrial land (92.53%)
		The rate of Hi-tech industrial land (92.52%)
	Land use intensity (98.09%)	General floor-area ratio (98.31%)
		Building density (98.13%)
		General floor-area ratio of industrial land (97.39%)
		Building density of industrial land (98.65%)
Land output efficiency (96.90%)	Input–output efficiency of industrial land (96.90%)	The intensity of industrial investment in fixed assets (95.29%)
		Output intensity of industrial land (94.84%)
		Output intensity of Hi-tech industrial land (100%)
Land management performance (95.73%)	Regulation performance of land use (100%)	The rate of land disposal for maturity project (100%)
		The rate of idle land disposal (100%)
	The degree of marketization of land supply (90.06%)	The rate of compensative land use (94.69%)
		The rate of land transfer by using bidding, auction and listing (85.42%)

The general score of intensive land use is 96.44%

development gets a score of 96.21%, general floor-area ratio of industrial land gets a score of 97.39%, and all the other five indexes score more than 98%. It means that intensive land use level is quite high in Xi'an National Hi-tech Industrial Development Zone. However, at the same time, the rate of industrial land and the rate of Hi-tech industrial land should be increased in the future.

The third objective, land management performance, gets a score of 95.73%. One of its sub-objectives, the degree of marketization of land supply, gets a lower score of 90.06%. Table 3 shows that it is for the lower rate of land transfer by using bidding, auction and listing. The actual value of the index is 27.94%, the ideal value is 32.71%, and the score of degree of realization is 85.42%.

4 Conclusions

Through the evaluation, the focuses and directions of intensive land use management in Xi'an National Hi-tech Industrial Development Zone are identified: (1) Taking the initiative to introduce Hi-tech industry, upgrading the existing industry and enhancing the proportion of Hi-tech industrial land and output intensity of Hi-tech industry. (2) Strengthening engineering construction management, and paying more attention to industrial land input–output intensity. Setting the bottom line of building density and fixed investment about industrial land. (3) Giving priority to the supply of industrial land and Hi-tech industrial land, improving the rate of industrial land and the rate of Hi-tech industrial land. (4) Enhancing the rate of land transfer by using bidding, auction and listing in the future.

References

1. Yang Dong-lang, An Xiao-li (2007) Colligation evaluation of Xi'an urban-land intensive use. Economic Geography:470–475
2. Long Hua-lou, Cai Yun-long, Wan Jun et al. (2000) The sustainability of land use in the developing areas of china: The case of Kunshan Economic & Technological Development Area. Acta Geographica Sinica:719–727
3. He Shu-jin, Su Guang-quan (2001) Causal mechanism and classification of idle land in China's development area. Resources Science:17–22
4. Zhai Wen-xia, Huang Xian-jin, Zhang Qiang et al. (2006) Intensive land use potential in urban development zones: A case study in typical urban development zones in Jiangsu Province. Resources Science:54–60
5. Zhai Wen-xia, Huang Xian-jin, Zhang Qiang et al (2006) Land intensive use in city development zones based on analytic hierarchy process: A case study of Jiangsu Province. Journal of Nanjing University (Natural Sciences):96–102
6. Lau S.S.Y, Giridharan R, Ganesan S (2005) Multiple and intensive land use: case studies in Hong Kong. Habitat International: 527–546

Industrial Planning, Macro-economic Control and Government's Role in the Perspective of Economic Crisis

Bo Cao and Yang Yu

Abstract In the context of the economic crisis, this could be taken as a study on function of the government's macro-control and industrial planning. Theoretical analysis shows that under the condition of information lack on industry planning, it would be very difficult to have entrepreneurs to carry out effective investment, making it impossible to achieve rapid economic recovery and development. With the Chinese government in industrial development, behavioral characteristics, this paper argues, industrial planning should, together with fiscal and monetary policies, as a means of macroeconomic control and become a part of government functions. In carrying out industrial planning, the government should do its own functional position, the quality of the information industry, the proportion of profitable projects, as well as the level of social benefits, is the government in the formulation of industrial planning should focus on variables.

Keywords Control · Industrial planning · Macro-economic analysis

1 Introduction

In order to tackle the economic crisis and prevent the rapid decreasing of China economy, at the beginning of 2009 the State Council successively issued industrial changing planning of ten industries. The National Development and Reform Commission have formulated regulations for the program of the 10 sections and make 76 missions and 120 policy measures clear. The measures which the Chinese government issued for the industrial planning share some similarities with the industrial development of Japan and South Korea in the period of world crude oil crisis and

B. Cao (✉) and Y. Yu
Economics and Management School of Beijing University of Technology, Beijing 100124, People's Republic of China
and
Research Center for Industrial Organization, Southeast University, Nanjing 211189, People's Republic of China
e-mail: caobobjut@163.com, yangyu.seu@gmail.com

D.D. Wu (ed.), *Modeling Risk Management in Sustainable Construction*,
Computational Risk Management, DOI 10.1007/978-3-642-15243-6_29,

Asian economic crisis. For example, during the period of crude oil crisis Japanese shipping building industry closed many manufactory factories in order to reduce ship building abilities. However, the South Korea government issued some plans for the revitalization of ship building industry and helped these corporations to promote productivity and competitiveness, coordinate the development from the comprehensive way. These plans greatly promoted the development of its ship building industry and South Korea has surpassed the Japan and became the second largest ship building industry in the world. Take culture industry for another example. The Japanese government has made a strategy of "culture industry" in the Asian economic crisis. At the present, the cartoon industry has become the third largest industry in Japan and its size only next to America's. At the same period, the South Korea has made the culture industry as the strategic pillar industry for the national economic development in the twenty-first century and regulated some laws, such as "Cultural Industry Promotion Basic Law", "Cultural Industry Development five-year Plans". Since 2001 the South Korea government has increased the portion of culture industry profit from 1 to 5% in the world market and become the fifth strongest country of culture industry in the world.

As viewing the macroeconomic theory, governments use some traditional measures of finance and currency to regulate and control the economy [1]. However, from the previous examples, the conclusion that industrial planning is necessary in the governmental macroeconomic regulation could be obtained. Take the Regan's presidency for example. The Strategic Defense Initiative was proposed at 1983 for the fail of revival plans with the taxation plan as a core. The development of the directed energy greatly increased the investment and promotion of technology-intensive industry [2, 3]. Except the political intentions, from the economic perspective, the effect of the industrial planning, with the industrial promotion as its core, has even surpassed the effect of financial policy. As to the government, whether or not the industrial planning is belong to one of its basic functions. The analysis of this question is not only meaningful to the study of macroeconomic theory, but also helpful to the change of the governmental functions. In the background of the economic crisis, the further discussion of the question that how to reinforce the function associating with the industrial policy and planning has many realistic values with emphasizing the macroeconomic control and the livelihood of the people by our government.

2 Theoretical Analysis: Functions of the Government in Industry Planning During the Economic Crisis

The immediate cause of the economic crisis is the abandonment of regulation, and in essence it is the information and incentive problems which relate to market failures [4, 5]. The influence of economic crisis has gradually shifted from the virtual to the real economy, from the export enterprises to the non-exporting ones.

The various transmission mechanisms lead to the bankruptcy of a large number of small and medium sized enterprises and the rise of the unemployment rate and so on. In this condition, because of the occurrence of the over production, the private-owned companies lose their confidence in investment. Therefore, accurately identify the right industries to invest could at last effectively strengthen the real economy. The investment and development of the industry is not only influenced by the short-term macroeconomic policies, but also by the long-term development strategy and the overall plan for the national economy. So the participation of the government in industry planning is really needed.

Here is a simple model, which would describe the behavioral characteristics of the private-owned enterprise, the government and some other main part in the economic crisis. And then, through this model we could analyze the problems concerning the investment behaviors of the entrepreneurs and the government's role in industry planning.

2.1 Assumption

First of all, we could assume that the ratio of the projects which could bring benefits to the entrepreneur is $\alpha \in (0,1)$, and at the same time private benefits $\pi > 0$ could be obtained. In addition, the profits of the entrepreneur's projects could be generally observed. Therefore, the social benefits $\Pi > \pi$ are produced. For the ratio of $1-\alpha$ of the projects which are non-profitable, the level of private benefits and social benefits are all as zero.

The entrepreneur and government do not have complete information about the profitability of the different projects. The entrepreneur is risk-neutral. The cost of finding the profitable project is recorded as C_e and C_g by entrepreneur and government separately. When the cost of government regulation is relatively too high or tax revenue is distorted by industry policies, $C_e < C_g$. However, when the entrepreneur is faced with project risks, or the capital market is imperfect, $C_e \geq C_g$.

For a particular industry, the signals observed about whether a project is profitable or not could be denoted as s_i^{π} and s_i^0, $i \in \{e, g\}$, and represents the entrepreneur and the government separately [6]. For signal s_i^{π}, the conditional probability of the project to be profitable is $p\langle \pi \mid s_i^{\pi} \rangle = q_i + (1-q_i)\alpha, q_i \in (0,1)$ denoting the quality of the signal and the ability of the entrepreneur and the government. The ability of the government also reflects the quality of the published industry planning. For simplicity, suppose that $p(s_i^{\pi}) = p(\pi)$. Meanwhile, assume that the signals received by the entrepreneur and the government are irrelative, it means $p(s_e^{\pi}|k, s_g^{\pi}) = p(s_e^{\pi}|k, s_g^0), k \in \{0,\pi\}$ and $p(s_g^{\pi}|k, s_e^{\pi}) = p(s_g^{\pi}|k, s_e^0), k \in \{0,\pi\}$. The overall welfare effect brought by the industry planning is $W = \int_e w_j(s_g)de$. Supportive the planning is, its expectancy effect would be $w_1(s_g) = p(\pi|s_g)\Pi - c_g$, $s_g \in \{s_g^0, s_g^{\pi}\}$. Otherwise, the effect is $w_0(s_g) = 0$.

Assume that the welfare factors are always taken into account when the government decides to support the particular kinds of enterprises, meanwhile its utility

$U = \int_e u_j(s_g)de$ is maximized. The expectancy effect of supporting a particular kind of company is $w_1(s_g) = p(\pi|s_g)\Pi - c_g$. Otherwise, $u_0(s_g) = 0$. Assuming $\alpha\Pi < \min\{c_e, c_g\} < \Pi$, which means that the average investment cost of the projects is lower than the social welfare, the profitable projects could increase the welfare.

2.2 The Situation Without Industry Planning

Then the situation without the industry planning imposed by government is to be analyzed: Under this condition, the entrepreneur obtains the signal of $s_e \in \{s_e^0, s_e^\pi\}$, with the investment cost as C_e. Under the circumstances of private net income expectation satisfies $p(\pi|s_e)\pi - c_e > 0$, a bad signal of s_e^0 would decline any investment, because $p(\pi|s_e^0)\pi \leq \alpha\pi \leq \alpha\Pi < c_e$.Yet a good signal s_e^π is obtained, if and only if $q_e > q_e{}' = \dfrac{c_e - \alpha\pi}{(1-\alpha)\pi}$ is satisfied, the enterprise would invest. Because $\alpha\pi < c_e, \alpha < 1, q_e{}' > 0$, if and only if $\pi > c_e$ is satisfied, $q_e{}' < 1$. It could be observed that $q_e{}' \in (0, 1)$ would increase simultaneously with c_e, and decrease while α and π go oppositely. Therefore, the proposition can be reached as follows:

If there is not any industry planning, the entrepreneur who get the good signal would pay the cost of investment when $q_e > q_e{}'$, otherwise there would be no one to invest.

2.3 Lacking of Investment Motivation

Next, measurements of increasing welfare and promoting economic development are to be depicted under the condition $q_e \leq q_e{}'$ when social investment is lack of motivation. Because the expected welfare effect for supporting a project is $E(w_1) = \alpha\Pi - c_g$. According to the assumption, the value is negative. When in the face of the bad signal s_g^0, the expected welfare effect is: $w_1(s_g^0) = p(\pi|s_g^0)$ $\Pi - c_g = (1-q_g)\alpha\Pi - c_g < E(w_1) < 0$. By contrary, $w_1(s_g^\pi) = p(\pi|s_g^\pi)\Pi - c_g =$ $[q_g + (1-q_g)\alpha]\Pi - c_g$. Therefore, if and only if $q_g > q_g{}' = \dfrac{c_g - \alpha\Pi}{(1-\alpha)\Pi}$, social welfare would increase.

Similarly, once $q_g{}' > 0$, if and only if $\Pi > c_g$, $q_e{}' < 1$ could be get; $q_e{}' \in (0, 1)$ would increase when c_e increase, and decrease when α and Π increase. Therefore the proposition is obtained as follows: When social investment is lack of motivation, if and only if $q_g > q_g{}'$, in other words, when the government has sufficient capacity, it would implement the industry planning in order to enhance the welfare. Further indication of the condition is: Government must have stronger ability in mastering the information of industry investment, only in this way the welfare would be enhanced. The higher the investment cost c_g is, the lower the ratio of the profitable projects α and the social benefits Π is.

The analysis of the theoretical model in this section indicates that: when the private entrepreneur face with an uncertain market environment, especially under the condition of economic crisis, subjected to the capacity of themselves, the proportion of the profitable projects and the low ratio of the private benefits, there would be a serious shortage of the investment motivation in the market. At this moment, government should strengthen of industry regulation, and provide supports to the private enterprise through industrial investment in order to enhance the social welfare.

3 The Orientation of the Chinese Government Function in the Development of Industry

In the models mentioned above, the key variables for the government are the quality of the information the government could acquire, the proportion of profitable projects and the level of social earnings. This section analyses the function orientation of the Chinese government in the development of industry and macro-control and regulation with those variables.

3.1 The Quality of Information

Effective distribution of resources requires making the most of various kinds of information. The rational choice each individual makes in the market economy could effectively regulate the balance between supply and demand in some industries and markets. However, under the situation of economic recession caused by the malfunction of market, essentially by the unbalanced distribution of information, one of the government's duties is to remedy the limitations of market. Industry planning aims at providing relevant information and measures to the main part of market investment so as to intervene in the economic activity of industry and perfect the allocation of resources. However, in the actual government departments, there are excessive administrative departments, thus resources are loosely distributed the management is confused. The ultimate result is the inefficiency of communication, low quality of information and the ineffectiveness of industry planning. The local government should exercise economic measures such as industry planning to regulate the economic operation, provide accurate information for the market main bodies steer the orientation of micro-economic main body operations and ensure the stable growth of economy, in conformity with the united plan of the central government and the local realities. Several mega data center, literature resources center and scientific information data base to provide some scientific references for the government decisions and supply the industries and the society with basic data, product data, scientific literature, the standard of technique, and information of human resources. Moreover, some industrious associations possess abundant information resources, thus the government may allocate part of its power to intermediary agencies, realizing the indirect support for the industries.

3.2 The Proportion of Profitable Projects

The local government put much emphasis on allocation of funds and the approval of projects, neglecting the research for the industrial policies and planning, thus they do not consider that critical variable. In the context of economic downturn, the orientation of government function should be adjusted, shifting from the emphasis on trade and investment promotion to that on encouraging native industries. In the aspect of industry steering, comprehensive uses of policy measures like tax, credit, import and export, and adjusting the proportion of profitable projects to effectively guide the individualistic decisions of investments. The government should strengthen supervision in industrial services, make full use of the integration of platforms of each industry to remedy the lacking profit of some industries on short terms. Meanwhile, attention should be paid to the problems of investment impulse and overcapacity which might be incurred by improvement of profits relevant to planning. For example, before the publication of the planning of revitalizing the new energy industry, there have been excessive PV and wind power enterprises. Therefore, the control of the proportion of profitable project should be the primary concern of government industrial planning.

3.3 The Level of Social Earnings

As a measure of macro control and regulation, the formulation of industrial planning is closely related to the general situation of social and economic development. The local government should formulate industry planning, comprehensively taking industry layout, the orientation of industry and transformation and upgrade into consideration in conformity with the medium to long term program of national economic and social development. The government should clarify the relations among the dominant project and accessory projects, manufacturing projects, R&D, and sales, the second and the third industry, and try hard to maximize social welfare. During the process of trade and investment promotion, the government should avoid short sight, bureaucracy, and law violations which are detrimental to the public interest and market development in the long run. In some of the industry planning, the government set a goal of strengthening the ability of self-innovation and boosting the innovative development of industries. However, because of the eternality of R&D, R&D and sales promotion are less profitable than the average level. Thus, the government should encourage the innovation staff by increasing their earnings to the average level so as to ensure the healthy development of industries.

4 Conclusions

This paper is written in the background of economic crisis. Combined the theoretical studies with the discussion of the practice in industrial planning of Chinese government, the author believes that the industrial planning should be taken as one of the macroeconomic measures, like financial and currency policy. The government should play an appropriate role at the industrial planning, and pays a great attention to the variable factors of industrial planning, such as the quality of industrial information, proportion of profit programs and the average level of the social income. This paper emphasizes that the macroeconomic regulation, the policy of industrial planning and the function of public administration have the different roles and functions in the economic development, and also proposes that the government should reinforce its position in the industrial planning. By the issue of the industrial planning policy, the government could make a promise to the society, and provide the correct information to the entities of micro-investment which are lack of information and conduct their investment in order to avoid the situation of both lacking of investment motives and surplus of investment. Besides, the industrial planning of social benefit could regulate the governmental behaviors.

Acknowledgments Sponsored by Science & Technology Innovation Platform, PXM2010_014204_09_000048.
Sponsored by Key Project of National Science Foundation "Research on the Structure and Operation of Government in China" (No. 70833002).

References

1. Langdana FK (2002) Macroeconomic policy: demystifying monetary and fiscal policy. Springer.
2. Lichtenberg FR (1989) The impact of the strategic defense initiative on US civilian R&D investment and industrial competitiveness. Social Studies of Science, 19(2): 265–282.
3. Harvey B (1986) The strategic defense initiative as science policy. International Security, 11(2):177–184.
4. Kanaga R (2009) Financial deregulation at root of current global crisis. Third World Network. http://www.twnside.org.sg/title2/finance/2009/twninfofinance20090305.htm. Accessed 26 May 2009.
5. Stiglitz JE (2008) The financial crisis of 2007/2008 and its macroeconomic consequences. United Nations Public Administration Network. http://unpan1.un.org/intradoc/groups/public/documents/apcity/unpan033508.pdf. Accessed 06 May 2009.
6. Hodler R (2009) Industrial policy in an imperfect world. Journal of Development Economics, 90(1): 85–93.

Evaluation and Simulation for Ecology Risk of Urban Expansion Based on SERA Model

Taking Selangor, Malaysia as an Example

Xiaoxia Shi, Yue Wu, and Han Zhang

Abstract This article aims to study the correlation between urbanization of space and the ecological environment and, from the change of pressure, resulting from urban expansion over temporal series, on regional ecology risk, judge the sustainability of urbanization, providing scientific basis for appraisal of the sustainable development of urbanization. First of all, with supports of spatial information technologies such as GIS and RS, and through the analysis of spatial mechanism of ecology risk, this study establishes the Spatial Ecology Risk Remote Sensing Evaluation Model (SERA) of urban expansion and analyses the concrete realizations of its relevant factors; after that, on the basis of the relevant data of the actual space and property of Selangor, Malaysia, this article carries out simulation of different pressures brought to regional ecology risk by the changes of urban expansion in four different periods from 1990 to 2002 in the research area; finally, this article verifies the model by utilizing the method of degree of interference on the landscape ecology. The results have shown that, from 1990 to 2002, the pressure rating of the regional ecology risk in that research area had been rising continually. These results comply with relevant laws of correlativity between urbanization and regional ecology in the research area. SERA model can properly appraise the pressure of regional ecology risk of urban expansion and provide scientific means to appraisal of the sustainable development of urbanization.

Keywords Ecology risk · SERA · Urban expansion · Urbanization

X. Shi (✉)
Beijing Key Laboratory of Logistics Systems and Technology, Beijing 101149, People's Republic of China
and
Beijing Wuzi University School of Logistics, Beijing Wuzi University, Beijing 101149, People's Republic of China
e-mail: shixx897@gmail.com

Y. Wu, and H. Zhang
Beijing Key Laboratory of Logistics Systems and Technology, Beijing 101149, People's Republic of China
e-mail: wuyue@m165.com, zhanghan56@263.net

D.D. Wu (ed.), *Modeling Risk Management in Sustainable Construction*, Computational Risk Management, DOI 10.1007/978-3-642-15243-6_30,

1 Introduction

The development of urbanization is primarily incarnated by extension of urban space. Through the spoliation of space of ecological environment and resource, it breaks the pattern and layout of landscape of the ecological system and influences the ecological safety of regional space. The sustainable development of ecological environment is one of the important measurements of the sustainable development of urbanization. Study on the correlation between them will provide a scientific basis for appraisal of the sustainable development of urbanization. Study on the correlation of urban expansion and ecological environment has gone through the phases of qualitative description to quantitative description. At present, it is mainly represented by three aspects: (1) Study on the correlation of pattern of urban space and landscape and ecological environment (Li et al. 2008). (2) Study on the correlation of urban expansion and ecological environment based on the thermal environment of space (Lo et al. 1997). (3) Study on the correlation of urban expansion and ecological environment with introduction of the index of ecological environment. (Wilson et al. 2003; Yue et al. 2006).

By judging from the current remote sensing investigation of the correlation between urbanization and ecological environment, the ecological appraisal carried out from the perspective of regional pattern of space fails to properly reflect the relation of space urbanization and ecological environment; the appraisal of ecology risk with flat scale no longer can satisfy needs of research; introduction based on remote sensing index is far too simple. According to the means of remote sensing, this article establishes the Spatial Ecology Risk Remote Sensing Evaluation Model (SERA). It appraises the ecology risk of space of the research area by considering specific incarnations of such factors and using Salengor, Malaysia as an example. 2 SERA Model2.1 Establishment of SERA Model.

The Spatial Ecology Risk Remote Sensing Evaluation Model (SERA) in this study is an evaluation model based on landscape cell (x, y). The ecology risk pressure P which is subjected to the macro-scale landscape cell (x, y) is represented by the common interaction of risked space driving force of the landscape cell P_A, factor of influence of the macro regional space of driving force P_{AI}, the space risk resistance (P_R) which is subjected to the landscape cell (x, y), factor of influence of the macro regional space of resistance P_{RI}, landscape cell (x, y)'s characterization factor of ecology risk P_E (based on remote sensing), comprehensive factor of influence of the regional ecology risk appraisal (P_{SI}) and the model adjustment coefficient P^0. The ecology risk pressure P is expressed by the following (1):

$$P = \frac{(P_A P_{AI} - P_R P_{RI}) + P_E}{2} \cdot P_{SI} \cdot P^0 \tag{1}$$

The spatial driving force of landscape cell P_A includes the correlation of DR (the relation between the landscape cell and the nearest road), DG (the relation between the landscape cell and the geometrical center of gravity of major patches of the land for construction), *FL* (the relation between the landscape cell and the land for construction) and *DW* (the relation between the landscape cell and the space heat environment). Among the driving force of space landscape, *DR* (the relation between the landscape cell and the nearest road) and *DG* (the relation between the landscape cell and the geometrical center of gravity of the land for construction) both represent the influence of distance and function jointly; *FL* (the relation between the landscape cell and the nearest land for construction) and *DW* (the relation between the landscape cell and the space heat environment) both represent the relation of distance and area and function jointly. The factor of influence of the macro regional space of driving force P_{AI} includes the area index of patches of land for city-building in the research area *SA* and the shape index of patches of land for city-building in the research area *SF*. The risked resistance of the space of landscape cell P_R includes the self-stability of landscape cell, namely, the density index for patches of land within the landscape cell *SD* and slope *SI*; neighborhood stability of the landscape cell *NS*. The factor of influence of the landscape of resistance of regional space P_{RI} is mainly determined by the influence coefficient of degree of fragmentation of ecological landscape *FN*. Characterization factor of the ecology risk of the landscape cell P_E is primarily represented by the index of ecological environment which is based on remote sensing. In this study, it is expressed by the leaf area index *LA*, which represents the net primary production force of the earth surface and energy exchange, and the cover degree of optical vegetative cover *CW*, which reflects soil erosion and biological mass. Comprehensive factor of influence of the model is represented by the pressure which is subjected to the ecological environment by human activity *UZ* and reflected by the large amount of waste materials produced by economic growth. Accordingly, the remote sensing evaluation model for ecology risk pressure based on the landscape can be expressed by the following (2):

$$\begin{aligned} P &= (P_A P_{AI} - P_R P_{RI}) \cdot P_{SI} \cdot P^0 \\ &= \frac{1}{2}\left[\left(\frac{1}{n_{Ai}}\sum_{i=1}^{n} P_{Ai}\right)\cdot\left(\frac{1}{n_{AIj}}\sum_{j=1}^{n} P_{AIj}\right) - \left(\frac{1}{n_{Ri}}\sum_{i=1}^{n} P_{Ri}\right)\cdot\left(\frac{1}{n_{RIj}}\sum_{j=1}^{n} P_{RIj}\right) + P_E\right]\cdot P_{SI}\cdot P^0 \\ &= \frac{1}{2}\left[\begin{array}{l} \sqrt{\frac{1}{2}\left[\frac{1}{2}(DR+DG)+\frac{1}{2}(FL+DW)\right]\times\frac{1}{2}[SA+SF]} \\ \quad -\sqrt{\frac{1}{3}(SD+SI+NS)\times FN)}+\frac{1}{2}(LA+CW) \end{array}\right]\cdot(UZ)\cdot P^0 \end{aligned} \tag{2}$$

Among them, $P > 0$

1.1 Realization of the SERA Model

1.1.1 Realization of the Driving Force Factors and Resistance Factors

(1) Factor of transportation and the geometrical center of gravity of the town. Expressions of the risk pressure which is subjected to the landscape cell (x, y) due to the influence of factor of transportation and the distance from the geometrical center of gravity of the land for city-building can be the same (3):

$$DR = DG = \frac{1}{1 + \frac{D}{a}} \tag{3}$$

where D represents the distance between the landscape cell and the nearest traffic artery and geometrical center of gravity of land for city-building; as a coefficient, a is about the attenuation of corrected range. It represents the degree of influence of traffic artery and geometrical center of gravity of cities on each land utilization type.

(2) Relation of land for city-building and relation of thermal environment. The driving effect of land for city-building on the ecology pressure of landscape cell (x, y) is represented as follows: As for random landscape cell (x, y), the larger the distance between it and the land for city-building, the more severe the risk pressure would be; the area of the nearest patches of land for city-building also has an impact on the degree of risk which is subjected to the object element. The larger the area, the more severe the risk would be and vice versa. When the distances between the landscape cell (x, y) and many patches of land for city-building are similar, the effect is deemed as equivalent combined action.

Influence of the heat space environment: First of all, persons concerned should obtain the T value of information about the heat island strength through the DN value of Landsat TM6. Then to determine the central patch of the space heart environment T and then by utilizing (4) to materialize the influence of the heat space environment within the flat space on ecological environment of the landscape cell.

$$DW = 1 - \frac{D_W}{M_W} \tag{4}$$

where D_W represents the distance between the landscape cell and the nearest heat center patch; M_W represents the area of heat center patch which is nearest to the landscape cell. The final result should be standardized to be between 0 and 1.

(3) Patch area index and patch shape index of city and town construction land. The patch area index SA for the factor of influence of driving force. This research reflects the area index of city and town construction land. If the whole research area is used as a construction land of city and town for landscape purpose, its value is 1; if the whole research area is used as a place other than the construction land of city and town, its value is 0.

The patch shape index of city and town construction land *SF* represents the landscape shape index on the landscape ecology. In this research, it represents the landscape shape index for city and town construction land within the area (Yue et al. 2006; Fu 2001).

(4) The patch density index for landscape resistance represents the patch density index within the landscape cell (x, y). According to the requirements of urban construction and planning, under the normal circumstances, when gradient exceeds 25°, the land shall be seen as a soil and water conservation region and is forbidden to be reclaimed. The neighbourhood stability can be decided through the theory of cellular automation. In the model, the influence coefficient of landscape fragmentation means the influence of fragmentation on the macroscopic ecological landscape for the land other than city and town construction land.

1.1.2 Realization of Ecology Risk and Social Economy Factor

(1) Leaf area index *LA* and optical vegetation coverage *CW* are the average values of pixel on the landscape cell. Leaf area index *LA* is the result of (5). Its range is regulated to 0–1 through modified coefficient L^0. Optical vegetation coverage *CW* is the result of (6). Its range is between 0 and 1.

$$LAI = \sqrt{\left(\mathrm{NDVI} \cdot \frac{1 + \mathrm{NDVI}}{1 - \mathrm{NDVI}}\right)} \tag{5}$$

$$C_w = 0.00579B_4 - 0.00308B_2 - 0.002482B_3 - 0.08905 \tag{6}$$

NDVI means normalized difference vegetation index; B_4, B_2 and B_3 are the composite spectral brightness of the certain pixel with the wave band TM 4, 2 and 3.

(2) The relation between urbanization *UZ* and ecological environment can be seen as the relation between economic development *ED* and ecological environment. This research shows us about the influence of social economy on ecology risk pressure through atmospheric pollutant discharge. Atmospheric pollution are usually caused by automotive emission, static goods' emission and waste material combustion. In the SERA model, the factor of influence of social economy P_{SI} can be expressed though (7):

$$P_{SI} = \frac{PA}{n \cdot S} \tag{7}$$

where *PA* represents the discharge of atmospheric pollutant in the research area. *S* represents area of research area. *n* represents modified coefficient. The result is regulated to 0–1.

2 Ecology Risk Evaluation for Selangor, Malaysia

The space of research area reaches 8,214 km^2, including Selangor, Kuala Lumpur, KL (capital) and Putrajaya (administrative capital). In the SERA model, the landscape cells with the size of 300 × 300 m and 900 × 900 m is used. The spatial ecology risks of the research area for the years 1990, 1991, 1994, 1996, 1998 and 2002 were evaluated. Their result range is between 0 and 1. The result values were divided into five levels. They are 0–0.2, 0.2–0.4, 0.4–0.6, 0.6–0.8 and 0.8–1. Figure 1 (a–c) are the evaluation result chats of spatial risk in 1990, 1994, 1998 and 2002 respectively, using 300 × 300 m cell size; (d) is the evaluation result chats of spatial risk in 2002 which cell size is 900 × 900 m.

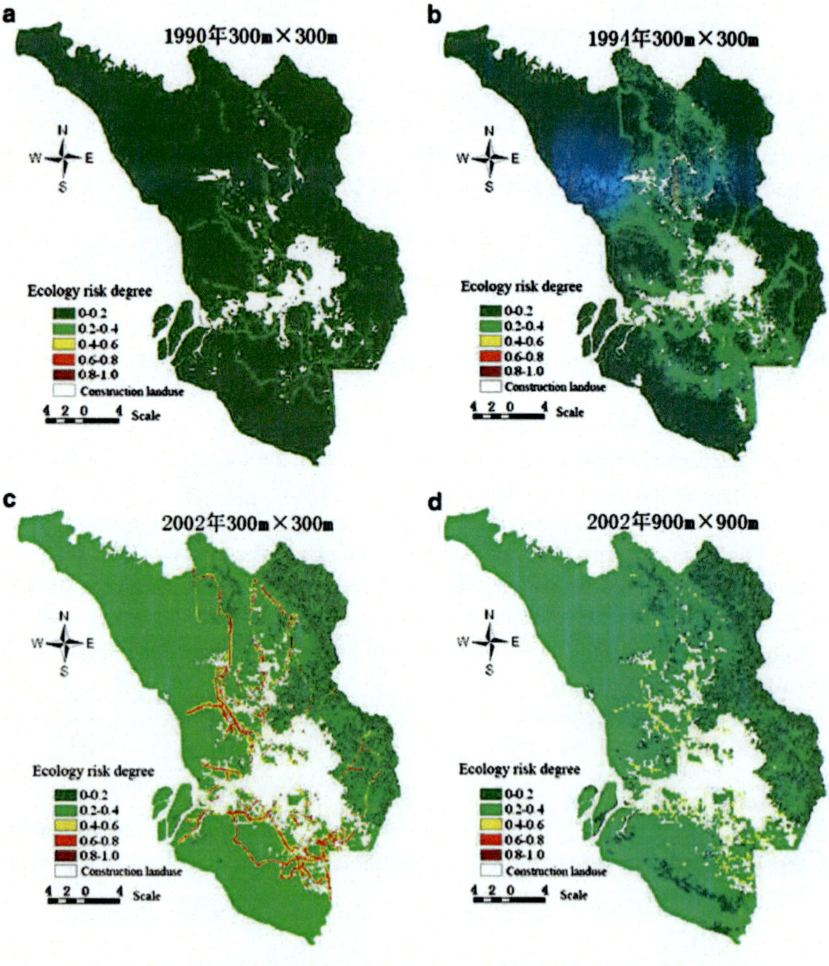

Fig. 1 Ecology risk change in space of study area from 1990 to 2002

3 Result and Conclusion

Based on the ecology risk evaluation values (see Fig. 1) for the research area made by SERSRS model each year, we can see that the change of city expansion and regional spatial ecology risk closely interlink with each other, and that the risk change is seriously influenced by humanity.

(1) Through, we can see that, within the landscape cell with the size of 300 × 300 m in the research area, the spatial ecology risk in 1990 was divided into two risk levels (i.e. 0–0.2 and 0.2–0.4), while in 1994, a new risk level (i.e. 0.4–0.6) was added and in 2002, another risk level was added based on the above three risk levels. The increasing ecology risk level is caused by the massive discharge of waste material brought by the rapid expansion of city and town construction area and rapid economic growth. While the city and town construction land continues to expand, the areas of forest land and arable land decreases, which increase the ecology risk of research area.

(2) According to Table 1, we can learn from the simulated result of ecology risk for research area that the ecology risk for research area at present is relatively high, but no indication of ecology risk at high level is found. During the model operation, we find some negative values from the result values. But these negative values only appear in the maintain area with high gradient. This means that the relatively high spatial risk resistance in this area greatly helps to protect the ecological environment.

(3) By comparing the two landscape cells with the sizes of 300 × 300 m and 900 × 900 m which are applied in the research area in 2002, we can see that though the spatial ecology risk values for these two landscape cells concentrate on the risk level 0.2–0.4, the risk level for the landscape cell with the larger size is lower than that of the landscape cell with the small one in 2002. So, in the ecology risk evaluation conducted at the same period for research area, the spatial ecology risk value for the landscape cell with the large size is lower than that of the landscape cell with the small one.

An SERA model combines the effect of landscape size with the characteristics of remote sensing index to forecast remote sensing simulated ecology risk evaluation under the condition of city expansion. This model, by applying the remote sensing index to ecology risk evaluation, not only overcomes the shortcoming in which the needs of macro feature for ecology risk evaluation are hard to be satisfied, but also realizes the remote sensing evaluation for spatial ecology risk, laying a foundation for direct application of remote sensing index to ecology risk evaluation model. The application verification of SERA model in the research area proves that the simulated result of this model complies with the correlation between urbanization and regional ecology in the research area.

References

Fu Bojie: (2001) *Landscape Ecology Theory and Application* (Science Press, Beijing)

Li Jinggang, He Chunyang and Aobing. (2008) Landscape Ecological Risk Assessment of Natural/ Semi-natural Landscapes in Fast Urbanization Regions – A Case Study in Beijing, China. Journal of Natural Resources, vol. 23, p. 33

Lo CP, Quattrovhi DA and Luvall JC. (1997) Application of high resolution thermal infrared remote sensing and GIS to assess the urban heat island effect. International Journal of Remote Sensing, vol. 18, p. 287

Wilson JS. Clay M, Martin E, Risch KV. (2003) Evaluating environmental influence of zoning in urban ecosystems with remote sensing. Remote Sensing of Environment, vol. 83, p. 303

Yue Wenze, Xu Jianhua, Xu Lihua. (2006) An analysis on eco-environmental effect of urban land use based on remote sensing images: a case study of urban thermal environment and NDVI. Acta Ecologica Sinica, vol. 5, p. 1450

Part VI
Financial Risk

The Gerber–Shiu Discounted Penalty Function for the Credit Risk Model with Dependent Rates of Interest

Dan Peng and Zaiming Liu

Abstract In this paper, we consider the credit risk model with dependent rates of interest. The rates of interest $\{I_n, n = 1, 2, \ldots\}$ are assumed to have an autoregressive structure, we obtained the integral equations for the penalty function by using the analysis methods in probability. Furthermore, the finite time ruin probability, the joint distribution of surplus immediately before ruin and the deficit at ruin are also obtained.

Keywords Credit rating · Penalty function · Rate of interest · Risk theory

1 Introduction

In this paper, we consider a firm which could be either a financial corporation or an insurance company. At the beginning of each time interval, a rating agency will provide a credit rating to assess the firm's abilities in meeting its debt obligations. We use a Markov chain to model the firm's credit ratings. Let I_t be a time-homogeneous Markov chain with a state space of $N = 1, 2, \cdots, k$; where state 1 represents the highest credit class and state k be the lowest. Let $q_{ij} = P\{I_{t+1} = j | I_t = i\}$, $i, j \in N$, $t = 0, 1, \cdots$ be the one-step transition probabilities, the transition matrix of the Markov chain I_t can be

D. Peng (✉)
School of Mathematics, Hunan University of Science and Technology, Xiangtan 411201, People's Republic of China
e-mail: danpengdanpeng@126.com

Z. Liu
School of Mathematics, Central South University, Changsha 410075, People's Republic of China
e-mail: math_lzm@csu.edu.cn

D.D. Wu (ed.), *Modeling Risk Management in Sustainable Construction*,
Computational Risk Management, DOI 10.1007/978-3-642-15243-6_31,

$$Q = \begin{pmatrix} q_{11} & q_{12} & \cdots & q_{1k} \\ q_{21} & q_{22} & \cdots & q_{2k} \\ \cdots & \cdots & \cdots & \cdots \\ q_{k1} & q_{k2} & \cdots & q_{kk} \end{pmatrix}.$$

Hailiang Yang [1] builds a new risk model for a firm which is sensitive to its credit quality. In his model, A Markov chain is to depict the credit rating, Recursive equations for finite time ruin probability and distribution of ruin time are derived. Inspired by Yang [1], we consider a discrete time risk model, in which the surplus process is expressed by a equation

$$U_n = u \prod_{k=1}^{n} (1 + R_k) + \sum_{m=1}^{n} (X_m^{I_{m-1}} \prod_{i=m+1}^{n} (1 + R_i)) \tag{1}$$

where u is the initial surplus of an insurance company, X_n^i is the portfolio change in the nth time interval if the firm's credit rating in time interval n is of class i. $\{R_i, i = 1, 2, \cdots\}$ are assumed to have a dependent autoregressive structure of order 1, i.e. R_n satisfies:

$$R_n = aR_{n-1} + w_n$$

where $0 \leq a < 1$ and $R_0 = r_0$ are constant. $\{w_n, n = 1, 2, \cdots\}$ is a sequence of i.i.d. nonnegative random variables, they have common distribution functions $G(w) = P(w_i \leq w)$. We will assume $X_n^i, i = 1, 2, \cdots, n = 1, 2, \cdots$ are independent random variables. For any fixed $i = 1, 2, \cdots, k, X_n^i, n = 1, 2, \cdots$ are identically distributed. $X^1, X^2, \cdots X^k$ are independent but have different distributions. We will denote the distribution of X^i by $F_i(x)$. We also assume that the portfolio change in the nth time interval depends on I_{n-1}, the firm's credit rating in time $n-1$.

Let $T = \inf\{n : U_n < 0\}(\inf \phi = \infty)$ be the ruin time, U_T^- be the surplus before ruin and $|U_T|$ be the deficit at ruin. Let $\omega(x_1, x_2), 0 \leq x_1, x_2 < \infty$ be a nonnegative function. For $\delta \geq 0$, define

$$M(u, i_0, r_0) = E[e^{-\delta T} \omega(U_T^-, |U_T|) I(T < \infty) | U_0 = u, I_0 = i_0, R_0 = r_0] \tag{2}$$

where $I(T < \infty) = 1$ if $T < \infty$ and $I(T < \infty) = 0$ otherwise. The function $M(u, i_0, r_0)$ in (2) is useful for deriving results in connection with joint and marginal distributions of $T, U_T^-, |U_T|$. While δ may be interpreted as a force of interest, the function (2) may also be viewed in terms of a Laplace transform with δ serving as the argument. In particular, if we let $\omega(x_1, x_2) = 1$, (2) is the Laplace transform of the time of ruin T. If we let $\delta = 0$ and $\omega(x_1, x_2) = I(x_1 \leq x)I(x_2 \leq y)$, (2) becomes the joint distribution function of the surplus before ruin and the deficit at ruin. Furthermore, if $\delta = 0$ and $\omega(x_1, x_2) = {x_1}^n$, we obtain the nth moment of the surplus before ruin and the deficit at ruin.

2 Integral Equations for Penalty Functions

Assume that at time 0, $I_0 = i_0, R_0 = r_0$. From (2) we obtain:

$$M(u,i_0,r_0) = E[e^{-\delta T}\omega(U_T^-,|U_T|)I(T<\infty)|U_0 = u, I_0 = i_0, R_0 = r_0]$$

$$= \sum_{n=1}^{\infty} E[e^{-\delta T}\omega(U_T^-,|U_T|)I(T=n)]$$

$$= \sum_{n=1}^{\infty} E[e^{-\delta n}\omega(U_{n-1},|U_n|)I(\bigcap_{i=1}^{n-1}(U_i \geq 0, U_n < 0)]$$

$$\triangleq \sum_{n=1}^{\infty} m_n(u,i_0,r_0)$$

Theorem 2.1 $M(u,i_0,r_0)$ satisfies the following equation:

$$M(u,i_0,r_0) = m_1(u,i_0,r_0) +$$

$$e^{-\delta}\sum_{i=1}^{k} q_{i0\bar{i}} \int_0^{\infty}\int_{-u(1+ar_0+w)}^{+\infty} M(\bar{u},\bar{i}_0,\bar{r}_0)dF_{\bar{i}0}(x)dG(w)$$

where $m_1(u,i_0,r_0) = e^{-\delta}\int_0^{\infty}\int_{-\infty}^{-u(1+ar_0+w)} \omega(u,|\bar{u}|)dF_{i0}(x)dG(w)$, $\bar{u} = (u+X_1^{i0})$ $(1+ar_0+w), \bar{r}_0 = ar_0 + w$.

Proof Define: $w_1 = w, X_1^{i0} = x, \bar{u} = u(1+ar_0+w) + X_1^{i0}$

$$m_1(u,i0,r_0) = E[e^{-\delta}\omega(U_0,|U_1|)I(U_0 \geq 0, U_1 < 0)]$$

$$= E[e^{-\delta}\omega(u,|U_1|)I(u \geq 0, U_1 < 0)]$$

$$= e^{-\delta}\int_0^{\infty}\int_{-\infty}^{-u(1+ar_0+w)} \omega(u,|\bar{u}|)dF_{i0}(x)dG(w) \tag{3}$$

If $u(1+ar_0+w) + X_1^{i0} < 0$, i.e. $X_1^{i0} < -u(1+ar_0+w)$, then $P\{U_1 \geq 0|U_0 = u, I_0 = i0., R_0 = r_0\} = 0$. which implies that: for $n \geq 2$,

$$E\left\{e^{-\delta n}\omega(U_{n-1},|U_n|)I\left(\bigcap_{i=1}^{n-1}(U_i \geq 0, U_n < 0)\right)\right\} = 0.$$

To evaluate the Gerber–Shiu penalty function, we need to consider the auxiliary model.

Let $\{\overline{w}_n, n=1,2,\cdots\}, \{\overline{X}^i_n, n=1,2,\cdots\}$ be independent copies of $\{w_n, n=1,2,\cdots\}$ and $\{X^i_n\}$, Furthermore by [2] we know that:

$$\begin{aligned} R_n &= a^n R_0 + a^{n-1} w_1 + \cdots + a w_{n-1} + w_n \\ &= a^{n-1}(a r_0 + w) + a^{n-2} w_2 + \cdots + a w_{n-1} + w_n \end{aligned}$$

$\{\overline{R}_n, n=1,2,\cdots\}$ has a similar autoregressive structure to that of $\{R_n, n=1,2,\cdots\}$. i.e. $\overline{R}_n = a\overline{R}_{n-1} + \overline{w}_n, n=1,2,\cdots$, but with a different initial rate $\overline{R}_0 = a r_0 + w$.. Then we define the other process as:

$$\overline{U}_n = \overline{u} \prod_{k=1}^{n} (1+\overline{R}_k) + \sum_{m=1}^{n} (\overline{X}_m^{\overline{I}_{m-1}} \prod_{i=m+1}^{n} (1+\overline{R}_i))$$

where $\{\overline{U}_n, n=1,2,\cdots\}$ has a similar structure to that of $\{U_n, n=1,2,\cdots\}$ except for a different initial surplus $\overline{u} = (u + X_1^{i0})(1 + a r_0 + w)$, a different interest $\{\overline{R}_n, n=1,2,\cdots\}$ and a different initial credit rating $\overline{I}_0$. Furthermore$\{\overline{I}_{m-1}, m=1,2,\cdots\}$ is also a time-homogeneous Markov chain with a state space of $N=\{1,2,\cdots,k\}$. Hence, if $X_1^{i0} > -u$, then $P\{U_1 \geq 0 | U_0 = u, I_0 = i0, R_0 = r_0\} = 1$.For $n=2$,

$$\begin{aligned} m_2(u,i0,r_0) &= E\{e^{-2\delta} w(U_1,|U_2|) I(U_1 \geq 0, U_2 < 0) | U_0 = u, I_0 = i0, R_0 = r_0\} \\ &= e^{-\delta} E[e^{-\delta} \omega(U_1,|U_2|) I(U_1 \geq 0, U_2 < 0)] \\ &= e^{-\beta} \sum_{i=1}^{k} q_{\overline{i}_0 \overline{i}} E[e^{-\delta} \omega(\overline{u}, |\overline{U}_1|) I(\overline{u} \geq 0, \overline{U}_1 < 0)] \\ &= e^{-\delta} \sum_{i=1}^{k} q_{\overline{i}_0 \overline{i}} \int_0^{\infty} \int_{-u(1+ar_0+w)}^{+\infty} m_1(\overline{u}, \overline{i}_0, \overline{r}_0) dF_{\overline{i}_0}(x) dG(w). \end{aligned} \tag{4}$$

Similar to the proof (3) and (4), if $X_1^{i0} > -u$, $m_n(u,i0,r_0) = E\{e^{-n\delta} \omega(U_{n-1},|U_n|) I(\bigcap_{i=1}^{n} (U_i \geq 0, U_n < 0))\}$

$$\begin{aligned} &= e^{-\delta} \sum_{i=1}^{k} q_{\overline{i}_0 \overline{i}} E\left[e^{-(n-1)\delta} \omega(\overline{U}_{n-2}, |\overline{U}_{n-1}|) I\left(\bigcap_{i=1}^{n-2} (\overline{U}_i \geq 0, \overline{U}_n < 0)\right)\right] \\ &= e^{-\delta} \sum_{i=1}^{k} q_{\overline{i}_0 \overline{i}} \int_{-u}^{+\infty} m_{n-1}(\overline{u}, \overline{i}_0, \overline{r}_0). \end{aligned}$$

Therefore, we get

$$M(u,i0,r_0)=\sum_{i=1}^{k}m_n(u,i0,r_0)=m_1(u,i0,r_0)+\sum_{n=2}^{\infty}m_2(u,i0,r_0)$$

$$=m_1(u,i0,r_0)+e^{-\delta}\sum_{i=1}^{k}q_{\bar{i}_0\bar{i}}\int_0^{\infty}\int_{-u(1+ar_0+w)}^{+\infty}M(\bar{u},\bar{i}_0,\bar{r}_0)dF_{\bar{i}_0}(x)dG(w)$$

which proves Theorem 2.1.

3 Some Special Cases

In this section, we discuss several special cases. Especially expressions for the probability of ruin, the joint distribution of surplus just before ruin and the deficit at ruin in the discount free case.

In model (1), if $\delta=0$, we can get the joint distribution of surplus just before ruin and the deficit at ruin. Define

$D_{i0}(u,x,y)=P\{U_T\leq -y,U_{T-1}\geq x,T<\infty|U_0=u,I_0=i0\}(x>0,y>0)$. By Theorem 2.1, we get the following corollary:

Corollary 3.1 The function $D_{i0}(u,x,y)$ satisfies the following equations:

$$D_{i0}(u,x,y)=d_{1i0}(u,x,y,)\sum_{i=1}^{k}q_{i0i}\int_0^{\infty}\int_{-u(1+ar_0+w)}^{\infty}D_i(u(1+ar_0+w)$$
$$+z,x,y,ar_0+w)dF_{i0}(z)dG(w)$$

where

$$d_{1i0}(u,x,y,r_0)=\begin{cases}\int_0^{\infty}F_{i0}(-u(1+ar_0+w)-y)dG(w) & x<u;\\ 0 & x\geq u.\end{cases}$$

If $\delta=0$, $\omega(x,y)=1$, we get the ruin probability of the model (1).

Define

$\psi_{ni0}(u,r_0)=P\{U_n<0|U_0=u,I_0=i0,R_0=r_0\}$, $\phi_{ni0}(u,r_0)=1-\psi_{ni0}(u,r_0)$, Thus we get

Corollary 3.2 The no ruin probability of the model (1) is:

$$\varphi_{1i0}(u,r_0)=1-\int_0^{\infty}F_{i0}(-u(1+ar_0+w))dG(w);$$

$$\varphi_{ni0}(u,r_0)=\sum_{i=1}^{k}q_{i0i}\int_0^{\infty}\int_{-u(1+ar_0+w)}^{\infty}\varphi_{(n-1)i}(u(1+ar_0+w)+s),$$
$$ar_0+w)dF_{i0}(s)dG(w)n=2,3,\cdots$$

Proof $\varphi_{1i0}(u,r_0)=P\{U_1>0|U_0=u,I_0=i0,R_0=r_0\}=P\{X_1^{i0}>-u(1+ar_0+w_1)\}$

$$=1-P\{X_1^{i0}\leq -u(1+ar_0+w_1)\}$$

$$=1-\int_0^{\infty}F_{i0}(-u(1+ar_0+w_1))dG(w).$$

When $n=2$,

$$\varphi_{2i0}(u,r_0)=P\{U_1>0,U_2>0|U_0=u,I_0=i0,R_0=r_0\}$$

$$=P\{X_1^{i0}>-u(1+r_1),X_1^{i0}(1+r_2)+X_2^{I_1}>-u(1+r_1)(1+r_2)\}$$

$$=P\{X_1^{i0}>-u(1+ar_0+w_1),X_1^{i0}(1+a(ar_0+w_1)+w_2)$$
$$+X_2^{I_1}>-u(1+ar_0+w_1)(1+a(ar_0+w_1)+w_2)\}$$

$$=\sum_{i=1}^{k}q_{i0i}\int_0^{\infty}\int_{-u(1+ar_0+w)}^{\infty}P\{X_2^{i}>-(u(1+ar_0+w)+s)$$

$$g(1+a(ar_0+w)+w_2)\}dF_{i0}(s)dG(w)$$

$$=\sum_{i=1}^{k}q_{i0i}\int_0^{\infty}\int_{-u(1+ar_0+w)}^{\infty}\varphi_{1i}(u(1+ar_0+w)+s,ar_0+w)dF_{i0}(s)dG(w)$$

$$=\int_0^{\infty}(1+t)\sum_{i=1}^{k}q_{i0i}\int_{-u}^{\infty}\varphi_{1i}((u+y)(1+t))dF_{i0}(y)dM_r(t).$$

Similarly we get

$$\varphi_{ni0}(u,r_0)=P\{U_1>0,U_2>0,\cdots,U_n>0|U_0=u,I_0=i0,R_0=r_0\}$$
$$=\sum_{i=1}^{k}q_{i0i}\int_0^{\infty}\int_{-u(1+ar_0+w)}^{\infty}\varphi_{(n-1)i}(u(1+ar_0+w)+s),ar_0+w)dF_{i0}(s)dG(w).$$

Corollary 3.3 In corollary 3.2, if $R_n = 0, n = 0, 1, 2, \cdots$, no ruin probability of the model (1) satisfies the following equation:

$$\phi_{1i0}(u) == 1 - F_{i0}(-u)$$

$$\phi_{ni0}(u) = \sum_{i=1}^{k} q_{i0i} \int_{-u}^{\infty} \phi_{(n-1)i}(u+y)dF_{i0}(y).$$

$$n = 2, 3, \cdots$$

Remark: If $R_n = 0, n = 0, 1, 2, \cdots$ the model (1) is the case of credit risk model without rates, corollary 3.3 is consistent with theorem 3.1 in Yang [1].

Acknowledgment This research was fully supported by a grant from National Natural Science foundation of China (NSFC10971230) and supported by Scientific Research Fund of Hunan Provincial Education Department (08C346).

References

1. Yang, H.L., Ruin theory in a financial corporation model with credit risk, Insurance: Mathematics and Economics, 2003, 32, 345–358.
2. Yang, H.L., Non-exponential bound for ruin probability with interest effect included, Scandinavian Actuarial Journal, 1999, 66–79.

A Risk-Sensitivity Analysis on NPV Model of Investment Projects

Xiansheng Qin, Xuyao Ma, and Hongwei Bai

Abstract NPV (Net Present Value) is a preferred method of feasibility study to describe uncertainty of risk-sensitivity. Sensitivity analysis is an important and indispensable process. In addition to single factor sensitivity analysis, Risk-sensitivity analysis takes into account of probability distribution, control and relativity of risk factors, making the traditional sensitivity analysis more uniform and more objective. This paper briefly describes NPV, sensitivity analysis method, and discusses concepts about risk factors distribution factor, and controllability factors. It also demonstrates operability of an integrated sensitivity analysis through the establishment of NPV model and case analysis.

Keywords Investment projects · Monte Carlo simulation · NPV · Sensitivity

1 Introduction

In the feasibility study of an investment project, NPV analysis is also known as 'financial net present value method', it is an important investment project evaluation index and received extensive attention. The financial benefits of investment projects are assessed by comparing the present value of income and expenditure [1]; moreover it is necessary to consider how changes of key factors impact the project evaluation index. Uncertainty analysis includes profit and loss analysis, sensitivity analysis, and probability analysis and so on. Risk-sensitivity analysis, combining with multi-factor analysis and Monte Carlo simulation, has increasingly been an important choice to decision makers.

X. Qin (✉) and X. Ma,
Northwestern Polytechnical University, Xi'an, People's Republic of China
e-mail: qinxiansheng@163.com; maxuyao@sina.com

H. Bai
Shaanxi Fast Gear Co., Ltd, Xi'an, People's Republic of China
e-mail: hevin_bai@163.com

D.D. Wu (ed.), *Modeling Risk Management in Sustainable Construction*, Computational Risk Management, DOI 10.1007/978-3-642-15243-6_32,

2 Sensitivity Analysis Based on NPV Model

2.1 NPV Model

$$NPV = \sum_{t=0}^{n} (CI - CO)_t (1 + i_c)^{-t} = \sum_{t=0}^{n} \frac{C_t}{(1 + i_c)^t} - I \tag{1}$$

NPV is Net Present Value; CI is cash inflow; CO is cash outflows; $(CI\text{-}CO)_t$ is the net cash flow of year t; n is life cycle of the project; i_c is benchmark interest rate; I is present value of cash outflows.

In definite state, the manager's mission is to maximize shareholder's value through commitment of the investment with a positive NPV [2]. But in uncertain state, because of existence of risk, the project cash flow needs some risk premium. However, NPV in those instances are estimated by its independent variables. If the manager is a passive recipient, then the adjusted NPV model is:

$$NPV = \sum_{t=0}^{n} \frac{E(C_t)}{(1 + k_t)^t} - I \tag{2}$$

E (Ct) is cash inflow year t; Kt is discount rate of year t.

2.2 Multi-factor Sensitivity Analysis

The basic principle of sensitivity analysis is to assume that only one risk factor changed and the others remain unchanged [3].

$$E_i = \frac{\Delta NPV(x_i)/NPV(x_i)}{\Delta x_i/x_i},$$

Then

$$\Delta NPV(X_i) = \Delta NPV(X_i)(\Delta X_i/X_i)E_i \tag{3}$$

x*i* is a risk factor; E*i* is sensitivity index of xi; NPV(xi)is Net Present Value, a function of xi; NPV(xi) is variable quantity of NPV(xi).

Single factor sensitivity analysis helps to identify and control key risk factors to evaluation index, but deficiency is that each time only one variable is considered and interaction between variables are neglected [4].

2.3 Multi-factor Sensitivity Analysis

$$F_t = NPV(X_t)R_iE_iC_i \tag{4}$$

Fi is risk-sensitivity index; Ri is distribution index of risk factors; Ci is controllability index of risk factors, which can be derived from Fuzzy Evaluation Method or Delphi Method.

If probability density function of x_i is $x_i(t)$ and $E(x_t)$ is the expectation of xi, then the probability density function of $\frac{\Delta x_i}{x_i}$ is $\frac{x_i(t) - E(x_i)}{E(x_i)}$. If variable range of $\frac{\Delta x_i}{x_i}$ is [a, b], then its probability $\beta_t = \int_a^b \frac{x_i(t) - E(x_i)}{E(x_i)} dt$, Ri is defined as $\frac{1}{2}\beta_i \frac{|a-b|}{E(x_i)}$. In addition, the interaction among uncertainties should be considered in the actual analysis.

The combined impact of multiple factors can be simulated by Monte Carlo method [5]. The method can effectively resolve multiple variables decision-making problems, even if there is interaction between these variables. It is hard to understand interdependence among the factors, to determine the discount rate, and to distinguish system risk and project risk. Although it is difficult to apply dynamic programming in actual analysis, Monte Carlo simulation is still the most effective method.

3 Case Analysis

A new project was completed with a total investment of 75 million RMB (value at the end of first year), operated and reached its productivity of 10,000 transmissions in the second year. Operation duration is 10 years, the residual value is 10 million RMB, the unit price of a transmission is 10,000 RMB, the variable cost of a transmission is 8,000 RMB, Fixed Cost is 1.5 million RMB each year, standard profitability is 12%. Relationship of Investment (G), Residual Value (G'), Fixed Cost(Ct), Production(Qt), Price(Pt), Variable Cost(Vt) are: $G' = 0.1333G$, $C = 0.02G$.

Table 1 is a computational process that shows of risk-sensitivity indexes. In this project, controllable key risk factors are: sales price, variable cost, production, and investment.

Estimated NPV (calculated in accordance with expectations of each risk factor).

$\text{NPV} = \sum_{t=1}^{11} (Q_tP_t - Q_tV_t - C_t)(P/F, 12, t) + G'(P/F, 12, 11)$-G=16[mil. RMB]

By using Monte Carlo simulation method, sample the price, variable cost, investment, and production in a normal distribution, then calculate NPV of each sample.

Table 1 Main risk factors and its risk-sensitivity index on NPV

No.	x_i	$M(x_i)^a$	[a, b]	$E(x_i)^b$	β	R_i	$\|E_i\|$	C_i	F_i	Sort
1	G[mil. RMB]	75	[50,100]	75	1	0.333	3.99	0.20	4.26	4
2	G'[mil. RMB]	10	[6. 7,13.3]	10	1	0.333	0.18	0.20	0.19	6
3	C_t[mil. RMB]	1.5	[1,2]	1.5	1	0.333	0.47	0.15	0.37	5
4	Q_t[mil.]	0.01	[0.005,0.012]	0.0095	1	0.368	5.64	0.15	4.99	3
5	P_t[mil. RMB]	0.01	[0.008,0.011]	0.01	1	0.368	30.04	0.15	26.61	1
6	V_t[mil. RMB]	0.008	[0.007,0.01]	0.008	1	0.184	24.40	0.15	10.80	2

[a]Note: $M(x_i)$ means most probable value of x_t in the case
[b]$E(x_i)$ is reduced by PERT (Performance Evaluation Review Technique) method

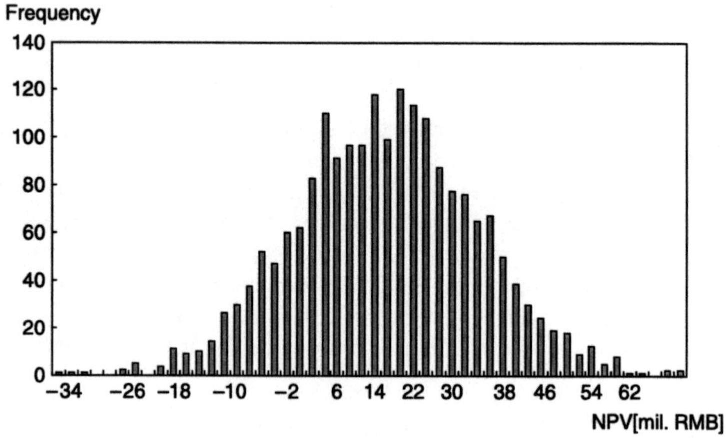

Fig. 1 Frequency histogram after 2,000 simulation

After 2,000 simulations, we analyzed each NPV sample and plotted frequency histogram (see Fig. 1). According to the Central Limit Theorem, NPV of the project accords with the normal distribution.

3.1 Risk Analysis

Statistics of NPV of the 2,000 simulations sample suggested that the mean value is 16.1112 million for a standard deviation of 14.5559 million and cumulative probability P (NPV $>$ 0) $=$ 0.899. From these data, we concluded that the project has a certain amount of investment value, but a large standard deviation also showed the project has certain risks. For feasibility study of the project, a conservative policy-maker over-valued risk requires stable expected NPV. Based on the principle of utility, a risk-preference decision-maker thinks that the cash flow value is not high and lack of good investment value.

3.2 *Model Accuracy and Test of Stability*

A NPV sample of 4,000 simulations (mean of 15.7861 and a standard deviation of 14.5515) is used instead of total test results of 2,000 simulations.

If E(X) is the mean expectation value of totality and σ is the standard deviation of totality, according to the Central Limit Theorem, when $n \to \infty$, $P\left\{\frac{\bar{x}-E(X)}{\frac{\sigma}{\sqrt{n}}} \leq \chi\right\} \to \frac{1}{\sqrt{2\pi}} \int_{-\infty}^{\chi} e^{-\frac{u^2}{2}} du$ When n is large enough, $P\left\{\frac{\bar{x}-E(X)}{\frac{\sigma}{\sqrt{n}}} \leq 2\right\} \approx \frac{1}{\sqrt{2\pi}} \int_{-2}^{2} e^{-\frac{u^2}{2}} du = 0.95$. So in a probability of 0.95,

$$|\bar{x} - E(X)| \leq \frac{2\sigma}{\sqrt{n}} \tag{5}$$

Insert the mean expectation value and the standard deviation of 2,000 simulations and 4,000 simulations in (5). If it is tenable, it passed the Accuracy test. $|16.1112 - 15.7861| = 0.3251 < \frac{14.5515 \times 2}{\sqrt{2000}} = 0.9203$. It passed the probability test.

Probability of NPV is positive after 2,000 simulations is $P1 = 0.899$, Probability of 4,000 simulations is $P2 = 0.898$. $\frac{|P_1 - P_2|}{P_2} \times 100\% = 0.44\% < 1\%$, Therefore, it passed the stability test Based on the above test results, it is concluded that the model is accurate and stable.

4 Conclusion

The Risk-sensitivity Analysis takes into account probability distribution, controllability, and relevance, more unified and more comprehensive than traditional uncertainty analysis.

Application of Monte Carlo Simulation techniques and expected utility theory are very effective to evaluate investment projects. They help decision-makers to understand more about the investment project and to make final decisions.

References

1. Peter H. Rossi, H. E. Freeman, Mark W. Lipsey, Evaluation, A Systematic Approach 2002
2. Miao Changrun, An Yaqin, Chen Jingwu, The Investment Project Risk Evaluation, Hebei University of Technology, 2001 [4]
3. Matthew J. Liberatore, Bruce Pollack-Johnsn, Colleen A. Smith, Project Management in Construction, Software Use and Research Directions Journal of Construction Engineering and Management, 2001 [2]
4. Zhou You, Defects and Improvement to Investment Project Evaluation of the Present Value of Net Flows, Technical and Economic, 2004 [4]
5. Annan JD. Modeling under Uncertainty, Monte Carlo Methods for Temporally Varying Parameters, Ecological Modeling, 2001, 136 (23), 297–302

Research on Appraisal of High-Tech Entrepreneurial Risk Based on Osculating Value Method

Yan-Rong Wang and Qiao-Ling Xu

Abstract Entrepreneurial risk, throughout the entire business process, is inevitable for all enterprises, and with characteristics of high-tech such as high technology content, big demand for fund, rapid technological updating, high growth nature and so on, high-tech entrepreneurial risk should be paid more attention. Therefore, the paper, in combination with characteristics of high-tech, builds evaluation index system of high-tech entrepreneurial risk, and chooses osculating value method for evaluation. The empirical result shows that osculating value method is simple, easy to operate, and relatively objective.

Keywords Entrepreneurial risk · High-tech · Osculating value method

1 Introduction

High-tech doesn't simply mean new technology, which is a general term for latest and most advanced technology in the field of contemporary science and technology, including biotechnology, information technology, new energy technology, new materials technology, space technology, marine technology and so on. Since 1990s, along with depth of reform and opening up and rapid economic development, China's high-tech enterprises have appeared and developed in large numbers. However, entrepreneurial success ratio of high-tech is very low, which indicates that high-tech faces high entrepreneurial risk. Throughout the entire process of entrepreneurial activity, entrepreneurial risk is inevitable, which start-ups have to face. Especially with characteristics such as high technology content, big demand

Y.-R. Wang (✉) and Q.-L. Xu
North China University of Water Conservancy and Electric Power, Zhengzhou 450011, People's Republic of China
e-mail: wyr223@126.com; qiaoling1026xu@126.com

D.D. Wu (ed.), *Modeling Risk Management in Sustainable Construction*, Computational Risk Management, DOI 10.1007/978-3-642-15243-6_33,

for fund, rapid technological updating, high growth nature, entrepreneurial risk of high-tech takes on greater uncertainty, which should be paid more attention. Therefore, in order to ensure the smooth progress of entrepreneurial activity and gain obvious advantages of market competition, the entrepreneurs must timely identify and evaluate business risks, and take effective measures to avoid risks.

2 Related Research

In theory, entrepreneurship research is still in its initial stage, without a universally accepted concept of entrepreneurship. Peter Drucker, Form perspective of innovation, held that entrepreneurship was an innovative process. During this process, opportunities of new product or new service would be recognized, and finally been developed to create new wealth. He thought anyone could learn to be an entrepreneur with entrepreneurial spirit [1]. Robert Ronstadt, from perspective of wealth creation, thought that entrepreneurship was a dynamic process of creation and growth of wealth [2]. Howard Stevenson, based on view of entrepreneurial opportunities and entrepreneurial risk-taking, believed that entrepreneurship was a process of tracking and capturing opportunities, which can be understood from six aspects, such as chance discovery, strategic orientation, commitment to opportunity, resource allocation process, resource control and return policy [3]. Chinese scholar Yu Yi-hong believed that entrepreneurship was an process to discover and capture opportunities, and thereby create innovative products or services to achieve its potential value [4]. The benevolent see benevolence and the wise see wisdom, different scholars have different views from different perspectives. This paper, based on related research, considers that entrepreneurship is a process of searching and capturing opportunities, then developing innovative products and services in order to achieve their specific business objectives [5].

Entrepreneurial risk mainly results from uncertainty of relevant factors during entrepreneurial activities. But as for definition of entrepreneurial risk, there is no uniform point of view. Present studies just center upon certain angle, and define entrepreneurial risk just by adding concept of entrepreneurship and concept of risk together. Timmons and Devinney regarded entrepreneurial risk as an important factor of entrepreneurial decision-making environment, including handlement of decision-making environment of new businesses or new markets, as well as introduction of new products [6]. Zhao Guang-hui, mainly from perspective of entrepreneurial talents, believed that entrepreneurial risk existed in some process during which people start new business. It is some possibility and corresponding result of deviation from the desired objectives due to uncertainty of entrepreneurial environment, complexity of entrepreneurial opportunities and entrepreneurial business, and limited nature of entrepreneurial abilities and strength of entrepreneur and entrepreneurial team [7]. Some scholars divided entrepreneurial risk into systematic risk and non-systematic risk. In sum, although they expressed entrepreneurial risk from different angles, but all of them reflect common characteristics of entrepreneurial risk, such as objective existence, uncertainty, dual nature of profit and loss, relevance, variability and so on.

With regard to studies on entrepreneurial risk assessment, academic studies at home and abroad take on big difference according to study perspective. At present, as for high-tech entrepreneurial risk assessment, traditional assessment methods have been widely used, which, based on risk identification, through collection and collation of data and with the help of probability theory and mathematical statistical methods, estimates extent of risk, but this method lacks applicability premise during evaluation process of high-tech entrepreneurial risk. Some scholars began to use comprehensive evaluation methods to evaluate business risk, such as analytic hierarchy process, fuzzy comprehensive evaluation method and so on. Song Feng-ming divided entrepreneurial risk into process risk and environmental risk, established corresponding evaluation index system and carried on evaluation by use of analytic hierarchy process [8]. Zhao Guang-bing and Wan Wu, according to aspects such as self-trend of high-tech venture, entrepreneurial environment of regional high-tech, industry environment and market conditions, builds evaluation index system and chooses multi-level fuzzy evaluation model for evaluation [9]. Zhang Ren-jun, Liu Xiang-qin thought entrepreneurial risk included technology risk, market risk, financial risk, management risk, personnel risk and environmental risk, established corresponding evaluation index system of entrepreneurial risk about hi-tech SMEs, applied improved analytic hierarchy process and fuzzy comprehensive evaluation model for evaluation, and analyzed possible risk and occurrence probability of entrepreneurial process of high-tech SMEs [10]. However, AHP and fuzzy comprehensive evaluation method have such shortcomings as complex calculation and subjective weight. Therefore, the paper proposes osculating value method for evaluating entrepreneurial risk, which could overcome above shortcomings.

3 Evaluation Index System of Entrepreneurial Risk

For entrepreneurial risk involves many factors, the paper, following some principles such as objectivity, scientificalness, comparability, operability, and combination of quantitativity and qualitativity, builds multi-level evaluation index system of entrepreneurial risk.

3.1 Opportunity Risk

Opportunity risk is possibility of potential loss entrepreneurs would suffer when giving up other options for venture, which is a reflection of current interests and future value of entrepreneurs, mainly including wage income (A_{11}), venture pressure (A_{12}), expected income (A_{13}), social benefits (A_{14}) and so on.

3.2 Market Risk

Market risk is possibility of loss which venture would suffer and failure of start-ups, due to changes in market demand or products not been fully accepted by market, specifically including market stability (A_{31}), market development difficulty (A_{32}), market demand conditions (A_{33}), product market competition (A_{34}), product life-cycle (A_{35}) and so on.

3.3 Management Risk

Management risk is related to management level, which is caused by non-adaptability of management and staff, ranging from overall quality and experience of entrepreneurs (A_{41}), maturity of management mechanism (A_{42}), scientific level of decision-making (A_{43}), coordination of management team (A_{44}) and so on.

3.4 Capital Risk

Capital risk is possibility of account chaos, funding difficulties, loss of solvent and financial crisis during financial activities, and uncertainty of owners' earnings, mainly including capital structure (A_{51}), fund-raising capacity (A_{52}), fund recovery situation (A_{53}), financial management standardization (A_{54}), income level (A_{55}) and so on.

3.5 Environment Risk

Environmental risk is possibility of business losses or failure resulting from changes in social environment, legal environment and national and local policies or because of an unexpected disaster beyond control during entrepreneurial process, such as political environmental risk (A_{61}), legal environmental risk (A_{62}), macroeconomic conditions (A_{63}), social and cultural risk (A_{64}) and so on.

4 Entrepreneurial Risk Assessment Model

Osculating value method is an optimization method of multi-objective decision-making, which needn't calculate weight. This method integrates multiple target system into a single goal strength and weakness of which can be measured overally, and lists priority. Basic idea is as followed: First, sort out the optimum point and the inferior point from a large number of evaluation objects, then calculate the distance between the optimum point and the inferior point of each evaluation object, and list priority of high-tech entrepreneurial risk accordingly. Specific evaluation procedures are as follows:

4.1 Establishment of Index Matrix and Standardization

Supposed that value of program set Ai ($i = 1, 2, ..., m$) under index S_i ($j = 1, 2, \ldots, n$) is a_{ij}, obtain index matrix $A = (a_{ij})_{m \times n}$. Since the program index is so numerous, which take on complex relationship between each other. Among them, there are positive indicators (the higher the index value, the stronger the ability) and reverse indicators (the higher the index value, the worse the ability). What's more, each indicator has different dimension. Therefore, in order to better compare, the paper carries out standardized treatment on index matrix.

Supposed:

$$x_{ij} = \begin{cases} \dfrac{a_{ij}}{\sqrt{\sum\limits_{i=1}^{m} (a_{ij})^2}} & \text{When } j \text{ is positive indicator} \quad (1) \\ \dfrac{-a_{ij}}{\sqrt{\sum\limits_{i=1}^{m} (a_{ij})^2}} & \text{When } j \text{ is reverse indicator} \end{cases} \tag{2}$$

Get standardized index matrix $X = (x_{ij})\ m \times n$.

4.2 Determine the Optimum Point and the Inferior Point of Program Set

Supposed:

$$X_j^+ = \max\{X_{ij}\} \quad X_j^- = \min\{X_{ij}\} \tag{3}$$

$(j = 1, 2, \ldots, n)$
Then:
Optimum point set: $A^+ = (x_1^+, x_2^+, \ldots, x_n^+)$
Inferior point set: $A^- = (x_1^-, x_2^-, \ldots, x_n^-)$
Satisfied program is focused on identifying decision-making point, which is nearest the optimum point and furthest away from inferior point.

4.3 Calculation of Osculating Value of Each Program

Osculating value of Program A_i as:

$$C_i = d_i^+/d^+ - d_i^-/d^- \tag{4}$$

and:

$$d_i^+ = \left[\sum_{j=1}^{n} (X_{ij} - X_j^+)^2\right]^{1/2} \tag{5}$$

$$d_i^- = \left[\sum_{j=1}^{n} (X_{ij} - X_j^-)^2\right]^{1/2} \tag{6}$$

$$d^+ = \min\{d_i^+\}, \quad d^- = \max\{d_i^-\} \tag{7}$$

d_i^+ represents Euclidean distance between program A_i and optimum program A^+, and d_i^- between program A_i and inferior program A^-. d^+ and d^- respectively shows minimum among m optimum point distances and maximum among m inferior point distances.

Size of C_i reflects deviation degree of program set from optimum point. When $C_i > 0$, Ai is deviated from optimum point, and the bigger the value is, the further the deviation is. When $C_i = 0$, A is closest to the optimum point. Size of C_i is regarded as decision-making criteria, the smallest size of C is thought to be satisfied program.

5 Empirical Analysis

In order to test scientificalness and effectiveness of evaluation index system and evaluation method, the paper selects such four high-tech enterprises as A, B, C and D, and evaluate their entrepreneurial risk by osculating value method.

Among evaluation index system established of entrepreneurial risk, qualitative index are predominated. For some quantitative index, the paper directly gets data from the company's financial department, human resources and technical centers or through calculation of relevant index. After arrangement and analysis, the paper gets standardized data shown in Table 1.

According to (3) and Table 1, the paper obtains optimum point (A^+) and inferior point (A^-):

$A^+ = (x_1^+, x_2^+, \ldots, x_n^+)$, $A^- = (x_1^-, x_2^-, \ldots, x_n^-)$, shown in Table 2

According to (5) and (6), calculate d_i^+ and d_i^-, then in combination with formula (7), calculate osculating value of each enterprise, and according to size of osculating value, the paper lists priority of high-tech entrepreneurial risk, please see Table 3.

We can see $C_D < C_B < C_C < C_A$, which demonstrates that entrepreneurial risk of A is biggest, much smaller is C and B, and entrepreneurial risk of A is smallest. The evaluation result is in accordance with the real situation.

Table 1 Standardized data of each enterprise

Index data		Standardized data of each Enterprise			
Index	Sub-indicator	A	B	C	D
Opportunity risk	A_{11}: wage income	0.53	0.45	0.52	0.52
	A_{12}: venture pressure	0.49	0.40	0.42	0.51
	A_{13}: expected income	0.51	0.50	0.50	0.53
	A_{14}: social benefits	0.43	0.52	0.46	0.51
Technology risk	A_{21}:technology progressivity	−0.49	−0.51	−0.38	−0.59
	A_{22}: technology maturity	−0.50	−0.51	−0.46	−0.53
	A_{23}: technology applicability	−0.47	−0.63	−0.37	−0.49
	A_{24}: technology replaceability	0.64	0.52	0.48	0.50
	A_{25}: technology life cycle	−0.45	−0.50	−0.45	−0.65
Market risk	A_{31}: market stability	−0.60	−0.53	−0.55	−0.57
	A_{32}: market development difficulty	0.46	0.51	0.32	0.72
	A_{33}: market demand conditions	−0.51	−0.53	−0.49	−0.59
	A_{34}:product market competition	0.47	0.66	0.44	0.65
	A_{35}: product life-cycle	−0.41	−0.50	−0.81	−0.44
Management risk	A_{41}:overall quality of entrepreneur	−0.61	−0.42	−0.48	−0.66
	A_{42}:maturity of management mechanism	−0.52	−0.52	−0.52	−0.57
	A_{43}: scientific level of decision-making	−0.47	−0.52	−0.44	−0.56
	A_{44}: coordination of management team	−0.49	−0.50	−0.44	−0.54
Capital risk	A_{51}: capital structure	−0.43	−0.54	−0.46	−0.60
	A_{52}: fund-raising capacity	−0.50	−0.50	−0.54	−0.49
	A_{53}: funds recovery situation	−0.60	−0.51	−0.72	−0.43
	A_{54}:financial management standardization	−0.56	−0.48	−0.63	−0.67
	A_{55}: income level	−0.42	−0.50	−0.56	−0.61
Environment risk	A_{61}: political environmental risk	0.50	0.43	0.49	0.56
	A_{62}: legal environmental risk	0.46	0.53	0.48	0.49
	A_{63}: macroeconomic conditions	−0.54	−0.50	−0.54	−0.55
	A_{64}: social and cultural risk	0.55	0.48	0.42	0.41

Table 2 Optimum point and inferior point of evaluation system

Index	Sub-indicator	j = 1,2, ... 26	x_j^+	x_j^-
Opportunity risk	A_{11}: wage income	1	0.53	0.45
	A_{12}: venture pressure	2	0.51	0.40
	A_{13}: expected income	3	0.53	0.50
	A_{14}: social benefits	4	0.52	0.43
	A_{21}:technology progressivity	5	−0.59	−0.38
Technology risk	A_{22}: technology maturity	6	−0.53	−0.46
	A_{23}: technology applicability	7	−0.63	−0.37
	A_{24}: technology replaceability	8	0.64	0.48
	A_{25}: technology life cycle	9	−0.65	−0.45
	A_{31}: market stability	10	−0.60	−0.53
Market risk	A_{32}: market development difficulty	11	0.72	0.32
	A_{33}: market demand conditions	12	−0.59	−0.49
	A_{34}:product market competition	13	0.66	0.44
	A_{35}: product life-cycle	14	−0.81	−0.41
	A_{41}:overall quality of entrepreneur	15	−0.66	−0.42
Management risk	A_{42}:maturity of management mechanism	16	−0.57	−0.52
	A_{43}: scientific level of decision-making	17	−0.56	−0.44
	A_{44}: coordination of management team	18	−0.54	−0.44
	A_{51}: capital structure	19	−0.60	−0.43
Capital risk	A_{52}: fund-raising capacity	20	−0.54	−0.49
	A_{53}: funds recovery situation	21	−0.72	−0.43
	A_{54}:financial management standardization	22	−0.67	−0.48
Environment risk	A_{55}: income level	23	−0.61	−0.42
	A_{61}: political environmental risk	24	0.56	0.43
	A_{62}: legal environmental risk	25	0.53	0.46
	A_{63}: macroeconomic conditions	26	−0.55	−0.50
	A_{64}: social and cultural risk	27	0.55	0.41

Table 3 Osculating value and evaluation result

enterprise	d_i^+	d_i^-	C_i	priority
A	0.69	0.436	0.713118	1
B	0.635	0.489	0.539736	3
C	0.728	0.555	0.626244	2
D	0.534	0.753	0	4

6 Conclusion

Along with economic development and support of national policy, the threshold of high-tech venture is decreasing, but success ratio is very low because of inevitable entrepreneurial risk which leads to entrepreneurial failure. Therefore, how to identify and evaluate entrepreneurial risk and take corresponding measures is very vital. Considering numerous factors of high-tech entrepreneurial risk, and subjectivity and ambiguity of evaluation process, the paper chooses osculating value method to evaluate high-tech entrepreneurial risk. Osculating value method is an optimization method of multi-objective decision-making of system engineering, easy to calculate and comparably objective. Empirical result shows that osculating value method to assess high-tech entrepreneurship risk is desirable.

References

1. Peter Drucker. Innovation and Entrepreneurship [M]. New York: Harper Row, 1985:16.
2. Robert Ronstadt. Network Support and the Success of Newly Founded Business [J]. Small Business Economics; 2000(3): 213–215.
3. Howard Stevenson. Venture Corporate Finance [M]. Beijing: China Renmin University Press, 2002:31.
4. Robert D. Hisrich. Entrepreneurship [M]. Shanghai: Fudan University Press, 2000:134.
5. Wang Yan-Rong. Entrepreneurship-Theory and Methods [M]. Xi'an: Shanxi People's Publishing House, 2004:12.
6. Jeffery A.Timmons. New Venture Creation [M]. London: Irwin McGraw-Hill, 1999:45–58.
7. Zhao Guang-hui. Government Function Innovation of Private High-Tech Enterprises Innovation System Research of Private High-Tech Entrepreneur [J]. Technology Entrepreneurial Monthly Publication. 2005 (18):21–22.
8. P.E. Petrakis. The Effects of Risk and Time on Entrepreneurship [J]. Int Entrep Manag J. 2007 (3):277–291.
9. Vesa Kanniainen, Mikko Leppämäki. Union power, Entrepreneurial Risk, and Entrepreneurship [J]. Small Bus Econ. 2009 (33):293–302.
10. Zhang Ren-jun, Liu Xiang-qin. Evaluation Study on High-tech SMEs Venture [J]. Mod Manag Sci. 2009 (3):68–69.

An Approach to Overseas Iron Ore Investment Risk Assessment Based on Fuzzy Neural Network

Li Guo, Caiwu Lu, and Zhen Yang

Abstract The iron ore investment overseas influenced by a variety of risk factors including geological reserves risk, market risk, the risk of the investment environment, political and legal risks, and etc. Based on the theory of risk assessment, this paper firstly analyzed the risk from the asset influence and frequency of threat, set up risk level structure of overseas iron ore investment, and presented the membership matrices for judgment set. Then, the neural network and fuzzy reasoning theory were applied to evaluate the risk of overseas iron ore investment to obtain its risk grade. Finally, a calculation example was used to show how the method works, and the error analysis was applied to detecting effectiveness and reliability of the model performance.

Keywords Fuzzy neural network · Iron ore investment risk oversea · Risk assessment

1 Introduction

With the rapid development of China's steel industry, the shortage of domestic iron ore resources becoming an increasingly serious problem which lead to a substantial increase in imports of iron ore in successive years. But in recent years, pricing right of China's imports of iron ore loss, imports of iron ore prices and sea freight are rising, seriously affects the healthy development of China's steel industry. The serious situation urgently requires our country to invest in overseas iron ore actively and to obtain more mineral rights. For the specificity of iron ore resources, there are

---

Imbursed by Shaanxi province specialties fund of importance subject building

L. Guo (✉), C. Lu, and Z. Yang
School of Management, Xi'an University of Architecture & Technology, Xi'an, Shanxi 710055, People's Republic of China
e-mail: fair@126.com; lucaiwu@126.com; yangzhen-2005@hotmail.com

D.D. Wu (ed.), *Modeling Risk Management in Sustainable Construction*, Computational Risk Management, DOI 10.1007/978-3-642-15243-6_34,

many overseas iron ore investment risks, such as mineral resources risk, investment environment risk, which all need investors to consider seriously and do the full depth and meticulous research.

2 Risk Factors of the Overseas Iron Ore Investment

Iron ore exploration and development is a very complex process. There is a considerable difference between overseas and domestic iron ore exploration and development in the investment environment, operating environment, cultural environment, political environment, and the relationship between resources sovereign state and investor. At present, the risk existed in the overseas iron ore exploration and development project can be classified into following four aspect by the nature of venture capital: geological reserves risk, market risk, the risk of the investment environment, political and legal risk [1, 2], such as Fig. 1.

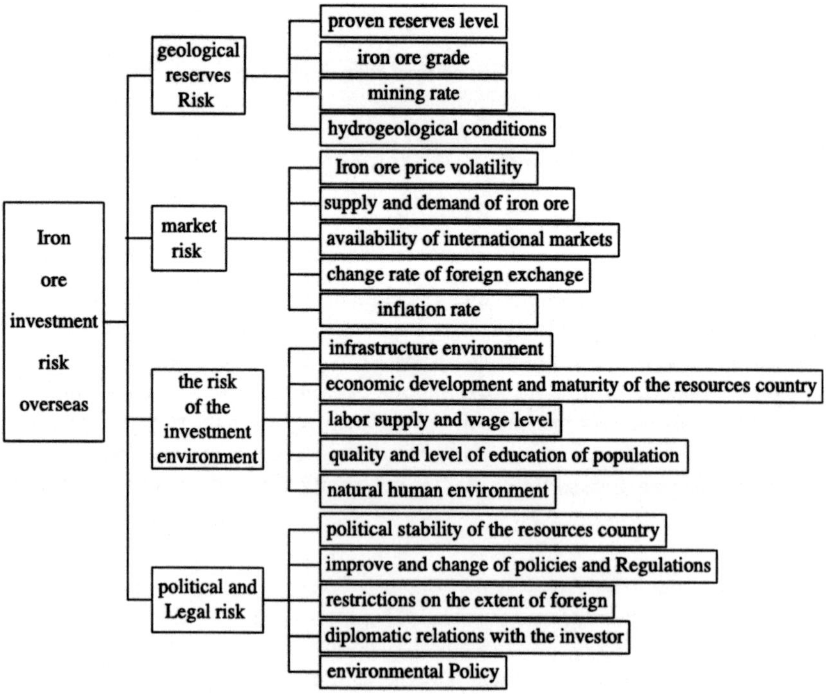

Fig. 1 Risk factors of overseas iron ore investment

3 Risk Assessment of Overseas Iron Ore Investment Based on Fuzzy

3.1 Fuzzy Sets and Membership Matrix

In the risk assessment of the overseas iron ore investment, we identify the degree of the risk according to the evaluation of possibility and negative effects of the risks event. Overseas iron ore investment risk R is seen as the function of asset and threat frequency. That is $R = g(c, t)$, where c for the assets affected, t as the threat frequency. In other words, the overseas iron ore investment risk is divided into the two aspects: the assets affected and the threat frequency.

The estimated of assets affected and threat frequency all have a certain degree of vagueness. So the paper analyzes and deals with the various factors with fuzzy theory [3].

First, established a risk factors set. Suppose $A = \{a_1, a_2, \cdots, a_n\}$, in which n is the number of elements in the factors set ; constructed evaluation set, for the assets and threats frequency this two elements may establish a different evaluation set $B = \{b_1, b_2, \cdots, b_m\}$, in which m is the number of elements in the corresponding evaluation.

Secondly, assess the various factors in the set A reference evaluation set B, given the comments of various factors, structural fuzzy mapping. $f : A \rightarrow F(B)$, $F(B)$ is the fuzzy set of all B, $a_i \rightarrow f(a_i) = (P_{i1}, P_{i2}, \cdots, P_{im}) \in F(B)$. Where the map f denotes that the level of support of the risk factors a_i to the reviews of various evaluation set, the attached to the vector of the risk factors a_i on the evaluation set B $P_i = (P_{i1}, P_{i2}, \cdots, P_{im})$, i = 1,2, ..., n, was attached to the matrix:

$$P = \begin{bmatrix} P_{11} & P_{12} & \cdots & P_{1m} \\ P_{21} & P_{22} & \cdots & P_{2m} \\ \vdots & \vdots & & \vdots \\ P_{n1} & P_{n2} & \cdots & P_{nm} \end{bmatrix}$$

The various factors of overseas iron ore investment risk relative to the level of the assets influence and threat frequency are attached to different membership matrix, them are P_c and P_t. Corresponding weight vector of each factor is $\Phi = (\varphi_1, \varphi_2, \cdots, \varphi_n)$. We can obtain the target weight vector $U = (u_1, u_2, \cdots, u_{n_1})$ for giving corresponding weight to the factors of evaluation set, where n_1 is the number of elements in the evaluation set of the assets influence. That the assets influence can be expressed as $R_c = \Phi \cdot P_c \cdot U^T$.

Similarly, the evaluation set index weight vector of threat frequency is $V = (v_1, v_2, \cdots, v_{n_2})$, where n_2 is the number of elements in the evaluation set of the threat frequency. That the threat frequency can be expressed as $R_t = \Phi \cdot P_t \cdot V^T$.

3.2 Investment Risk Rating

By the algorithm given above can be obtained the asset influence value R_c and the threat frequency value R_t. Then integrate the risk value of the various elements using the system integration method. So we can calculate the investment risk value $R = g(c,t) = k_1R_c + k_2R_t$. Where: $k1$, $k2$ respectively the relative importance of two elements, and $k1 + k2 = 1$. The grade of membership of investment risk as follows: 0–0.2 lower, 0.2–0.4 low, 0.4–0.6 medium, 0.6–0.8 high, 0.8–1 higher. The risk level can be used to guide the investors to analysis and decision making in investment.

4 Neural Network Model

4.1 Fuzzy BP Neural Network Design

Single three layers BP neural network can simulate any nonlinear input–output relationship, it can approximate arbitrary continuous function and the nonlinear mapping. Therefore, the paper designs d (d is the number of subsystems) three layers BP neural network, input layer is the element values in fuzzy membership matrix of various risk factors in overseas iron ore investment; output layer is a single node output which output the subsystem risk value. Then output of d sub-network as the input of next network, in order to complete the risk assessment of overseas iron ore investment.

For the number of hidden nodes, using empirical formula to calculate: $l = \log 2n$. Where: n is the number of input nodes; l is the number of hidden nodes.

4.2 Learning Process of Single BP Neural Network

Let the learning sample group of input is k, set the allowable error is e and the learning rate is α, the learning process [4] as follows.

Step 1: Determine the input and output layers.

Input layer: the input $X_i^{(q)}$ of node i is the element values in fuzzy membership matrix of each risk factor through the fuzzy quantification. The input $X_i^{(q)}$ is to output $a_{ij}^{(q)}$ through the input layer nodes. In the input layer, the input and output are equal, that is $X_i^{(q)} = a_{ij}^{(q)}$, $i = 1,2,\ldots,n$, $j = 1,2,\ldots,l$, $q = 1,2,\ldots,m$.

Hidden layer: the input of hidden layer node k is the weights sum of output variables of the input nodes, that is $u_k^{(q)} = \sum_{i=1}^{n} w_{ik}a_{ik}^{(q)}$, where w_{ik} is the connection weights of the input layer node i to the output layer node k, $w_{ik} \geq 0$, $k = 1,2,\ldots,l$;

The output of hidden layer node k is $b_k^{(q)} = f(u_k^{(q)})$, f is Sigmoid function, that is $f(x) = 1/(1+e^{-x})$.

Output layer: The output layer only has one node, the input of the output node is the weights sum of all output variables in the hidden layer, that is $\sum_{k=1}^{l} v_k b_k^{(q)}$, The final output of network is $y^{(q)} = f\left[\sum_{k=1}^{l} v_k b_k^{(q)}\right]$, $q = 1,2,\ldots,m$, v_k is the weights that hidden layer node k connect to the output node, f is Sigmoid function.

Step 2: Calculate the output error and deviation of the output layers.

Square error function is used to calculate the error $E_q = (t_j^{(q)} - y_j^{(q)})^2/2$ of a single sample q and the system Average error $E = 1/m \cdot \sum_{q=1}^{m} E_q$ of m training samples.

It is necessary to adjust the network from behind to front when the actual output value of output layer is inconsistent with the expectations. The δ learning rules is used in BP neural network: Deviation of the output layer is $\delta^{(q)} = \partial E_q/\partial v_k = y^{(q)}(1-y^{(q)})(t^{(q)}-y^{(q)})$; Deviation of the hidden layer is $e_k^{(q)} = \partial E_q/\partial w_{ij} = b_k^{(q)}(1-b_k^{(q)})\sum_{k=1}^{l} v_k \delta^{(q)}$, $k = 1,2,\ldots,l$.

Step 3: Calculate the weight correction.

The weights correction that hidden layer connects to output layer is $\Delta v_k = a \cdot b_k^{(q)} \cdot \delta^{(q)}$;

The weights correction that input layer connects to hidden layer is $\Delta w_{ik} = a \cdot a_{ik}^{(q)} \cdot e_k^{(q)}$.

It makes the square error of the network output and the actual value of the training sample reduces through the iterative algorithm of neural network, to gain a stable network structure and connection weights.

5 Case Studies

Takes an iron ore investment project in Philippines as an example, conducts a risk assessment, the market risk is the main consideration here. It will construct the BP network model of market factors for risk assessment. First of all, assesses the market risk using the methods of fuzzy theory to obtain the valuation which as the network data set, and then completes the assessment using trained network.

1. Construct factor set and evaluation set, seek membership matrix P_c and P_t, calculate the target weight vector.
   Factor set $A = \{a_1, a_2, a_3, a_4, a_5\}$, where a_i ($i = 1,2,\ldots,5$) denotes the market risk factors respectively: "iron ore price volatility", "supply and demand of iron ore", "availability of international market", "change rate of foreign exchange" and "inflation rate". The evaluation set is constructed as $\mathrm{B_c} = \{b_{c1}, b_{c2}, b_{c3}, b_{c4}, b_{c5}\}$, $\mathrm{B_t} = \{b_{t1}, b_{t2}, b_{t3}, b_{t4}, b_{t5}\}$.

Firstly, give the opinions about various risk factors by the experts, then calculate the probability of the risk factors belonging to the index to get the matrix P_c and P_t. The corresponding weight vector of each factor is calculated by the entropy coefficient: $\Phi_c = \{\varphi_{c1}, \varphi_{c2}, \varphi_{c3}, \varphi_{c4}, \varphi_{c5}\} = (0.450, 0.284, 0.146, 0.064, 0.056)$. $B_t = \{b_{t1}, b_{t2}, b_{t3}, b_{t4}, b_{t5}\} = (0.295, 0.205, 0.164, 0.186, 0.150)$.
The target weights of evaluation set are: U = (1/15,2/15,1/5,4/15,1/3), V = (1/15,2/15,1/5,4/15,1/3).

2. Construct a three layers BP neural network, the input layer with 25 neurons, received respectively the five factors to constitute the fuzzy membership matrix with 25 elements value; calculated $l = \log_2 25 \approx 5$, the hidden layer with five neurons; output layer with one neuron, corresponding to the risk assessment result.
Twenty-one sets of samples as the training set, one as the testing set. Meanwhile, set the square error of average output of the training samples e equal to 10–4, and

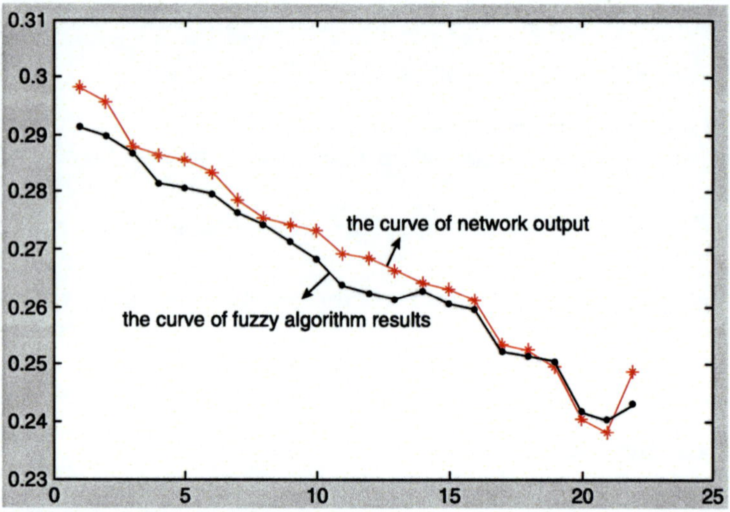

Fig. 2 Relationships between FT and FNN

Table 1 Results of FT and FNN assessment for samples

	1	2	3	4	5	6	7	8
FT	0.2912	0.2898	0.2867	0.2813	0.2805	0.2795	0.2763	0.2742
FTT	0.2983	0.2957	0.2879	0.2864	0.2856	0.2833	0.2785	0.2756
	9	10	11	12	13	14	15	16
FT	0.2713	0.2683	0.2637	0.2623	0.2612	0.2627	0.2603	0.2595
FTT	0.2744	0.2732	0.2692	0.2685	0.2664	0.2642	0.2631	0.2611
	17	18	19	20	21	22	–	–
FT	0.2521	0.2513	0.2502	0.2416	0.2403	0.2429	–	–
FTT	0.2536	0.2525	0.2496	0.2404	0.2382	0.2487	–	–

the learning rate α of 0.05. Impact of assets influence of the market risk, the results of FT and FNN assessment for samples are shown in Table 1.
Plots Fig. 2 according to Table 1, we can see that the risk output values of neural network approach the fuzzy risk assessment values with strong adaptability and high accuracy.

3. The comprehensive integration of assessment value.
Similarly, the risk value of the threat frequency can also be calculated. The corresponding risk values of the geological reserves risk, market risk, and the risk of the investment environment, political and legal risk can be also calculated by building their BP neural network model. The risk value of overseas iron ore investment can be calculated according to the degree of importance of different risk factors, this does not repeat. Finally, the calculation of the value of its integrated risk grade belongs low. So, the investment risk grade belongs low.

6 Conclusions

A risk assessment model of overseas iron ore investment is established in this paper by combining the fuzzy theory and neural networks, and the model has been tested by data simulation. The result shows that the model improves the performance of risk assessment through the adaptive of the network, and the data processing is realized by Matlab, it is accurate and fast. So the research provides an effective way for intelligent assessment of the overseas iron ore investment risk.

References

1. Hou Yubin and Yang Juan (2010) Risk analysis on fuzzy Synthetical Judgment of iron Investment Oversea. China Mining Magazine 2: 61–63
2. Han Enze and Zhu Yingchao (2010) Evaluation of overseas investment risk for Chinese Oil Corporation based on fuzzy-AHP. Henan Science 2: 235–239
3. Fu Yu and Wu Xiaoping (2010) An approach to information systems security risk assessment based on fuzzy-combinatorial neural network. Journal of Naval University of Engineering 1: 18–23
4. Xiao Long and Fang Yong (2006) Risk evaluation of information system based on fuzzy neural net-work. Research on Computer Application 5: 137–139

Analysis on Structure Risk and Its Countermeasures of International Trade Corridor in Inland China

Xiao-dong Xie, Mao-zeng Xu, Shun-yong Li, and Li Huang

Abstract Based on the structure of trade, structure of transportation corridor, structure of transportation mode and structure of port, this paper analyzes the structure risk of International Trade Corridor(ITC) in Inland China (for example in Chongqing) and puts forward a new corridor system which including four chief and six accessorial corridors. This countermeasure can help to evade or resolve the corridor structure risk and ensure the construction and management of ITC in Inland China easily.

Keywords Corridor structure · Corridor system · International trade · Risk analysis

1 Introduction

The international trade corridor (ITC) in inland China refer to available inland corridors with strategic significance, which have played a leading role in international trade transportation and customs declaration, would cause great losses when

X.-d. Xie (✉)
College of Economy & Business Administration, Chongqing University, Chongqing 400044, China
and
School of Management, Chongqing Jiaotong University, Chongqing 400074, People's Republic of China
e-mail: xiexd@cquc.edu.cn

M.-z. Xu and S.-y. Li
School of Management, Chongqing Jiaotong University, Chongqing 400074, People's Republic of China
e-mail: xmxzrzhy@cquc.edu.cn, lsypub@gmail.com

L. Huang
International Office, Chongqing Jiaotong University, Chongqing 400074, People's Republic of China
e-mail: orioleli@hotmail.com

D.D. Wu (ed.), *Modeling Risk Management in Sustainable Construction*, Computational Risk Management, DOI 10.1007/978-3-642-15243-6_35,

they are blocked [1]. At present, the inland provinces and cities in China all pay great attentions to the ITC, and a variety of media and academia have concerned and discussed it hotly [2, 3]. However, until now, nobody presents a clear judgment on the structural risk of the ITC, or the hidden dangers in it, which then make the relevant departments facing enormous risks in constructing and managing it. Therefore, based on the in-depth analysis of the structure of the ITC (Taking Chongqing as an example), this paper reveals structural risks of the existing corridor, and further proposes the countermeasure of avoiding or defusing the risks, thus ensuring the construction and management of ITC smoothly.

2 Structural Characteristics Analysis of ITC in Inland China (Chongqing as an example)

2.1 Structural Characteristics of Chongqing International Trade Orientation

Table 1 reflects the general flow of goods in international trade of Chongqing in recent years. The biggest three orientations are to America, the Europe except Eastern part and the Northeast Asia, and their total value of import and export accounted for about 71%. With the ports in Europe and the West Coast ports in U.S. growing congestion, the risk of block may undoubtedly worsened [4].

Table 1 Distribution of import and export value in Chongqing in years of 2006–2008 (million U.S. dollars)

Area	Total import and export value		Export value		Import value	
	Total value in the 3 years	Rate (%)	Total value in the 3 years	Rate (%)	Total value in the 3 years	Rate (%)
America	499,664	28.5	321,376	18.4	188,288	10.8
Europe except Eastern part	470,116	26.8	139,216	8.0	330,837	18.9
Northeast Asia	275,711	15.7	70,572	4.0	205,139	11.7
South-Eastern Asia	123,265	7.0	97,484	5.6	25,781	1.5
Western Asia	105,343	6.0	100,119	5.7	5,224	0.3
Africa	81,416	4.6	72,136	4.1	9,280	0.5
Hong Kong, Macao and Taiwan	76,588	4.4	45,220	2.6	31,367	1.8
Eastern Europe	60,989	3.5	52,338	3.0	8,650	0.5
Southern Asia	34,996	2.0	30,297	1.7	4,699	0.3
Oceania	22,863	1.3	12,147	0.7	10,716	0.6

Source: Chongqing foreign trade and economic relations commission

2.2 Composition and Characteristics of the Main Transport Corridors

There are six corridors undertaking the above-mentioned trade tasks. Their characteristics are shown in Table 2. Among them, the main transport corridor is the Yangtze River waterway from Chongqing to Shanghai [5]. However, the middle reach of the Yangtze River and the Three Gorges Dam have become a potential bottleneck, which increases the risks in corridor structure.

2.3 Structural Characteristics of Transshipment Port

The structure of Chongqing International Trade transshipment port is shown in the following table. Table 3 shows that the trans-shipment volume of Shanghai Port accounts for 87.2% of the total, and it is the largest import and export port of Chongqing. Recently, Shanghai Port has undertaken a heavy customs declaration task of the Yangtze River Delta region. If Chongqing is still over-reliant on Shanghai Port, it would be of great risks for its international trade.

2.4 Transport Modes of Chongqing International Trade

Water transport is absolutely the dominate way of Chongqing's foreign trade. Its total traffic volume accounts for more than 97% of the total foreign trade, and other means of transport accounts for a very small part (as shown in Tables 4 and 5).

Table 2 The basic situation of main transport corridors

No.	Starting and ending point	Destination	Trans mode	Transportation mileage (km)	Transit time (days)
1	Chongqing–Shanghai	Europe, America, Africa, and Asia-Pacific Areas	Waterway	2,336	6–7
2	Chongqing–Shenzhen	Europe, Africa, Asia-Pacific Areas	Railway	2,135	4–5
3	Chongqing–Hekou in Yunnan province	Southeast Asian Areas	Expressway	1,583	3–4
4	Chongqing–Pingxiang in Guangxi province		Expressway	1,219	2–3
5	Chongqing–Alashankou port	West Asia, Eastern Europe	Railway	3,835	16–17
6	Chongqing–Tianjin	Northeast Asia	Railway	1,510	5–6

Source: Ministry of Communication of the People's Republic of China, and the literature [6–9]

Table 3 The major trans-shipment ports of Chongqing international trade

Area	Transshipment port	Port amount	Rate of transship volume (%)
Shanghai	Pujiang Customs, Wusong Customs, Shanghai Airport Customs, Waigaoqiao Customs, Waigang Customs, Pudong Airport, Shanghai Express, Yangshan Port	8	87.2
Jiangsu	Lianyungang Customs, Nantong Customs, Zhenjiang Customs Xingshengyu Customs, Yangzhou Customs, Jiangyin Customs, Lukou machine Office, Customs Changshu, Taicang Customs	9	5.6
Guangdong	Guangzhou Customs, Guangzhou Xingfeng, Guangzhou Airport, Transit Center, Huanggang Customs, Shekou Customs, Sungang Customs, Dapeng Customs, Shengguan Airport, Meilin Customs, Hengqin Customs, Xia Shan Customs, Zhanjiang Hai Xia Customs	13	3.7
Beijing	Airport documentation	1	1.4
Xinjiang	Alashankou, Uganda Airport Customs	2	0.83
Guangxi	Fangcheng Customs, Pingxiang Customs	2	0.5
Sichuan	Chengdu Airport Customs, Chengdu Airport Express	2	0.4

Source: Chongqing foreign trade and economic relations commission

Table 4 The import and export transportation volume in Chongqing from 2006 to 2008 (Ton)

Mode	2006		2007		2008	
	Volume	Rate (%)	Volume	Rate (%)	Volume	Rate (%)
Waterway	1,701,504	97.70	3,286,942	98.69	4,368,244	98.86
Railway	34,358	1.97	34,002	1.02	41,208	0.93
Airway	4,739	0.27	7,711	0.23	8,554	0.19
Highway	944	0.05	1,810	0.05	443	0.01
Total	1,741,545	100	3,330,465	100	4,418,449	100

Source: Chongqing statistical yearbook

Table 5 The import and export transportation value in Chongqing from 2006 to 2008 (million dollars)

Mode	2006		2007		2008	
	Value	Rate (%)	Value	Rate (%)	Value	Rate (%)
Waterway	363,113	86.97	516,387	87.31	684,204	88.36
Railway	14,803	3.55	14,659	2.48	17,753	2.29
Airway	38,474	9.21	58,445	9.88	70,639	9.12
Highway	1,141	0.27	1,965	0.33	1,715	0.22
Total	417,531	100	591,456	100	774,311	100

Source: Chongqing statistical yearbook

Chongqing will face huge security risks if relying on shipping heavily, because of the congestion in the Panama Canal, Suez Canal, the Strait of Gibraltar and the Strait of Malacca as well as the piracy and terrorist threats [10].

3 Structural Risks and Countermeasures of ITC in Inland China (Chongqing as an Example)

3.1 Main Structural Risk of the ITC in Chongqing

According to the above analysis and our early researches [6], the structural risks of inland ITC (such as Chongqing) as following:

1. There is a potential bottleneck, because the middle Waterway of the Yangtze River waterway is too shallow and the maximum carrying capacities as designed of the Three Gorges Dam and Gezhouba Dam are too small.
2. Right now, all straits around the world are very congested. The overdependence on waterway may cause a serious unbalance in transportation structure. It may bring a huge calamity in a way, once the Three Gorges Dam is suddenly blocked and wars breaks out along the coast, coupled with piracy and terrorist threats.
3. At present, the main destinations of Chongqing foreign trade are America, Europe and Northeast Asia when their major ports have become increasingly congested. It will make the situation worse if Chongqing rely heavily on the current transport corridors however.
4. On the one hand, a large number of transshipment ports of Chongqing concentrate in the east part of China, which may cause a huge transshipment risk once these ports have an accident. On the other hand, the backward infrastructure and inadequate staffing in local ports could cause congestion in customs declaration.

3.2 Countermeasures of Solving Structural Risks

For the above structural risks, the inland areas (taking Chongqing as an example) should further improve its corridor structure, adjust or reconstruct the Four Main-corridor System and the Six Auxiliary Corridor System (i.e. '4 Main + 6 Auxiliary' Corridor system, and the distribution of foreign trade of which is 8:2), to form a balanced, safe and expedite international trade system.

3.2.1 Four Main Corridors (Core Corridor System)

The four main corridors, which based on the shipping center of the upper reaches of the Yangtze River and the Lianglu Cuntan bonded port area, would be a core corridor system with structural stability and small structural risks (as in Fig. 1). The four corridors as following:

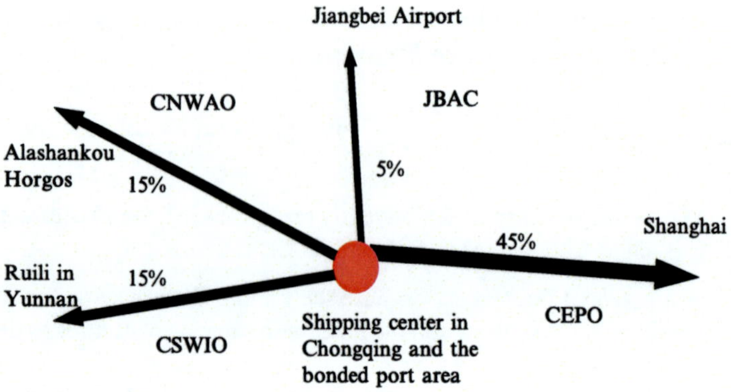

Fig. 1 The core corridor system of the ITC of Chongqing

1. Corridor East to the Pacific Ocean (CEPO). Which includes the Yangtze River, the high- speed railway along it, Chongqing-Shanghai expressway and Shanghai – Chengdu expressway.
2. Corridor South-west to the Indian Ocean (CSWIO). which includes those corridor to Southeast Asian Nations (especially Myanmar). The carried cargo can cross Myanmar into the Indian Ocean, forming the most convenient access to the Indian Ocean in the southwest.
3. Corridor Northwest to the Atlantic Ocean (CNWAO). Which take the advantage of the new Eurasian Continental Bridge into the Atlantic Ocean.
4. Jiangbei Airport Corridors (JBAC). Through which the international cargo flights direct connect the big cities in Europe, the United States and Asia-Pacific areas.

Among them, the CEPO, the CSWIO and the CNWAO are the core ITC in Chongqing. It is known as Chongqing's "one River with two Wings" strategic corridor.

From Fig. 1, we can see the core corridor system is more balanced in the structure. From the task allocation, this will greatly ease the structural imbalance of Chongqing international trade by sharing burden to the two western corridors. Meanwhile, the JBAC can make immediate supplement to other corridors, which upgrade the stability of the whole system.

3.2.2 Six Auxiliary Corridors (Auxiliary Corridor System)

The other six auxiliary corridors (shown in Fig. 2) as follows:

1. Tianjin Corridor (mainly based on railways). It is via Tianjin Port to Japan, South Korea, and North Korea in the Northeast Asia and forms a sea-rail intermodal access.

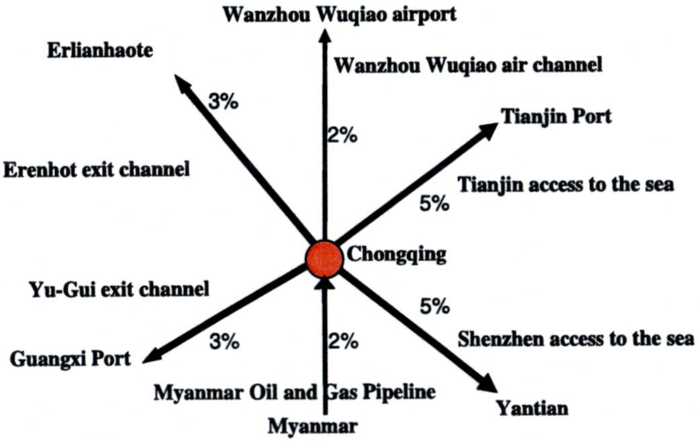

Fig. 2 The six auxiliary corridors of Chongqing ITC

2. Shenzhen Corridor (mainly based on railways). It is via Yantian Port in Shenzhen to the South China Sea and then into the Pacific Ocean.
3. Chongqing-Guangxi corridor (mainly based on railways). It is through the northern gulf in Guangxi or through the Pingxiang Port and forms a land corridor access to the Association of Southeast Asian Nations.
4. Erenhot Corridor (mainly based on railways through the Yu-Zheng Railway and the Northern rail network). It starts from Erenhot Port via Mongolia, Russia into Europe and finally into the Atlantic Ocean.
5. Sino-Burmese Oil and Gas Pipeline Corridor. It begin from Myanmar's Sittwe Port, through Mandalay, Ruili in Yunnan, Kunming to Chongqing.
6. Wanzhou Wuqiao Air Corridor. It can expand the direct international travel routes and form a aviation cargo network connecting major cities in ASEAN countries.

In Fig. 2, the Tianjin and Shenzhen Corridor are the important supplements to the CEPO which bears the greatest share of foreign trade, so it needs two auxiliary corridors to support. When the CEPO faces an emergency, the two auxiliary corridors can quickly replace it's functions and ensure the safety and smooth of Chongqing international trade.

Similarly, the Chongqing-Guangxi and Erenhot Corridor are supplements to the CSWIO and the CNWAO, while the Wanzhou Wuqiao Air Corridor is an important supplement to the JBAC. Finally, the Sino-Burmese Oil and Gas Pipeline can be used for the supplement to the ground corridors and the air corridors in crisis to ensure the energy security in the southwest China.

Figure 2 shows the auxiliary corridor system has a comparatively balanced structure and the task allocation is also more reasonable than before. Furthermore, the various auxiliary corridors can also support each other and jointly safeguard the realization of supplement function.

3.2.3 Integration of the Four-Main-Corridors and the Six-Auxiliary-Corridors

After the formation of the four-main-corridor system and the six-auxiliary-corridor system, the core corridor system will further enhance its stability and play a leading role in the transportation with the help of the auxiliary corridor system. With the main corridor system bears the responsibility of 80%, the auxiliary corridor system can function with ease, activeness and flexibility. An integrated structure can be formed by the mutual support of the two systems. The integration of the main corridor system and the auxiliary corridor system can meet the different needs, and ultimately reach an systems with truly balance, safety and smooth, which can effectively reduces the structural risks of the ITC of Chongqing.

4 Conclusion

In this paper, we present the structural risks of ITC of Chongqing based on the in-depth analysis of its structure, and further proposes to build a new type of "4 main +6 secondary" ITC system, so as to really form an ITC with balance, perfection, safety and smooth to evade its structural risks, to ensure the construction and management of the ITC in Inland China, which have a great strategic significance in accelerating a open inland and realizing the development of the western region in China.

References

1. Xie XD, Xu MZ, Xie J and Li SY (2010) Analysis on the Structure and Character of International Trade Corridor in Chongqing. Work paper:1
2. Wang YW (2006) West constructs the international big channel with to develop the central Asian market. Journal of ILi Normal University 4:53–58
3. Li Q and Chen X (2008) Research on Yunnan international corridor' s pushing action on the 3rd Eurasia Land Bridge. Journal of Inquiry into Economic Issues 1:7–10
4. Che TL (2005) New channels of container transportation in Sino-American trade. Continental Bridge View 9:38–39
5. Xu MZ Yu D and Li SY (2005) How to Solve the Delivery Channel of Chongqing foreign Trade. Journal of Logistics Technology 1:17–18
6. Chongqing Commerce Commission (2009) Inland International Trade Corridor Strategies, Chongqing
7. Cao XF (2006) On the surrounding environment for the construction of the great international passage in Yunnan and its countermeasures. Journal of Around Southeast Asia 6:58–59
8. Hu AG, Wen J and Wang Z (2001) Building of southwest international channels and implementational trade freedom in China. Journal of China Soft Science 6:6–7

9. Chongqing Commission of Chinese Farmer and Worker Democratic Party (2008) Building a Corridor from Chongqing to Indian Ocean to Push forward the Great Development of Southwest China, Chongqing
10. Li BL and Zhang JP (2005) Challenges and trend of the war on terror in southeast Asia and the measures to be taken to build Yunnan International grand passageway. Journal of Around East Asia 1:58–59

Part VII
Sustainable Risk Management Tools

Asphalt Pavement Surface Penetrate Rejuvenate Restore Technology: Application and Evaluation

Xiaohong Guo and Bangyin Liu

Abstract This paper discussed the applicability of Asphalt Pavement Surface Penetrate Rejuvenation Restore Technology (SPRR) in preventive maintenance, probed into the infiltration mechanism, rejuvenation mechanism, hermetic closure mechanism of micro-cracks, closed pavement mechanism and bonding mechanism of discrete aggregate, and put forward the relevant construction technology and requirements as well as its acceptance index. The actual case application has proved that the SPRR can better repair the surface damage of asphalt pavement, restore pavement performance and extend the service life. It is an important technology that achieves sustainable development in the highway operations and maintenance.

Keywords Asphalt pavement · Rejuvenation · Restore · Surface · Sustainable

1 Introduction

Asphalt pavement extremely presents the early surface damages after a period of time and seriously impacts the pavement service life. Asphalt Pavement Surface Penetrate Rejuvenate Restore Technology (SPRR) is a preventive maintenance technology of asphalt pavement. It can repair the tissue strain in pavement surface, restore pavement performance and extend the pavement

X. Guo (✉)
School of Management, Chongqing Jiaotong University, Nan'an, Chongqing 400074, People's Republic of China
e-mail: chq-gxh@126.com

B. Liu
Chengban Science and Technology Development Ltd, Nan'an, Chongqing 400060, People's Republic of China
e-mail: bpl99@hotmail.com

D.D. Wu (ed.), *Modeling Risk Management in Sustainable Construction*, Computational Risk Management, DOI 10.1007/978-3-642-15243-6_36,

service life. The technology could maintain the well operating state of road system longer and slow down the destruction in the future [1]. And it is an important technology that achieves sustainable development in the highway operations and maintenance.

2 The General Description of Technologies

The SPRR is applied when the asphalt pavement structure has sufficient strength and the pavement condition is still good. Without changing the asphalt pavement surface structure, the special Rejuvenate solution (asphalt pavement Rejuvenate curing compound) is sprayed on the asphalt pavement by use an appropriative distribution truck. Then through a series of physical, chemical reaction between the Rejuvenate materials and the aged layer of pavement, it would rejuvenate and restore the aged layer of the asphalt pavement surface within a certain depth ($\leq$8 mm) and format an irregular stable space network structure which consistent with the road surface deformation in pavement surface.

3 Asphalt Pavement Conditions for the Application of SPRR Technology

3.1 The Choose of Applicable Timing

1. *Macroscopic state of roads*: The indicator of macroscopic state of roads contains three items: pavement structural strength index (PSSI), riding quality index (RQI) and pavement condition index (PCI). PSSI and RQI are the test ratings, PCI is the judgment target. That is, when the PSSI and RQI fulfill the requirement, the PCI is taken as a standard to judge whether asphalt pavement needs pre-maintenance [2, 3]. The macroscopic state of SPRR technology should suit for asphalt pavement which accord with the stipulations in Table 1.
2. *Microscopic state of roads*: Damaged type and classification criteria of pavement that adapt to SPRR technology see in Table 2 [2].

Table 1 Macroscopic state of roads

Indicator of roads	Macroscopic state of roads for pre-maintenance	
	Expressway	Primary secondary highway
PSSI	85–100	82–100
RQI	90–100	80–100
PCI	85–95	82–92

Table 2 Damaged type and classification criteria of pavement that adapt to SPRR technology

Damaged type and name	Classification	Definition
Blocky crack	Light	Thin crack, none fallouts in crack areas, the width of crack less than 3 mm, most of the crack area is bigger than 1.0 m
Slitting	Light	Thin crack, none or few fallouts around crack wall, none or few branch-crack, the width of crack less than 3 mm
Transversal crack	Light	Thin crack, none or few fallouts around crack wall, none or few branch-crack, the width of crack less than 3 mm
Pitting surface	–	Small calking filler lost, present coarse pitting surface
Loose	Light	Fine aggregate lost, pavement surface coarse and pitting
Rut	Light	Depth < 10 mm
Settlement	Light	Depth <10 mm, no obvious uncomfortable in riding
Polish	Light	Original structure depth of pavement wear away or loss lightly, the anti-slide capacity of expressway and primary highway is SFC ≥ 40 or BPN ≥ 40

3.2 *The Request of the Original Pavement on Asphalt Pavement SPRR Technology*

The SPRR technology neither changes the structural strength of original pavement nor increases its structural-load-carrying capacity, so it provides the following requirements for the original pavement when apply the technology, which are sufficient strength and stiffness, good overall stability and surface keep smooth and clean.

4 The Material Requirements for Asphalt Pavement SPRR Technology

As long as the material meet its technical function, such as significantly rejuvenating the aged asphalt pavement surface, renewably replacing aged asphalt, sealing off micro cracks and so on, it can be used for the technology. In the implementation of Asphalt Pavement SPRR Technology, pavement maintenance enterprise can use specific asphalt rejuvenate agent that made by specialized manufacturers.

5 Mechanism of Asphalt Pavement SPRR Technology

There are four main technical principles for asphalt pavement SPRR technology to realize pavement pre-maintenance.

5.1 Penetration Mechanism

During the implementation of the asphalt pavement SPRR technology, Rejuvenate materials which infiltrate into the pavement surface via the gap between loose aggregates and the micro-cracks vigorously would penetrate and absorb the contiguous asphalt mixture constantly, and take the active ingredient in Rejuvenate materials to deepen into the pavement. After the opening of maintenance pavement, the active ingredient in Rejuvenate materials always maintains a state of infiltration under the dynamic load of vehicle continuously. The air that once remained in cracks and the original gap was squeeze out through the vertical stress, horizontal stress and lateral stress generated by the action of vehicle dynamic load. When the stress is gone, the fluid around the gap gathered to fill the space left out by the air in order to achieve the balance of forces owing to the effect of negative pressure and makes the bond between binder and aggregate tighter.

5.2 Rejuvenate Mechanism

After the implementation of the asphalt pavement SPRR technology, the infiltration agent would bring the rejuvenate agent into the depth of pavement (<5–8 mm). Then the rejuvenate agent supplies the aged asphalt with the oleaginous base. The organic synthesis, polymerization and a series of physical and chemical reactions would rejuvenate the contacted aged asphalt. In this way, the components of aged asphalt would distribute in a rational proportion and then reach the new asphalt standard. The penetration map of maintenance agent is shown in Fig. 1.

Table 3 shows the rejuvenate performance requirements for the rejuvenate maintenance agent that used in the asphalt pavement SPRR technology. The rotary pellicle aging experience of base asphalt was carried under the conditions of 163°C in laboratory.

5.3 Mechanism of Micro-cracks Sealing

Through these micro-cracks and original gaps, the rejuvenate materials would bring asphalt infiltrate into the depth quickly, heal the tiny fracture automatically, replenish the detached asphalt binder because of aging and enwrap and bond the exposed

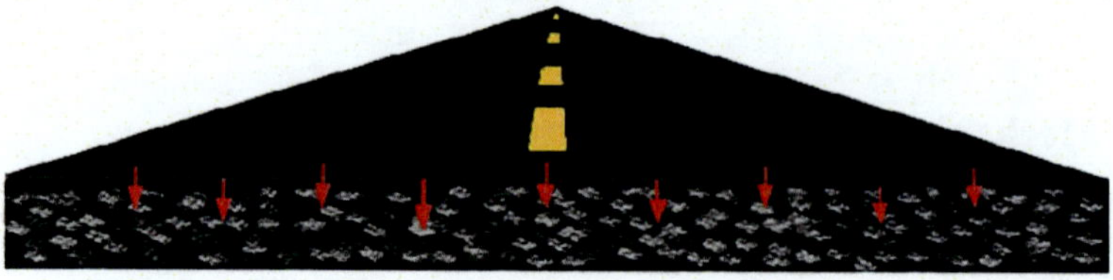

Fig. 1 The penetration of asphalt pavement maintenance agent

Table 3 The technical requirements of rejuvenate maintenance agent for the SPRR

Sort test item	Unit	Technical index recovery degree		Permissible error (%)	Test method
		One cycle	Two cycles		
Penetration degree (25°C)	0.1 mm	>90%	>75%	±5	T0604-2000
Ductility (15°C)	cm	>90%	>5%	±5	T0605-1993
Softening point	°C	±3°C	±5°C	±5	T0606-2000

Note: the recovery degree of softening point in the table is the difference between the rejuvenate asphalt and crude asphalt, which has been undergo the rotary pellicle aging experience of asphalt for one cycle (or two cycles)

asphalt aggregate binder again. Figure 2 is the sketches that the mechanism of micro cracks sealing.

5.4 *Mechanism of Closing Pavement and Bonding Loose Aggregate*

Through combining the aggregate and the rejuvenate asphalt binder together closely in the way of bridge, the rejuvenate material could maintain a consistent temperature changing rate. Meanwhile, it forms a compact whole of three-dimensional network interpenetrating structure on the pavement surface so as to improve the waterproof properties and the overall performances of the pavement.

6 Construction of Asphalt Pavement SPRR Technology

6.1 *The Determination of Sprayed Amount of Rejuvenate Maintenance Agent*

Before the implementation of SPRR technology, the design of the sprayed amount of rejuvenate maintenance agent should fully consider the use requirements, the original pavement situation, the traffic, the climate condition and so on. The performance indicators of the rejuvenate maintenance agent in the construction of asphalt pavement SPRR technology should satisfy the requirements in Tables 3 and 4.

6.2 *Construction*

During the construction process, it should notice the followings: (1) the rejuvenate maintenance agent should be mixed evenly and then poured into the storage tank of

Table 4 The physical performance technical requirements of rejuvenate maintenance agent for the SPRR

Sort test item	Unit	Technical indexes	Test method
Character	–	Black liquid	Visual observation
Specific gravity	–	>1.0	T0603-1993
Brookfield viscosity	pa s	$>2 \times 10^{-2}$	T0625-2000
Distillation residue (300°C)	%	≥45	T0641-1993

professional distribution truck; (2) when the professional distribution truck on site, the mixer in the storage tank tart should continually mixed for 30 min. (3) Setting the spray width as the road width of the pending construction, selecting the direction of construction and adjusting the position of professional distribution truck. (4) Conducting a formal spray after completing the experimental spray.

6.3 The Pavement Maintenance

There should be enough time for maintenance forming after the construction as the weather conditions. In general, when the pavement is dry and inadhesive to test paper, the professional people will take off the protective membrane which covered the traffic mark line and then the traffic could be open. The open time of traffic should at least ensure that it is at least 4 h at normal temperature and the relative humidity of air is less than 70%.

6.4 Implementation Effects and Evaluations

In order to verify the effect of asphalt pavement SPRR technology to treat the early disease of asphalt pavement, we combined the pavement maintenance project of Chongqing Yu-Wu expressway and selected road K15 + 000–K16 + 000 as the test section (SMA asphalt pavement).

6.4.1 Technology Results

Before the construction of the test section, the pavement tectonic depth, the friction coefficient, the Anti-skid value of British pendulum number and the coefficient of infiltration were detected. Then these indicators were detected again after the restored traffic about 1 month. The contrast of testing data are shown in Tables 5–8.

Table 5 The tectonic depth statistics before and after the construction

	Before construction (mm)	After construction (mm)	Decrease after construction (mm)	Rate of decrease (%)
Mean value	0.787	0.684	0.103	13.109
Variance	0.002	0.001	0.001	8.334
Mean square deviation	0.047	0.035	0.026	2.887

Table 6 The anti-skid value statistics of BPN before and after construction

	Before construction (BPN)	After construction (BPN)	Decrease after construction	Rate of decrease (%)
Mean value	49.420	47.320	3.500	6.441
Variance	23.002	2.944	–	–
Mean square deviation	4.796	1.716	–	–

Table 7 The statistics of coefficient of infiltration. Before and after the construction

	Before construction (mL/min)	After construction (mL/min)	Decrease after construction	Rate of decrease (%)
Mean value	9.525	1.219	9.469	84.939
Variance	46.048	0.345	–	–
Mean square deviation	6.786	0.587	–	–

Table 8 The infiltration depth of asphalt pavement *Maintenance agent*

Serial number	1	2	3	4	5	6	7	8	Average
The infiltration depth infiltration depth (mm)	5.06	5.11	6.33	5.23	5.54	6.03	6.12	5.67	5.64

6.4.2 Technology Evaluation

1. According to the Tables 5 and 6, it can be seen from that through the construction of this technology, the original pavement value reduces some extents, but still fit the standard and the requirements. The variance decline illuminates that this technology improves the pavement performances.
2. According to the regulation, the infiltration coefficient of the ordinary asphalt pavement surface is less than 300 mL/min and the infiltration coefficient of the SMA asphalt pavement surface is less than 200 mL/min. It can be seen from the Table 7 that before and after construction, the cross-section of experimental sections could achieve the requirements. However, before construction, the

infiltration coefficient and variability of the cross-section are bigger. After the application of the maintenance technology, the pavement was closed and the infiltration coefficient was decreased 84.94% on average. The variance decline of infiltration coefficient means that the homogeneity of infiltration coefficient in the pavement is improved.

3. From Table 8, we can see that after applying the technology in construction, the average penetration depth in asphalt pavement surface could reach 5.6 mm.

6.4.3 Intuitionistic Visual Evaluation

The respective status of the pavement surface before construction and after construction are: before construction, the pavement shows blushing phenomenon, the coarse aggregate exposes obviously in a rough state and the surface marking was not clear under the sunshine. Moreover during the rainy day, the dusk and the night, the marking was even fuzzy due to the dark light. Meanwhile, the asphalt membrane in surface peel off, most of the fine aggregate miss, a large amount of small pits appear on the pavement and parts of the aggregate become loose in pavement surface. After the construction, it closes the micro-cracks and gaps in the pavement surface, updates and protects the original asphalt pavement, deepens the color of asphalt pavement, prevents the loose of asphalt pavement, increases the contrast of markings and asphalt pavement and improves the riding quality as well.

7 Economic Efficiency

If adopting the asphalt pavement SPRR technology to treat the early disease of asphalt pavement, the one-off construction cost is 15–20 Yuan/m^2 and the cured pavement could maintain a good condition in 3 years. In other word, this could ensure the treatment cost per square meter is 15–20 Yuan in 3 years and the average annual cost is 5–7 Yuan/year. m^2, it is about 1/4–1/5 of the traditional mat coat or renovation cost.

References

1. Ministry of Communications in People's Republic of China, Highway Asphalt Pavement recycling technical specifications (JTG F41 -2008). Beijing: People's Communications Press (2008).
2. California Department of Transportation (CADOT), "Fog Seal Guidelines", Caltrans Division of Maintenance, October, 2003.
3. Guo Xiaohong: The mechanism, construction and evaluation of Asphalt Pavement SPRR technology, Road Machinery and Construction Mechanization. 2009.26 (3) 16–23.

A Study of Construction Project Conflict Management Based on Evolutionary Game Theory

Jie Ding

Abstract In the implementation of construction project, conflict inevitably occurs due to different interests of all the participants, which brings about the negative control over project progress, quality, and cost etc. The evolutionary game theory is applied in order to produce a comprehensive analytic framework for solving such problem. Based on this theory, evolutionary game model is established and the evolutionary stable strategy (ESS) is obtained under different circumstances. The results show that, project builder can gets higher revenue when they take aggressive strategy, and driven by economic interests, project owner may take the high hand in order to maximize its revenue. At last, in light of these problems, several suggestions are given in order to solve the construction project conflict problems.

Keywords Conflict management · Construction project · Evolutionary game theory

1 Introduction

In the implementation of construction project, conflict inevitably occurs due to different interests of all the participants, which brings about the negative control over project progress, quality, and cost etc. Though many factors contribute to the uncertainties of construction project, conflict between the project participants is usually regarded as a definite phenomenon. Various conflicts can be divided into three categories: individual interests colliding with whole project, different organizations benefits clashed, and projects interests going against the community.

Game theory attempts to mathematically capture behavior in strategic situations, in which an individual's success in making choices between conflict and

J. Ding
School of Economics and Management, Tongji University, Shanghai 200092, People's Republic of China
e-mail: dingjie_2010@126.com

D.D. Wu (ed.), *Modeling Risk Management in Sustainable Construction*,
Computational Risk Management, DOI 10.1007/978-3-642-15243-6_37,

cooperation depends on the choices of others. Construction project is a kind of game activities involving several interest-related parties and thus conflicts and contradictions caused by different interests inevitably happened. Therefore, the conflict of optimum revenue between individual and collective, consists in individual's strategies under interacting external economic circumstances. The evolutionary game theory can be used to analyze mutual influence of different organizational behaviors, conflicts and coherence of different organizational interests, as well as cooperation and competition.

2 Evolutionary Game Model of Compensation System

2.1 Evolutionary Game Theory

Evolutionary game theory, originated from the combination of biology evolutionism and classical game theory, reveals a dynamic process describing how players adapt their behavior over the course of repeated plays of a game. The central concept of an evolutionarily stable strategy (ESS) was introduced by Maynard Smith and Price (1973) and developed further in Maynard Smith's (1982) influential Evolution and the Theory of Games (Samuelson 2002) [1–3].

In classical game theory, game player must be rational decision-maker. But, faced with the complex practical problems, because of information deficiency and interference of irrational factors, it's hard for game player to be perfect rational. Evolutionary game theory differs from classical game theory by focusing on the dynamics of strategy change more than the properties of strategy equilibria. Based on evolutionary game model, continuous replicator equations assume infinite populations, continuous time, complete mixing and that strategies breed true. Then, the evolutionary stable strategy (ESS) is obtained [4].

2.2 Evolutionary Game Model

Construction project conflict is a kind of game activities involving several interest-related parties. This paper established a Hawk–Dove game. This game, shown in Fig. 1, involves two players (project owner and builder). In which, A1 and B1 represent aggressive strategy; A2 and B2 represent acquiescent strategy. V_1, V_2, D_1 and D_2 represent project owner payment in terms of construction. C_3, C_4 represent the costs of project builder if they choose aggressive strategy. C_1, C_2 represent the costs of project owner's coping strategy when project builder choose aggressive strategy (Table 1).

If project owner is aggressive (Hawk) and the other acquiescent (Dove), then the former gets -V_2 and the latter V_2; if project builder is aggressive (Hawk) and the

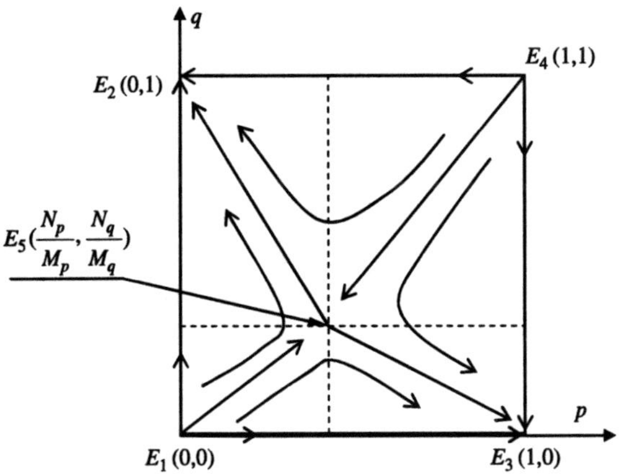

Fig. 1 Phase diagram of equilibrium points

Table 1 Hawk–Dove game

Project builder	Project owner	
	A1	A2
B1	$V_1 - C_3,\ -V_1 - C_1$	$D_1 - C_4,\ -D_1 - C_2$
B2	$V_2,\ -V_2$	$D_2,\ -D_2$

other acquiescent (Dove), then the former gets D_1-C_4 and the latter -D_1-C_2; if both are aggressive, with mutual aggression causing each to incur an injury cost of V_1-C_3 and -V_1-$C_1$with probability; if both are passive, then the former gets D_2 and the latter -D_2. According to the actual situation, there is inequality relation between the parameters above:

$$\begin{cases} V_1 > V_2 & D_1 > D_2 \\ D_1 > V_1 & D_2 > V_2 \\ C_1 > C_2 & C_3 > C_4 \end{cases} \tag{1}$$

Under the assumption that the project owner may in q probability of taking A1 strategy, in (1 − q) probability of taking A2 strategy; project builder may in p probability of taking A1 strategy, in (1 − p) probability of taking A2 strategy; On the case of demolition, we use negative revenue represent expenditure, and the marginal expected revenue when project owner carry out A1 strategy is U_{A1}:

$$U_{A1} = (-V_1 - C_1)p - V_2(1-p) \tag{2}$$

Marginal expected revenue when project owner carry out A2 strategy is U_{A2}:

$$U_{A2} = (-D_1 - C_2)p - D_2(1-p) \tag{3}$$

Expected revenue of project owner is U_A:

$$U_A = U_{A1}q + U_{A2}(1-q) \tag{4}$$

Marginal expected revenue when project builder carry out B1 strategy is U_{B1}:

$$U_{B1} = (V_1 - C_3)q + (D_1 - C_4)(1-q) \tag{5}$$

Marginal expected revenue when project builder carry out B2 strategy is U_{B2}:

$$U_{B2} = V_2 q + D_2(1-q) \tag{6}$$

Expected revenue of project builder is U_B:

$$U_B = U_{B1}p + U_{B2}(1-p) \tag{7}$$

According to evolutionary game theory, the growth rate of a strategy equals to its relative adaptability. As long as a strategy's adaptation higher than the average adaptability, this strategy will develop. So, the growth rate of aggressive strategy taken by project builder is:

$$\begin{aligned}\frac{dp}{dt} &= p(U_{B1} - U_B)\\ &= p(1-p)[(V_1 - V_2 + D_2 - D_1 + C_4 - C_3)q + D_1 - D_2 - C_4]\\ &\underline{\underline{\text{def}}} F(p,q)\end{aligned} \tag{8}$$

The growth rate of Hawk strategy taken by project owner is:

$$\frac{dp}{dt} = p(U_{A1} - U_A) = q(q-1)[(V_1 - V_2 + D_2 - D_1 + C_1 - C_2)p + V_2 - D_2] \underline{\underline{\text{def}}}\, G(p,q) \tag{9}$$

3 Model Analysis

The simple discussion on autonomous systems of differential equations above can be shown as follows:

$$\begin{cases}\frac{dp}{dt} = p(1-p)(M_p q - N_p)\underline{\underline{\text{def}}}F(p,q)\\ \frac{dq}{dt} = q(q-1)(M_p p - N_q)\underline{\underline{\text{def}}}G(p,q)\end{cases} \tag{10}$$

In which

$$M_p = V_1 - V_2 + D_2 - D_1 + C_4 - C_3, \; N_p = D_2 - D_1 + C_4$$

$$M_q = V_1 - V_2 + D_2 - D_1 + C_1 - C_2, \; N_q = D_2 - V_2$$

According to the qualitative theory of ordinary differential equations, points meet the equation below are equilibrium points of (10):

$$[F(p,q)]^2 + [G(p,q)]^2 = 0 \tag{11}$$

Range of p and q are both [0, 1], thus $E_1(0,0), E_2(0,1), E_3(1,0)$ and $E_4(1,1)$ are equilibrium points of (10); If the two equations also meet:

$$\begin{cases} 0 \le \frac{N_p}{M_p} \le 1 \\ 0 \le \frac{N_q}{M_q} \le 1 \end{cases} \tag{12}$$

So, there exists the fifth equilibrium point $E_5\left(\frac{N_p}{M_p}, \frac{N_q}{M_q}\right)$. According to the way discussed above, we can get two eigenvalues:

$$\lambda_{1,2}^5 = \pm\sqrt{\frac{N_pN_q}{M_pM_q}\left(M_q - N_q\right)\left(N_p - M_p\right)} \tag{13}$$

Through practical investigation, we find that relocation household can get higher compensation when they take aggressive strategy. So, in this model, $N_p = D_2 - (D_1 - C_4) < 0$. According to (12), we can get:

$$M_p \le N_p < 0, M_q \ge N_q > 0 \tag{14}$$

Equilibrium point $E_1(0,0)$, $\lambda_1^1 = -N_p > 0$, $\lambda_2^1 = N_q > 0$, unstable equilibrium point;

Equilibrium point $E_2(0,1)$, $\lambda_1^2 = M_p - N_p \le 0$, $\lambda_2^2 = -N_q < 0$, stable equilibrium point;

Equilibrium point $E_3(1,0)$, $\lambda_1^3 = N_p < 0$, $\lambda_2^3 = N_q - M_q \le 0$, stable equilibrium point;

Equilibrium point $E_4(1,1)$, $\lambda_1^4 = N_p - M_p \ge 0$, $\lambda_2^4 = M_q - N_q \ge 0$, unstable equilibrium point;

Equilibrium point $E_5\left(\frac{N_p}{M_p}, \frac{N_q}{M_q}\right)$, $\lambda_{1,2}^5 = \pm\sqrt{\frac{N_pN_q}{M_pM_q}\left(M_q - N_q\right)\left(N_p - M_p\right)}$, Saddle Point.

Plane $S = (p,q)$ is the dynamic game process between project owner and project builder, in which $(0 \le p,q \le 1)$. Shown in the phase diagram above, the dynamic game process runs to $E_2(0,1)$or $E_3(0,1)$ If project builder can get higher revenue when they take aggressive strategy, on one hand, if $\frac{N_p}{M_p}$ step up, and moreover, $\frac{N_q}{M_q}$

taper off, equilibrium point runs to $E_3(1,0)$; on the other hand, if $\frac{N_p}{M_p}$ taper off, and moreover, $\frac{N_q}{M_q}$ step up, equilibrium point runs to $E_2(0,1)$ That is, when one player is aggressive (Hawk) and the other acquiescent (Dove), then the game achieve balance.

4 Conclusion and Suggestions

Construction project conflict is a kind of game activities involving several interest-related parties. Based on evolutionary game theory, this paper gain such conclusion: only if one player is aggressive (Hawk) and the other acquiescent (Dove), the game can achieve balance. What's more, in this circumstance, driven by economic interests, project owner may use its powers and take the high hand.

In light of these problems, several suggestions are put forward: Firstly, using formal authority or other power that project owner possess to satisfy his concerns. Secondly, allowing project builder to satisfy their concerns while neglecting project owner. Thirdly, attempting to resolve a conflict by identifying a solution that is partially satisfactory to both parties, but completely satisfactory to neither. Fourthly, cooperating with the other party to understand their concerns and expressing your own concerns in an effort to find a mutually and completely satisfactory solution (win–win).

Acknowledgments This work was supported by the National Natural Science Foundation of China (Grant No. 70903051).The author are grateful to Daizhong Tang for his guidance that helped to significantly improve this paper from its earlier versions. All remaining errors are my own.

References

1. JM. Smith, GR. Price, The Logic of Animal Conflict. Nature, Vol. 246 (1973), p. 15–18.
2. JM. Smith, Evolution and the Theory of Games. Cambridge: Cambridge University Press (1982).
3. L. Samuelson, Evolution and Game Theory. Journal of Economic Perspectives, Volume (Month) (2002): 2 (Spring) p. 47–66.
4. D. Friendman, On economic applications of evolutionary game theory. Evolutionary Econometrics (1998), p. 15–42.

Study on the Management Mechanism of Emergency Telecommunication in China

Zhenyu Jin, Xiaoyu Wan and Xingming Yang

Abstract In recent years, unconventional emergencies bring serious challenges to emergency telecommunication in China. So, creating a scientific and rational management system of emergency telecommunications has become the key point of improving capability of emergency telecommunications. And, the study on management mechanism of emergency telecommunications can provide a strong theoretical basis for building management system of emergency telecommunications. Above all, this article analyzes the status of emergency management, then, clarifies the feature and content of emergency telecommunications according to the character of emergency telecommunication. Finally, an earthquake is taken as an example, elaborates the interaction relationship between the various mechanisms in the mechanism system of emergency telecommunication management.

Keywords Emergency management · Emergency telecommunications · Mechanism system

1 Introduction

With the rapid development of the national economy, the continued expansion of production scale and increasing of social wealth and losses caused by disasters are rising year after year, and it is a serious threat to social security. Telecommunications industry as a vital basis of the national economy, directly affects timely distribution of national important information and the smooth implementation of relief work. In addition, telecommunications industry is related to people's daily life, once the telecommunications network goes wrong, it will give great inconvenience to people's work and life, sometimes may lead to social chaos, endanger

Z. Jin (✉), X. Wan and X. Yang
School of Economic & Management, Chongqing University of Posts and Telecommunications, Chongqing 400065, People's Republic of China
e-mail: jzy_860818@hotmail.com, wanxy@cqupt.edu.cn, Xinming.Yang@alcatel-sbell.com.cn

D.D. Wu (ed.), *Modeling Risk Management in Sustainable Construction*, Computational Risk Management, DOI 10.1007/978-3-642-15243-6_38,

national security, and result in incalculable consequences. So, combined with Chinese national conditions, exploring management mechanism for emergency communication under emergencies will provide a useful reference for improving emergency management system, and it has high practical value.

2 Status of Emergency Telecommunications Management

Modern emergency management is a set of theories, methods and technology system which is in order to reduce the hazards of emergencies, based on the reasons causing emergencies, the occurrence and development of emergencies and the scientific analysis of negative impact, effectively integrates resources of all sectors in society, effectively responds, controls and treats to emergencies by modern technical means and management methods.

For a long time, the concept of emergency communications management is rated in the narrow space of telecommunication rescue, and management tools are scarce, the methods of different periods and stages are difficult in forming a coherent system. Thus, the relevant work of emergency telecommunications management can easily fall into a passive defensive disadvantage. Both the telecom regulators and telecom operators are taking remedial measures after a disaster. The same results of telecommunication barriers caused by different public emergencies are difficult in distinguishing, and they are often removed by a single technical means. Due to the absence of clear and perfect mechanism system, it is difficult to deeply understand the role and importance of various aspects or elements of emergency telecommunications as a result the focus of management work is not prominent.

3 Study on Mechanism of Emergency Telecommunications Management

Mechanism is inherent logic and rules followed by something. For emergencies, after analyzing the mechanism of the incident, you can find the source of events, and discover the law of the formation and the momentum of promoting the development of events, and find appropriate coping strategies in emergency management. The diversity of emergencies means of telecommunication and telecommunication content directly leads to the type and complex process of disasters. In order to make reasonable and accurate classification for emergency telecommunications, the content contained in emergency telecommunication must be scientifically summed up, and the mechanism system should be objectively summarized, that is the internal logic and rules between the various parts.

3.1 Feature and Content of Emergency Telecommunications

After the earthquake in Wenchuan, the emergency management is very important for natural disasters and public safety incidents and so on. Putting forward higher requirements to telecommunications security, emergency telecommunications are given more responsibility, and it emphasizes telecommunications security which is related to information transfer in emergency management. As the emergency telecommunications plays an important role in emergency management, its role is not just limited to the telecommunication of special circumstances, it includes all activities that are related to information transfer after emergencies. Therefore, it is necessary to establish the relational model of emergency telecommunications in the emergency management system, shown in Fig. 1.

In the relational model chart of emergency handling and technical support, we can clearly see that the model is consisted of three layers, which are the layer of emergency managers, the layer of decision-making and the layer of technical support, on the map the dependent relationship of three layers from top to bottom is that upper are dependent on the lower. The working process is following: emergency information collected through various means is transmitted to the layer of decision-making by different ways from the layer of technical support. The layer of decision-making analyzes, contrasts and judges the information, makes

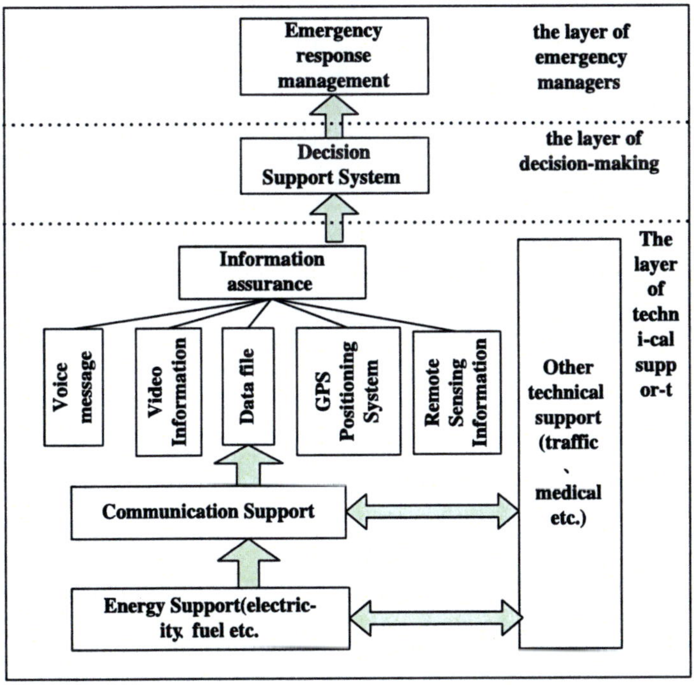

Fig. 1 Relational model chart of emergency handling and technical support

the appropriate conclusions to the administrator, then implements relevant action according to the orders of administrator, starts related plans, and issues command by means of technical support [1].

3.2 Mechanism System of Emergency Telecommunications

The objects of management are sure after clarifying the meaning of emergency telecommunications that are activities of telecommunication during the disposal process of emergencies. In "Response Act of Chinese People's Republic"(2007), our country divides public emergencies into four main categories: natural disasters, accident disasters, public health incidents, social security incidents. Although different types of public emergencies have different need and impact on telecommunications support, there are still some universal inherent logic and laws, and it is necessary to study management strategies of emergency telecommunication management in the different situations which is the trade mechanism system of emergency telecommunications management.

According to the feature of emergency telecommunications, the trade mechanism system is divided into several layers, shown in Fig. 2.

In Fig. 2, the mechanism of emergencies mainly refers to professional mechanism of different types of emergencies, the management mechanism of emergency telecommunications is consisted of two parts: one is the professional mechanism of telecommunication, referring to the necessary professional and technical principles, for example, a complete telecommunication system should include access, transmission, switching and control layer, and specific electrical and physical characters of various telecommunications equipment. The other part is the management mechanism, it has the general mechanism of emergency management, contains four types, which are principle, theory, process and operational mechanism [2].

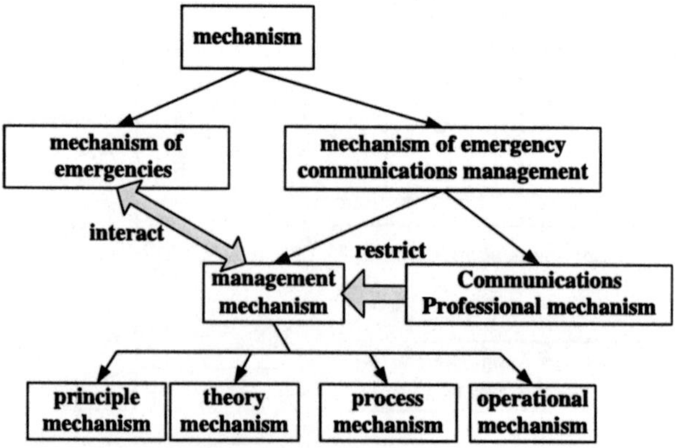

Fig. 2 Mechanism system of emergency telecommunications

The relationship among emergency mechanism, management mechanism and telecommunication professional mechanism is shown in Fig. 2: emergency mechanism and management mechanism are the interaction, while telecommunication professional mechanism restricts management mechanism. Because the type, occurrence and development of emergencies are different, requirement for the level of telecommunications security has differences, meanwhile, the impact or damage of the telecommunication system that is caused by emergencies which are certainly need to be distinguished. Therefore, principle, theory, process and operational mechanism of the management mechanism should change and adjust for the type of emergencies. Accordingly, the path of evolution will transfer, because some strategies are adopted in development process of emergencies, and management mechanism has the reaction in emergency mechanism. On the other hand, management mechanism is limited by the principle of telecommunications professional on some extent. Due to different technical means, its theory mechanism of management mechanism would present different regularity, and this directly leads to the difference in substance between process mechanism and operational mechanism. Figure 3 takes earthquake as an example, and describes the relationship of interaction among the three.

It can be seen from Fig. 3 that after the earthquake, I and II evolutionary path will be produced, and through the amplification of telecommunications professionals mechanism, the different behaviors of two paths will lead to the same result, that is telecommunication trouble. However the principles of trouble that two types of behaviors lead to are different.

Abnormal telecommunication behavior, interpreted that a large-scale public launch call at the same time after disaster has occurred, which does not cause the physical damage of telecommunication equipment, just cause call failure due to limited frequency resources and limited ability of switch service. Because this

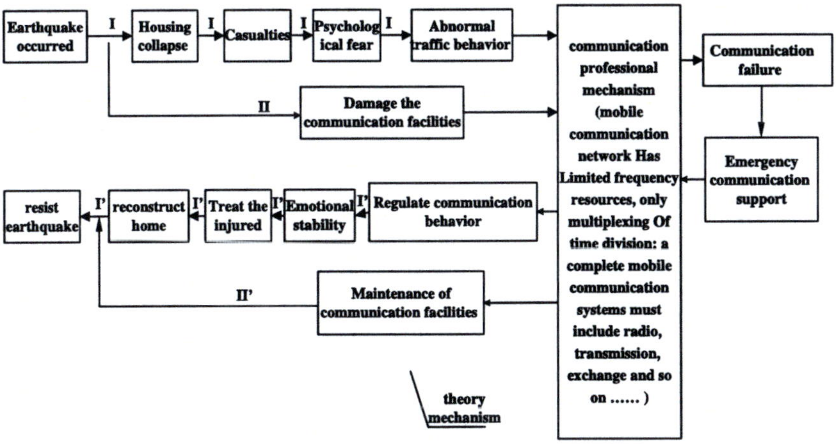

Fig. 3 Flow of mechanism system in the situation of earthquake

telecommunication trouble is controlled, for this type of emergency telecommunication, you can use assessment model of "may slow down" to evaluate [3]. So managers can assess probability of such behavior and severity in advance, and take appropriate preventive measures, formulate relevant emergency public telecommunications standard to reduce the occurrence of abnormal telecommunication behavior when emergencies occur.

However, the damage of telecommunication equipment mainly refers to the base station, transmission cable or switches are destroyed physically in the earthquake, such as the collapse of the base station, transmission cable fault and switches to be buried and so on. This telecommunication trouble is difficult to restore in the short term, in addition to take a number of measures in advance to enhance the device's physical disaster level, more work is the assessment of "recoverability" after disaster, so that emergency telecommunication managers can assess general time to the restore telecommunications facilities destroyed, which can provide reference for the emergency rescue.

In addition, we can observe that after taking security measures of emergency telecommunication, through the feedback of telecommunications professionals mechanism. According to different principles mechanism, there are also two different evolution paths, I′ and II′, which is the reaction of the management mechanism to the emergency mechanism. The two evolution paths are to standardize the telecommunications action and maintain telecommunications facilities. Emergency managers, under the guidance of measure of emergency telecommunication support, on the one hand standardize positively public communication behavior, so that so many telecommunication resources can be used in emergency rescue, on the other hand, assess the "may slow down" of existing telecommunication facilities that are damaged, order and repair the telecommunication facilities damaged following the priority, which will allow emergency telecommunication managers to implement emergency telecommunications targeted relief.

On the other hand, on the aspect of telecommunications mechanism, because the general emergency telecommunication includes mobile telecommunications, fixed telecommunications, HF telecommunications, satellite telecommunications and Internet telecommunications and so on. The different technical characteristics need to be unified and summarized. Developments of new technology should also continue to be enriched to professional mechanism, which can continuously improve the management mechanism of emergency telecommunications system.

4 Conclusion

This paper introduces the concept of mechanism system into the study on emergency telecommunication management, constructs a mechanism system of the emergency telecommunication that centers on emergency mechanism, management mechanism and telecommunication professional mechanism on the basis of clarifying the features and contents of emergency telecommunication, and then elaborates the interaction between various mechanisms in the mechanism system of emergency telecommunication management by specific examples. This paper argues that you must scientifically summarize the content that emergency telecommunication contains to create a comprehensive management system of emergency telecommunication. Only clarify the character and content of emergency telecommunication, that are objects and links of emergency telecommunication, we can reasonably conclude the mechanism system of emergency telecommunication management that is internal logic and rules between the various parts. Therefore, the more scientific and perfect mechanism system of emergency telecommunication we construct the greater role for our research and creating emergency telecommunication system. So mechanism system of emergency telecommunication management can provides a powerful theoretical foundation and theoretical gist for creating management system of emergency telecommunication, also can provide decision-making reference for the relevant government departments in formulating the policies of emergency telecommunication.

References

1. Shangguan Yanqiu, Chen An, Salvability Measurement Model and Application in Earthquake Disaster Rescue[J], Transactions on Emergency Management, 2008.7, 3(4), p 34–41 (Ch)
2. Chen An, Mechanism System on Emergency Management [J], Anquan, 2007.6, p 10–12
3. Wan Xiaoyu, Sun Sanshan, Lu Anwen, On the National Emergency Communication Management of Serious National Disaster [J], Journal of Chongqing University of Posts and Telecommunications (Social Science), 2009.1, 21(1), p 29–34

Forewarning for Urban Sustainable Development Based on Fuzzy Matter Element Model: Taking Nan Tong City for Example

Wen-jin Zhang and De-shan Tang

Abstract A forewarning model was set up to evaluate the process of urban sustainable development based on fuzzy matter element theory. Taking status of Nan Tong city from 2004 to 2007 as an example, we set up an index system of forewarning in the process of urban sustainable development in Nan tong and established the forewarning standards, limits and degrees.

Keywords City · Forewarning model · Fuzzy matter element · Sustainable development

1 Introduction

The forewarning system of Urban Sustainable Development is a complicated system combined with society, economy, environment, resources; aims to prevent the city developing deviated from its sustainable route; to foresee the trend and speed of the inverse change to the Sustainable Development; to avoid serious conflicts between urban development and environment protection [1]. This essay sets up a forewarning model for the urban sustainable development, bases on the reference to related research. It takes the forewarning model of Nantong urban sustainable development as an example, uses the Analytic Hierarchy Process to set the weight of index to conduct a forewarning analysis of the Nantong urban sustainable development in 2004–2007.

W.-j. Zhang (✉)
Business School, Hohai University, Nanjing 210098, People's Republic of China
e-mail: zhangwenjin@yahoo.cn

D.-s. Tang
College of Water Conservancy and Hydropower, Hohai University, Nanjing 210098, People's Republic of China
e-mail: tds808@163.com

D.D. Wu (ed.), *Modeling Risk Management in Sustainable Construction*, Computational Risk Management, DOI 10.1007/978-3-642-15243-6_39,

2 Urban Sustainable Development Forewarning Model

2.1 Fuzzy Matter Element Model and Composite Fuzzy Matter Element Mode

Take a matter N, the magnitude of its character c is v. If we use triad R = (N, c, v) to describe the matter. We can call it matter element. If its magnitude v is fuzzy, then we can call it fuzzy matter element. The magnitudes for different characters c_1, c_2, … , c_n are v_1, v_2, … ,v_n therefore we say R is an N dimensions fuzzy matter element, the triad R = (N, c, v). If we have M matters with N dimensions combined together, we will get R_{mn}. If we change the magnitude of R_{mn} to fuzzy matter element magnitude, then we will have M fuzzy matters with N dimensions combined together, we will get:

$$Rmn = \begin{bmatrix} & M_1 & M_2 & \cdots & Mn \\ c_1 & u_{11} & u_{21} & \cdots & u_{m1} \\ c_2 & u_{12} & u_{22} & \cdots & u_{m2} \\ \vdots & \vdots & \vdots & \vdots & \vdots \\ c_n & u_{1n} & u_{2n} & \cdots & u_{mn} \end{bmatrix} \tag{1}$$

In the formula above, R_{mn}, is M fuzzy matters with N dimensions; Mi is the ith matter. i = 1, 2… m; ck is the Kth character, k = 1, 2… n; u_{ik} is the corresponding fuzzy matter element magnitude of the ith matter the kth character. Apparently, the presentation of the concept of the matter element created a new way to determine the level of category ascription according to the magnitude of its character.

2.2 The Establishment of the Forewarning Standard

In order to do the research, we divide the forewarning into four degrees, that is no alert, light alert, mid-degree alert, heavy alert, and in the range 0–10 level within the division. For the smaller the more superior type, the correlation between forewarning criteria and indicators range in Table 1, S_1, S_2, S_3 is an indicator of forewarning threshold of the criteria, correspondingly, there are four levels index value, which respectively establishes correspondence with index range of indicators standard. Similarly, the index range of the bigger the worse superior type can be concluded [2, 3].

Table 1 The correlation between alert degree and index

Alert degree	No alert	Light alert	Mid-degree alert	Heavy alert
Forewarning index	[0,2.5)	[2.5,5)	[5,7.5)	[7.5,10)
Index range	$<S_3$	$[S_3,S_2)$	$[S_2,S_1)$	$\geq S_1$

2.3 Standard Fuzzy Matter-Element

On the basis of determining fuzzy matter-element, combined with forewarning standards, we calculate the standard forewarning indicators of evaluation index, then establish a new standard fuzzy matter-element. concerning the smaller the more superior type of indicators, take S_1, S_2, S_3 in Table 1 for examples, evaluation index corresponding fuzzy matter-element of the forewarning indicators can be calculated in accordance with the following formula:

No alert: $X_{ij} = 2.5 + 2.5 \times \frac{(U_{ij} - S_3)}{S_3} \quad (S_3 \succ U_{ij})$

Light alert: $X_{ij} = 5 + 2.5 \times \frac{(U_{ij} - S_2)}{(S_2 - S_3)} \quad (S3 \prec U_{ij} \prec S2)$

Mid-degree alert: $X_{ij} = 7.5 + 2.5 \times \frac{(U_{ij} - S_1)}{(S_1 - S_2)} \quad (S_2 \prec U_{ij} \prec S_1)$

Heavy alert: $X_{ij} = 7.5 + 2.5 \times \frac{(U_{ij} - S_1)}{S_1} \quad (S_1 \prec U_{ij})$

If $X_{ij} < 0$,then the value is 0;if $X_{ij} > 10$,then the value is 10. U_{ij} is the value of indicators. By the same token, the bigger the more superior type of indicators can be calculated, received the standard fuzzy matter-element as follows:

$$R_{ij} = \begin{bmatrix} & M_1 & M_2 & \cdots & M_m \\ c_1 & X_{11} & X_{21} & \cdots & X_{m1} \\ c_2 & X_{12} & X_{22} & \cdots & X_{m2} \\ \vdots & \vdots & \vdots & \vdots & \vdots \\ c_n & X_{1n} & X_{2n} & \cdots & X_{mn} \end{bmatrix} \tag{2}$$

In the above formula, the R_{ij} represents matter i's c_j th character fuzzy matter element, i = 1, 2, ... ,m; j = 1,2, ... ,n.

2.4 The Determining of Forewarning Index Weights

In this paper, we use analytic hierarchy process to determine the relative importance order between the evaluation indexes, thus get the weight of evaluation of index, and prior to normalization in the synthesis, namely:

$$\sum_{i=1}^{n} wi = 1 \quad (wi \geq 0, i = 1, 2, \cdots, n)$$

2.5 Comprehensive Forewarning Model

A comprehensive forewarning analysis for the SD system is the key method to measure development status of system comprehensively. Based on fuzzy matter-element matrix and the index weight set, weight n-dimensional matter-element, calculate comprehensive forewarning indicators, the calculation model as follows:

$$I_i = W_j \times R_{ij} = W_j \times \begin{bmatrix} & M_1 & M_2 & \cdots & M_m \\ c_1 & X_{11} & X_{21} & \cdots & M_{m1} \\ c_2 & X_{12} & X_{22} & \cdots & M_{m2} \\ \vdots & \vdots & \cdots & \vdots & \cdots \\ c_n & X_{1n} & X_{2n} & \cdots & M_{mn} \end{bmatrix} \\ = (\sum_{j=1}^{n} W_j X_{1j}, \sum_{j=1}^{n} W_j X_{2j}, \cdots, \sum_{j=1}^{n} W_j X_{mj}) = (I_1, I_2, \cdots \mathrm{I_m}) \quad (3)$$

According to index range corresponding to forewarning level in forewarning standards, judge *m one matter's* comprehensive forewarning indicators $I_i(i = 1,2, \ldots, m)$ belongs to the alert degree, then publishing a forewarning report.

3 SD Forewarning Evaluation of Nantong City

3.1 Forewarning Index System

To establish a forewarning index system, we must select quantifiable indicators and obtain some statistical data, meanwhile, the change of index has a bigger impact on sustainable development. In this paper, based on the reference to related research, we select 15 evaluations from economics, society, environment three aspects to establish system [1, 4]. The indicator hierarchy is shown in Table 2.

3.2 The Determining of Forewarning Index Weights

According to index hierarchy in Table 2, based on the relative importance order between the evaluation indexes that determined by specialists, we use AHP to build comparison matrix, then calculate index weight level by level, take consistency tests, results are in Table 2.

3.3 Forewarning Standards Setting

Combined with it's own characteristics of Nan tong urban development, in accordance with favorable membership degree principle in forewarning reference

Table 2 SD forewarning index system and weight of Nan tong city

Target level	Module level	Guidelines level	Element level			
	Index	Weight	Index	Weight	Index	Weight
SD forewarning index system of Nan tong city A	Environmental index B1	1/3	Current situation index C1	0.50	Park green area per capita /m^2 (D1)	0.500
					Green coverage ratio/% (D2)	0.500
			Management index C2	0.50	Domestic sewage treatment rate/% (D3)	0.110
					Compliance rate of industrial wastewater discharge % (D4)	0.300
					Comprehensive utilization rate of solid waste/% (D5)	0.480
					The proportion of good air quality days/% (D6)	0.110
	Economic index B2	1/3	Economic income C3	0.75	Per capita GDP (yuan/people.year) (D7)	1.000
			Economic structure C4	0.25	GDP, the proportion of tertiary industry/% (D8)	1.000
	Social index B3	1/3	Medical and public health C5	0.20	Million people have the number of beds (D9)	1.000
			Material life C6	0.40	Per capita living space/m^2 ‘D10)	0.480
					10,000 people have public transport vehicles/S (D11)	0.088
					Per capita road area/m^2 (D12)	0.230
					Per cargo throughput/million tons (D13)	0.202
			Population quality C7	0.40	Million people in the school number of students (D14)	0.170
					Population density (people/km^2) D15	0.830

standards setting, based on reference to related research results, this paper determines the limits of different indexes, results can be seen in Table 3.

3.4 Evaluation of Forewarning Results

According to above comprehensive forewarning module of fuzzy matter-element, in accordance with forewarning reference standards, combined with indexes from

Table 3 Reference standards and alert degrees of Nan tong urban SD

Alert degree	No alert	Light alert	Mid-degree alert	Heavy alert
Forewarning index range	[0,2.5)	[2.5,5)	[5,7.5)	[7.5,10]
D1	>20	[20,10)	[10,5)	[5,0)
D2	>60	[60,30)	[30,20)	[20,0)
D3	>80	[80,60)	[60,30)	[30,0)
D4	100	[100,80)	[80,60)	[60,0)
D5	>90	[90,70)	[70,50)	[50,0)
D6	>90	[90,80)	[80,60)	[60,0)
D7	>50000	[50000,20000)	[20000,10000)	[10000,0)
D8	>70	[70,60)	[60,50)	[50,0)
D9	>60	[60,40)	[40,20)	[20,0)
D10	>15	[15,12)	[12,6)	[6,0)
D11	>10	[10,5)	[5,3)	[3,0)
D12	>30	[30,10)	[10,8)	[8,0)
D13	>20000	[20000,10000)	[10000,5000)	[5000,0)
D14	>2000	[2000,1500)	[1500,1000)	[1000,0)
D15	<700	[700,5000)	[5000,10000)	>10000

Table 4 The result of comprehensive evaluation of Nan tong urban SD forewarning

Forewarning index	2004	2005	2006	2007
D1	6.05	5.60	5.35	4.93
D2	4.11	4.04	4.03	4.02
D3	4.69	3.10	2.49	2.45
D4	2.71	2.69	2.60	2.53
D5	2.44	2.36	2.39	2.33
D6	2.93	2.95	3.00	2.88
D7	3.75	3.60	3.12	1.83
D8	7.01	6.62	6.37	6.25
D9	2.14	1.78	1.92	1.80
D10	0.67	0.15	0.10	0.00
D11	3.40	2.45	2.43	2.15
D12	5.00	4.70	4.40	4.31
D13	6.39	5.84	4.90	4.42
D14	4.64	4.51	4.74	5.02
D15	3.48	3.49	3.51	3.52
I_i	3.88	3.64	3.44	3.03
Alert degree	Light alert	Light alert	Light alert	Light alert

2004 to 2007 of Nan tong city, we calculate fuzzy forewarning indexes of the bigger the more superior and the smaller the more superior type of indicators respectively, at last come out the fuzzy comprehensive forewarning indexes of Nan tong urban sustainable development (Table 4).

4 Conclusions

As we can see from the calculated outcome of index (Table 4), the majority of factors are showing a good development trend, there is no deterioration development trend, but the individual indicator such as population density and the number of students in school per 10,000 people are still in mild deterioration. On the whole, the comprehensive forewarning index of Nan Tong urban SD from 2004 to 2007 is 3.88, 3.64, 3.44, 3.03, which shows a declining trend. The SD shows a stable and harmonious trend, which means the efforts for harmonious development of social-economic and ecological environment has achieved certain results. However, from the perspective of alert degree, comparing integrated forewarning index to standard forewarning index interval indicates Nan tong urban SD was still in light alert state in the latest 4 years, which requires, Nan tong should raise vigilance and prevent the reverse development, and earnestly implement the scientific concept of development, adhere to the path of sustainable development in order to achieve regional socio-economic development and natural environment co-ordination and a virtuous circle.

References

1. Jing Ping, Jia Hai-feng, Xu Bi-xia: Trend Forecasting and Forewarning Method for Urban Sustainable Development. *Journal of Chongqing Jianzhu University*, Vol. 30, No.2 (2008) p. 116–120
2. Fu Juan-lin, Qiao Biao: Ecological Early-warning Model and Its Application in the Process of Urbanization Based on Fuzzy Matter Element Theory, Advances in Earth Science, Vol. 23, No. 9 (2008) p. 990–995
3. Henderson V: The Urbanization Process and Economic Growth: The So-What Question, Journal of Economic Growth, Vol. 8, No.1 (2003) p. 47–71.
4. Pan Feng, Liang Chuan: Fuzzy Matter-Element Model for Evaluating Sustainable Utilization of Regional Water Resources, *Advances In Water Science*, Vol. 14, No. 3 (2003), p. 271–275

Resident Population Prediction Based on Cohort-Component Method

Biyu Lv, Jiantong Zhang, and Hong He

Abstract Resident population prediction is very important to sustainable urban construction. Population forecasts by age group and sex can be derived through cohort-component method. This method requires at least two consecutive censuses data, but in this paper we will address the problem of how to apply this method to predict population with only one census data. Furthermore, there are no firsthand materials about fertility rate, and the form of migration rate is not suitable for the cohort-component model directly. Under these circumstances, we have to do some processing to those data in order to better model the method. It is proved that this method performs well in population prediction.

Keywords Cohort analysis · Population prediction · Sustainable urban construction

1 Introduction

An important aspect in sustainable urbanization is a reasonable population size and structure of a city. Thus effective prediction of the size and structure of the resident population is crucial. By integrated considering its own constrains and the predictions, the size and structure of population of the city is able to be guided, adjusted and directed to a sustainable way.

Demographic forecasting has a long history [1]. Forecasts of the size and structure of the population are central to social and economic planning [2]. Fertility fluctuations of the past are the major drivers of the population ageing process, and the declining mortality is also significant. One response to population ageing has been an increase in immigration to make up for past shortfalls in births [3]. Immigration has thus become a major driver of population change.

B. Lv (✉), J. Zhang, and H. He
School of Economics and Management, Tongji University, 1239 Siping Rd, Shanghai, People's Republic of China
e-mail: eabesy2529@163.com; zhangjiant@163.com; sophiestream@hotmail.com

D.D. Wu (ed.), *Modeling Risk Management in Sustainable Construction*,
Computational Risk Management, DOI 10.1007/978-3-642-15243-6_40,

The population is disaggregated by age and sex to provide the necessary detail. Forecasting demographic change is difficult because accuracy depends on the particular situation or trends, but it is not clear when a method will perform best [4]. Population forecasting is also highly uncertain: as Keyfitz [5] remarked, "The best demographers do it, but none would stake their reputation on the agreement of their forecasts with the subsequent realization."

A simple version of the cohort-component method was developed that requires data only from two consecutive censuses and a set of simple calculations [6]. The city we concern, Beilun, is districted in 1984 in Ningbo Zhejiang province. And a census of population is taken every 10 years. Consequently and unfortunately, there is only one census data we could obtain in Beilun statistics.

In this paper, the projections are constructed using the well-known cohort-component method, in which births, deaths, and migration are projected separately by age group and sex.

2 Cohort-Component Method for Population Prediction

2.1 Cohort-Component Model

Cohort-component method is a system of demographic accounting in which the population is advanced forward in time through the application of time-specific survivorship ratios by age and sex and the derivation of births from time-specific fertility rates of women by age; migration by age and sex can also be incorporated [7]. The basic theory of demographic and a lot of facts of population changes show that, when an area's population reaches a large enough scale the time-varying changes of population by age group and sex generally have a relatively stable characteristic. Cohort-component method is just to utilize this characteristic to predict a certain region's population.

Here, we group population according to the age interval of five (up to age 85 and over). The prediction interval is 5 years. We introduce the definition and illustrate the model as following:

$M_{x,t}$: Male population of age group of $x \sim x + 4$ in year t,

$F_{x,t}$: Female population of age group of $x \sim x + 4$ in year t,

where x = 0, 5, 10, ... 80, $M_{85,t}$ and $F_{85,t}$ denote elderly population of men and women over the age of 85 respectively.

B_t: The number of babies born between yeat t and year $t + 5$,

r: Sex ratio at birth between yeat t and year $t + 5$,

$B_{t,m}$: The number of male babies born between yeat t and year $t + 5$,

$B_{t,f}$: The number of female babies born between year t and year $t + 5$,

$d_{x,t}^{m}$: Death rate for males of age group of $x{-}5 \sim x{-}1$ in year t,

$d_{x,t}^{f}$: Death rate for females of age group of $x{-}5{\sim}x{-}1$ in year t, where $d^m_{0,t}$ and $d^f_{0,t}$ denote the death rate of male babies and female babies who born between year t and year $t + 5$ respectively, while $d^m_{85,t}$ and $d^f_{85,t}$ denote the death rate of male and female population of age group of 80–84 in year t respectively.

$b_{x,t}$: Fertility rate for females of age group of x~$x + 4$ in year t,

$m^m_{x,t}$: Net migraion rate for males of age group of $x-5$~$x-1$ between year t and $t + 5$,

$m^f_{x,t}$: Net migraion rate for females of age group of $x-5$~$x-1$ between year t and $t + 5$,

According to the above definition, we can calculate the population of each age group in year $t + 5$ based on the population of each age group in year t by the following equations:

$$M_{x,t+5} = (1 - q^m_{x,t} + m^m_{x,t}) \cdot M_{x-5,t}, \quad 5 \le x \le 80 \tag{1}$$

$$F_{x,t+5} = (1 - q^f_{x,t} + m^f_{x,t}) \cdot F_{x-5,t}, \quad 5 \le x \le 80 \tag{2}$$

$$B_t = \sum_{x=15}^{49} (F_{x,t}+F_{x,t+5}) \cdot b_{x,t} \times \frac{5}{2} \tag{3}$$

$$B_{t,m} = B_t \times (\frac{r}{100 + r}), \quad B_{t,f} = B_t - B_{t,m} \tag{4}$$

$$M_{0,t+5} = (1 - q^m_{0,t} + m^m_{0,t}) \cdot B_{t,m} \tag{5}$$

$$F_{0,t+5} = (1 - q^f_{0,t} + m^f_{0,t}) \cdot B_{t,f} \tag{6}$$

2.2 Data Sources

This paper aims to apply cohort-component method to produce population prediction of 2015 by age group and sex. Though the simplest version of the cohort-component method requires data from two consecutive censuses, we can only get one group of census population numbers by age group and sex from Beilun statistics. Apart from this, we also have the following useful data: death rate in 2000 by age group and sex, average annual growth rate of the life expectancy, age-sex-specific migration rate in 2000, and population numbers of both registered population and floating population number by age group and sex at the end of 2005 and 2009. About fertility, there is nothing we could collect.

2.3 Rate of Change

There are three components in cohort-component method. They are fertility rate, death rate and migration rate, which are essential to the change of population number.

Traditional population projections typically comprise three deterministic scenarios, based on combinations of assumptions about death rate, fertility rate and migration rate.

2.3.1 Death Rate

According to the data of death rate in 2000, we can plot a chart about it as shown in Fig. 1.

As we know, in Beilun, the average annual growth rate of the life expectancy since 1990 is about 0.4%, expecially after 2000. In the light of this, we assume that the average life expectancy in Beilun from 2000 to 2010 still continue to follow the 0.4% growth rate, so the average life expectancy of males and females, respectively, are 79.82 years old and 84.29 years old in 2010. Then the growth rate gradually slows down. From 2010 to 2015 it reduces to 0.3%. In accordance with this assumption, the average life expectancy of males and females in 2015, respectively, are 81.02 years old and 85.57 years old.

2.3.2 Fertility Rate

In the cohort-component model, $b_{t,\,x}$ denotes fertility rate. It is used to predict the number of new-born babies. However, there is no direct data about fertility rate. Fortunately, we can address this issue by another way. Here, we introduce another notation cw which denotes the children–women ratio. It refers to every 1,000 women at the age of 15–49 corresponding to the number of children less than 5 years old in a certain year. This indicator can be obtained in the census or sample surveys, so it can provide data on fertility levels on condition of having no detailed births statistics. Thus (3) can be replaced by

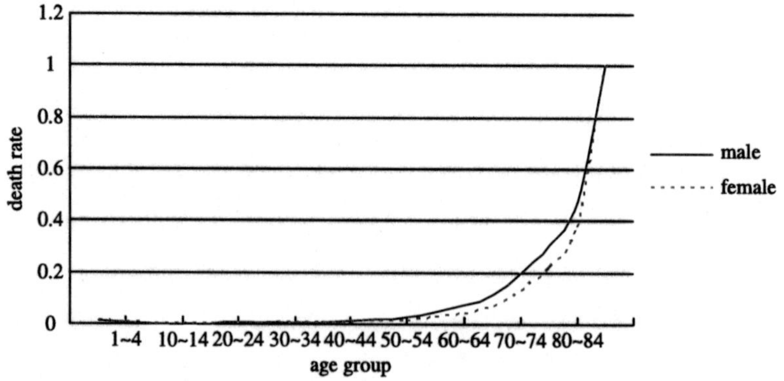

Fig. 1 Death rate of resident population by age group and sex in Beilun in 2000

$$B_t = \sum_{x=15}^{49} \left(F_{x,t} + F_{x,t+5}\right) \cdot cw \tag{7}$$

2.3.3 Migration Rate

Figure 2 indicates the migration rate of resident population by age and sex in Beilun in 2000. As showed in it, the migration rate is age-sex-specific, but what we want is by age group and sex. So we must transfer the age-sex-specific migration rate by age group and sex firstly. Here, we take an example to further illustrate how to calculate the migration rate of population by age group of 0 year old to 4 year old as showed in Table 1.

It is wrong to just directly add up the migration rate of age of 0–4. The relatively accurate way to calculate the migration rate by age group is shown as follows:

The migration rate of male by age group 0–4 is:

$$(1 + 0.0266)(1 + 0.0229)(1 + 0.0211)(1 + 0.0192)(1 + 0.0174) = 1.1119$$

The migration rate of male by age group 0–4 is:

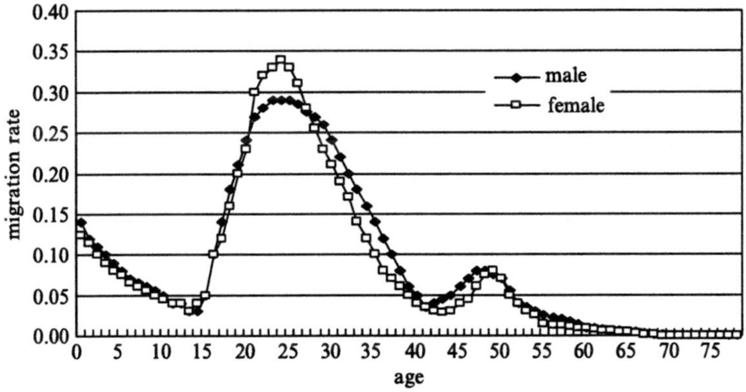

Fig. 2 Migration rate of resident population by age and sex in Beilun in 2000

Table 1 Migration rate of age 0–4

Age	Migration rate	
	Male	Female
0	0.0266	0.0238
1	0.0229	0.0220
2	0.0211	0.0192
3	0.0192	0.0174
4	0.0174	0.0155

Table 2 Total population in year 2000, 2005 and 2009

Year	Total population	Registered population	Floating population
2000	382,276	330,090	52,186
2005	585,823	349,879	235,944
2009	841,818	373,171	468,647

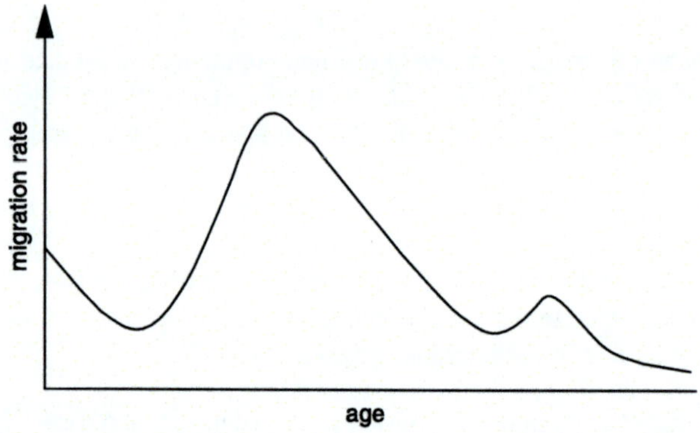

Fig. 3 Migration age table of population formed by Rogers, an American famous population professor, in 1978

$$(1 + 0.0238)(1 + 0.0220)(1 + 0.0192)(1 + 0.0174)(1 + 0.0155) = 1.1018$$

Beilun was districted in 1984. Its floating population grows very slow in first 15 years. However, with the economy developed, as Table 2 illustrates, the floating population grow rapidly between 2000 and 2009. The number of floating population in 2009 is almost nine times to 2000. As for registered population, there is relatively pedestrian.

By comparison, we found that Figs. 2 and 3 are very similar. Therefore, it is reasonable for us to set the migration rate of Beilun between 2000 and 2010 under these two migration age table of population.

2.4 Population Prediction

In order to better forecast the resident population, we first examine the method by predictions of 2005 and 2010.

Since we can only get one census data, we have no idea about how the migration rate changed in the last 15 years. As a result, when forecast the resident population of Beilun in 2005 and 2010, we try to get the migration rate, changes of migration and the change trends between 2000 and 2010 by constantly adjust migration rate to best fit the number of population which we have already known according to the population size and the approximate ratio of some age groups in 2005 and 2009.

Table 3 Resident population prediction in Beilun in year 2015

Age group	High		Medium		Low	
	Male	Female	Male	Female	Male	Female
0–14	54,315	51,541	52,982	50,290	51,648	49,039
15–34	178,302	186,857	166,679	175,306	155,057	163,754
35–59	233,158	192,003	228,135	188,776	223,112	185,551
60–84	431,06	418,44	43,059	41,808	43,012	41,771
>=85	1,385	2,071	1,385	2,071	1,385	2,071
Total	510,266	4,74,318	4,92,240	4,58,252	4,74,215	44,2187
Total population	984,584		950,492		916,402	

Through many times of simulation, we find out that if the migration rate between 2000 and 2005 is five times to 2000 in the age groups of 15–34, and other age groups is three times, then the resident population prediction in 2005 is 585,267. The prediction error is only 556 people, and the error rate is 0.95%. When the migration rate between 2005 and 2010 was the same as 2000 in the age groups of 15–34, and other age groups is 0.8 times, then the resident population prediction in 2005 is 862,762. We know the total population in 2009 is 841,818. Considering the growth at present, the population increase 21,922 in 2010 is very reasonable compared with 2009.

On the basis of the simulation of prediction in 2005 and 2010, we can conclude that the migration rate have slowed down from 2005 to 2010. In cohort-component method, there are always three scenarios called the high, medium and low scenarios. By doing this, the Savants can make the prediction perform better. Here, we assume that there are three probabilities of the migration rate in between 2010 and 2015 too. For the high scenario the migration rate is 0.6 times of 2010 at all age groups. For the medium scenario, the migration rate is 0.8 times of the high, and the low scenario is 0.6 times of the high. The results of predictions and the details are showed in Table 3 as following:

3 Summary

The above analysis has demonstrated how to apply cohort-component method to forecasting resident population when there are only one census data. In this paper, we also illustrates how to calculate the births without any information on the fertility, how to calculate the migration rate by age groups based on the age-sex-specific migration rate. The changes of migration rates which is absent in the statistics are obtained by simulations of population which we can get.

Just as we know, the population prediction is highly uncertain. So errors are bound to exist. Cohort-component method is a well-established one for population projection. Though we consider the changes of fertility, mortality and migration in the future according to some certain statistical data, but subjective factors is still in existence, especially when we forecast death rate, fertility rate and migration rate. So in the future, we can strive for better methods for forecasting these three components.

Acknowledgments The authors gratefully acknowledge financial support from the project of Research on Population Size and Structure Based on Urban Development of Beilun (Project No: 1200242168). We would also like to thank the professors and classmates who are in the same group with us for their helpful comments, suggestions, which significantly improved an earlier version of this paper.

References

1. De Gans HA. (1999). *Population forecasting 1895–1945: The transition to modernity.* Dordrecht: Kluwer Academic.
2. Hyndman RJ and Booth H. (2008). Stochastic population forecasts using functional data models for mortality, fertility and migration. *International Journal of Forecasting*. 24, 323–342.
3. United Nations (2001). Replacement migration: is it a solution to declining and aging population? *No. ST/ESA/SER.A/206, United Nations, New York.*
4. Booth H. (2006). Demography forecasting: 1980 to 2005 in review. *International Journal of Forecasting*. 22(3), 547–581.
5. Keyfitz N. (1996). Foreword. In: W. Lutz (Ed.). *The future population of the world: What can we assume today*? (revised edition). London: Earthscan.
6. Hamilton CH and Perry J. (1962). A short method of projecting population by age from one decennial Census to Another. *Social Forces*. 41, 163–170.
7. Preston SH, Heuveline P, and Guillot M. (2001). *Demography: Measuring and modeling population processes*. (pp. 119–129). Oxford: Blackwell.
8. Yang Chaoyong. (2003). *Cohort-component method and population prediction of Zhejiang*. Thesis of Master Degree. Zhejiang, China.
9. Tayman J and Swanson DA. (1996). *Demography*. 33(4), 523–528.
10. Smith SK. (1997). Further thoughts on simplicity and complexity in population projection models. *International Journal of Forecasting*. 13, 557–565.

Dynamic Monitoring of Land Utilization Security of Mining City

Jin-sheng Zhou

Abstract While accelerating industrialization, urbanization and regional economy, the mining city has been confront with security problem of land utilization. In this paper, firstly, the valuation index system is established based on connotation of land utilization security of mining city. The main contents of evaluation, which include reserves security of mineral resources, land sustainable utilization security, eco-environmental security and security of geological hazards triggered by mining. Secondly, remote sensing should be the main method of dynamic monitoring of land utilization security in mining city, and statistical information and survey data are parts of monitoring results too. Finally, this paper builds early warning model of land utilization security of mining city, and presents an analysis of prediction way for security level.

Keywords Early warning · Land security · Mining city · Monitoring · Remote sensing

1 Introduction

Mining city is the city which develops by exploiting local mineral resources [1], Land utilization security is a relatively new term derived from national security. Mining City has played a crucial role in the promotion of industrialization, the urbanization process and the speeding up regional economic development, as the mine is one of the largest regional disturbed by human, land security caused by the exploitation of mineral resources has received a great concern to our community. Dynamic monitoring the mining city land utilization security through advanced technology and methods and providing timely warning are the basic starting point to guarantee the sustainable development of mining cities.

J.-s. Zhou
China University of Geosciences, Beijing, People's Republic of China
e-mail: zhoujinsheng001@163.com

D.D. Wu (ed.), *Modeling Risk Management in Sustainable Construction*, Computational Risk Management, DOI 10.1007/978-3-642-15243-6_41,

There are many studies on the mining city at home and abroad, but most of them concentrate in mining city's economic restructuring and environmental pollution problems caused by mineral resources development [2–4]; meanwhile, the mining environment has exceeded its ecological connotations and is being more and more noticed by scholars as it is an important component of land security. Mining city ecological environmental quality is divided into natural ecological environment quality, socio-ecological environment quality and economic ecological environmental quality by Liu Zhi-hui and other experts [5]. Na-wei and other experts also believe that man-land system of mining city has the vulnerability, and it is specifically manifested in the economic system vulnerability, the social system vulnerability and the natural systems vulnerability, and the root causes of the vulnerability is that the development of mineral resources is a kind of activity which strongly influence man-land systems and highly interfere the natural [6]. Remote sensing and other advanced methods build up a broad prospect for land utilization security research of mining city. Starting from pressure on resources ecological environment, resources, ecological environment situation and the human impact on the environment and using 1994 and 1998 TM image data, Wu Yan-bin [7] evaluates the changes of ecological security of Huainan in Anhui Province. Using land-use vector images interpretation of 1986 and 2000 TM images, Gu Kang-kang analyzes Land-use changes of that period in mining City of Liaoning, and the results shows that woodland and grassland have a downward trend when construction land increasing [8]. Using CBERS images, Du Pei-jun studies the landscape pattern changes of Xuzhou from 2001 to 2007, and points out that the occupation of cultivated land and green spaces destroys the natural ecological balance to a certain extent [9].

Without the limit of Mining city, the connotation of land utilization security is very extensive, so the scholars often study land-use security and land resources security. Some scholars divide land utilization secure into the quantity secure, quality secure and regional security [10], some scholars divide land resources security into economic security, social security and ecological security [11], Pan Cheng-rong analyzes the land-use ecological security of Anhui Province from cultivated land ecological security, forest land ecological security and mine ecological security [12].

Remote sensing technology, especially high-resolution satellite remote sensing is rapidly extended in the area of land use monitoring because of its accurate, fast and covering. In the RS and GIS support, Liao Ke dynamically monitors the land use changes in Changping District, Beijing [13]. Using remote sensing images, Yang qing-hua gets land use changes of 51 county areas around Beijing quickly and accurately [14]. Remote sensing technology is also playing an increasingly important role in the evaluation of mineral resources. Jin Qing-hua analyzes the application principles of hyper-spectral remote sensing technology in the evaluation of mineral resources and mine environmental monitoring, and specific cases in prospecting of porphyry copper, hydrothermal gold deposit, in-situ leach able sandstone-type uranium ore, oil and gas, diamond, and in the area of mine waste pollution monitoring [15]. The use of remote sensing techniques in the mine exploitation monitoring had begun in 1960s in the foreign. In the United States, the mine environment and disaster monitoring project carried out in 1969 which uses remote sensing technology to dynamically monitor gangue heap generated by coal mining and land reclamation, and it achieves remarkable effects of disaster prevention and mitigation [16].

The fundamental purpose of dynamic monitoring is early warning, and the early warning mainly includes warning sources analysis, warning signs recognition, dynamic monitoring of warning intelligence, warning degree of prediction and control decision-making. Domestic and foreign scholars have done a theoretical and practical exploration in land resource security warning from different angles. Jeffrey analyzes the land security situation from the effects on land of agro-ecological environmental changes [17]; taking the Red River Valley of Canada as an example, C. EmadHaque discusses the risk of land resources from the inflow and outflow of ecosystems matter and energy in the river basin [18]; Liu You-zhao analyzes the warning intelligence, warning sources, warning signs and warning degree of China's cultivated land security warning [19] ;Wu Wen-sheng proposes evaluation index system of cultivated land resource security and security standards, and conducts an evaluation and early warning of China's cultivated land [20].

Mining cities are special cities. Many cities become failure when mine is exhausted, and also many cities transform successfully. How to analyze mining city's survival and development from the global point of view including resource, environmental, economic, social factors and dynamic monitoring and early warning of land utilization security in the process of mining city's development are the root of solving many problems in mining cities, and they are also the weakness of the current theoretical research.

2 The Land Use Security Elements of Mining City

2.1 The Development Situation of Mining City

According to preliminary statistics, there are 426 mining cities of county level and above in China. Among them, there are 178 of city level, 212 of county level and 36 of town level [1]. Mining cities have made great contributions to the country's economic, social development and the improvement of people's living. They provide the state with more than 93% of the coal, more than 90% of the oil, more than 80% of the iron ore and 70% of natural gas and they have indelible historical contributions to regional economic development, improving living and social stability as the regional economy market centers and regional radiation centers.

But we should also see that, with the development and utilization of resources, the mining cities are facing twin threats of the mineral resources reserve security and ecological security, and the regional economic security and social stability security issues it brings have become increasingly prominent. The reduction in reserves is a direct threat to the supply of industrial raw materials, the vegetation destruction, water pollution, air pollution caused by mineral development seriously damage the ecological environment, the endogenous and exogenous soil acidification, alkalization, heavy metal pollution are serious threats to the land quality security, and secondary geological disasters such as collapse, ground collapse, landslide, debris flow are threats to the life and property safety of residents.

Therefore, studying the land utilization security issues of mining cities not only relates to the mining city's own survival, development and demise, but also relates to the country's industrial base and mineral resources strategies, the regional economic development and the construction of a harmonious society.

2.2 The Connotation of Land Utilization Security of Mining Cities

Land is a broad concept. It means the territory of the State in the "Advanced Chinese Dictionary" and means territorial possessions or property in English. Land security was first used for military and means to protect the country's territorial integrity against external violation, the connotation of land security often said now has been greatly expanded. The concept of land utilization security is first the opposite of external aggression, and it refers to the land security issues caused by human disturbance while using and transforming. Land utilization security of mining city positions the ordinary land utilization security in mineral resources development and utilization, and its security issues are directly or indirectly associated with mining activities.

It have not had a clear definition of the land utilization security of mining city in the literature, but many scholars have discussed the "land resource security" and "homeland resources security" whose connotation is similar with it. Land resources security refers to land resources Status and capacity of a country or region can continue to access and ensure biological communities (human) efficient production and high quality life [21]. Homeland resources security is the state of effective defense when a country's land resources are facing threat, destruction of land resources' safety and the effective supply of the economy [22].

Drawing on the above definition, in this article, land utilization security of mining city will be defined as follows: in mineral resource development and utilization activities, the sustainable development health status of biological communities (human) which rely on the land, and the status mainly includes four content: the security status of mineral resources reserves; the security status of the sustainable use of land resources; the security status of ecological environment; the security status of secondary geological disasters. The mining cities' economic security and social security are derived from land utilization security of mining city.

2.3 The Evaluation Indexes of Land Utilization Security of Mining City

Homeland security involves resources, environment, economy and many other factors, it is a complex system interrelated by a number of factors, and a comprehensive set of indicators are needed to judge it. Therefore, this article builds the evaluation index criteria layer based on the connotation of land utilization security of mining city, and builds evaluation indexes based on the criteria layer; and uses many relative mutative indexes in order to reflect the characteristics of dynamic.

1. *The security evaluation indexes of mineral resources reserves*: The security of mineral resources reserves can be evaluated in static and dynamic areas, the reserve production ratio and reserve consumption ratio reflect the security degree of static, the ore-forming conditions and growth rate of exploration investment affect the prospecting potential and they dynamically reflect the mineral resources security of mining cities.
2. *The security evaluation indexes of land resources sustainable utilization*: The security evaluation of land resources sustainable utilization can be evaluated in quantitative and qualitative areas, and the indexes can be selected have the land reclamation rate, the reduction rate of the cultivated area, the change rate of soil organic matter and so on.
3. *The security evaluation indexes of ecological environment*: the damage to the ecological environment causing by mineral resource development is one of the greatest threats to the land utilization security of mining city, and the contents of its evaluation are very complex. The following indexes can be selected: the standard-reaching rate of waste discharge, the reduction rate of green space, the reduction rate of species, the governance rate of ecological environment, the investment growth rate of ecological environment governance.
4. *The security evaluation indexes of secondary geological disasters*: The secondary geological disasters of mining cities mainly include landslides, subsidence, landslides, debris flows, and their frequency and destroying degree constitute the security evaluation indexes of secondary geological disasters.

Of the above indexes system, there have positive trend indexes, such as the reserve production ratio, the larger of its value is, the higher of the security degree of land utilization is; there also have negative trend indexes, such as the reduction rate of green space, the larger its value is, the lower of the security degree of land utilization is. The index system constructed in this paper is only a coarse outline. Some indexes need to be further subdivided in the practical application, and even another set of index system is needed to evaluate one of the indexes. The evaluation indexes of land utilization security of mining city are summarized in the Table 1.

Table 1 The valuation index system of land utilization security of mining city

Target layer	Criterion layer	Index layer	Sub-index layer
A the evaluation indexes of land utilization security of mining city	B1 the factor of mineral reserves security	C01 the reserve production ratio	(Omission)
		C02 the reserve consumption ratio	
		C03 the ore-forming conditions	
		C04 the growth rate of exploration investment	
	B2 the factor of land resources sustainable utilization security	C05 the land reclamation rate	
		C06 the reduction rate of the cultivated area	
		C07 the change rate of soil organic matter	
	B3 the factor of ecological environment security	C08 the standard-reaching rate of waste discharge	
		C09 the reduction rate of green space	
		C10 the reduction rate of species	
		C11 the governance rate of ecological environment	
		C12 the investment growth rate of ecological environment governance	
	B4 the factor of secondary geological disasters security	C13 the growth rate of collapse	
		C14 the growth loss rate of collapse	
		C15 the growth rate of subsidence	
		C16 the growth loss rate of subsidence	
		C17 the growth rate of landslide	
		C18 the growth loss rate of landslide	
		C19 the growth rate of debris flow	
		C20 the growth loss rate of flow	

3 The Land Utilization Security Monitoring Methods and Contents of Mining Cities

The direct purpose of land utilization security monitoring is to obtain land dynamic information. These information service directly to the security evaluation indexes and they are basic data for calculating the values of evaluation indexes. Usually, there are three ways to obtain the land dynamic changes data and they are field survey, statistical analysis and remote sensing monitor. Field survey is limited to region, manpower and money, and statistical information is limited to the statistical indexes, so they cannot be the main method of large-scale and cyclical land dynamic information extraction. Remote sensing technology not only has macro, economic, rapid and efficient advantages on the surface information collection, but also shows broad prospects in the underground information collection through inversion, so remote sensing has become a main method to monitor the land utilization security of mining cities. In particular, the integration of remote sensing (RS) and geographic information systems (GIS) can quickly get a more satisfactory land dynamic monitoring results [23].

Remote monitoring takes a variety of remote sensing data as a data source, and gets land utilization dynamic spatial and temporal information through information extraction and simulation. The main steps are as follows:

1. Select the appropriate remote sensing data source. Now the commonly used remote sensing data sources are the United States TM data, the French SPOT data, India IRS data, and CBERS data. The data choice needs to consider the key monitoring surface elements, monitoring precision, data amount and cost and so on. The dynamic monitoring of land utilization security is a very complex system, and usually needs two or more data sources to compensate for the lack of one single data source and improve the quality of information.
2. The processing and synthesis of remote sensing images. It includes atmospheric correction, geometric correction, image enhancement and the image synthesis of different bands.
3. The extraction of remote sensing information. Based on the preliminary interpretation and through field investigation, establish the remote sensing image interpretation signs and extract the remote sensing information. At present, visual interpretation and man-computer interactive interpretation are usually combined to extract the land utilization change information.
4. Accuracy judgment and data correction. Through field verification, it needs to revise the interpretation results if the extracted information does not meet the predetermined precision.

We can easily and regularly get the land utilization security information of most of the mining cities by remote sensing, but remote sensing is not omnipotent under current technology. The land utilization security monitoring needs remote sensing information, and at the same time, it needs statistical information and field survey data's support. The nature of remote sensing monitoring is to identify the land cover, ecological environment and other elements' change processes of land utilization security of mining cities through the principle of the images at different times have different spectral characteristics. It can directly reflect the reduction in green area, the number and scope of secondary geological disasters, solid waste dumping, mining land reclamation and other information, and can also roughly determine the soil composition changes, the atmosphere changes and water resources changes through the inversion method. But, the resources exploration investment, eco-environmental recovery investment, secondary geological disasters, losses, reserves and other information must be obtained through statistical data analysis and field surveys. The land utilization security monitoring methods and contents of mining cities are shown in Fig. 1.

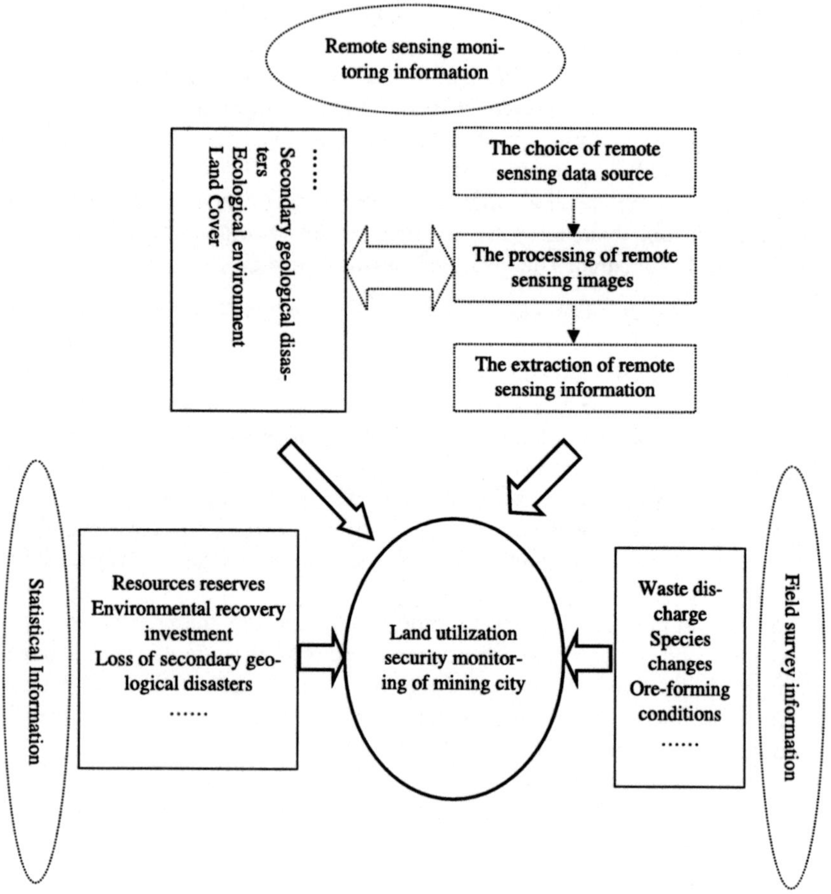

Fig. 1 Monitoring methods and contents of land utilization security of mining city

4 The Land Utilization Security Warning of Mining Cities

4.1 The Ideas of Land Utilization Security Warning of Mining Cities

The basic idea of resources warning of is: find the warning source → clarifies the warning situation → analyze the warning signs → forecast the warning degree [24]. The warning source of land utilization security warning of mining cities is obvious, that is, the irrational behavior of human in the process of mineral resources development; the warning situation can be clarified through the land utilization dynamic monitoring; warning signs are closely related to the warning situation and they are external representation of the warning situation t deterioration; therefore, the focus of land utilization security warning of mining cities is forecasting the, and the core of warning degree forecasting is the warning model.

4.2 The Warning Model of the Land Utilization Security Warning of Mining Cities

This paper selects the evaluation indexes of land utilization security of mining city as the warning indexes and comprehensive index method as warning model. Its calculation formula is expressed as:

$$E = \sum_{i=1}^{n} E_i * W_i \quad (\mathrm{i} = 1, 2 \ldots \mathrm{n}) \tag{1}$$

In the formula, E is integrated value of the land utilization security warning of mining cities, E_i is the evaluation value of index i, W_i is the weight of index i. In the model calculations, determine the index weight using AHP and it requires the comparison of monitoring value and evaluation criteria to get the evaluation warning value. Evaluation criteria are usually determined based on the following principles: (a) international and national standards; (b) development planning and land planning of country or study area; (c) international or community recognized standards; (d) research results of experts and scholars; (e) historical data [25]. The warning process of land utilization security warning of mining cities is shown in Fig. 2.

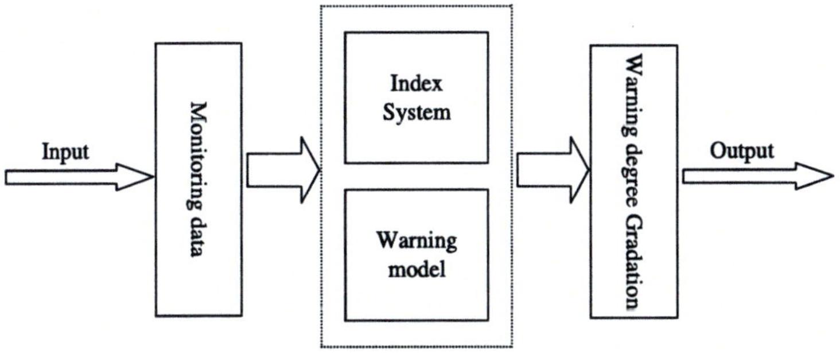

Fig. 2 The warning process of land utilization security warning of mining cities

4.3 *Warning Degree Prediction of Land Utilization Security of Mining City*

Warning degree reflects the degree or intensity of warning indexes value changes. Warning degree is usually divided into five levels: no warning, light warning, moderate warning, serious warning, and huge warning. As the integrated warning value of land utilization security of mining city is between 0 and 1, so the warning degree interval can be roughly divided by 0.2 (can be adjusted depending on the circumstances). Different color lights represent the warning degree grade when predicting warning degree, as shown in Table 2.

5 Conclusions

Land utilization of mining city is a very complex system, and land utilization security has a direct impact on the economic security and social security of mining city. Therefore, the comprehensive study of the land utilization security of mining city is of great practical significance. Land utilization security of mining city includes four connotations: mineral resources reserves security, land security, ecological security, and secondary geological disasters security.

The evaluation indexes of land utilization security of mining city are built on the basis of the connotations, and they are both the indexes of the land utilization dynamic monitoring and land utilization security warning. Remote sensing should be the main method of dynamic monitoring of land utilization security in mining city, and added with statistical information and survey data. Comprehensive index method is appropriate to build the warning model of the land utilization security warning of mining cities, and the output value of warning system is the composite index of land utilization security. The composite warning index value is divided into different intervals according to certain principles to reflect the different warning degree, and different color lights represent the warning degree grade.

Table 2 Warning degree prediction of land utilization security of mining city

Warning degree interval	[0.0,0.2]	(0.2,0.4]	(0.4,0.6]	(0.6,0.8]	(0.8,1.0]
Warning degree grade	Huge warning	Serious warning	Moderate warning	Light warning	Non warning
Color of signal lights	Black	Red	Yellow	Blue	Green
Show of signal lights	•	•	•	•	•

References

1. Zhu Xun. The study of mining city restructures [M]. Beijing: China Land Press, 2005: 22–25.
2. Liu Yao-bin, Song Wen-jun. Alternative industries progress and prospects of domestic mining cities [J]. Coal Economic Research, 2008, (12): 16–19.
3. Zhu Qing, Luo Zhi-hong. Comparison and reference of the mining city transformation of china and other countries [J]. China Mining Magazine, 2007, 16 (12): 15–18.
4. Ding Zhi-Ping. Status of geological environment of mining cities and protecting measures [J]. Resources and Industries, 2003, 5 (1): 45–46.
5. Liu Zhi-hui, Lai Yong-bin, Sun Cui-ling. General Assessment on the Ecological Environmental Quality of Mineral-Rich Cities [J]. Journal of Liaoning University of Petroleum & Chemical Technology, 2004, 24 (3): 39–44.
6. Na Wei, Liu Ji-sheng. Research on the vulnerability and the evaluation of the human-earth system in mining cities [J]. Urban problems, 2007, (7): 43–48.
7. Wu Yan-bin, Peng Su-ping, Jin Yi. Study on ecological security for sustainable development in the mining cities [J]. China Mining Magazine, 2006, 15 (4): 26–36.
8. Gu Kang-kang, Liu Jing-shuang, Dou Jing-xin. Land use change in mining cities of Central Liaoning [J]. Chinese Journal of Ecology, 2007, 26 (8): 1265–1270.
9. Du Pei-Jun, Yuan Lin-shan, Zhang Hua-peng. Urban landscape pattern change based on Multi-temporal CBERS imagery – taking Xuzhou City as an Example [J]. Journal of China University of Mining & Technology, 2009, 38 (1): 106–113.
10. Liu Yan-sui. Strategies to guarantee land resources safety in China [J]. Bulletin of Chinese Academy of Sciences, 2006, 21 (5): 379–384.
11. Wang Nan-jun, Wu Qun, Chen Cheng. A research into index system of land resource security evaluation in the process of urbanization [J]. Scientific and Technological Management of Land and Resources, 2006, (2): 28–31.
12. Pan Cheng-rong, Zhang Zhi-yuan, Jia Liang-qing. An analysis of eco-safety of land use in Anhui Province [J]. Journal of Anhui Agricultural University, 2004, 31 (4):495–500.
13. Liao Ke, Cheng Xi-fang, Wu Jian-sheng. High resolution remote sensing image used in land use change dynamic monitoring [J]. Science of Surveying and Mapping, 2006, 31 (6):11–15.
14. Yang Qing-hua, Zeng Fu-nian, Cao Wen-yu. The application of remote sensing technology to environment and resources monitoring in the peripheral areas of Beijing [J]. Land Resources Remote Sensing, 2007, (4):76–84.
15. Jin Qing-hua, Zhu Li-li, Zhang Li-xin. Examples of using hyperspectral remote sensing technology for mineral resource evaluation and mining environment monitoring [J]. Geological Bulletin of China, 2009, 28 (2–3):278–284.
16. Qian Li-ping. Application of remote sensing technology to the dynamic monitoring of mine environment [J]. Safety and Environmental Engineering, 2008, 15 (4):5–9.
17. Lockwood J.A. Agriculture and biodiversity: Finding our place in this world [J]. Agriculture and Human Values, 1999, 16 (4):365–379.
18. EmadHaque C. Risk assessment, emergency preparedness and response to hazards: The case of the 1997 Red River Valley Flood, Canada [J]. Natural Hazards, 2000, 21 (2–3):225–245.
19. Liu You-zhao, Ma Xin, XU Mao. Preliminary study on the early warning of cultivated land quality [J]. China Land Science, 2003, 17 (6):9–12.
20. Wu Wen-sheng, Zhu Jun, Hao Zhi-jun. An evaluation and prediction on the safety of cultivated land resources [J]. Areal Research and Development, 2003, 22 (5):46–49.
21. Wu Ci-fang, Bao Hai-jun, Qian Na-li. Theory and method of land resources security research [M]. Beijing: China Meteorological Press, 2004:1–5.
22. Meng Xu-guang, Li Xiang-ju. Analysis on plan and budget examination of geological survey program [J]. China Geology & Mining Economic, 2002, (1):31–34.

23. Chen Jian-ping, Wang Gong-Wen, Ding Huo-ping. Desertification evolution simulation and evaluation in Beijing [M]. Beijing: The Geological Publishing House, 2004:41.
24. Bu shan-xiang, Meng Xu-guang, Song Wei. Research on mineral resources warning of China [M]. Beijing: The Geological Publishing House, 1998:19–21.
25. Wang Rui-ling, Chen Yin-jun. An early warning system for farmland eco-environment quality – a case of Zhengzhou city [J]. Acta Pedologica Sinica, 2007, 44 (6):994–1002.

Risk Assessment of Water Transportation in Three Gorges Reservoir Through Approaches of System Engineering

Dan Zhang, Liwen Huang, and Xiaobiao Fan

Abstract Water transportation is system engineering, including four aspects: staff, vessel, environment and management. The four main aspects are affected by many unspecific factors. An unascertained measure model for evaluating the risks of water transportation in Three Gorges Reservoir was proposed on the basis of system engineering method in this paper, and the risk factors in the water area were identified and quantitative analysis of risk were done. In terms of the defects of traditional analytic hierarchy process (AHP) and entropy method in confirming weight, a composed method was proposed to determine the weight of indexes based on the improved analytic hierarchy process and information entropy. The application shows that the unascertained measure model based on system engineering can quantify the risk of water transportation system, and also be conducive to decision-making of the risk control.

Keywords Risk assessment · System engineering · Three Gorges reservoir · Water transportation

---

D. Zhang (✉)
College of Navigation, Wuhan University of Technology, Wuhan 430063, People's Republic of China
and
Maritime College, Chongqing Jiaotong University, Chongqing 400074, People's Republic of China
e-mail: ekindan@tom.com

L. Huang
College of Navigation, Wuhan University of Technology, Wuhan 430063, People's Republic of China
e-mail: lwhuang@whut.edu.cn

X. Fan
Maritime College, Chongqing Jiaotong University, Chongqing 400074, People's Republic of China
e-mail: fanxiaobiao@sina.com

D.D. Wu (ed.), *Modeling Risk Management in Sustainable Construction*, Computational Risk Management, DOI 10.1007/978-3-642-15243-6_42,

1 Introduction

The water transportation in Three Gorges Reservoir has played a significant role in increasing shipping capacity in China's Yangtze River. Cargo transportation by shipping in Three Gorges area increased greatly. The risk assessment of water transportation has been especially important and necessary in Three Gorges Reservoir. Risk assessment is a process of risk identification, risk estimation and risk evaluation to provide information for the purpose of system security (Timothy and Eirik 2000).

Water transportation is system engineering, including four aspects: staff, vessel, environment and management. The four main aspects are affected by many unspecific factors. The main risk factors were identified and quantitative analyzed in this paper to estimate the possibility of accident occurrence using an unascertained measure model (Liu et al. 1999) based on system engineering theory to provide the scientific basis for decision-making.

2 Water Transportation Risk Evaluation Index System Through Approaches of System Engineering Theory

According to the water transportation situation in Three Gorges Reservoir and research results of some experts and scholars, the operable second class indexes were established based on the first class index including staff, vessel, environment, and management for risk evaluation (Zheng and Li 2008). The factor of staff is centrally reflected in the professional skills of the crew, so the ratio of the crew breaking the rules and regulations, certificated crew, and the staff working more than 3 years are main evaluation index. The factor of vessel refers to the age of the ship, maneuverability, stowage of goods, etc. The ratio of old vessels, vessels overloaded, vessels carrying dangerous cargo and the vessels detained for safety check can be chose as evaluation index. Natural environment refers to the influence of wind, rain, fog, flow, etc. Channel environment can be influenced by the fluctuation of water level, the bend of channel, geologic hazard, etc. Navigational environment can be affected by the factors such as vessel traffic flow, navigation aids, traffic control, etc. (Veldhuyzen and Morrien 1997). Therefore, wind scale, visibility, variation of water level, concentration of vessel can be chose as environmental evaluation index. The factor of management refers to the management of maritime department, channel bureau, harbor department, and shipping companies. Therefore, traffic control and the number of aids to navigation can be tested as the last evaluation index.

Combined with the research of the experts and scholars, the scale of water transportation risk can be determined by five levels, put simply, low risk, relatively low risk, medium risk, relatively high risk, and high risk in accordance with the urgency of accidents, damage degree, area of influence and water transportation safety early warning mechanism of Three Gorges Reservoir.

3 Unascertained Measure Model for Water Transport Safety Assessment in Three Gorges Reservoir

3.1 *Single-Index Unascertained Measure*

Supposing $\mu_{ijk} = \mu(x_{ij} \in c_k)$, μ_{ijk} is the degree of estimate scale c_k, and μ satisfies the following equations:

$$0 \leq \mu(x_{ij} \in c_k) \leq 1 \tag{1}$$

$$\mu(x_{ij} \in \bigcup_{l=1}^{p} c_l) = \sum_{l=1}^{p} \mu(x_{ij} \in c_k) \tag{2}$$

$$\mu(x_{ij} \in U) = 1 \tag{3}$$

In the above equations, $i = 1, 2, ..., n; j = 1, 2, ..., m; k = 1, 2, ..., p$.

Single-index measure evaluation matrix can be expressed as:

$$(\mu_{ijk})_{m \times p} = \begin{array}{c} \begin{matrix} c_1 & c_2 & \cdots & c_k \end{matrix} \\ \begin{bmatrix} \mu_{i11} & \mu_{i12} & \cdots & \mu_{i1k} \\ \mu_{i21} & \mu_{i22} & \cdots & \mu_{i2k} \\ \vdots & \vdots & \vdots & \vdots \\ \mu_{im1} & \mu_{im2} & \cdots & \mu_{imk} \end{bmatrix} \end{array} (i = 1, 2, ..., n) \tag{4}$$

3.2 *Determination of Index Weight*

On the one hand, the value of index weight gained objectively by the means of entropy method was short of the expert's judgments on different evaluation indexes, on the other hand, the index weight gained by the means of analytic hierarchy process (AHP) method which analyze the different evaluation indexes given by the experts was too subjective. Based on the improved analytic hierarchy process and information entropy, a new combination weighting approach was proposed to determine the weight of indexes. The combination weighting approach utilized the advantages of both methods. The weight calculated by combination weighting approach was more rational and reliable (Xu 2007).

3.2.1 Entropy Method

Entropy is a measure of the uncertainty associated with a random variable. The uncertainty of system is increased with the rising entropy. The entropy of evaluation indicator x_{ij} can be expressed as $h_j = -\sum_{k=1}^{p} \mu_{ijk} \cdot \ln \mu_{ijk}$. Difference coefficient can be expressed as $e_{ij} = 1 - k \cdot h_j$. The degree of e_{ij} reflects the degree of importance of the index x_{ij}. The weight of index can be expressed as the following equation: $w_{ij} = e_{ij} \Big/ \sum_{j=1}^{m} e_{ij}$.

3.2.2 The Improved Analytic Hierarchy Process

The analytic hierarchy process (AHP) can be improved by the means of 0–1 scaling method. Consistency check is not needed in judgment matrix with the improved AHP. In the 0–1 scaling method, 0 indicates that A is inferior to B, 0.5 indicates that A is equal to B, and 1 indicates A is superior to B. Complementary judgment matrix $F = (f_{ij})_{m \times n}$ can be expressed by the means of 0–1 scaling method. Suppose $r_i = \sum_{j=1}^{m} f_{ij}$, $r_{ij} = (r_i - r_j)/2m + 0.5$, the fuzzy consistent matrix can be expressed as $R = (r_{ij})_{m \times n}$.

3.2.3 Determining the Weight of Index with the Combination Weighting Approach

Suppose w_i^1 stands for weight determined by entropy method, w_i^2 stands for weight determined by the improved AHP method, the combined weight can be expressed as $W_i = w_i^1 \cdot w_i^2 \Big/ \sum_{i=1}^{m} w_i^1 w_i^2$.

3.3 *Multi-index Measure of Evaluation*

Multi-index unascertained measure can be gained by single-index unascertained measure and the weight of index (Yang 2000), namely, $\mu_{ik} = \sum_{j=1}^{m} w_{ij} \mu_{ijk}$. Multi-index unascertained measure evaluation matrix can be expressed as following:

$$(u_{ik})_{n\times p} = \begin{pmatrix} \mu_{11} & \mu_{12} & \cdots & \mu_{1p} \\ \mu_{21} & \mu_{22} & \cdots & \mu_{2p} \\ \cdots & \cdots & \cdots & \cdots \\ \mu_{n1} & \mu_{n2} & \cdots & \mu_{np} \end{pmatrix} \tag{5}$$

3.4 *Identification and Evaluation of System Security*

The identify criteria of confidence measure recognition can be used for testing the system security. We usually get 0.6 or 0.7 for confidence measure λ ($\lambda \geq 0.5$).

$$k_0 = \min_k \left| k : \sum_{j=1}^{k} \mu_{ij} \geq \lambda, k = 1, 2, \cdots, p \right| \tag{6}$$

3.4.1 Application of Unascertained Measure Model in Risk Assessment

According to the unascertained measure evaluation model, the study on the risk assessment of water transportation was carried out in Three Gorges Reservoir. According to the reality conditions, the measure data of risk conditions was shown in Table 1.

According to the definition of unascertained measure model and the reality conditions we construct the unascertained measure function (Fig. 1).

From the data in Table 1 and measure functions, the evaluation matrix of single index measure can be obtained as follows:

$$\mu_1 = \begin{vmatrix} 0.5 & 0.5 & 0 & 0 & 0 \\ 0.25 & 0.75 & 0 & 0 & 0 \\ 0 & 0 & 0 & 0.4 & 0.6 \end{vmatrix} \quad \mu_2 = \begin{vmatrix} 0 & 0 & 0.96 & 0.04 & 0 \\ 1 & 0 & 0 & 0 & 0 \\ 0.6 & 0.4 & 0 & 0 & 0 \\ 1 & 0 & 0 & 0 & 0 \end{vmatrix}$$

$$\mu_3 = \begin{vmatrix} 1 & 0 & 0 & 0 & 0 \\ 0 & 0 & 0.375 & 0.625 & 0 \\ 1 & 0 & 0 & 0 & 0 \\ 1 & 0 & 0 & 0 & 0 \end{vmatrix} \quad \mu_4 = \begin{vmatrix} 1 & 0 & 0 & 0 & 0 \\ 0.111 & 0.889 & 0 & 0 & 0 \\ 0 & 0.555 & 0.445 & 0 & 0 \end{vmatrix}$$

Table 1 The measure data of index for water transportation risk assessment

Evaluation index	I_1	I_2	I_3	I_4	I_5	I_6	I_7	I_8	I_9	I_{10}	I_{11}	I_{12}	I_{13}	I_{14}
Value	3%	95%	62%	23%	3%	18%	0.8%	4	500	0.5	9	0.5	90%	95%

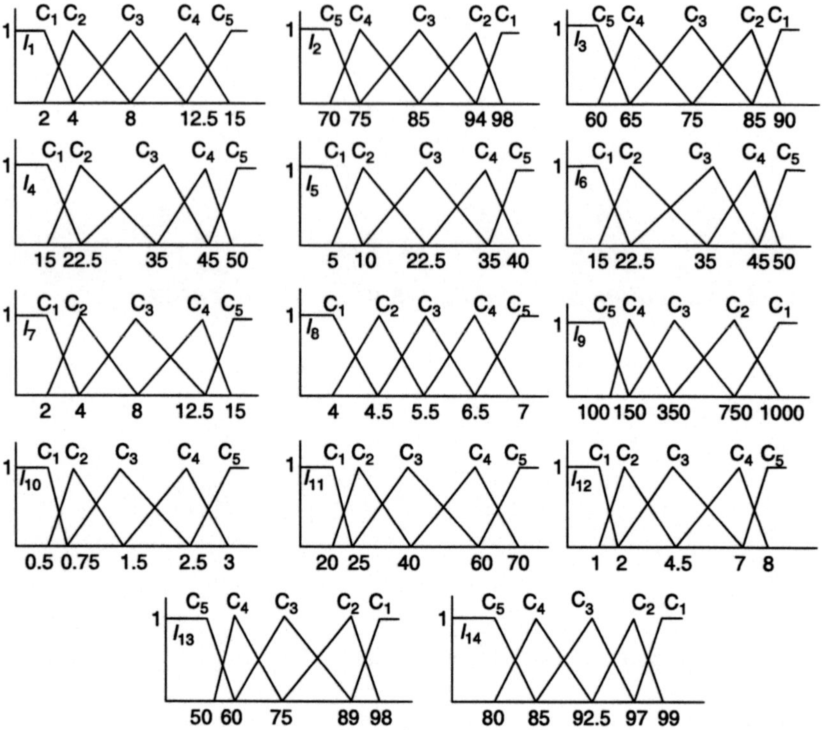

Fig. 1 Measure functions of indexes

The weight of a single index can be defined by combination weighting method as follows:

$$
\begin{aligned}
&(w_1, w_2, w_3, w_4, w_5, w_6, w_7, w_8, w_9, w_{10}, w_{11}, w_{12}, w_{13}, w_{14},) \\
&\quad = (0.0935, 0.0888, 0.0794, 0.0584, 0.0817, 0.0434, 0.0829, 0.0574, 0.0411, \\
&\qquad 0.0659, 0.0654, 0.0983, 0.0862, 0.0575).
\end{aligned}
$$

According to (5), the integrative appraise matrix can be calculated as follows: $I_{jk} = (0.5562, 0.2393, 0.0971, 0.0598, 0.0476)$. Taking $\lambda = 0.6$ (λ is confidence). We can know the risk of water transportation in Three Gorges Reservoir was relatively low, which showed that the conditions of water transportation was improved after reservoir storage and the conclusions were consistent with the actual situation. However, security was a relative concept, and the resources of human talents working for water transportation and the navigational environment and management especially in the water level changing area should be improved at present.

4 Summary

Water transportation safety is a systematic project involving multiple factors. An unascertained measure model for evaluating the risks of water transportation in Three Gorges Reservoir was established based on system engineering method in this paper. A composed method was proposed to determine the weight of indexes based on the improved analytic hierarchy process and information entropy. The qualitative analysis and quantitative evaluation were done for the risk assessment. The application shows that the unascertained measure model based on system engineering can quantify the risk of transportation system, and can also be conducive to decision-making of the risk control.

Acknowledgments The research was supported by Fundamental Research of the Ministry of Transport, China under the contract number 2008-319-814-060 and also by Western Science and Technology Construction Project, China, with the contract number 200732822242.

References

Kaidi Liu, Heqin Wu, Yanjun Pang (1999) Uncertain Information Processing and Application of Mathematics (pp. 160–191). Beijing: Science Press.

Timothy G. Fowler, Eirik Sørgård (2000) Modeling Ship Transportation Risk. Risk Analysis. doi:10.1111/0272-4332.202022.

W. Veldhuyzen, A.B. Morrien (1997) Application of Risk Models in the Assessment of the Effects of Vessel Traffic Management. SAFECO WP II.2.3, Port of Rotterdam and Marine Safety International, Rotterdam b.v., The Netherlands.

Yingjia Xu (2007) Research on Safety Assessment and Trend Analysis of Xiang River. Wuhan University of Technology.

Zhimin Yang (2000) Unascertained information on the mathematical approach. China Management Science, 11 (8): 192–196.

Zhongyi Zheng, Hongxi Li (2008) Study of Navigation Safety Evaluation in navigable Waters. Navigation of China, 31(2): 30–35.

Damaged Bridges over Watercourses and Stream Order Flood Analysis

Marek Mihola

Abstract The paper describes how data about floods and bridges, which were damaged by the floods, were used for analysis. The paper is focusing on determination of watercourse segments with higher risk of exceeding 100-year flow level. This is important because bridges are designed for n-year recurrence flood flow, generally for 100-year flow. Two analyses were performed. Data were analyzed from hydrometric stations about n-year recurrence flood flows and extreme (real) flood flows. Watercourses were evaluated by Strahler's stream ordering method and confronted with bridges damaged by floods.

Keywords Bridge · Damage · Flood · Flow rate · Q100 · Strahler · Stream order · Water course

1 Introduction

The Czech Republic is a specific inland state about 78,000 sq.km in central Europe with three main drainage divides to Baltic, North and Black Sea. Floods are common here after winter when snow melts or in summer due to high precipitation. However, floods in 1997 and 2002 were extreme because of slow moving cyclones, which prolonged normal rain period for as twice as long. For example in northeast region of the country, in Jeseniky Mountains, the precipitation in 5 days reached over 600 mm of water column, which is about half the annual rainfall. The flow rate in rivers Odra and Morava rose above 150- and even 500-year level [1]. Flow rate on rivers in South bohemian region exceeded 1,000-year flow in several hydrometric stations in 2002 (see Fig. 1).

M. Mihola (✉)
Faculty of Civil Engineering, VSB – Technical University of Ostrava, Ludvika Podeste 1875, 70833 Ostrava, Czech Republic
e-mail: marek.mihola@vsb.cz

D.D. Wu (ed.), *Modeling Risk Management in Sustainable Construction*, Computational Risk Management, DOI 10.1007/978-3-642-15243-6_43,

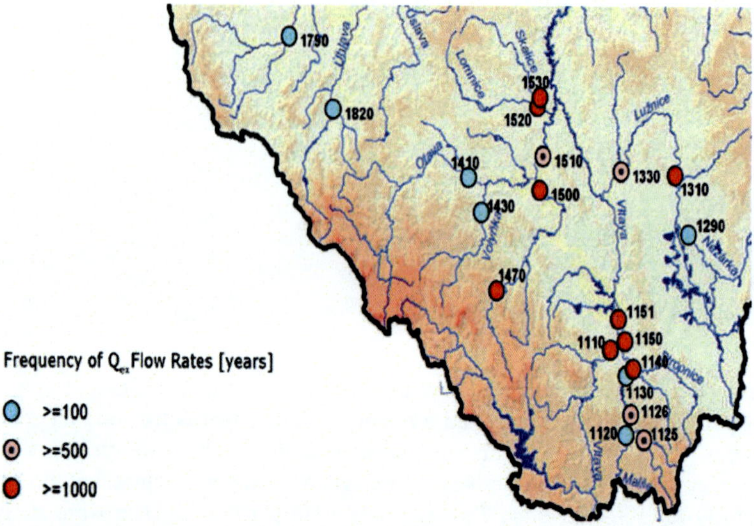

Fig. 1 Frequency of Qex in South bohemian region during flood in 2002 [2]

Flow rate is a stochastic value. Among others, it depends on prediction of frequency of maximum precipitation. This was underestimated in the Czech Republic. Since that time flow rates have been recalculated and refined several times.

2 Bridges

These floods put bridges over watercourses and inundation areas to the test. Though bridges are built according to the Czech Technical Standards for building bridges [3], some were damaged or destroyed during the floods. The bridges are generally built for 100-year flow (Q100) and should have 0.5 m free space from Q100 water level in the bridge opening. This is a standard design.

The problem is that every time flow rates are recalculated and changed, bridges can't be rebuilt. Flow rate higher than Q100 may damage the bridge sub- or superstructure; as stated in [4] scouring is generally listed among the most frequent reasons of bridge failures during floods.

As 85% of all the bridges in the Czech Republic are located over water courses, it is essential to deal with the matter. The paper is focusing on determination of watercourse segments with higher risk of exceeding the Q100 level on the basis of flood damage in recent years.

3 Hydrometric Stations

There are four categories (I–IV) indicating precision of input data for n-year recurrence flood flow Qn along with the technical standard [5]. Category I includes segments of water courses adjacent to the hydrometric station. These segments are not affected by any significant inflow. Category II includes segments with significant inflow such as confluence down the stream from the hydrometric station. Category III includes upper stream segments of observed and lower stream segments of unobserved water courses. Flow rate in category IV is determined by calculation only (upper streams, washes, etc.). The uncertainties for each category are defined in Table 1.

The most accurate data about n-year recurrence flow and extreme (real) flood flows can be retrieved from hydrometric stations. But the stations are often available only for areas of hundreds of square kilometers and are limited to a number of watercourses. The analysis of the flood flow rate at the crossings with bridges would be inaccurate.

But the data about floods can be used in a different way. To identify potential risks an analysis was performed [7] to demonstrate relationship between long-term observed and determined values of 1-year flow (Q1), 100-year flow (Q100) and the real extreme flood flow (Qex). There were found 67 out of 114 hydrometric stations with known Q1 and Q100 (from year 1996) and known Qex (data from [2, 5]). On 37 of them the Q100 level was exceeded.

The data from stations on Fig. 2 is sorted by Q100/Q1 from the highest to the lowest (circles; left Y axis) and corresponding value of Qex/Q100 (squares; right Y axis) ratio is shown. The X axis is used for station identification only. No relation was found. We cannot use Q100/Q1 ratio to differentiate bridges with lower exceeding from higher exceeding of Q100.

4 Stream Order

The Strahler's method [8] was used for watercourses classification. This method describes environmentally similar segments of watercourses and does not produce so many distinct orders like Shreve's ordering method [9]. Horton's [10] and Hack's [11] ordering methods were not found suitable for the analysis.

Table 1 The uncertainties of flow rates according to technical standards [6]

Category	Root mean square error for n-year flow (Q_n) (%)	
	Q_1–Q_{10}	Q_{20}–Q_{100}
I	10	15
II	20	30
III	30	40
IV	40	60

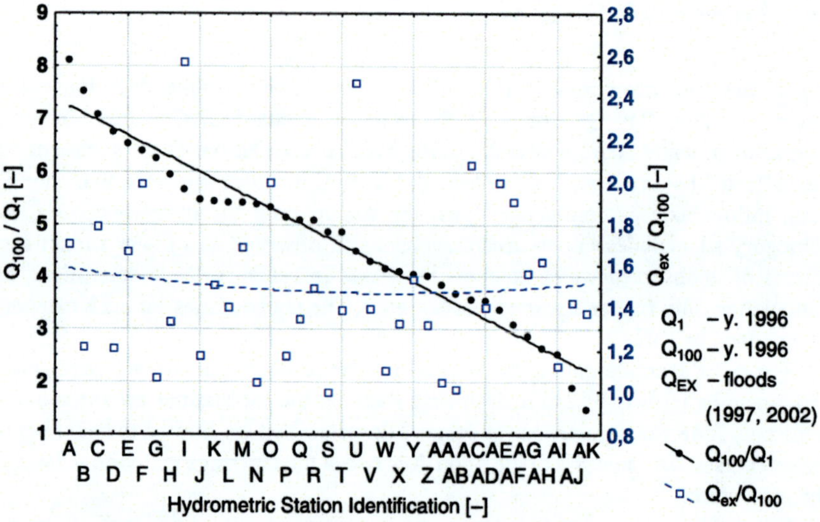

Fig. 2 Flow ratios Q_{100}/Q_1 and Q_{ex}/Q_{100} from hydrometric stations [7]

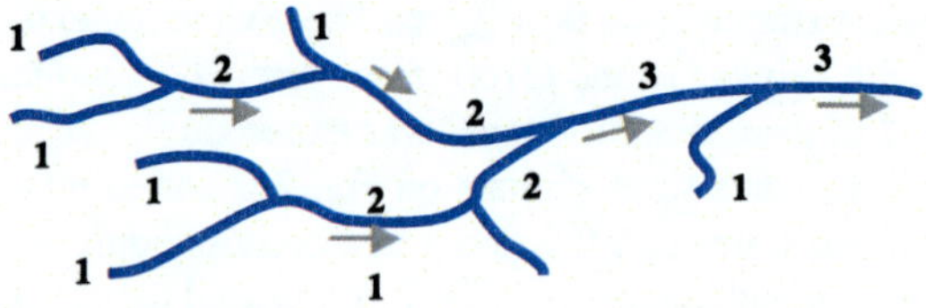

Fig. 3 Stream order, Strahler's method

The Strahler's method assesses values to the structure of natural segments of water courses in the following way (see Fig. 3):

- First segment – first order,
- In case of confluence of segments with the same order, next segment's order is higher by one,
- In case of confluence of segments with different order, next segment's order is the higher one of them.

Analysis has been carried out in two regions: Region 1 – South bohemian region with 1,207 bridges and Region 2 – Jeseniky Mountains with 917 bridges [12].

Region 1 has a representative sample of bridges in the Czech Republic according to [4]. Both mountains and lowlands with inundation areas are common here. There were 105 out of 1,207 bridges damaged or destroyed during flood in 2002. Maximum stream order in the region is 7 according to the Strahler's method.

Region 2 can be described as extreme in the Czech Republic. It is mountainous and hilly area with high slopes. During flood in 2002 there were 75 out of 917 bridges damaged or destroyed. Maximum Strahler's stream order in this region is 6.

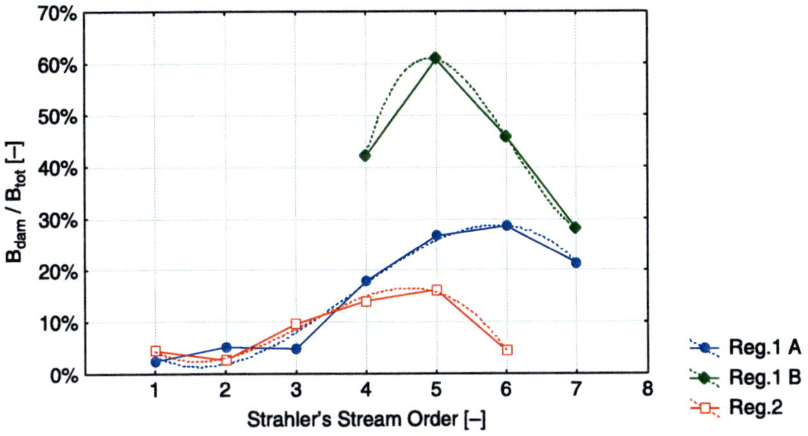

Fig. 4 Damage to bridges according to Strahler's stream order

Number of damaged bridges (Bdam) to total number of bridges (Btot) for each stream order is shown in Fig. 4. There is data about both regions (referred as Reg. 1A and Reg. 2) with addition of (Reg. 1B), which is alternation for region 1. The alternation consists in selecting only bridges, which were situated on watercourses where we are certain of exceeding the Q100 during flood. There were 73 out of 230 bridges damaged. It was not possible to determine Qex and Q100 on streams of lower orders. Hence there are only data from fourth to seventh stream order available.

The difference between Reg. 1A and 1B suggests that lower stream orders 1–3 are much less likely to experience flow rate exceeding. The damage on higher stream orders is caused by 500-year flow and higher.

5 Conclusions

Designing bridges over watercourses for the 100-year flow may be insufficient. There are high levels of uncertainty arising from position of the bridge to the hydrometric station and also from the prediction of frequency of maximum precipitation in the river-basins. When constructing bridges on important roads or on roads with high traffic intensity it is recommended that the bridge design flow should be multiplied by safety factor γQ. Value of safety factor should be set circa from 1.2 to 1.7 (that would mean approx. 200–500-year flow) depending on road importance, extra expenses for bridge failure scenario and Strahler's stream order. There is higher risk of exceeding the 100-year flow as well as higher risk of damage of the bridges on stream orders 4 and higher. In mountain areas this applies from stream order 3 and higher, in lowlands this might apply to higher stream orders.

Acknowledgement This outcome has been achieved with the financial support of the Ministry of Education, Youth and Sports of the Czech Republic, project No. 1M0579, within activities of the CIDEAS research centre. This outcome has been achieved with the financial support of the Regional authority of the Moravian-Silesian Region.

References

1. O. Brosch: Povodi Odry (Anagram, s.r.o, Czech Republic 2005)
2. Ministry of the Environment of the Czech Republic: Katastrofalni povoden v Ceske republice v srpnu 2002 (VUV T.G.M. Praha, 2003)
3. Czech standard institute: CSN 736201 Projektovani mostnich objektu, Cesky normalizacni institut (2008)
4. V. Tomica, F. Struhár: Poruchy mostů po povodních, Stavební obzor, No. 6, (2004), p. 181–185
5. Czech Hydrometeorological Institute: Hydrologicke charakteristiky vybranych vodomernych stanic Ceske republiky, CHMU (1996)
6. Czech standard institute: CSN 751400 Hydrologicke udaje povrchovych vod, Praha: Cesky normalizacni institut (1997)
7. M. Mihola, V. Tomica: Flood Damage to Bridges Analyzed within a Geographic Information System In Proceedings of the Eleventh International Conference on Civil, Structural and Environmental Engineering Computing, Civil-Comp Press. p. 197 (2007)
8. A.N. Strahler: Quantitative analysis of watershed geomorphology, Transactions of the American Geophysical Union 8 (6): p. 913–920 (1957)
9. J. Hack: Studies of longitudinal stream profiles in Virginia and Maryland, U.S. Geological Survey Professional Paper, 294-B, (1957)
10. R.E. Horton: Erosional development of streams and their drainage basins: hydro-physical approach to quantitative morphology, Geological Society of America Bulletin 56 (3): p. 275–370 (1945)
11. R. Shreve: Statistical Law of Stream Numbers, Journal of Geology, 74, (1966), p. 17–37.
12. Tomica, V. et al.: 1F55A/012/120 Odolnost a provozni bezpecnost mostnich objektu nad vodnimi toky jako soucasií pozemnich komunikaci, VSB – TU Ostrava (2005)

Part VIII
Enterprise Risk Management Modeling

Understanding Commuters' Daily Travel Time: Application of a Hazard-Based Duration Model

Zhicai Juan, Jianchuan Xianyu, and Linjie Gao

Abstract Travel behavior researchers have long been intrigued by the amount of time people allocate to travel in a day. This paper revisits this issue by introducing the hazard-based duration model to travel time analysis. In the hazard-based duration model daily travel time is analyzed through the likelihood of ending the duration depends on the length of elapsed time since start of the duration, which incorporates the impacts of covariates and enables the test of travel time dependence on the elapsed time. Using travel data from the Beijing Third Comprehensive Transport Survey, this paper sheds new light on daily travel time by analyzing the relationships between daily travel time and socio-demographic attributes and activity and travel characteristics. Furthermore the estimated results illustrate that the behavior of most commuters can be represented by travel minimization mechanism. It is demonstrated that hazard-based duration model, integrating the notion of temporal dynamics, is a suitable tool for duration data analysis in travel behavior research.

Keywords Commuter · Daily travel time · Hazard-based duration model · Travel time minimization

Z. Juan (✉)
Antai College of Economics & Management, Shanghai Jiao Tong University, 535 Fahua Zhen Rd., Shanghai, People's Republic of China
e-mail: zcjuan@sjtu.edu.cn

J. Xianyu
College of Economics and Management, Shanghai Dianji University, 88 Wenjing Rd., Shanghai, People's Republic of China
e-mail: jianchuanxy@gmail.com

L. Gao
School of Naval Architecture, Ocean and Civil Engineering, Shanghai Jiao Tong University, 800 Dongchuan Rd., Shanghai, People's Republic of China
e-mail: ljgao@sdju.edu.cn

D.D. Wu (ed.), *Modeling Risk Management in Sustainable Construction*, Computational Risk Management, DOI 10.1007/978-3-642-15243-6_44,

1 Introduction

Efficient transport policy calls for the understanding of travel choices and the precise quantifying of traveler's responses to changes of transportation environment. Traveling is the integral part of our everyday lives. And the amount of time available for the participation of an activity is largely dependent on the amount of time needed to reach the destination. So travel is one of many attributes of an activity and competes for the scarce resource of time. The increasing concern in several municipal cities about the level of traffic congestion in China, combined with the conceptual deficiencies of the trip-based approach has led to the rapid development of activity-based approach in travel behavior analysis. The activity-based approach views travel as a demand derived from the need to pursue activities over space.

Travel behavior researchers have devoted a considerable effort to conceptualize and understand the amount of time that people allocate to travel in a day, i.e., the daily travel time expenditure. And in this paper we revisit the issue of the daily travel time (DTT) by introducing the concept of conditional probability of termination of travel duration. The focus of this paper is to analyze the DTT of Chinese commuters using the hazard-based duration model with the guidance of activity-based approach. It supports a discussion of the relationships between DTT and covariates relative to socio-demographic and activity attributes. Furthermore, it permits the analysis of the link between DTT and activities duration and the test of the travel minimization behavior mechanism.

The remainder of this paper is organized as follows. The next section provides a brief review of related literature. Then the data set are described, followed by the modeling methodology, model estimation, and results explanation. Finally, conclusions are drawn and directions for further research are discussed in the last section.

2 Literature Review

Zahavi [1] was one of the first who raised the concept of a stable travel time budget. And a few studies [2, 3] have been carried out to examine the regularities of travel time cost. These studies generally supported the notion of a spatially and temporally stable DTT.

Despite the early evidence, many researchers have observed that the daily travel time cost is not constant. Kumar and Levison [4] investigated the allocation of time and trip-making across time-of-day, day-of-week. They found time spent in travel on each weekend day exceeded that on any weekdays. Mokhtarian and Solomon [5, 6] have further explored issues of travel time budgets and show that travel time expenditure can be related to personal and household characteristics, activity duration, and residential location. And more recently, researchers do suggest that daily travel budgets are indeed changing over time and space [7, 8].

With regard to the analysis of time as a continuous variable, four econometrics techniques can be distinguished: the single linear equation approach, structural equations model, linear and multinomial models, and duration analysis model. Early researches on travel time expenditures were generally limited to the one-dimensional linear model [9, 10]. Subsequently, Golob [11] used a dynamic structural equations model in an examination of car ownership and travel time expenditures by different travel modes. Recently duration models are introduced to travel behavior analysis. But most of the applications are concerned with the activity durations, excluding travel [12–14].

Hazard-based duration models represent a class of analytical methods which are appropriate for modeling data that have as their focus and end-of-duration occurrence, given that the duration has lasted to some specified time [15]. This concept of conditional probability of termination of duration recognizes the dynamics of duration. It recognizes that the likelihood of ending the duration depends on the length of elapsed time since start of the duration [16]. Therefore this technique is suitable to deal with duration data that are non-negative and can be censored and time-varying.

In this paper a duration model is applied to analyze commuters' daily travel time (DTT). It permits to examine how DTT is dependent on individual and household socio-demographics, and individual travel and activity characteristics. Furthermore, the hypotheses of the stability and the minimization of travel time are also tested.

3 Modeling Methodology

Let T be a non-negative random variable representing the daily travel duration time of an individual. The hazard at time t on the continuous time-scale, $h(t)$, is defined as the instantaneous probability that the travel duration under study will end in an infinitesimal time period Δt after time t, given that the duration has not elapsed until time t. A mathematical definition for the hazard function is as follows:

$$h(t) = \lim_{\Delta t \to 0^+} \frac{P(t \leq T < t + \Delta t | T > t)}{\Delta t} \tag{1}$$

Let $f(\cdot)$ and $F(\cdot)$ be the density and cumulative distribution function for T respectively. Then the probability of ending in an infinitesimal interval of range Δt, after time t is $f(t) \cdot \Delta t$. And the probability that the process lasts at least t is given by the survival function,

$$S(t) = P(T > t) = 1 - F(t) \tag{2}$$

And so the hazard function can be further expresses as:

$$h(t) = \frac{f(t)}{S(t)} = \frac{dF(t)/dt}{S(t)} = \frac{-dS(t)/dt}{S(t)} = \frac{-d\ln S(t)}{dt} \tag{3}$$

The hazard function and the survival function describe the duration process. And the shape of the hazard function has important implications for duration dynamics. One may adopt a parametric shape, a semi-parametric shape, or a non-parametric shape.

Since the distribution of daily travel time is unknown, the non-parametric method Kaplan–Meier product limit estimator is used to explore the covariates effects and the potential distribution to be used in the parametric approach first. And then accelerated failure time (AFT) model is developed to examine the linkages between travel time and covariates relative to individual and household, and attributes of activities and travel.

KM Estimator: The KM estimator produces an empirical approximation of survival and hazard, but hardly models any covariate effects. It is similar to an exploratory data analysis. Denote the distinct failure times of n individuals as $t_1 < t_2 < \ldots < t_n$ then the KM estimator of survival at time at time t_j is computed as the product of the conditional survival proportions:

$$S_{KM}(t_j) = \prod_{k=1}^{j} \frac{r(t_k) - d(t_k)}{r(t_k)} \tag{4}$$

where $r(t_k)$ is the total population at risk for ending at time t_k, $d(t_k)$ is the number of individuals stopping at t_k.

AFT Model: AFT model belongs to the parametric approach. It permits the covariates to affect the duration dependence. The survival function is given as:

$$S(t) = S_0[t\exp(-\boldsymbol{\beta}'\mathbf{X})] \tag{5}$$

where $S_0(\cdot)$is the baseline survival function. And the corresponding hazard function is:

$$h(t) = \frac{-\partial S(t)/\partial t}{S(t)} = h_0[t\exp(-\boldsymbol{\beta}'\mathbf{X})]\exp(-\boldsymbol{\beta}'\mathbf{X}) \tag{6}$$

The AFT model can be expressed as a log-linear model:

$$\ln t = \boldsymbol{\beta}'\mathbf{X} + \boldsymbol{\varepsilon} \tag{7}$$

4 Data Description

The data set used to estimate the daily travel time duration model is derived from the household travel survey of Beijing Third Comprehensive Transport Survey conducted in 2005. Detailed individual and household demographic characteristics and activity and trip information for a 24-h period are provided. A subsample of families surveyed on Tuesday to Thursday is first obtained. Then after sampling, data checking and cleaning the final data used for analysis and model estimation consist of 4,822 commuters. The summary statistics of the sample is presented in Table 1.

5 Model Estimation Results

The KM estimator is first used for exploration of the covariate effects and potential distribution function. The survival function and smoothed hazard curve are provided in Figs. 1 and 2 respectively. The hazard curve increases with travel time, which suggests that an AFT model with Weibull distribution will be appropriate.

Table 1 Statistics of commuters' daily travel time (min)

Sample Size	4,822	Mode	40	Quantile 75%	126
Mean	94.11	Quantile	50	Interquartile Range	76
Std. error	58.41	Median	83	Range	337

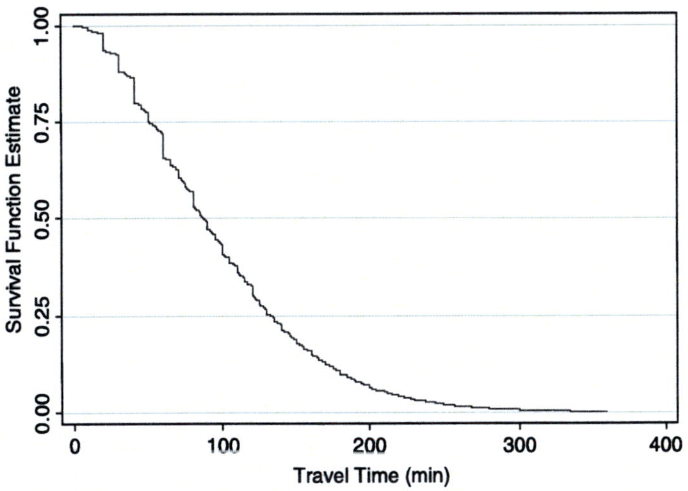

Fig. 1 Survival curve of daily travel time

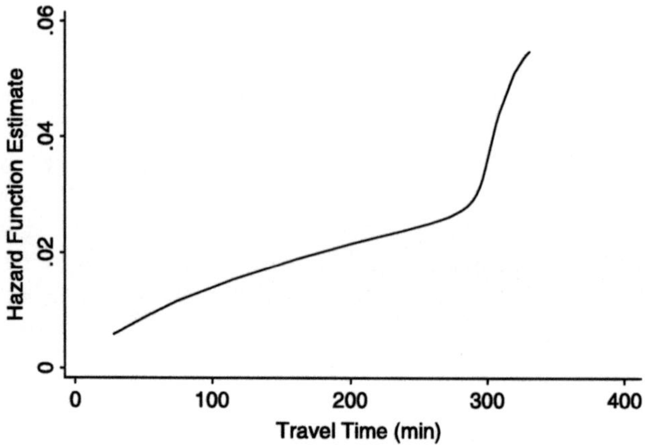

Fig. 2 Smoothed hazard curve

Table 2 ATF model estimates

Variable	Coefficient	t-Statistic
Constant	3.24	12.59
Male	0.05	4.54
Young (age: <=30)	0.02	6.22
Licensed driver	0.02	8.32
Wgzcn (one or more unemployed adults in the household)	0.02	3.61
Residence (resides within the fourth ring road)	−0.04	−4.02
Middle income (household monthly income: 2,501–5,500RMB)	0.014	5.83
High income (household monthly income: >5,500RMB)	0.022	1.94
Commute distance (in km)	0.050	46.61
Bike (No. of household bikes)	0.033	3.74
Ebike (No. of household e-bikes)	0.052	5.29
Transit user	0.38	4.91
Car user	0.25	5.62
Work duration (in min)	−0.00038	−8.10
Nact (No. of daily activities participated)	0.21	11.81
Live (No. of daily maintenance activities participated)	0.00068	3.28
p	2.79	12.97
N 4,822		
$LL(\beta)$ −2273.76		

The AFT model as shown in (7) is applied to the sample data. Based on the results of KM approach, Weibull distribution function is selected. Parameter estimates are calculated using Stata 10.0 and presented in Table 2.

All of the covariates are significant at the 95% confidence or more and have the expected signs. In AFT model exponential of the estimates can be interpreted as expected time ratio. As illustrated the DTT of men is about 4% higher than that of women. Young commuters have high DTT. And the presence of unemployed adults increases the DTT. The commuters of high household income are characterized by high DTT. The residential location also affects the DTT. Commuters who live within the fourth ring, namely around the city central, have low DTT. The principal modes of commute travel are highly influent. They are indicators of accessible travel speeds. Activity participation related variables also improved the likelihood of the model. Number of daily activities especially maintenance activities has a positive effect on DTT. And work duration affect DTT negatively. Finally the estimated scale parameter p is above unity, which means the hazard rate increases with travel time increase. And this confirms that most commuters can be represented by the travel time minimization mechanism.

6 Conclusions and Discussion

In this paper a survival analysis is presented to study the daily travel time of commuters using the non-parametric estimator and the parametric approach. Covariates relative to individual and household socio-demographics and activity and commute travel attributes are found significant. These influent variables show relative instability of individual DTT. And the model results also support the travel time minimization hypothesis for most commuters. To gain more meaningful results several directions for future research can be identified. First, it is better to bring more variables relative to residence and work locations to improve the explanatory capability of the model. The current research fails to consider the interaction between travel times and activity need. And future research should take the competition between travel and different activities for time resource into consideration.

Acknowledgments This research is supported by National Natural Science Foundation of China (50878129). The contents of the paper reflect the views of the authors who are responsible for the facts and accuracy of the information presented herein. The contents do not necessarily reflect the official views of the Antai College of Economics & Management, Shanghai Jiao Tong University.

References

1. Y. Zahavi, and A. Talvitie: The stability of travel components over time. Transportation Research Record Issue 750 (1980), p. 19–26
2. A. Schafer, and D.G. Victor: The future mobility of the world population. Transportation Research Part A, Vol. 34, Issue 3 (2000), p. 171–205
3. T. Schwanen, and M. Dijst: Travel-time ratios for visits to the workplace: the relationship between commuting time and work duration Transportation Research Part A, Vol. 36, Issue 7 (2002), p. 573–592
4. A. Kumar, and D. Levinson: Temporal variations on the allocation of time. Transportation Research Record, Issue 1493 (1995), p. 118–127

5. P.L. Mokhtarian, and C. Chen: TTB or not TTB, that is the question: a review and analysis of the empirical literature on travel time (and money) budgets. Transportation Research Part A, Vol. 38, Issue 9–10 (2004), p. 643–675
6. P.L. Mokhtarian, and I. Salomon: How derived is the demand for travel? Some conceptual and measurement considerations. Transportation Research Part A, Vol. 35, Issue 1 (2001), p. 695–719
7. A. Banerjee, Y. Xin, and R.M. Pendyala: Understanding travel time expenditures around the world: exploring the notion of a travel time frontier. Transportation, Vol.34, Issue 1 (2007), p. 51–65
8. L. Toole-Holt, S.E. Polzin, and R.M. Pendyala: Two minutes per person per day each year: an exploration of the growth in travel time expenditures. Transportation Research Record, Issue 1917 (2005), p. 213–219
9. A. Chumak, and J.P. Braaksma: Implications of travel-time budget for urban transportation: modeling in Canada. Transportation Research Record, Issue 794 (1981), p. 19–27
10. J.N. Landrock: Spatial stability of average daily travel times and trip rates within Great Britain. Transportation Research Part A, Vol. 15, Issue 1 (1981), p. 55–62
11. T.F. Golob: The dynamics of household travel time expenditures and car ownership decisions. Transportation Research Part A, Vol. 24, Issue 6 (1990), p. 443–463
12. V. Peter, and B. Mark: A hybrid discrete choice departure time and duration model for scheduling travel tours. Transportation Research Record, Issue 1894 (2004), p. 46–56
13. C.R. Bhat, S. Srinivasan, and K.W: Axhausen. An analysis of multiple interepisode durations using a unifying multivariate hazard model. Transportation Research Part B, Vol. 39, Issue 9 (2005), p. 797–823
14. B. Lee, and H.J.P. Timmermans: A latent class accelerated hazard model of activity episode durations. Transportation Research Part B, Vol. 41, Issue 4 (2007), p. 426–447
15. D.A. Hensher, and F.L. Mannering: Hazard-based duration models and their application to transport analysis. Transport Reviews, Vol. 14, Issue 1 (1994), p. 63–82
16. C.R. Bhat, and A.R. Pinjari, *Duration modeling*, in Handbook of transport modeling, edited by D.A. Hensher and K.J. Button, Editors. Elsevier Science (2008)

Influence of Perceived Risk and Service Recovery on On-Line Shopping: A Dynamic Game of Incomplete Information

Yong Fang and Fengming Tao

Abstract Customers' perceived risk is an important content in risk research field. Recently, perceived risk is being widely used in decision making and customers' behavior explanation, and deserves a special recognition by scholars. Service failures are unavoidable for on-line shops because of their particularities. Certain deals being applied to win the customers satisfactory when service failures happen can benefit on-line shops to be competitive. With a two-stage dynamic game of incomplete information between on-line shops and customers, this paper discussed the relationship among the customers' perceived risk, on-line shops optimal strategies and customers' purchase behaviors.

Keywords Dynamic game of incomplete information · e-Commerce · Perceived risk · Service recovery

1 Introduction

The original concept of perceived risk derived from psychology by Bauer (1960). Afterwards, lots of scholars defined perceived risk from various points of view (Cox 1967; Cunningham 1967; Peter and Ryan 1976; Derbaix 1983; Murray 1991; Stone and Gronhaug 1993; Featherman and Savlou 2003). With the diversity of traditional definitions, there is no standard concept of perceived risk of on-line shopping. Some scholars have studied the influence of perceived risk on on-line shopping behaviors

---

Y. Fang (✉)
School of Management, Chongqing Jiaotong University, No. 66 Xuefu Road, Nanan District, Chongqing Municipality, People's Republic of China
e-mail: fangyongcqu@sohu.com

F. Tao
College of Mechanical Engineering, Chongqing University, No. 174 Shazheng Street, Shapingba District, Chongqing Municipality, People's Republic of China
e-mail: taofengming@cqu.edu.cn

D.D. Wu (ed.), *Modeling Risk Management in Sustainable Construction*, Computational Risk Management, DOI 10.1007/978-3-642-15243-6_45,

since the study of Jarvenpaa and Todd (1997). Identified perceived risk as the lack of safety and privacy; Salam et al. (1998) identified it as the subjective anticipation of on-line financial loss, base on the research of Peter and Ryna; identified it as the credibility or reliability of on-line seller; Sandra and Shi (2003) identified it as the subjective anticipation of loss of the current on-line purchasing.

If consumers apperceived certain risks in purchasing, they would be anxious to find out a way to reduce the risk. Increasing the certainty of consequence, such as buying famous brands, or decreasing the losses of consequences, such as after-sale service can reduce perceived risk (Hoover et al. 1978; Mitchell and Mc Goldrick 1996). Consumers will make decisions to purchase only when the perceived risks are as low as acceptable or totally disappear. Service recovery is one important guarantee to decrease the losses of consequences.

Service recovery is a management behavior of firms and an important topic of marketing. The 1970s witnessed the transformation from product consumption to service consumption. When the services could not satisfy consumers' expectation, firms could do nothing but apologize or compensate. 'Compensation' was substituted by 'recovery' by Etzel and Silverman (1981) in the analysis of customer maintainability, which was recognized broadly. In the middle of 1980s, Gronroos (1988) identified service recovery as the responses and reactions by service providers after service failures happened, and the other name of service recovery was 'deals for customers' complaints'.

Because of their particularities, service failures are unavoidable for on-line shops. Service failures and bad service recoveries may become the impediment to the growth of on-line market. Certain deals being applied to win the customer loyalty when service failures happen can benefit not only on-line shops but also the widening and deepening of on-line market. In this paper, a dynamic game of incomplete information was built up to explain how the perceived risk (including customers' judgment for service quality and type of on-line shop, possibility of on-line shop when service failure happened, and the expected economic loss or dissatisfaction result from service failure) and service recovery of on-line shops can influence their customers' purchasing behaviors.

2 Hypothesis and Model

Hypotheses 1: there are two types of on-line shops: θ_h with high service quality and θ_l with low service quality. The shops know their type θ, but customers only know that the probability of the two types, namely $\theta = \theta_h$ and $\theta = \theta_l$, are respectively μ and $1 - \mu$.

Hypotheses 2: The two types of on-line shops provide the same products, but with different service. Certain failures might appear in the process of service. The probability for θ_h having failures is p_h, and for θ_l is p_l; and $p_h < p_l$, that is, it is less possible for shops with high quality service to have failures than shops with low quality service. When failures appear, the disutility of failures is w_h for θ_h, and w_l

for θ_h; and $w_h < w_l$, that is, the severity of failures is greater for shops with low quality service than shops with high quality service.

Hypotheses 3: When failures happened, shops chose service recovery or not, that is $SR \in \{0, 1\}$. $SR = 1$ means service recovery was chosen, and $SR = 0$ means service recovery was not chosen. And the costs for θ_h and θ_l to take remedial action are respectively c_h and c_l. For the sake of simplicity, we assume that there is no utility loss in transmission process of service recovery, that is, shops directly pay customers money compensations as c_h or c_l. At the same time, for the consideration of credibility of long term game, we assume that two types are consistent in their choice of recovery or not. In real life, service recoveries frequently are kind of regulations, so it's time stability is reasonable.

Hypotheses 4: If deals are repeated, customers will decide whether or not purchase in the shops according to failures or not in last deals and the sellers responses when failures happened. We assume that, if there is no failure in the last deal, customers will still purchase in the shops; if there are failures in the last deal and sellers do nothing about service recoveries, customers will not purchase in the shops; if there are failures in the last deal and sellers do service recoveries, customers will or will not purchase in the shops.

Hypotheses 5: for sake of revealing real life and the differences between two types of on-line shops, we assume $u - b - w_h + c_h > 0$, $u - b - w_l + c_l < 0$, $u - b - w_h < 0$, $u - b - w_l < 0$. And the economic explanation is that: when failures appear, compensation from θ_h can guarantee customer to profit from purchases, but compensation from θ_l cannot. The latter two equations mean that if neither of the two types provides service recoveries, customers will not purchase next time.

In order to simplify calculation, we assume that the sum of purchase every time is b, and discount factor $\delta = 1$. At stage $t = 1$, customer encountered failures in on-line shopping at the first time (customers may shop on line first or not, but they never met service failure before, so they do not fix their prior probabilities of the two types). Then, customers complaint, shops may do service recoveries or do nothing.

If shops do service recoveries, the payoff for $\theta_i, i \in \{h, l\}$ at $t = 1$ is $\pi_{i,1} = b - c_i$, and customers' payoff is $R_{i,1} = u - b - w_i - c_i$. At stage $t = 2$, for θ_h, if customers purchase next time (customers loss w_h may happen at the probability of p_h, and shops will always do service recoveries), the expected payoff for θ_h is $\pi_{h,2} = p_h(b - c_h) + (1 - p_h)b = b - p_h c_h$.

And the expected payoff for customer is:

$$R_{h,2} = p_h(u - b - w_h + c_h) + (1 - p_h)(u - b) = u - b - p_h(w_h - c_h).$$

In the same way, for θ_l, if customers purchase next time, the expected payoff for θ_l is $\pi_{l,2} = p_l(b - c_l) + (1 - p_l)b = b - p_l c_l$.

And expected payoff for customer is

$$R_{l,2} = p_l(u - b - w_l + c_l) + (1 - p_l)(u - b) = u - b - p_l(w_l - c_l).$$

If shops do not do service recoveries, the payoff for two types at $t = 1$ are b, and customers' payoff is $u - b - w_i$. And at $t = 2$ payoff for shops and customers are 0 because customers do not purchase.

The extensive form of game is as follows.

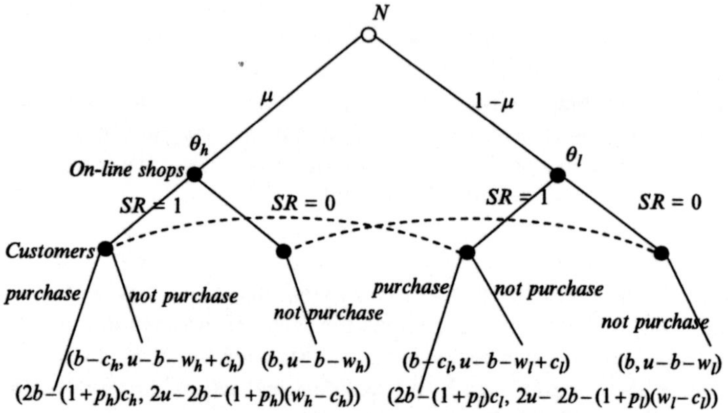

There are four possible equilibriums in the model, namely,

$$\begin{cases} \theta_h \to SR = 1, \theta_l \to SR = 1 \\ \theta_h \to SR = 1, \theta_l \to SR = 0 \\ \theta_h \to SR = 0, \theta_l \to SR = 1 \\ \theta_h \to SR = 0, \theta_l \to SR = 0 \end{cases}$$

We analyzed the possibilities and conditions of the four possible equilibriums as above, and got the four equilibriums as follows.

If

$$\begin{cases} u - b \geq \mu p_h(w_h - c_h) + (1 - \mu)p_l(w_l - c_l) \\ c_h \leq b/(1 + p_h) \\ c_l \leq b/(1 + p_l) \end{cases} \tag{1}$$

is satisfied, there is a pooling equilibrium: $\theta_h \to SR = 1$, $\theta_l \to SR = 1$, $\tilde{p}(\theta_h|SR = 1) = \mu, \tilde{p}(\theta_h|SR = 0) \in [0, 1]$; and customers will purchase at next time.

If

$$(1 + p_h)c_h \leq b \leq (1 + p_l)c_l \tag{2}$$

is satisfied, there is a separating equilibrium: $\theta_h \to SR = 1$, $\theta_l \to SR = 0$, $\tilde{p}(\theta_h|SR = 1) = 1$, $\tilde{p}(\theta_l|SR = 0) = 0$; and customers will purchase next time, if and only if they observe service recoveries provided by on-line shops.

If

$$\begin{cases} c_h \geqslant b/(1 + p_h) \\ c_l \geqslant b/(1 + p_l) \end{cases} \tag{3}$$

is satisfied, there is a pooling equilibrium: $\theta_h \to SR = 0$, $\theta_l \to SR = 0$, $\tilde{p}(\theta_h|SR = 1) \in [0, 1]$, $\tilde{p}(\theta_h|SR = 0) = \mu$; and customers will not purchase next time.

If

$$c_h < b/(1 + p_h) \tag{4}$$

is satisfied, there is a pooling equilibrium: $\theta_h \to SR = 0$, $\theta_l \to SR = 0$, $\tilde{p}(\theta_h|SR = 1) < \frac{p_l(w_l - c_l) - u + b}{p_l(w_l - c_l) - p_h(w_h - c_h)}$, $\tilde{p}(\theta_h|SR = 0) = \mu$; and customers will purchase next time, if and only if they observe $SR = 1$.

3 Economic Explanations of Equilibriums and Discussions

3.1 Pooling Equilibrium $\theta_h \to SR = 1$, $\theta_l \to SR = 1$

In this equilibrium, both shops choose to do service recoveries and customers choose to purchase next time. The realizable condition $c_h \le b/(1 + p_h)$, $c_l \le b/(1 + p_l)$ and $p_h > 0$, $p_l > 0$, tell us that both shops compensations are less than customers real payments. And because of $p_h < p_l$, the upper limit of service recoveries of θ_h is high than that of θ_l, and the more probabilities of failures, the lower is the upper limit. From this result, we can judge the service quality of shops according to their upper limit of compensation.

Because of $p_h < p_l$, $w_h - c_h < w_l - c_l$ and $\mu \in [0, 1]$,

$$u - b \ge \mu p_h(w_h - c_h) + (1 - \mu)p_l(w_l - c_l) \Rightarrow \mu \ge \frac{p_l(w_l - c_l) - u + b}{p_l(w_l - c_l) - p_h(w_h - c_h)}$$

If $u - b - p_l(w_l - c_l) \ge 0$, this condition changes into $\mu \ge 0$, and it is necessarily satisfied. This means that if customers' expected payoff at single period in θ_l which are willing to provide service recoveries is greater than zero, this pooling equilibrium has no requirement for the prior probability μ. Otherwise, the prior belief μ should not be too low if this pooling equilibrium is hoped to appear. In fact, parameters μ, p_h, w_h, p_l and w_l embody customers judgments of on-line shopping risks. This condition tells us that, while other conditions unchanged, the improvement of service quality of θ_h will reduce p_h and w_h, and then the requirement of the prior belief will be looser, this means that even if the possibility for customers to meet θ_h is not high, it does not matter. In the same way, the improvement of service quality of θ_l will reduce p_h and w_h, and then the requirement of the prior probability will be looser, too. In one word, improvement of service quality is good to stimulate customers to have on-line shopping for both types of shops. And this result is consistent with our intuitive perceptions.

The economic explanation of this equilibrium is that, only if customers perceive that there exist a high proportion of shops with high service quality in on-line shopping, they will purchase on-line. Shops know that failures and no deal to compensate failures will result in customers' discontent and customer forfeit, therefore, in view of maximization of long term profit, both types will do service recoveries when service failures happened. However, the sum of compensation should not surplus customers' real payment. And customers will repeat their purchases.

3.2 Separating Equilibrium $\theta_h \to SR = 1, \theta_l \to SR = 0$

Because of $(1+p_h)c_h \le b \le (1+p_l)c_l \Rightarrow \begin{cases} c_h \le b/(1+p_h) \\ c_l \ge b/(1+p_l) \end{cases}$ and $\theta_l \to SR = 0$, we get that $c_l = 0$, but it is contradictory with $c_l \ge b/(1+p_l)$. Therefore, this separating equilibrium impossibly exists. This means, customers can not distinguish the types of on-line shops simply by whether or not they have failure recoveries.

3.3 Pooling Equilibrium $\theta_h \to SR = 0, \theta_l \to SR = 0$

Just like the separating equilibrium $\theta_h \to SR = 1$, $\theta_l \to SR = 0$, the condition of equilibrium 3 $\begin{cases} c_h \ge b/(1+p_h) \\ c_l \ge b/(1+p_l) \end{cases}$ is contradictory with $c_h = c_l = 0$, therefore, this pooling equilibrium impossibly exists.

In equilibrium 4, because of $c_h = c_l = 0$, the existence condition is necessarily satisfied. This equilibrium results from the strict posterior probability that customers subjectively judge the shops are θ_h when service recoveries appear. If $u - b - p_l(w_l - c_l) \ge 0$, this equilibrium could not exist. This means that this pooling equilibrium impossibly exists if the customers' expected payoff in θ_l which are willing to provide service recoveries at single period is greater than 0, this pooling equilibrium impossibly exists. Otherwise, the posterior belief should not be high if this pooling equilibrium appears. This condition tells us that, while other conditions unchanged, the improvement of service quality of θ_h will reduce p_h and w_h, and then the requirement of the posterior belief will be stricter. In the same way, the improvement of service quality of θ_l will reduce p_h and w_h, and then the requirement of the posterior probability will be stricter, too. Therefore, from another side, we could find that improvement of service quality is good to stimulate customers to have on-line shopping for both types of shops.

Equilibrium 4 embodies that when customers are pessimistic toward on-line shopping, (namely, customers regard that most of on-line shops are with low service quality, they could not believe the on-line shops are with high service quality even service recoveries appear), neither of the two types will do service recoveries, customers will not repeat purchase, either.

4 Conclusions

1. Analyses above tell us, the two-stage game only has two pooling equilibriums: one is that both types choose to provide service recoveries, and this equilibrium requires prior probability; and the other is that neither chooses to do have service recoveries, and this equilibrium requires posterior belief. Both of which reveal the influence of customers' perceived risk in on-line shopping. Customers cannot distinguish the types of on-line shops simply by whether or not they have failure recoveries, since the separating equilibriums do not exist (namely, in view of maximization of long term profit, both types have service recoveries).
2. Both of the two pooling equilibriums suggest that improvement of service quality is positive to stimulate customers to have on-line shopping for both types of shops.
3. When service failures happen, neither of the two types will provide the compensation more than customers' real payment.
4. When both types of shops have service recoveries, the shops with high service quality provide a higher upper limit of service compensation than the shops with low service quality. And the more probabilities of failures, the lower are the upper limit.

References

Bauer, R.A. (1960). *Consumer behavior as risk raking*. Dynamic marketing for a Changing World, Proceedings of the 43rd Conference of the American Marketing Association.

Cox, D.F. (1967). *Risk taking and information handling in consumer behavior*. Boston: Graduate School of Business Administration, Harvard University Press.

Cunningham, S.M. (1967). The major dimensions of perceived risk. *Consumer Behavior*, 82–101.

Derbaix, C. (1983). Perceived risk and risk relievers: An empirical investigation. *Journal of Economic Psychology*, (3), 19–38.

Etzel, M.J., Silverman, B.I., (1981). A managerial perspective on directions for retail customer satisfaction research, *Journal of Retailing*, 57(3), 124–136.

Featherman, M., Savlou, P.A. (2003). Predicting e-services adoption: a perceived risk facets perspective. *International Journal of Human-Computer Studies*. 59, 451–474.

Gronroos, C. (1988). Service quality: The six criteria of good perceived service quality. *Review of Business*, 9(3), 10–13.

Hoover, R.J., Green, R.T., Saegert, J. (1978). A cross-national study of perceived risk. *Journal of Marketing*, 42(3).

Jarvenpaa, S.L., Todd, P.A. (1997). Consumer reactions to electronic Shopping on the Worldwide Web, *International Journal of Electronic Commerce*, (2), 59–88.

Mitchell, V.W., Mc Goldrick, P.J. (1996). Consumers-risk reduction strategies: A review and synthesis. *The International Review of Retail, Distribution and Consumer Research*, 6(1), 1–33.

Murray, K.B. (1991). A test of services marketing theory: consumer information acquisition activities. *Journal of Marketing*, 55(1), 10–25

Peter, J.D., Ryan, M.J. (1976). An investigation of perceived risk on brand level. *Journal of Marketing Research*, 13(2), 184–188.

Salam, A.F., Rao, H.R., Pegels, C.C. (1998). *Consumer-perceived risk in e-commerce transactions: the role of institutional trust and economic incentive in a social exchange framework*, Proceedings of the 4th Americas Conference on Information Systems.

Sandra, M.F., Shi, B. (2003). Consumer patronage and risk perceptions in internet shopping. *Journal of Business Research*, 56(11), 67–875

Stone, R.N., Gronhaug, K. (1993). Perceived Risk: Further Considerations for the Marketing Discipline. *European Journal of Marketing*, (3), 39–50.

Traffic Risk Assessment of Freeway On-Ramp and Off-Ramp Areas Based on Simulation Analysis

Ying Yan, Yan-ting Sheng, and Yu-hui Zhang

Abstract In order to improve safety of freeway on-ramp and off-ramp areas, the operating characteristics of traffic flows and accident cause on freeway on-ramp and off-ramp areas were analyzed. The risk level was changed from two-dimension vector to one-dimension variable based on the critical deceleration and unsafe degree. The deceleration risk and unsafe density parameter as traffic risk assessment index were put forward, and then the traffic risk quantitative assessment models were established. According to the safety risk management theory, the risk classification description and assessment were built up. Applying the microscopic traffic simulation technique, the suggested values of the traffic control standard of on-ramp and off-ramp areas were also proposed. At last, a case study was illustrated for the risk analysis through simulating the traffic flows. The results suggested that the traffic risk assessment index and the assessment method are accurate and effective. Furthermore, it can lay a theoretical foundation for the establishment of the dynamical traffic control and management measures.

Keywords Microscopic simulation · On-ramp and off-ramp areas · Speed control · Traffic risk assessment · Unsafe density parameter

Y. Yan (✉)
Traffic safety Laboratory, Automobile Institute, Chang'an University, Xi'an, People's Republic of China
e-mail: yanying2199@sohu.com

Y.-t. Sheng
China Airport Construction Group Corporation of CAAC Northwest Branch, Xi'an, People's Republic of China
e-mail: syt19831013@163.com

Y.-h. Zhang
Liaoning Communication Survey and Design Institute, Shenyang, People's Republic of China
e-mail: lu20009693@126.com

D.D. Wu (ed.), *Modeling Risk Management in Sustainable Construction*, Computational Risk Management, DOI 10.1007/978-3-642-15243-6_46,

1 Introduction

The freeway on-ramp and off-ramp areas are the special sections of the traffic flow diverging and converging. The vehicle acceleration and deceleration, lane changing and other complex traffic behavior likely to cause the drivers' wrong judgment and operation, then lead to traffic chaos, thus the probability of accident increases greatly. Generally, the accident rates per km of on-ramp and off-ramp areas is 4–5 times than the basic section [1]. They are the accident black spots where the traffic safety is very serious. However, the research of the on-ramp and off-ramp areas at home and abroad [2, 3] mainly concentrate on traffic capacity, service levels, the variable-speed lane, rare road safety. Therefore, according to the traffic characteristics, it is very necessary to analyze the road safety by the driving risk micro-analysis of these areas.

This paper analyzes the factors of greater influence on driving risk or combination factors. By means of changing the risk degree from two-dimensional vector into a one-dimensional variable, the driving risk assessment quantitative index and models are proposed, and then determine the appropriate risk classification. Using simulation technology to simulate the microscopic traffic flow, the paper calculates the risk of different traffic conditions in order to provide the basis for dynamic traffic control management.

2 Concept of Driving Risk

In the traditional safety evaluation, the accident risk is represented with the number of casualties and the predictable factors associated with accidents which belong to ex-post evaluation. The collection of raw data is extremely difficult and requires long time, while the correspondence is also uncertain.

Therefore, the paper proposes the concept of traffic risk which is defined as the probability and severity of accidents in the specific traffic conditions at a certain period of time on a section. The greater the likelihood of accidents, the higher severity, the greater risk, otherwise the risk is smaller. This factor can reflect the likelihood of an accident which was caused by drivers, vehicles, traffic conditions, thus to quantify the driving risk of this particular section of freeway.

3 Driving Risk Assessment Index and Risk Classification

The safety status description of on-ramp and off-ramp traffic flows is stable, smooth, small frequency and amplitude fluctuations. The driver can accelerate and decelerate calmly to driving expectations. Through the analysis of accident patterns and causes, it found that the risk was mainly due to changing lanes or sudden acceleration and deceleration. Considering the likelihood and the severity of the accident, the braking deceleration risk and unsafe density parameter as the safety micro-assessment index for the on-ramp and off-ramp of freeway were put forward.

4 Braking Deceleration Risk

The model assumed: the front car n brakes when meet an emergency, the rear car must brake to avoid rear-end collision, at last two cars need to maintain a certain safety distance, that is, the front vehicle braking distance $X_n(t+\Delta t)$ should be greater than or equal the distance of the braking distance $X_{n+1}(t+T)$ with safety distance L, namely:

$$X_n(t+\Delta t) - L \geq X_{n+1}(t+T) \tag{1}$$

$$V_2^2/2a_{n+1} - V_2 \cdot (\tau + \theta) - V_1^2/2a_n + S(t) - L \geq 0 \tag{2}$$

τ is driver's normal reaction time, θ can be considered as the response lag time. $\tau + \theta$ as the reaction time is the partial security. Gipps proved if premised $\theta = \tau/2$ and did not underestimate the braking strength, the vehicle would operate with a safe speed and distance, so chose $\theta = \tau/2$. From the above formula, it can get that:

$$a_n = \frac{V_n^2}{3\tau \cdot V_n + V_{n-1}^2/a_{n-1} - 2 \cdot (S(t) - L)} \tag{3}$$

a_n – the safety braking deceleration of vehicle n; V_{n-1} – the instant speed of vehicle $n-1$; V_n – the instant speed of vehicle n; L – the safe distance of front and rear car when braking, take 3 m; τ – the reaction time, take 1 s; S – the instant distance between front and rear car; a_{n-1} – the instant braking deceleration of vehicle $n-1$.

5 Unsafe Density Parameter UD

Swedish scholar proposed a safety evaluation index – Unsafe parameter U with the combination of microscopic traffic simulation and its calculation formula is as follows [4]:

$$U = v \cdot \Delta v \cdot a_d \tag{4}$$

U – unsafe parameter (m^2/s^2); v – crash speed of the following car (m/s); v – crash speed difference between the front and rear car (m/s); $a_d = a/a_{\max}$ – ratio of the deceleration and its maximum;

The crash that may occur can be divided into four cases:

1. The rear car (n + 1) driving as original, the front (n) braking but not stopping

$$V_{n+1}t + \frac{1}{2}a_{n+1}t^2 = V_n t + \frac{1}{2}a_{n,\max}t^2 + d\,,\ \mathrm{t} < \mathrm{t_0} \tag{5}$$

$$U = v \cdot \Delta v \cdot \frac{a_n}{a_{n,\max}} = v \cdot (v - v') \cdot \frac{a_n}{a_{n,\max}} \tag{6}$$

2. The rear car (n + 1) driving as original, the front (n) stopping

$$V_{n+1}t + \frac{1}{2}a_{n+1}t^2 = d + \frac{V_n^2}{2|a_{n,\max}|},\ \mathrm{t} < \mathrm{t_0} \tag{7}$$

$$U = v \cdot \Delta v \cdot \frac{a_n}{a_{n,\max}} = v^2 \cdot \frac{a_n}{a_{n,\max}} \tag{8}$$

3. The rear car (n) braking, the front (n) as the same

$$\begin{aligned} &V_{n+1} \cdot t_0 + \frac{1}{2}a_{n+1} \cdot {t_0}^2 + (V_{n+1} + a_{n+1} \cdot t_0) \cdot t + \frac{1}{2}a_{n+1,\max} \cdot t^2 \\ &= d + V_n \cdot t_0 + \frac{1}{2}a_{n,\max} \cdot {t_0}^2 + (V_n + a_{n,\max} \cdot t_0) \cdot t + \frac{1}{2}a_{n,\max} \cdot t^2;\ \mathrm{t} > 0 \end{aligned} \tag{9}$$

$$U = v \cdot \Delta v \cdot \frac{a_n}{a_{n,\max}} = v \cdot (v - v') \cdot \frac{a_n}{a_{n,\max}} \tag{10}$$

4. The rear car (n) braking but not stopping, the front (n) stopped

$$\begin{aligned} &V_{n+1} \cdot t_0 + \frac{1}{2}a_{n+1} \cdot {t_0}^2 + (V_{n+1} + a_{n+1} \cdot t_0) \cdot t + \frac{1}{2}a_{n+1,\max} \cdot t^2 \\ &= d + \frac{V_n^2}{2|a_{n,\max}|},\ \mathrm{t} > 0 \end{aligned} \tag{11}$$

$$U = v \cdot \Delta v \cdot \frac{a_n}{a_{n,\max}} = v^2 \cdot \frac{a_n}{a_{n,\max}} \tag{12}$$

The unsafe parameter U characterizes the safety level between two successive vehicles. But it only gives some safety information about a specific section of two cars. In order to have a complete understanding, the unsafe density parameter is defined as follows:

$$UD = \frac{\sum_{s=1}^{S_t}\sum_{n=1}^{N_t} U_{n,S} \cdot d}{T \cdot L} \tag{13}$$

The unsafe density parameter is quantitative, so it can compare the safety level and traffic control management measures of different sections of road network in different time periods. Thus, unsafe density index can be used as an important evaluation indicator.

6 Driving Risk Classification

It is difficult to eliminate the driving risk completely. How to control the risk in an acceptable range is the problem of risk assessment to be solved. The risk is divided into four grades "weak risk, low risk, medium risk, high risk", specific qualitative described as Table 1:

7 Simulation Analysis

Taking the traffic volume, speed and other parameters on traffic safety into account, the paper uses Vissim software to do a lot of simulation experiments [5]. Through qualitative analysis of the experimental data, the control standards recommendations were made.

8 Experiment Design

Based on direct observation and traffic flow simulation, the minimum traffic volume is taken to be 1,600 veh/h, the max 3,600 veh/h, 200 veh/h as the interval; the traffic volume ratio of mainline and ramp is 5:1; the expectation speed is set from 20 to 120 km/h, 10 km/h as intervals; the proportion of the small cars and large trucks is 70%: 30%, totally 132 kinds of cases, repeat five times for each case, the part of the experimental data recorded as follows (Table 2).

Table 1 Description of the driving risk classification

Risk classfication	Risk description	Risk accepted principles	Risk control measures
1	Weak	Totally accepted	A
2	Low	Conditional accepted	B
3	Moderate	Undesirable	C
4	High	Totally unaccepted	D

Table 2 Expectation speed at 100 km/h of on-ramp and off-ramp areas

Traffic volume (veh/h)	Off-ramp areas					On-ramp areas				
	1	2	3	4	5	1	2	3	4	5
1,600	0.043	0.032	0.039	0.035	0.053	0.037	0.031	0.042	0.034	0.025
1,800	0.056	0.045	0.078	0.044	0.054	0.048	0.061	0.077	0.048	0.040
2,000	0.081	0.070	0.086	0.072	0.077	0.061	0.120	0.079	0.076	0.083
2,200	0.077	0.108	0.082	0.108	0.120	0.137	0.105	0.151	0.147	0.123
2,400	0.139	0.137	0.122	0.104	0.134	0.149	0.193	0.173	0.163	0.177
2,600	0.183	0.163	0.160	0.187	0.185	0.213	0.213	0.208	0.242	0.174
2,800	0.187	0.216	0.239	0.289	0.236	0.227	0.248	0.249	0.258	0.263
3,000	0.295	0.273	0.259	0.290	0.346	0.235	0.199	0.243	0.251	0.264
3,200	0.316	0.347	0.298	0.296	0.269	0.243	0.248	0.254	0.230	0.240
3,400	0.342	0.280	0.281	0.325	0.346	0.236	0.261	0.268	0.235	0.262
3,600	0.354	0.289	0.250	0.330	0.310	0.226	0.265	0.258	0.236	0.245

9 Traffic Control Standards of Mainline

The traffic volume, speed and risk value of on-ramp and off-ramp areas of three-dimensional equivalent relationship are shown in Figs. 1 and 2.

The data of each test case of five times are averaged to calculate the corresponding maximum risk. Using the linear interpolation, the off-ramp and on-ramp critical values between adjacent risk levels are set. Speed control intervals are taken to be 5 km/h [6], traffic control interval 10 veh/h. the traffic control standard suggestions under various conditions are as follows (Tables 3 and 4).

10 Application Example

The alignment and traffic signs plant of the off-ramp of one freeway are shown in Fig. 3. The mainline design speed is 80 km/h, the ramp design speed 40 km/h, the variable speed lane length is 144 m, of which transition section length 63 m, deceleration lane length 81 m.

Assumed that the weather conditions, road environment, road performance are good, the length of simulated sections is 1.3 km. UD as a safety evaluation index, the simulation time step = 1 s, the length of time = 1,800 s. The UD results are shown in Table 5 and Fig. 4.

From Fig. 4, the UD peak is before 300 m of the diverging point, so the section is the most danger. The data in Table 5 and Fig. 4 both show that when unlimited, the entire off-ramp areas are middle risk zone, while the speed limit at 65 km/h and 70 km/h, the UD reduces to low risk area, the entire areas are at an acceptable risk region, so these two measures are feasible. Furthermore, when limit speed

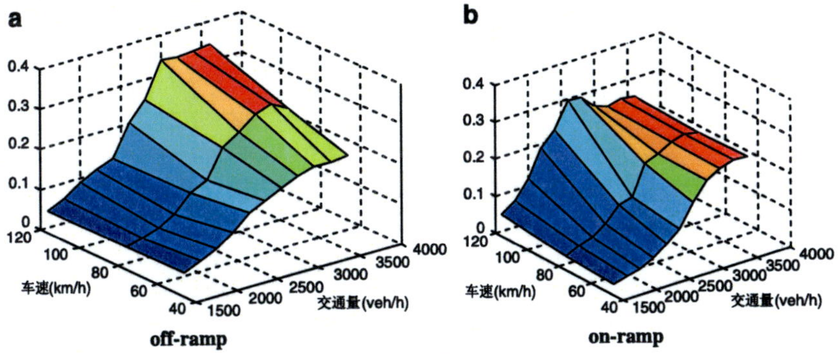

Fig. 1 Speed-traffic volume-risk relation

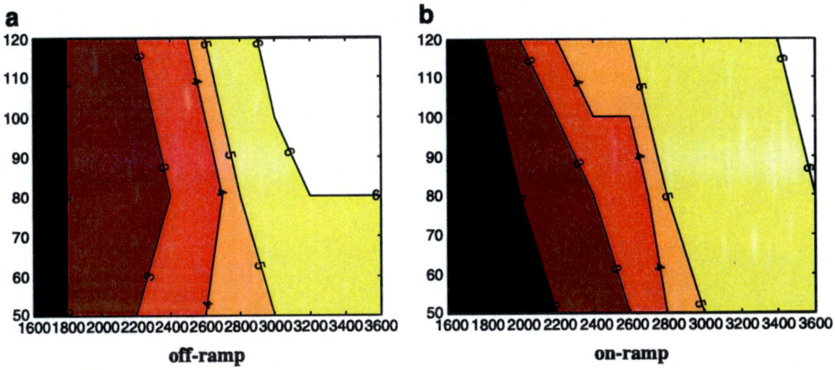

Fig. 2 Speed-traffic volume-risk equivalent values

Table 3 Speed control standard suggestions under each safety level

Traffic volume (veh/h)	Risk control level							
	Off-ramp				On-ramp			
	Weak	Low	Moderate	High	Weak	Low	Moderate	High
1,600	120	120	120	120	110	120	120	120
1,800	120	120	120	120	90	120	120	120
2,000	105	120	120	120	80	115	120	120
2,200	55	120	120	120	30	115	120	120
2,400	25	120	120	120	20	100	120	120
2,600	20	100	120	120	–	80	120	120
2,800	20	70	115	120	–	45	115	120
3,000	–	45	100	120	–	30	110	120
3,200	–	45	85	90	–	30	95	100
3,400	–	40	80	90	–	25	80	100
3,600	–	35	80	90		20	80	90

Note: "–" represents no matter what the value of traffic control is, are not able to control the risk in this level

Table 4 Traffic volume control standard suggestions under each safety level

Expectation speed (km/h)	Risk control level							
	Off-ramp				On-ramp			
	Weak	Low	Moderate	High	Weak	Low	Moderate	High
80	2,130	2,790	3,600	3,600	2,000	2,630	3,600	3,600
100	2,090	2,590	3,000	3,200	1,720	2,410	3,170	3,400
120	1,920	2,550	2,900	3,000	1,440	2,290	2,660	3,000

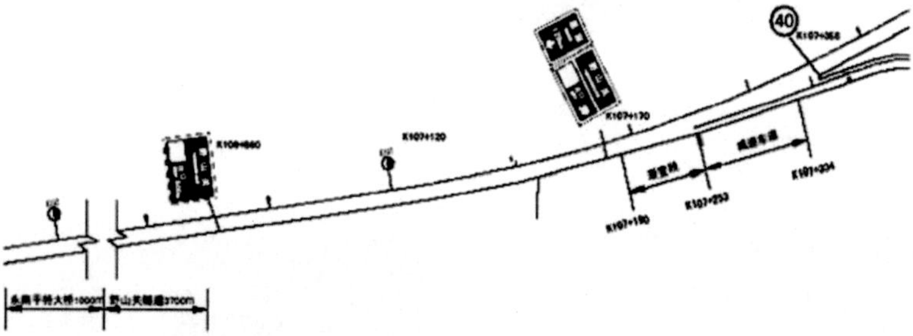

Fig. 3 Alignment and traffic signs arrangement

at 65 km/h, the average risk are the smaller, compared with the unlimited, the UD peak decreased 42.86%, the UD values of the other sections have different reduction. According to the mentioned risk classification, the reduced effects of driving risk after taking speed limit measures are shown in Fig. 5.

11 Conclusion

Taking microscopic traffic flow characteristics of the on-ramp and off-ramp of freeway with the starting point, the risk assessment index are put forward according the situations of people, vehicles and other factors before accidents. The status of the traffic risk classification description is determined. Using the traffic simulation technology, through varieties of experiments parameter setting and the risk calculation, the different security levels of speed and flow control recommended values are set for different traffic flow and design speed. At last, take the actual sections as an example, applying the micro-simulation software to simulate the traffic flow conditions under different speed limits measures; the paper compares the risk improved effect of use of different speed limit measures using the unsafe density index as a safety evaluation index.

Table 5 UD value of sections under each speed limit

Sections (m)		0–50	50–100	100–150	300–350	350–400	450–500	500–550	550–600	600–650
UD	Unlimited	0.024	0.023	0.026	0.031	0.029	0.028	0.031	0.031	0.032
	70 km/h	0.020	0.024	0.023	0.031	0.030	0.033	0.033	0.029	0.029
	65 km/h	0.025	0.022	0.027	0.031	0.030	0.030	0.032	0.032	0.033
	60 km/h	0.020	0.024	0.023	0.031	0.030	0.033	0.033	0.029	0.029
	55 km/h	0.020	0.024	0.023	0.031	0.030	0.033	0.033	0.029	0.029
	50 km/h	0.020	0.024	0.023	0.031	0.030	0.033	0.033	0.029	0.029
Sections (m)		650–700	700–750	750–800	950–1,000	1,000–1,050	1,100–1,150	1,150–1,200	1,200–1,250	1,250–1,300
UD	Unlimited	0.038	0.043	0.066	0.014	0.026	0.020	0.020	0.021	0.024
	70 km/h	0.035	0.037	0.039	0.046	0.015	0.021	0.018	0.021	0.020
	65 km/h	0.037	0.043	*0.064*	0.044	0.032	0.023	0.024	0.023	0.024
	60 km/h	0.035	0.037	0.039	0.064	0.012	0.020	0.018	0.018	0.019
	55 km/h	0.035	0.037	0.039	0.072	0.012	0.020	0.018	0.019	0.019
	50 km/h	0.035	0.037	0.039	0.076	0.010	0.019	0.019	0.019	0.019

Note: The units of UD are m/s^2, the units of limited speed are km/h

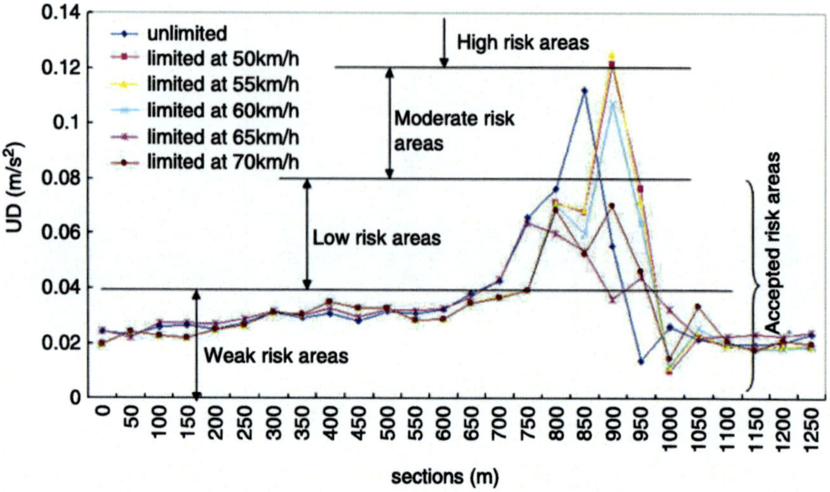

Fig. 4 UD comparison

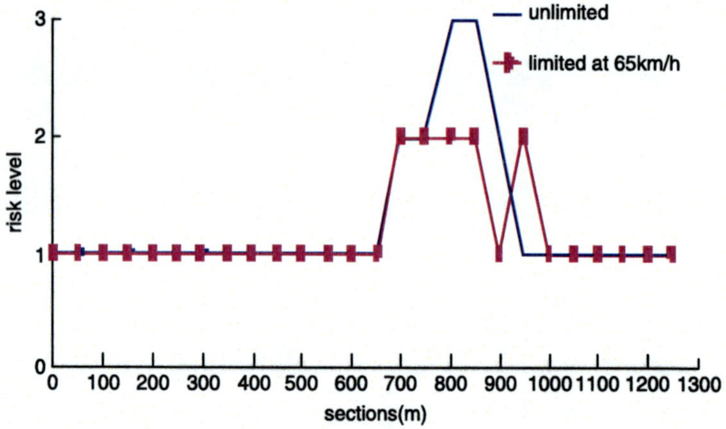

Fig. 5 Risk level comparison

References

1. Sheng Yan-ting. Traffic Safety Analysis of Freeway On-ramp and Off-ramp Areas Based on Microsimulation[D]. Shanghai: Tongji University, 2007
2. Michael J, Cassidy, Study of freeway traffic near an off-ramp, Transportation Research Part A, 2000
3. Thomas F, Golob, Tool to Evaluate Safety effects of changes in freeway traffic flow, Journal of Transportation Engineering, 2004

4. Frédérique Huguenin, Alexandre Torday, André-Gilles Dumont. Evaluation of traffic safety using microsimulation[R]. Swiss Transport Research Conference, 2005 (March 9–11)
5. VISSIM Version 4.0 Manual. PTV Planung Transport Verkehr AG. June 2004. 33–45; 152–158
6. Jun Zhi-cai, Yao Hong-wei. Expressway Socio-Economic Impact Assessment for Variable Speed Limits[J]. Journal of highway and transportation research, 2004, Vol. 21, No. 5, 104–108

Probe into the Effectiveness Connotation of Emergency Telecommunication Plan and Its Assessment Method Under Unconventional Emergency

Xiaoyu Wan, Zhenyu Jin, and Jinying Wei

Abstract Emergency Telecommunication is significant for the commanding, scheduling as well as the information transmission under the unconvention emergency which is based on the logical and effective of the emergency telecommunication plan. By the feature of telecommunication industry, scientific community presents the definition of emergency telecommunication plan based on the in-depth research on the domestic and overseas related documents, putting up the system about the effectiveness of emergency telecommunication plan by taking efficiency and effect as the clue. Moreover, the design ideas and methods of efficiency assessment model which provides the science basis on improving the effectiveness of the emergency telecommunication plan is proposed.

Keywords Assessment · Effectiveness · Emergency communication plan

1 Introduction

In recent years, various types of unconventional incidents indiscriminately occurred all over the world. The studies on "emergency" are becoming highly valued. Unconventional incident is emergency with inadequate premonition, obivious complexityand the derivative endenger, enormous destructive effect, so regular management has no good effect on it [1], such as the January 12th Hayti earthquke, the May 12th Wenchuan Seismic Disaster, the July 5th incident and the September 11th terrorist attacks.

Telecommunicaiton industry is the basic trade of the national economy. When the unconventional incidents come up, whether the telecommunication is clear or the damaged telecommunication system can be restored high-speedly, is the key

X. Wan (✉), Z. Jin, and J. Wei
School of Economic and Management, Chongqing University of Posts and Telecommunications, Chongqing 400065, People's Republic of China
e-mail: wanxy@cqupt.edu.cn, jzy_860818@hotmail.com, wjynjupt@163.com

D.D. Wu (ed.), *Modeling Risk Management in Sustainable Construction*, Computational Risk Management, DOI 10.1007/978-3-642-15243-6_47,

piont for the success of the emergency actions in the aspects of responsing, commanding schudling and rescuing [2]. Because the emergency plan is the foundation and the action guidance of the emergency actions, so whether the Emergency telecommunication Plan is logical, effective and feasible or not is significant for the quality of the guarantee of emergency telecommunicaitons in the face of incidents, and then, affects the whole rescuing process.

Based on above, this article aims to study the effectiveness connotation of our country's emergency telecommunication plan as well as its assessment methods based on the related theories, standards and methods. Thereby, it contributes to improve the operation capabilities of the emergency telecommunication plan.

2 Literature Review

2.1 Review of the Connotation of Effectiveness

In order to study Effectiveness, we must have deep knowledge of Effectiveness [3]. Otherwise, the study is blind and broad without effectiveness. In management, effectiveness of management [4] and the efficiency of leadership are two important knowledge points [5]. Their understandings on effectiveness lay on two aspects: efficiency and effect [6]. Efficiency refers to act correctly, while effect is to do the right thing. In the article *Performance Management and Effectiveness* Management, Feng Yingjun and Wang Dawei consider that the effectiveness management is a kind of behavioral characteristic which can reflect the fact that people can produce benefit due to the operating management. It reflect essentially the level of people effective efforts subjuctively. From that we can see, their understanding emphazise the effect, namely, the core point of the paper is performance. Luo Guoying (2006) thinks that the assessment on the effectivement should focus on the result, and to focus on the essence and the aim of effectiveness is to focus on performance [3]. Chen Hanwen (2008), in the angle of the source, considers the assessment on Internal Control effectiveness is whether the guaratee level for the related goals provided by Internal Control has reached or over the reasonable level [7]. In other words, under the Internal Control, whether the company risk has dropped to a reasonable level. We can see this definition explains effectiveness as effect. From literature reading, I find no matter the assessment on effecitveness is on efficiency or effect, the essence is to build a evaluation criterion or a system of evaluation. Xu Pei and Zhang Renjun (2006) assess the effectiveness of team from four dimensionalities: team circumstance, team composition, team orperation and team output [8]. In order to assess the enforcement of *Regulations of Shenzhen Special Economic Zone on Public Library*, He Yun (2008) builds an assessment criteria focusing on the basic facilities, open time, use ratio and investment. From these documents, we can see the premise to assess to effectiveness is to build related index system [9].

2.2 *Review Assessment Model of the Effectiveness of the Plan*

On the methods and theories of assessment, Liu et al. (2008) adopt the Fault Tree Analysis (FTA) to assess the completeness of natural disaster emergency plan. According to the characteritistics of emergency, they summerise that our country's natural disaster emergency plan contians 41 kinds of role types. Based on these, they build a emergency process and the Responsibility Matrixe and interpretational criteria among emergency personnel [10]. For the executive staff, the assessment on manipuility turns to the assessment on complexity, building a manipuility assessment methods on emergency plan structure. Gong Weiguo (2007) introduces fuzzy comprehensive evaluation, based on the feasibility and scientificity of emergency plan, as for the unquantitative description standerd, which can form the the assessment criteria through Quality Method of Forecast and experts' collective knowledge and experience. Meanwhile, He also studies and analyses the early warning [11].

3 Effectiveness Connotation of Emergency Telecommunication Plan

It is concluded that the academic concept of "effectiveness" is ambiguity from analyzing the literature, and most of which consider "effectiveness" as "efficiency" or "effect". Besides, only a few literature give a clear concept of effectiveness, and it is necessary to understand and analyze the connotation of Effectiveness, otherwise, the results would appear broad and messy. Additionally, there two types of ways to explain "efficiency", one is that input–output ratio and the other way considers it as response time or the rate of reflecting. But, the academic circles' understanding about "effect" is similar with each other, that is the level of achieving the desired goal. Some investigations also attempted to estimate that the "efficiency" and "effect" are two aspects of the same problem, which interact with each other (Liu Xiaoxuan 2004).

The indicator "effectiveness" is resolve into detailed indicators-"efficiency" and "effect". The efficiency of emergency telecommunication plan mainly means the time of implementing the plan and the The main criteria to measure it is the time. For example, presumably, earthquake, which lead the interruption of communication, occurs in a place, three kinds of time can be considered as the key indicators that could explain the "efficiency", they are the time from start of the earthquake to carry out emergency communications plan fully, the time from the operating of the plan to the time when all the emergency departments arrive at the spot, and the recovery time of the interrupted telecom network. And all of these can be summarized as the efficiency of carrying out the emergency telecommunication plan. On the other hand, the effect of the plan mainly means that comparing the condition before implementing the plan with that after implementing the plan. The critical

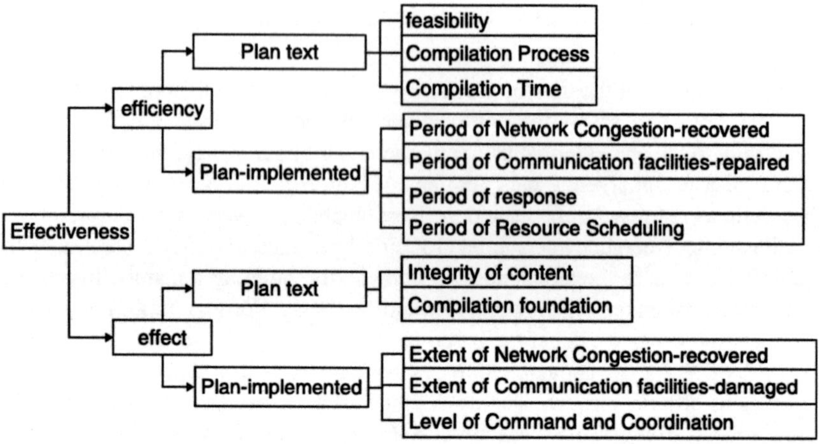

Fig. 1 The system of effectiveness connotation

indicators are the extent of network congestion-recovered, the level of command and coordination and so on.

Based on the above analysis, "efficiency" and "effect" are the two dimensions for us to resolve "effectiveness". At each dimension, there are two perspectives to make a further analysis.That is "plan text" and "pan-implemented". About the efficiency of emergency telecommunication plan, three indicators, which are "feasibility", "compilation process" and "compilation time" are the key indicators affecting plan text. And the indicators which affect "plan-implemented" are "Period of Network Congestion-recovered", "Period of Communication facilities-repaired", "Period of response" and "Period of Resource Scheduling". As to the effect of the plan, the indicators, which affect "plan text", are "Integrity Of content" and "Compilation foundation"; and the "plan-implemented" depends on three indicators- "Extent of Network Congestion-recovered", "Extent of Communication facilities-damaged" and "Level of Command and Coordination". The analysis above can be described as following Fig. 1:

4 The Method of Constructing the Model of Effectiveness

4.1 Divide Emergency Telecommunication into Different Categories and Levels

Dividing emergency telecommunication into different categories and levels is the fundation of the assessment. We can not give an assessment result only according to a certain kind of unconventional emergency. So, in order to evaluate the

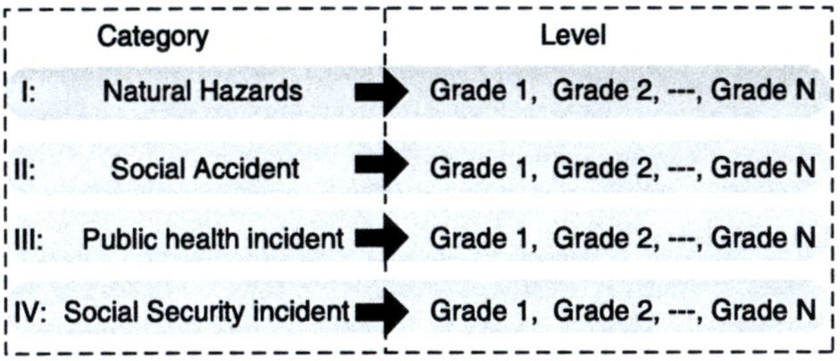

Fig. 2 Categories and levels of emergency telecommunication

effectiveness of the plan globally, emergency telecommunication should be divided into different categories and levels, which is displayed as the following Fig. 2.

Categories depend on the qualitaty of accidents or event, which arouse the telecommunication accident. This article divides emergency telecommunication into four categories: Natural Hazards (I), Social Accident (II), Public health incident (III), Social Security incident (IV). Levels means the extent of the damage of the communication systems, such as the size of the interrupted telecom network, the time of network congestion etc.

4.2 Construct the Model of "Efficiency" and Model of "Effect"

4.2.1 Model of "Efficiency" (M_1)

Suppose the indicators $x_{11}, x_{12}, x_{13}, \cdots, x_{1n}$, were some certain bottom indicators in the Fig. 1, such as "feasibility", "compilation process", "compilation time" and "Period of Network Congestion-recovered ", which consist of the Model of "efficiency" $M_1 : f_1(x_{11}, x_{12}, x_{13}, ..., x_{1n})$ From Fig. 2, According to each category and each level, the emergency telecommunication plan could be evaluated from the indicators $x_{11}, x_{12}, x_{13}, \cdots, x_{1n}$. Correspondingly, some real data will be got and put the data $x_{11}, x_{12}, x_{13}, \cdots, x_{1n}$ into model M_1, we can get η_{ij} that means the efficiency of the plan at a certain category and a certain level.

Take a certain emergency telecommunication plan for example, and evaluate it's efficiency at Category I, Grade 1. By investigation, $x'_{11}, x'_{12}, x'_{13}, \cdots, x'_{1n}$ (such as "compilation time" and "Period of Network Congestion-recovered" etc.) can be calculated out. Then, put them into modelM_1, so efficiency at Category I, Grade 1 is calculated out as a result of η_{I1}. The efficiency of the same plan, similarly, should be evaluated at Category I, Grade 2, and $x''_{11}, x''_{12}, x''_{13}, \cdots, x''_{1n}$can also be calculated out, and the efficiency at Category I, Grade 2 is calculated out as a result of η_{I1} by model M_1. And so forth, a set $Q_1\{\eta_{I1}, \eta_{I2}, \cdots, \eta_{In}, \eta_{II1}, \eta_{II2}, \cdots, \eta_{IIn}, \cdots\}$, which means the efficiency of the plan at every category and every grade, is work out. The analysis above is described as Fig. 3.

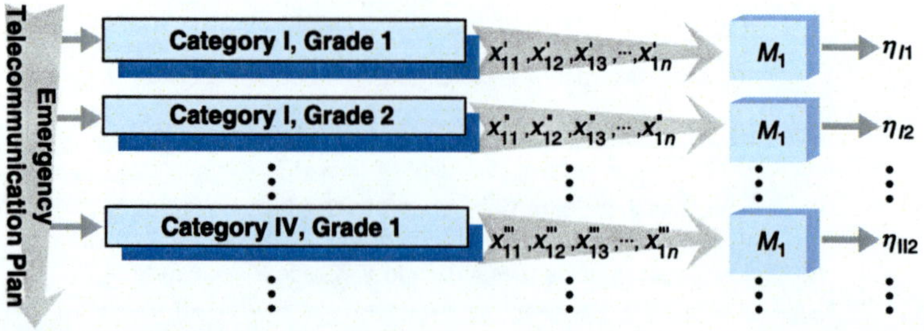

Fig. 3 Principium of model of "efficiency"

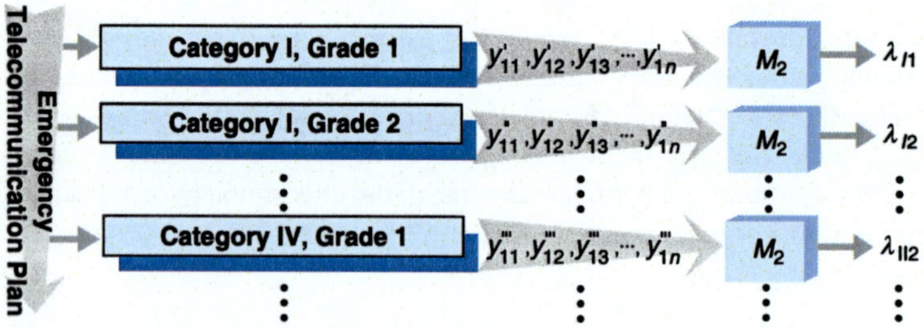

Fig. 4 Principium of model of "effect"

4.2.2 Model of "Effect" (M_2)

Analogously, the parameters "$y_{21}, y_{22}, y_{23}, \cdots, y_{2n}$", which can be on behalf of the indicators, such as "Integrity Of content" and "Compilation foundation" etc., construct the model. And the model can be expressed as $M_2 : f_2(y_{21}, y_{22}, y_{23}, ..., y_{2n})$, which is to evaluated the effect of the plan. Equally, the emergency telecommunication plan could be evaluated from the indicators "$y_{21}, y_{22}, y_{23}, \cdots, y_{2n}$" at every category and every level. After getting the numerical value of the indicators, put them into model M_2, we can get η_{ij} that means the effect of the plan at a certain category and a certain level.

Take a certain emergency telecommunication plan for example, and evaluate it's effect value at Category I, Grade 1. The numerical value of the parameters $y'_{11}, y'_{12}, y'_{13}, \cdots, y'_{1n}$, which aim to be put into model M_2, can be got by investigation. Then, the effect value of the plan is calculated out as the result of λ_{I1}. Similarly, as to the effect value of the plan at Category I, Grade 2, λ_{I2}can be got by putting $y''_{11}, y''_{12}, y''_{13}, \cdots, y''_{1n}$ into model M_2. Finally, a set $Q_2\{\lambda_{I1}, \lambda_{I2}, \cdots, \lambda_{In}, \lambda_{II1}, \lambda_{II2}, \cdots, \lambda_{IIn}, \cdots\}$, which means the effect of the plan at every category and every grade, is work out. The analysis above is described as Fig. 4.

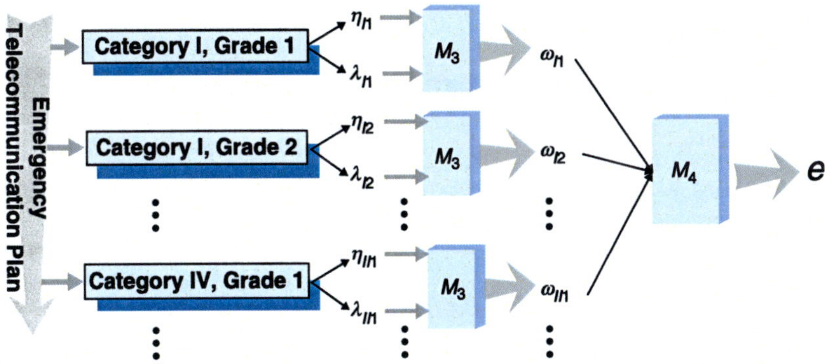

Fig. 5 Integration model M_3 and the full model M_4

4.2.3 Integration Model of "Efficiency" and "Effect" (M_3) and the Full Model (M_4)

According to the above, two numerical values, which are efficiency value (η) and effect value (λ), will be calculated out for every category and every level of an emergency telecommunication plan. The ω is calculated by Model M_3, which is established to integrate η with λ, and ω reflects the effectiveness value of the plan at a certain category and level. The final result of the effectiveness assessment of the plan, e, which is calculated by model M_4, is worked out by each ω of every category and every level. The process of analyzing is described as Fig. 5.

5 Conclusion

According to the features of telecommunications industry, the connotation of effectiveness of emergency telecommunication plan is analyzed after in-depth research in the domestic and overseas literature, so the connotation system beginning with the entry point "Efficiency" and "effect" is proposed. Then, emergency telecommunication is resolved into different categories and different levels, based on which, the methods for constructing the model of efficiency, the model of effect, the integration model of "efficiency" and "effect" and the full model are designed. All the above provides a scientific scheme and feasible ideas to improve the effectiveness of emergency telecommunication plan of our conutry. However, this is the primary stage of studing the effectiveness of emergency plan, and the some correlative quantitative models and empirical studies are the following difficulties and the next research direction.

References

1. Han Zhiyong. Background, Targets, and Organization of the Major Research Plan "Study on Unconventional Emergencies Management"[J]. Bulletin of National Natural Science Foundation of China, 2009 23(4)
2. Wan Xiao-yu, Sun San-shan, Lu An-wen. On the National Emergency Communication Management of Serious Natural Disaster[J]. Journal of Chongqing University of Posts and Telecommunications: Social Science Edition, 2009.1
3. Luo Guoying. Effectiveness Connotation and Denotation of Quality Management System[J]. China Quality, 2006(2):8–12
4. Feng Yingjun et al. Performance Management and Management Efficiency [J]. China soft science, 2003(4)
5. Li Chaoping, Meng Hui, Shi Kan. The Effects of Transformational Leadership on Organizational Citizenship Behavior[J]. Psychological Science, 2006, 29(1):175–177
6. Wan Jieqiu, Zhao Yachun. The Nature of Growth from Incentives[J]. Academic Journal of Suzhou University (Philosophy and Social Sciences), 2009(4):31–34
7. Chen Jian-kai, Chen Han-wen. Company Characters, Audit Demand and Factors Driving Local Accounting Firm Selection[J]. The Theory and Practice of Finance and Economics, 2009, 30(5)
8. Xu Pei, Zhang Renjun. Effectiveness of R&D team Construction of Evaluation System[J]. Science & Technology Progress and Policy, 2006, 23(12)
9. he Yun. Effect Evaluation and Revelation of the Regulations of Shenzhen Special Economic Zone on Public Library[J]. Library Tribune, 2008, (4):137–140
10. Liu Ji-fu, Zhu Jing-jing. Study on Evaluation Method of Natural Disaster Emergency Plan in China (PartII): Responsibility Matrix Evaluation[J]. China Safety Science Journal, 2008 18 (4):5–15
11. Gong Weiguo. Public Emergency Plans for Assessment and Analysis of Early Warning Alerts [J]. Journal of Hunan Business College, 2007, 14(6)

Risk Assessment of Levee Engineering Based on Triangular Fuzzy Number and Analytic Network Process and Its Application

Feng Li, Zong-Kun Li, and Chuan-Bin Yang

Abstract The levee engineering is the most important part of flood control system in China, the existing levee engineering has many uncertain facts in technology, economic natural and social environment. The risk factors are interdependence and interaction, and which are hard to quantization, at the same time, to considerate the uncertainty and fuzziness of judgments to the influencing factors made by the people, a risk analysis method based on analytic network process and triangular fuzzy number is built in the paper, and also a detailed exposition to the solution of the model. In the end, its rationality is confirmed by a case, and the result shows that fuzzy-ANP can treatment the complex effect between each risk factors and which can provide the important basis to the risk control and management to levee engineering.

Keywords Analytic network process · Risk assessment · Super matrix · Triangular fuzzy number

F. Li (✉)
School of Water Conservancy and Environment, Zhengzhou University, Zhengzhou, Henan Province 450002, People's Republic of China
and
Henan Province Water Conservancy Scientific Research Institute, Zhengzhou, Henan Province 450000, People's Republic of China
e-mail: lifeng9406@126.com

Z.-K. Li
School of Water Conservancy and Environment, Zhengzhou University, Zhengzhou, Henan Province 450002, People's Republic of China
e-mail: ramones123@126.com

C.-B. Yang
The Second Water Bureau of Henan Province, Zhengzhou, Henan Province, 450016, People's Republic of China
e-mail: yangchuanbin@126.com

D.D. Wu (ed.), *Modeling Risk Management in Sustainable Construction*, Computational Risk Management, DOI 10.1007/978-3-642-15243-6_48,

1 Introduction

On the process of levee engineering construction, we have faced with many aspects of uncertainty, such as technology, natural environment, social environment and organization management. Because of the theoretical limitations, the probability analysis method cannot considerate the multiple criterion factors comprehensively, and it cannot solve the problem. To the decision analysis and comprehensive evaluation of complex system which have multi-objective multi-criteria, multivariate, the analytic hierarchy process is a practical and effective method, which has widely used in various fields risk analysis [1]. But because the basic premise of AHP is that the elements of each level are independent, the AHP has limitation when dealing with interdependence elements of complex system. The risk factors of levee engineering involved a variety of technical, organizational management, natural and social environment are often interrelated and affect each other, so the elements AHP-related issues cannot be linked to better reflect its nature. The Analytic Network Process which is developed on the basis of AHP can precisely address elements of feedback and interactive in nature, making up for deficiencies caused by AHP [2]. Now, with the gradual development and improvement of ANP, it has been used in some areas of the complex systems, selection or indicators to assess the program has been applied, but in the field of risk analysis, applied research is still limited [3]. In this paper, the risk factors analysis of the levee engineering will be made based on ANP, taking into accounted the uncertainty and fuzziness when people in the decision-making to the risk factors, triangular fuzzy numbers will be the introduced into ANP method, which constitutes a fuzzy analytic network process (Fuzzy-ANP), with the analysis to the levee engineering risk factor by using of Fuzzy-ANP method, an important reference to further risk controlling can be provided.

2 Basic Principal

2.1 A Basic Principal of Analytic Network Process

ANP was built by Professor Saaty in 1996, to be different from the AHP, which looks the criteria as for separate and distinct, ANP considers an alternative to the guidelines from time to time exist between the role of the non-independence and feedback. The purpose is to get through the rating scale and predict the precise internal relations of all the criteria, objectives, programs, and their interaction under the action of the various groups, the element weight.

The elements of the system are divided into two parts by ANP method: the first part of the layer known as the control elements, including the issue of goals and decision-making criteria, all decision-making criteria are considered independent of one another, and only controlled by the goal of domination, controlling elements can be have no decision-making criteria, but at least there is a goal, the weight of each criterion in Controlling layer can be obtained using conventional AHP. The second part is divided into the network layer, which is dominated by all the elements under control layer composed of interdependence between elements of each other dominant, elements, and between levels within the non-independent, hierarchy in each of the criteria is not a dominant a simple internal and independent elements, it is a mutually dependent feedback network structure. Controlling layer and network layer hierarchy composed of a typical ANP [4], as shown in Fig. 1.

The decision-making process of ANP is as follows [5]:

Phase 1 as the standard comparison between their assessment process is in turn to each element separately to evaluate the dimensions between elements within this group an important degree, as well as other relevant elements of groups of pair-wise comparison between the importance degree, the general form of pair-wise comparison matrix is as follows:

$$A = [a_{ij}]_{n\times n} = \begin{bmatrix} 1 & a_{12} & \cdots & a_{1n} \\ a_{21} & 1 & \cdots & a_{2n} \\ \mathrm{M} & \mathrm{M} & \mathrm{M} & \mathrm{M} \\ a_{n1} & a_{n2} & \cdots & 1 \end{bmatrix} \tag{1}$$

where $a_{ij} = a_{ji}^{-1}, i, j = 1, 2, 3, ..., n$. Calculated the characteristic vectors of each pair-wise comparison matrix, then the characteristic vectors of each of the pair-wise comparison matrix are summarized in a matrix, to form a completed integrated matrix, known as the super-matrix, the form is:

$$W = \begin{array}{c} \\ C_1 \\ C_2 \\ \vdots \\ C_m \end{array} \begin{array}{c} \begin{array}{cccc} C_1 & C_2 & \cdots & C_m \end{array} \\ \left| \begin{array}{cccc} W_{11} & W_{12} & \cdots & W_{1m} \\ W_{21} & W_{22} & \cdots & W_{2m} \\ \vdots & \vdots & \vdots & \vdots \\ W_{m1} & W_{m2} & \cdots & W_{mm} \end{array} \right| \end{array} \tag{2}$$

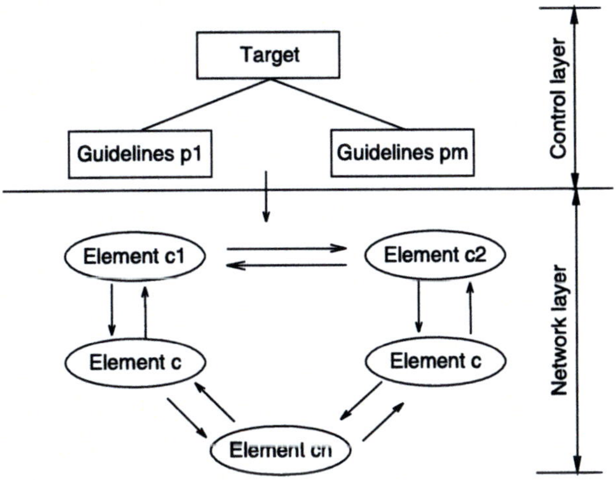

Fig. 1 A typical analytic network process

Among them, W_{ij} is said that the influence which each element of the i layer to the j layer, known as the block of super-matrix, which have the following matrix form:

$$W_{ij} = \begin{bmatrix} W_{i_1,j_1} & W_{i_1,j_2} & \cdots & W_{i_1,j_{nj}} \\ W_{i_2,j_1} & W_{i_2,j_2} & \cdots & W_{i_2,j_{nj}} \\ \vdots & \vdots & \vdots & \vdots \\ W_{i_{n1},j_1} & W_{i_{n2},j_2} & \cdots & W_{i_{ni},j_{nj}} \end{bmatrix} \quad (3)$$

Levels of various elements within the guidelines of a sort that can be used by super-matrix, in the super-matrix, each level of each column is normalized, but it did not take into accounted the impact of other levels of this criteria, so each column is not normalized in super-matrix.

To reflect the sort accurately, we must consider the influence between the levels, that is, to consider the feedback effects of the specific approach, that is: as an element of each level for a certain layer, to compared each other and calculate the weight of the corresponding sort. If we use a_{ij} to indicate the affect weight of the i layer to the j layer, $\widetilde{W}_{ij} = a_{ij}W_{ij}$, then $\widetilde{W}_{ij}$ is named weighted super-matrix, in weighted super-matrix, the sum of elements of each column are one, such matrix has random, which makes the cumulative effect exists and finite.

After the weighted super-matrix be multiplied many times, it will converge to a fixed value, that is, the matrix row vector is the same, while the column vector sum to 1, which named the ultimate super-matrix, from the ultimate super-matrix, we can get the relative weigh of the elements, that is, an element of the final impact on the ultimate goal [6].

2.2 Basic Principal of Triangular Fuzzy Number

Definition 1, set $M \in F(R)$ to a fuzzy number.

There is $x_0 \in R$, making $\mu_M(x_0) = 1$.

For arbitrary $\alpha \in [0, 1]$, $A_\alpha = \lfloor x, \mu_{A_\alpha} \geq \alpha \rfloor$ is a closed interval. Here $F(R)$ is for all of the fuzzy number set; R for the set of real numbers.

Definition 2, Based on the domain U is real number field, M is for linear triangular fuzzy number, its membership function is $\mu_A(x)$, triangular fuzzy number algebra is relatively easy, its membership function is as follows [7].

$$\mu_A(x) = \begin{cases} 0 & x < a \\ L(x) = \dfrac{x-a}{m-a} & a \leq x < m \\ 1 & x = m \\ R(x) = \dfrac{b-x}{b-m} & m \leq x < b \\ 0 & x > b \end{cases} \quad (4)$$

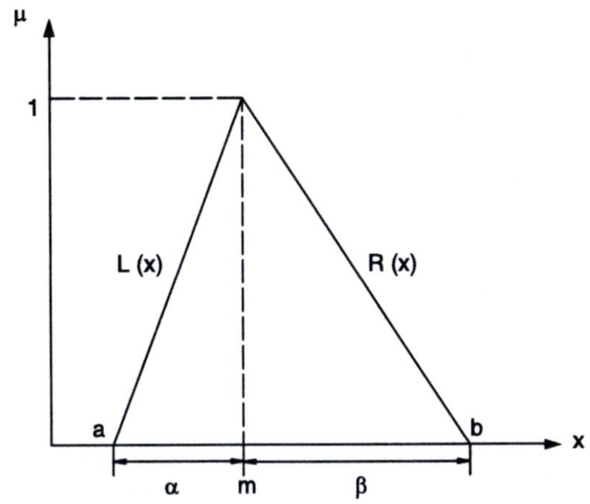

Fig. 2 Triangular fuzzy number membership function representation

We can see from Fig. 2, the linear triangular fuzzy number can be consist of $(m-\alpha, m, m+\beta)$ by fuzzy number triples, order $a = m-\alpha, b = m+\beta$, then the fuzzy number recorded as follows: $M = (a, m, b)$.

Setting up two triangular fuzzy number, M_1 and M_2, $M_1 = (a_1, m_1, b_1)$, $M_2 = (a_2, m_2, b_2)$ then the algebraic algorithms of fuzzy numbers are as follows:

- Linear triangular fuzzy number addition

$$M_1 + M_2 = (a_1, m_1, b_1) + (a_2, m_2, b_2) = (a_1 + a_2, m_1 + m_2, b_1 + b_2) \tag{5}$$

- Linear triangular fuzzy number subtraction

$$1 - M_1 = (a_1, m_1, b_1) = (1 - b_1, 1 - m_1, 1 - a_1) \tag{6}$$

$$M_1 - M_2 = (a_1, m_1, b_1) - (a_2, m_2, b_2) = (a_1 - b_2, m_1 - m_2, b_1 - a_2) \tag{7}$$

- Linear triangular fuzzy number multiplication

$$M_1 \times M_2 = (a_1, m_1, b_1) \times (a_2, m_2, b_2) = (a_1 a_2, m_1 m_2, b_1 b_2) \tag{8}$$

$$\begin{gathered}(\lambda, \lambda, \lambda) \times (a_1, m_1, b_1) = (\lambda a_1, \lambda m_1, \lambda b_1) \\ \lambda > 0, \lambda \in R\end{gathered} \tag{9}$$

- Linear triangular fuzzy number division

$$M_1 \div M_2 = (a_1, m_1, b_1) \div (a_2, m_2, b_2) = (a_1 \div a_2, m_1 \div m_2, b_1 \div b_2) \tag{10}$$

$$(a_1, m_1, b_1)^{-1} \approx (1/a_1, 1/m_1, 1/b_1) \tag{11}$$

Set $X = \{x_1, x_2, \ldots, x_n\}$ is a set of objects, $U = \{u_1, u_2, \ldots, u_m\}$ is a goal set, the i objects to meet the m target value for the required degree of $M_{E_i}^1, M_{E_i}^2, M_{E_i}^m$, then the "weight sum" type of fuzzy synthetic extent of the value of [8]:

$$S_i = \sum_{j=1}^{m} M_{E_i}^j \otimes \left[\sum_{i=1}^{n} \sum_{j=1}^{m} M_{E_i}^j \right]^{-1} \quad i = 1, 2, \ldots, n \tag{12}$$

The theory related to triangular fuzzy number:
1, setting up $M_1 = (a_1, m_1, b_1)$, $M_2 = (a_2, m_2, b_2)$ are two triangular fuzzy numbers, then the possibility of degree of $M_1 \geq M_2$:

$$V(M_1, M_2) = \begin{cases} 1 & m_1 m_2 \\ \dfrac{a_2 - b_1}{(m_1 - b_1) - (m_2 - a_2)} & m_1 < m_2, b_1 \geq a_2 \\ 0 & others \end{cases} \tag{13}$$

2, the possibility of the degree that triangular fuzzy number M is greater than other triangular fuzzy numbers is defined as [9]:

$$V(M \geq M_1, M_2, \ldots, M_k) = \min_{i=1,2,\ldots,k} V(M \geq M_i) \tag{14}$$

Supposed:

$$d'(A_i) = \min V(S_i \geq S_k) \tag{15}$$

Weight vector was:

$$W' = (d'(A_1), d'(A_2), \ldots, d'(A_n))^T \tag{16}$$

Normalized available, we can get:

$$W = (d(A_1), d(A_2), \ldots, d(A_n))^T \tag{17}$$

The main steps of fuzzy-analytic network process based on triangular fuzzy number are:

1. According to the problem of the overall objective, establish the ANP model
2. Constructed fuzzy pair-wise comparison matrix which consisting of triangular fuzzy numbers between the various decision-making criteria, and respectively to calculate the weight vector
3. Constructed fuzzy pair-wise comparison matrix with triangular fuzzy numbers in decision-making among the indicators, and respectively to calculate the weight vector
4. Integration and calculation of super-matrix

5. Total sorts of the relative importance degree of indicators weight

2.3 Case study

Chen Wan Jieshou section of Shayinghe River has 185.5 km length, there are 136 parts of dangerous works on the two sides such as bank collapse, landslide, seepage, etc. and there has one on average 1.4 km river and the dangerous works cumulative total length of about 62 km, accounting for the current 18% of the total length of a dike, which Zhoukou City dike segment elevation is about 51.2–51.8 m, the top width is 6m, outside of the dike distribute of multi-level scarp, bank collapse, beaches width is 0–100 m, river elevation is 36.7 m. Inside of dike is Zhoukou city, the ground elevation is about 46.0 m. The project area of ground motion peak acceleration is 0.05 g, the basic earthquake intensity is 6°.

Zhoukou City section dangerous works hydrological conditions are complicated, bank partial upper re-silty clay loam with low levels, in order to light silty loam, clip pink sand soil thin-layer, impact is poor; Xiangong sweep in which the right bank of pandemic edge, embankment scour the Bund to retreat, dangerous works in engineering design, construction and operation and management will encounter a large number of risk factors (uncertainty factors) influence, therefore, this paper make the level of decision-making criteria as the economic risk (M), natural hazards (E), technical risk (T), management risk (S).

1. ANP model of evaluation index system Under the decision-making criteria for evaluation, a number of indicators are included, which constitute the decision-making index system. With ANP model, we can get influence the relationship the evaluation index associated with each other and which shown in Fig. 3.

2. Construction of the decision-making criteria for the fuzzy pair-wise comparison between the matrix By using fuzzy semantic scale to describe the various criteria for paired comparisons between the relative importance, refer to 1–9 decision criteria of AHP method to determine evaluation criteria, specifically as shown in Table 1 [10]. Respectively, let all the evaluation criteria as the assessed object, then establish the fuzzy pair-wise comparison matrix of decision-making guidelines. Technical risk decision-making criteria for assessed object, for example, under which the pair-wise comparison matrix is listed in Table 2.

By (12), we can calculate important integrated value under each criterion compared with the other criteria:

$$S_{TM} = (0.178, 0.248, 0.322)$$

$$S_{TE} = (0.044, 0.052, 0.07)$$

$$S_{TT} = (0.064, 0.095, 0.136)$$

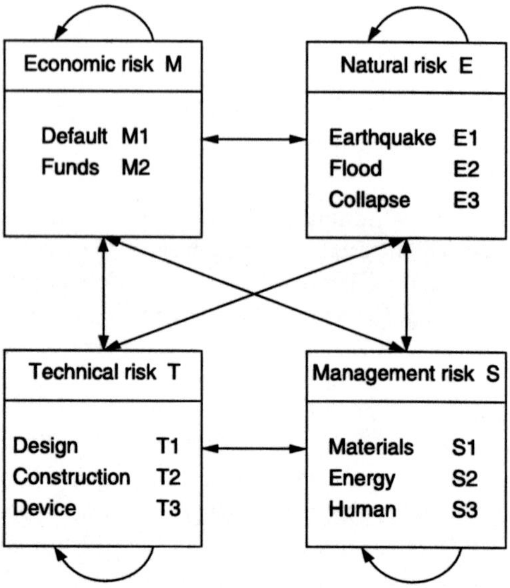

Fig. 3 ANP model for dike risk decision-making index system

Table 1 1–9 decision criteria

Scale	Meaning
1	To compared with each other, the two factors have the same importance
3	To compared with each other, the one is ratherish importance than the other
5	To compared with each other, the one is obviously importance than the other
7	To compared with each other, the one is strongly importance than the other
9	To compared with each other, the one is extremely importance than the other
2, 4, 6, 8	Intermediate value of adjacent judgment of the above

Table 2 Fuzzy pair-wise comparison matrix of the criteria layer under technical risk assessment object

Technical risk	M	E	T	S
M	(1, 1, 1)	(3, 4, 5)	(2, 3, 4)	(1, 2, 3)
E	(1/5, 1/4, 1/3)	(1, 1 ,1)	(1/3, 1/2, 1)	(1/4, 1/3, 1/2)
T	(1/4, 1/3, 1/2)	(1, 2, 3)	(1, 1, 1)	(1/3, 1/2, 1)
S	(1/3, 1/2, 1)	(2, 3, 4)	(1, 2, 3)	(1, 1, 1)

$$S_{TS} = (0.107, 0.161, 0.223)$$

By (13), we can calculate the possibility level of a triangular fuzzy number is greater than other fuzzy numbers:

$$V(S_{TM} \geq S_{TE}) = 1, \quad V(S_{TE} \geq S_{TM}) = 0$$

$$V(S_{TM} \geq S_{TT}) = 1, V(S_{TT} \geq S_{TM}) = 0$$

$$V(S_{TM} \geq S_{TS}) = 1, V(S_{TS} \geq S_{TM}) = 0.341$$

$$V(S_{TT} \geq S_{TS}) = 0.315, V(S_{TS} \geq S_{TT}) = 1$$

$$V(S_{TT} \geq S_{TE}) = 1, V(S_{TE} \geq S_{TT}) = 0.122$$

$$V(S_{TS} \geq S_{TE}) = 1, V(S_{TE} \geq S_{TS}) = 0$$

By (14), we can calculate important integrated value under the evaluation criteria is important to other criteria:

$$d'(S_{TM}) = \min V(S_{TM} \geqslant S_{TS}, S_{TE}, S_{TT}) = 1, d'(S_{TE}) = 0, d'(S_{TS}) = 0.341,$$
$$d'(S_{TT}) = 0$$

Thus, according to formula (16), $W_T' = (1,\ 0,\ 0.341,\ 0)$ when normalized, $W_T = (0.746, 0, 0.254, 0)$.

Similarly, we can get the relative importance of various criteria under to use other criteria to assess the object, which is showed as follows: $W_M = (0.545, 0.136, 0.081, 0.238)$, $W_E = (0.402, 0.188, 0, 0.41)$, $W_S = (0.238, 0, 0.421, 0.341)$.

The affect weight matrix between the criteria as follows:

$$W = \begin{bmatrix} 0.545 & 0.402 & 0.746 & 0.238 \\ 0.136 & 0.188 & 0 & 0 \\ 0.081 & 0 & 0.254 & 0.421 \\ 0.238 & 0.41 & 0 & 0.341 \end{bmatrix}$$

3. Construction of the fuzzy pair-wise comparison matrix between the elements of Indicators is still in accordance with the above steps, taking "human S3" evaluation index, for example, for the technical risk group is associated with it, the fuzzy pair-wise comparison matrix between the elements of Indicators is showed in Table 3 When calculated: $S_{S3T1} = (0.249,\ 0.373,\ 0.497)$, $S_{S3T2} = (0.146,\ 0.178,\ 0.306)$, $S_{S3T3} = (0.079,\ 0.0.088,\ 0.106)$ $d'(S_{S3T1}) = 1$, $d'(S_{S3T2}) = 0.421$, $d'(S_{S3T3}) = 0$ $W'_{S3T} = (1, 0.421, 0)$, $W_{S3T} = (0.704, 0.296, 0)$

Through the integration of the weight vectors of all fuzzy pair-wise comparison matrix, we can get the weighted super-matrix, and then by calculating the weighted super-matrix, we can get the limit super-matrix, as listed in Tables 4 and 5.

According to the results of the above limit super-matrix, the weight coefficients of decision-making indicators of "capital M2", "cave E3" "Design T1", "Construction T2" is highest, which is the key factors influencing in the levee engineering risk

Table 3 Fuzzy pair-wise comparison matrix of the technical risk criteria relevant indicators under "human S3" assess object

Human S3	Design T1	Construction T2	Device T3
Design T1	(1, 1, 1)	(1, 2, 3)	(3, 4, 5)
Construction T2	(1/3, 1/2, 1)	(1, 1, 1)	(2, 3, 4)
Device T3	(1/5, 1/4, 1/3)	(1/4, 1/3, 1/2)	(1, 1, 1)

Table 4 The weighted super-matrix

	M		E			T			S		
	M1	M2	E1	E2	E3	T1	T2	T3	S1	S2	S3
M1	0.000	0.235	0.000	0.378	0.000	0.000	0.013	0.000	0.136	0.234	0.265
M2	0.168	0.000	0.111	0.003	0.000	0.157	0.011	0.245	0.222	0.181	0.158
E1	0.050	0.000	0.000	0.000	0.298	0.027	0.000	0.102	0.000	0.153	0.000
E2	0.077	0.000	0.000	0.000	0.138	0.000	0.216	0.152	0.000	0.000	0.045
E3	0.022	0.198	0.062	0.018	0.000	0.256	0.119	0.157	0.026	0.132	0.116
T1	0.163	0.311	0.000	0.000	0.113	0.000	0.101	0.000	0.102	0.000	0.112
T2	0.076	0.000	0.224	0.000	0.000	0.000	0.000	0.198	0.000	0.139	0.000
T3	0.111	0.000	0.000	0.000	0.021	0.428	0.315	0.000	0.127	0.144	0.085
S1	0.078	0.178	0.312	0.409	0.316	0.121	0.225	0.018	0.000	0.010	0.210
S2	0.118	0.077	0.000	0.192	0.000	0.000	0.000	0.000	0.183	0.000	0.000
S3	0.137	0.000	0.290	0.000	0.114	0.011	0.000	0.131	0.203	0.000	0.000

Table 5 The limit super-matrix

	M		E			T			S		
	M1	M2	E1	E2	E3	T1	T2	T3	S1	S2	S3
M1	0.022	0.022	0.022	0.022	0.022	0.022	0.022	0.022	0.022	0.022	0.022
M2	0.183	0.183	0.183	0.183	0.183	0.183	0.183	0.183	0.183	0.183	0.183
E1	0.015	0.015	0.015	0.015	0.015	0.015	0.015	0.015	0.015	0.015	0.015
E2	0.056	0.056	0.056	0.056	0.056	0.056	0.056	0.056	0.056	0.056	0.056
E3	0.175	0.175	0.175	0.175	0.175	0.175	0.175	0.175	0.175	0.175	0.175
T1	0.174	0.174	0.174	0.174	0.174	0.174	0.174	0.174	0.174	0.174	0.174
T2	0.157	0.157	0.157	0.157	0.157	0.157	0.157	0.157	0.157	0.157	0.157
T3	0.031	0.031	0.031	0.031	0.031	0.031	0.031	0.031	0.031	0.031	0.031
S1	0.056	0.056	0.056	0.056	0.056	0.056	0.056	0.056	0.056	0.056	0.056
S2	0.013	0.013	0.013	0.013	0.013	0.013	0.013	0.013	0.013	0.013	0.013
S3	0.119	0.119	0.119	0.119	0.119	0.119	0.119	0.119	0.119	0.119	0.119

analysis (1) natural risk factors: the hydrological conditions are complicated of Zhoukou City's dangerous works, risk factors cannot be controlled easily, it can possibly Lead to significant losses to projects, and may trigger other risks, thus, we should to strengthen the pre-investigation, prediction and prevention when the projects carried out; (2) The investigation in the design and construction skills of technical risk category are also important risk factors, heavy silty clay loam on the top of the Slope is low ,which anti-impaction is poor and the uncertainties is large, resulting in the survey and design work may not be able to detect a significant geological flaws, and increasing difficulty to construction process, so we should pay attention to this work in future work, it is necessary to mobilize additional resources to prevent and control of these risks of the project caused by the uncertainty and disturbance; (3) a huge levee engineering investment have an enormous impact on society, so the smooth progress of the project is inseparable from reasonable financial management and control, so the management of funds in this project will also be facing significant risks, therefore to carry out engineering work is necessary to pay close attention to the dynamics of national policy, well the response measures are in advance to avoid the huge losses caused to the project when the risk occurrence.

Because these are most important risk factors in project, it is necessary to study and analyze them, and only in-depth analysis of these factors, then take the effective prevention and control measures, we can effectively reduce the project's overall risk level.

3 Conclusions

Fuzzy analytic network process is a quantitative method which can be used to deal with ambiguity, feedback and rely on the complex relationship between decision-making. It can adequately reflect the association and feedback relationship between the risk decision-making index system of levee engineering, the uncertainty and imprecision comparison of indicators is revised through triangular fuzzy numbers which is an effective tool for decision analysis in the levee engineering. According to the need of problems, after in-depth studying and improving of this model, it can be applied to all kinds of water conservancy and hydropower engineering risk analysis and evaluation of decision-making, therefore, this model has broad application prospects. Taking other forms of fuzzy number into this model and to consider the impaction of the degree of confidence will be the direction of further study, and because the calculation of the amount of ANP is very large, therefore, how to use computer resources to meet the additional levels of ANP application computing requirements arising is still to be a problem needed to in-depth study. Fundamentally speaking, scientific, simple way to establish the network control layer, the optimization of the structure of super-matrix to find fast, simple and convenient method, etc., are also key issues for future research works.

References

1. Wang Lian-fen. Analytic Network Process (ANP) of the theory and algorithms. Engineering Theory and Practice. 2001 (3): 44–50.
2. Mohammad A. Mustafa, Jamal F A I-Bahar. Project risk assessment using the analytic hierarchy process[J]. IEEE Transactions on Engineering Management, 1991, 38(1):46–52.
3. Prasanta Dey, Mario T. Tabucanon, Stephen O. Ogunlana. Planning for project control through risk analysis: a petroleum pipeline-laying project[J] International Journal of Project Management, 1994 12(1):23-33.
4. Wei Mo-mei, Chen Yi-hua. Research of technological innovation capability of enterprises valuation system based on ANP. Science and Technology Management Research, 2006 (4):59–61.
5. Zhong Deng hua, Cai Shao-kuan, Li Yu-qin. The hydropower project risk analysis based on ANP and its application [J]. Hydropower Journal, 2008, 2(3):11–17.
6. Cui Xiao-yan. Li Xu-hong. Logistics Alliance business cooperation in decision-making method of anp, 2008, 1(14).

7. Dodong Pangqinghua. Current comprehensive evaluation method [M] publishing house of Tsinghua University, 2005.
8. Yuanyinan. Supplier choice research based on the AHP/GRAD [J]. Technology and Innovation Management, 2007, 28(1).
9. Wu Qian, Wu Zeng-hai, Li Hui-min. Engineering project risk evaluation method. Xi'an University of Architecture and Technology, 2006 (4):258–262.
10. Zhangyunfei Zhoushujing. The use of Anp method in the international project risk analysis, 2006, 27(1).